VITAL
STATISTICS

VITAL STATISTICS

AN AMAZING COMPENDIUM OF FACTOIDS, MINUTIAE, AND RANDOM BITS OF WISDOM

BY PAUL GROBMAN

Design by Number Seventeen, New York

A PLUME BOOK

PLUME **PUBLISHED BY PENGUIN GROUP**

Penguin Group (USA) Inc., 375 Hudson Street, New York, New York 10014, U.S.A.
Penguin Group (Canada), 10 Alcorn Avenue, Toronto, Ontario, Canada M4V 3B2
(a division of Pearson Penguin Canada Inc.)
Penguin Books Ltd., 80 Strand, London WC2R 0RL, England
Penguin Ireland, 25 St. Stephen's Green, Dublin 2, Ireland
(a division of Penguin Books Ltd.)
Penguin Group (Australia), 250 Camberwell Road, Camberwell, Victoria 3124, Australia
(a division of Pearson Australia Group Pty. Ltd.)
Penguin Books India Pvt. Ltd., 11 Community Centre, Panchsheel Park, New Delhi – 110 017, India
Penguin Books (NZ), cnr Airborne and Rosedale Roads, Albany, Auckland 1310, New Zealand
(a division of Pearson New Zealand Ltd.)
Penguin Books (South Africa) (Pty.) Ltd., 24 Sturdee Avenue, Rosebank,
Johannesburg 2196, South Africa

Penguin Books Ltd., Registered Offices: 80 Strand, London WC2R 0RL, England

First published by Plume, a member of Penguin Group (USA) Inc.

First Printing, July 2005

10 9 8 7 6 5 4 3 2 1

PLUME

REGISTERED TRADEMARK—MARCA REGISTRADA

CIP data is available.
ISBN 0-452-28646-8

Printed in the United States of America
Set in Franklin Gothic, Berthold Akzidenz Grotesk, Clarendon BT & Brothers
Designed by Number Seventeen

BOOKS ARE AVAILABLE AT QUANTITY DISCOUNTS WHEN USED TO PROMOTE
PRODUCTS OR SERVICES. FOR INFORMATION PLEASE WRITE TO
PREMIUM MARKETING DIVISION, PENGUIN GROUP (USA) INC.,
375 HUDSON STREET, NEW YORK, NEW YORK 10014.

FOR
MICHELLE, MATTHEW, SUZANNA, AND KATIE

ACKNOWLEDGMENTS

It was either Mark Twain or Benjamin Disraeli who said that there are three levels of falsehood in the world: "lies, damn lies, and statistics."

Having spent six months poring over numbers of every imaginable variety, I share the sentiment that stats are often slippery things. Many are affected by a particular agenda or bias, others by shoddy research or methodology. The information in this book has been principally researched and compiled from books, newspapers, magazines, and other media outlets. Depending on one's viewpoint, some of the sources are more trustworthy than others.

While I vouch for what is between these covers, some information is included that even we found difficult to believe. What tipped the balance in these instances was that researchers actually cared enough to compile such arcane information in the first place, which we present to you so you can draw your own conclusions.

Many thanks to Michael Hilde, April Hayes, Ayleen Peled, Joe Basile, Crystal Proenza, Sun Park, Michael Garcia, Susan Lim, Lauren Milgrom, and Daniel Grobman for their invaluable help in researching and compiling Vital Statistics; to Julissa Herrera, Thu Nguyen, and Jeff French for their design assistance during the book's early stages; to my editor Jake Klisivitch for his judicious editing and general sage counsel and advice; to two extraordinary agents, Lisa Marks and Betsy Fitzgerald; to the fine designers at Number 17 for their hard work; and to my parents and siblings who, whenever asked, have never failed to lend an eye or an ear. Finally, a special thanks goes to my wife and kids, not only for their valuable advice and feedback, but also for tolerating my preoccupation during the writing of this book.

CONTENTS

VITAL STATISTICS

ADVERTISING

1. Amount spent on advertising in the U.S.: $141 billion (2004)

2. Top ad-spending categories, in order: cars, drugs, movies

3. Commercials watched by the average child each year: 20,000

4. Portion of every prime-time TV hour devoted to advertising: 16 minutes, 8 seconds

Sources: **1.** TNS Media Intelligence. **2.** Car companies spent $13.78 billion on ads in 2003, drug companies $12.13 billion, and entertainment companies $10.9 billion. (*Advertising Age*, 6/28/04). **3.** In the U.S., 72% of commercials aimed at children are for food, primarily candy and cereal. Some countries have placed limits or bans on ads aimed at children: Sweden and Norway forbid ads aimed at under-12s, and in the Netherlands, commercials touting candy must also include a shot of a toothbrush. (*Broadcasting and Cable*, 3/8/04; *San Francisco Chronicle*, 12/26/03; *Financial Times* [London], 12/17/02) **4.** It's even more in the daytime—20 minutes, 57 seconds of every hour consist of nonprogramming. (*Adweek*, 2/18/02)

LONGEST-RUNNING COMMERCIAL IN TV HISTORY: 28 YEARS

Discount Tire's "Thank you" ad has the longest broadcast history ever. Created in 1975, the spot has run, off and on, ever since in the states where Discount Tire operates. It stars a timeless granny rolling a tire toward a Discount Tire shop as a male voice states that unsatisfied customers can return their tires with no questions asked. The granny then throws her tire through the store window. (Copley News Service, 7/1/03)

LENGTH OF SHORTEST TV COMMERCIAL IN HISTORY: 1/14 OF A SECOND

The commercial for Frangos Chocolate, which ran in Seattle, Wash., on Nov. 29, 1993, had only four frames (there are normally 30 frames per second). Frame for frame, it was also one of the most expensive commercials ever broadcast, costing $3,780 for a commercial that ended in less than the blink of an eye. (*New York Times*, 11/23/93)

Number of brands recognized by the average American 3-year-old: 100

(*Albany Times Union*, 2/2/00)

TOP AD ICON OF THE 20TH CENTURY: MARLBORO MAN

According to *Advertising Age* magazine, the Marlboro Man beats out Ronald McDonald and the Jolly Green Giant as the most recognizable brand icon of the 1900s. Introduced in 1955 as a means of repositioning Marlboro from a "ladies' cigarette" to one with wider appeal, this powerful pitchman helped make Marlboros the best-selling cigarette brand in the world, despite the deaths of two Marlboro Men due to lung cancer. (*Advertising Age*, 3/29/99)

1. YEAR RAY CHARLES ENDORSED COKE: 1969
2. YEAR RAY CHARLES ENDORSED PEPSI: 1989

(*Entertainment Weekly*, 3/28/97)

1. FIRST ELECTRIFIED SIGN IN TIMES SQUARE: 1891

2. STATE WITH THE MOST BILLBOARDS:

FLORIDA

3. STATES WITH NO BILLBOARDS: ALASKA, HAWAII, MAINE, VERMONT

Sources: **1.** A man named O. J. Gude pioneered Times Square billboards—called "spectaculars" because of their dazzling display of lights. The first electric sign consisted of 1,457 lamps that said "Manhattan Beach Swept by Breezes." Gude's first true spectacular was created in 1905, featuring a young woman clad in a skirt made out of incandescent bulbs that made it appear as if her hem lifted with each passing breeze. (*Newsday*, 4/8/04; *Encyclopedia of New York*) **2.** Ohio and Michigan follow close behind. (*Detroit News*, 2/10/02) 3. *Miami Herald*, 7/8/04.

1. First radio station with an all-commercials format: WWAX, Duluth, Minn.

2. Number of days it lasted: 5

This radio station decided to shun typical talk and music formats in favor of all commercials, all the time. They mixed regular, revenue-earning ads with commercial parodies and old-time nostalgic ads. After 5 days, the format changed to "easy listening." (*St. Paul Pioneer Press*, 3/17/97)

FIRST USE OF SKYWRITING FOR ADVERTISING: 1922

During World War I, "Daily Mail" (the name of a popular newspaper) was scrawled across the skies in England to bolster readership. Six years later, people were encouraged to "Smoke Lucky Strikes" when they looked up at the New York skyline. (*New York Times*, 4/23/95; *Christian Science Monitor*, 1/25/00)

Most recent allegation of subliminal advertising:
George W. Bush's "Rats" commercial (2000)

In a commercial that briefly aired during the 2000 presidential campaign, Al Gore was criticized for his stand on prescription drugs for seniors as the word "bureaucrats" appeared in big white letters. Then, for 1/30 of a second, the last four letters of the word were broken off, displaying "RATS" in large blown-up letters. Republicans pulled the ad after the message was revealed, but denied that the word had been inserted intentionally. Interestingly, a recent study indicates that people exposed subliminally to the word "rats" before being shown the picture of a politician viewed the pol more negatively. (Salon.com, 3/16/04; *New York Times*, 6/20/04)

ODDS THAT A COMPANY'S STOCK WILL GO UP AFTER IT PUTS ITS NAME ON A STADIUM: 7 IN 10

In a study of 49 stadiums, 70% of companies that named a stadium (like Bank One Ballpark) saw their stock price increase after the naming. Such an advertising strategy demonstrates the company believes it will be around for a long time, and is considered more effective than sponsoring the Olympics or utilizing celebrities. (AP, 7/29/03)

FIRST AD DISPLAY ON THE SIDE OF COWS: 1984

In 1984, a Canadian farmer named Frazier Mohawk sold ad space on the sides of his Jersey heifers for $500 a year. Since then, several newspapers have reported on European farmers stenciling ads for radio stations and ice cream on the sides of their herds. (AP, 3/30/84)

Top American advertisers in 2003:
Procter & Gamble ($2.6 billion)
General Motors ($2.5 billion)
Time Warner ($1.9 billion)

The magazine *Advertising Age*, however, presents markedly different figures, saying that GM led the nation with $3.43 billion in total advertising in 2003, with P&G in second place with $3.32 billion. (*Adweek*, 3/15/04; *Advertising Age*, 6/28/04)

AFRICAN AMERICANS

1. Number of documented lynchings of blacks in America between 1882 and 1968: 5,000

2. States with the most lynchings: Mississippi (581), Texas (493), Georgia (431)

(Tuskegee University)

RACIST COMMENTS BY PRESIDENTS:

"Blacks in memory are equal to whites; in reason much inferior; in imagination, dull, tasteless and anomalous."

Thomas Jefferson

"There is a physical difference between the white and black races which I believe will forever forbid the two races living together on terms of social and political equality."

Abraham Lincoln, during his debate with Stephen Douglas (1858)

"This perfectly stupid race can never rise. The Negro has been kept down as much by a lack of intellectual development as by anything else."

Teddy Roosevelt

(Journal of Blacks in Higher Education, 1/31/00)

1. NUMBER OF BLACKS WHO HELD ELECTED OFFICE IN 1900: 50
2. NUMBER OF BLACKS WHO HOLD ELECTED OFFICE TODAY: 9,101
3. STATE WITH THE HIGHEST NUMBER OF BLACK ELECTED OFFICIALS: MISSISSIPPI

Sources: **1.** *USA Today,* 12/14/00. **2.** *Winston-Salem Journal,* 7/2/04. **3.** As of 2004, Mississippi had 892 black elected officials, Alabama 756, and Louisiana 705. (*Winston-Salem Journal,* 7/2/04)

1. Number of African Americans living in the U.S.: 36.4 million
2. Odds that an African American lives in the South: 1 in 2
3. State with the highest percentage of blacks: Mississippi (36.3%)
4. State with the lowest percentage: Montana (0.3%)

Sources: **1.** Blacks are the second largest minority group after Hispanics, comprising about 12.7% of the U.S. population. (*Boston Globe*, 1/4/04) **2.** U.S. Census Bureau, 2000. **3.** Louisiana has the second highest percentage of blacks, comprising 32.5% of the states population. Among American cities, Gary, Ind., has the highest percentage of blacks (84%). (*Washington Post*, 12/12/02) **4.** According to the 2000 census, only 2,692 African Americans lived in Montana, the lowest of any state, followed by Vermont, with 3,063 black residents. (U.S. Census Bureau, 2000)

PRICE PAID AT AUCTION FOR ROSA PARKS'S BUS: $492,000

The rusted, yellow-and-green 1936 General Motors bus received nearly 50 bids at a suburban Chicago auction house and was finally purchased by an anonymous institution. (UPI, 10/29/01)

1. YEAR CLASSES AT TAYLOR COUNTY HIGH SCHOOL IN BUTLER, GA., WERE DESEGREGATED: 1971

2. YEAR THE JUNIOR-SENIOR PROM WAS DESEGREGATED: 2002

3. NUMBER OF U.S. SCHOOLS THAT STILL HAD SEGREGATED PROMS AS OF 2004: 2

Sources: **1, 2.** Though most would have thought segregated dances were a thing of the past, habits persisted in Butler County until 2002, when students first moved for change, prompting a 2-to-1 vote in favor of an integrated prom. (*Washington Post*, 5/12/02) **3.** Both schools with segregated proms are located in Georgia—Johnson County High School and Toombs County High School. In fact, Toombs County High had three proms in 2004—one for whites, another for blacks, and a third for Hispanics. (*Macon Telegraph*, 4/13/04)

Most integrated city in America: Virginia Beach, Va.

According to a recent study, 38% of Virginia Beach residents live on a block that is at least 20% white and 20% black. (*Milwaukee Journal Sentinel*, 1/15/03)

1. ODDS THAT YOU WILL EXPERIENCE A MIDLIFE CRISIS: 1 IN 4

2. AGE GROUP REPORTING THE HIGHEST LEVEL OF SEXUAL SATISFACTION: 30 TO 39

3. PARTS OF YOUR BODY THAT GET BIGGER WITH AGE: FEET, NOSES, EARLOBES

4. PARTS OF YOUR BODY THAT GET SMALLER: GENITALIA

Sources: **1.** The term "midlife crisis" was coined by a French therapist named Elliot Jacques in 1965. (*Bergen Record*, 5/26/02) **2.** 30- to 39-year-olds were followed by: 20- to 29-year-olds; 40- to 49-year-olds; 50 to 59-year-olds; and those over 60. (Reuters, 2/10/00) **3.** *Los Angeles Times*, 2/7/95. **4.** *Washington Post*, 5/8/90.

OLDEST COUNTRY IN THE WORLD: JAPAN

The median age in Japan is 41.3, followed by Italy, Switzerland, Germany, and Sweden, each with a median age of about 40. (United Nations Population Division) Source: *New Straits Times*, 11/23/03

1. Amount a person shrinks between ages 30 and 40: 5/8 inch

2. Average gain in weight: 10 pounds

3. Age 40-year-olds would most like to be: 34

Sources: **1.** After 40, the body continues to shrink about 1/16 inch each year. (*U.S. News and World Report*, 6/9/97) **2.** The average person gains 1 pound each year after age 25. (*Physiology of Sport and Exercise*) **3.** *Good Housekeeping*, 8/1/96.

1. **Number of people over 100 in the world: 180,000**
2. **Percentage of centenarians who are women: 85%**
3. **Number of people worldwide over 110: 46**
4. **World's oldest person as of 2004: 114**

(Jendrikje Van Andel-Schipper, Netherlands)

Sources: **1.** Of these, some 48,000 live in the U.S. (*Miami Herald*, 10/8/03) 2. *St. Louis Post-Dispatch*, 7/18/04. 3. *Orange County Register*, 8/3/04. 4. Van Andel-Schipper eats herring and orange juice every day. According to the *Guinness Book of World Records*, "her eyesight and hearing are not as good as when she was 108." (*National Post*, 6/30/04)

1. **MEDIAN AGE IN THE U.S.: 35.3**
2. **OLDEST STATE IN THE U.S. BY MEDIAN AGE: FLORIDA (38.7)**
3. **YOUNGEST STATE: UTAH (27.1)**

Sources: **1.** *Salt Lake Tribune*, 1/9/04. **2.** Followed by West Virginia and Pennsylvania. (*Dallas Morning News*, 4/4/04; *Sarasota Herald*, 8/22/04) **3.** Followed by Alaska. (*Salt Lake Tribune*, 1/9/04)

1. **PERCENTAGE OF 70-YEAR-OLD MEN WHO STILL DAYDREAM ABOUT SEX: 72%**
2. **PERCENTAGE OF 70-YEAR-OLD WOMEN WHO DO SO: 43%**
3. **ODDS THAT A 70-YEAR-OLD SAYS THEIR SPOUSE GETS MORE ATTRACTIVE OVER TIME: 6 IN 10**
4. **ODDS THAT A 70-YEAR-OLD NEEDS GLASSES: 9 IN 10**
5. **RECENT INCIDENTS IN SUN CITY, ARIZ., OF RESIDENTS ENGAGING IN PUBLIC INTIMATE ACTIVITY: 24**
6. **AVERAGE AGE IN SUN CITY: 75**

Sources: **1–3.** *Palm Beach Post*, 8/4/99. **4.** *U.S. News and World Report*, 3/20/00. **5.** According to the *Arizona Republic*, the incidents have occurred in pools, golf courses, golf carts, park benches, and cars in parking lots. "We don't want to deny anybody their right to healthy sexual expression," said a Sun City spokesperson. "We just want them to do it in a more appropriate place." (*Arizona Republic*, 5/31/01) **6.** *New York Times*, 3/7/04.

AIRPLANES

1. **First airplane casualty in history:** Thomas Selfridge, September 17, 1908
2. **Odds of a U.S. commercial flight ending in a fatal crash:** 1 in 3.7 million
3. **Most dangerous month to fly in:** December
4. **Most dangerous place to fly:** Africa

Sources: **1.** Selfridge was a passenger on a plane piloted by Orville Wright when a propeller malfunctioned, sending the craft out of control. (*Washington Post*, 12/28/03) **2.** Only 25 commercial airliners crashed in fatal accidents in 2003, half the average of 50 fatal airline accidents a year, making it the safest year in airline history. The worst year for airliner accident fatalities was 1972, with 243 accidents, hijackings, etc., resulting in 2,556 deaths. (*Seattle Times*, 1/3/04; Knight Ridder, 1/3/04) **3.** *USA Today*. **4.** In 2003, nearly a third (28 percent) of fatal airliner accidents happened in Africa, though the continent accounts for only 3 percent of world aircraft departures. (*National Business Review* (NZ), 1/9/04)

Recent instances
in which passengers
got sucked into
airplane toilets: 1

In January 2002, a woman on an SAS flight from Oslo to New York made the mistake of flushing while she was still seated, creating such suction that the crew could do nothing to free her. It wasn't until she landed in New York seven hours later that ground technicians were able to pry her off. The story was featured in a London newspaper under the headline "PLANE GIRL'S LOO HORROR." (*Arlington Heights Herald*, 2/10/02; *The People*, 1/27/02)

NUMBER OF YEARS MERHAN KARIMI NASSERI HAS BEEN LIVING IN A TERMINAL AT CHARLES DE GAULLE AIRPORT: 16

After being expelled from his native Iran without a passport, Nasseri arrived at Paris's Charles de Gaulle Airport in 1988 but was refused entry into France because he had lost documents qualifying him as a refugee. For 11 years, Nasseri lived inside the terminal as lawyers argued over what should be done with him. Finally, in 1999, the French government permitted him to reside in France as a refugee. By that point, however, Nasseri refused to leave the terminal and resides there to this day. (*Hamilton Spectator*, 6/26/04)

1. First stewardess: Ellen Church (1930)
2. First film to be shown on a scheduled flight: *By Love Possessed* TWA, July 19, 1961
3. First American hijacking: 1961

Sources: **1.** Airlines had already been using small men (called "cabin boys") to load luggage and help passengers. But Church, a registered nurse, convinced Boeing Air that nurses could better deal with the sicknesses that frequently afflicted air travelers. The first stewardesses had to be single, trained as nurses, under five foot four, and between 20 and 26 years old. Things changed, of course. In the 1960s, stewardesses were presented as sex objects: Braniff Airlines clothed its stewardesses in mini-dresses, and its ads asked, "Does your wife know you're flying with us?" (*Bergen Record*, 12/14/03) **2.** There is some dispute as to when the first film of any kind was shown on a plane. *USA Today* says that a silent film was shown on a Lufthansa flight in April 1925, while the BBC says that *The Lost World* was shown in a converted World War I bomber during a thirty-minute flight near London. (*Entertainment Weekly*, 9/24/99; *USA Today*, 9/25/03; *BBC*, 10/31/02) **3.** In 1961, a National Airlines flight to Key West was hijacked to Cuba. Through the mid-1980s, one out of every three hijackers sought to go to Cuba. Indeed, in February 1991, a man arrested for attempting to hijack a Southwest Airlines plane from Oakland to Cuba answered this way when asked why he wanted to go to the island: "It's just a place that I read a long time ago that hijackers were going." (*Air Safety Week*, 2/21/2000; *Los Angeles Times*, 2/16/91)

1. PERCENTAGE OF PLANE ACCIDENTS THAT OCCUR DURING TAKEOFF: 35%
2. PERCENTAGE OF ACCIDENTS THAT OCCUR DURING APPROACH AND LANDING: 60%

Source: Boeing.com

1. FOOD BROUGHT BY LINDBERGH ON HIS TRANSATLANTIC FLIGHT: 5 SANDWICHES AND 2 CANTEENS OF WATER

2. FIRST MEAL SERVED ON A COMMERCIAL AIRLINE: KLM FLIGHT BETWEEN LONDON AND PARIS, OCTOBER 11, 1919

Sources: **1.** When King George V met Lindbergh after his record-setting flight, the king asked, "There is one thing I long to know. How did you pee?" (*Newsday*, 5/15/02; *Time*, 9/21/98) **2.** *USA Today*, 9/25/03

NUMBER OF HOMES HIT BY SEWAGE FALLING FROM PLANES IN THE PAST 25 YEARS: 28

For instance, in September 2002, a piece of what is euphemistically called "blue ice" crashed through a bathroom ceiling in Massapequa, New York. And in June 2003, a Santa Cruz, Calif., man was awarded $3,286 after frozen sewage from a passing commercial airliner crashed through the skylight of his boat. (*Newsday*, 9/7/02; *AP Online*, 6/15/03)

ALCOHOL

1. Odds that an American has had at least one drink in the past week: 7 in 10

2. Ratio of a beverage's "proof" to alcohol content: 2 to 1

3. Most popular mixed drink in the U.S.: Margarita

Sources: **1.** According to a September 2003 Gallup poll, 68% of Americans had at least one drink in the preceding 7 days, compared to 48% in 1992. Eight percent of men and 1% of women reported having more than 22 drinks in the past week. (*Chicago Sun-Times*, 9/20/03) **2.** Thus, a bottle of 50-proof whiskey contains 25% alcohol. The term "proof" comes from 17th-century England, when men poured liquor over gunpowder to determine its alcohol content. If the mixture sputtered, it was "proof" of low alcohol (and high water) content; if it burned evenly, it was "proof" of higher alcohol content. Incidentally, in England, proof is different—100 proof is 57.7% alcohol by volume. (*Boston Globe*, 8/28/03) **3.** However, the martini is the most popular cocktail in formal restaurants and hotels. (*Cheers On-Premise Handbook; Rocky Mountain News*, 11/25/03)

1. Date Prohibition was repealed: Dec. 5, 1933

2. Year Mississippi finally allowed liquor sales: 1966

3. Year you could first legally buy a mixed drink in Texas: 1972

Sources: **1.** One of the authors of the 18th Amendment, Texas Sen. Morris Sheppard, once said, "There's about as much chance of national prohibition being repealed as there is of a hummingbird flying to the planet Mars with the Washington Monument tied to its tail." Sheppard was wrong. At 5:32 P.M. on Dec. 5, 1933, after a 3-hour delay, Utah became the 36th state to ratify the repeal of the 18th Amendment, resulting in its invalidation. A headline from the *New York Times* stated, "Bartenders Poised for Drinkers' Rush," above a subheadline stating that "Orgies Are Frowned On." (*Washington Post*, 12/6/99; *New York Times*, 12/6/03) **2.** Mississippi was the last dry state in the union, after Oklahoma permitted liquor sales in 1959. (*Daily Oklahoman*, 4/18/99) **3.** Fifty-one of Texas's 254 counties are still completely dry—meaning no liquor or beer sales of any kind. (*New York Times*, 10/1/03)

Vice president who was drunk when he took his oath of office: Andrew Johnson (1865)

Johnson, Lincoln's vice-president during his short-lived second term, had not been feeling well in the days leading up to the inaugural, and thought several glasses of whiskey might be the cure. The *New York Herald-Tribune* called Johnson's inaugural address "a speech remarkable for its incoherence." Johnson ended his rambling speech only after the departing vice-president pulled on his coat. After taking the oath of office, Johnson put his hand on the Bible and blared, "I kiss this book in the face of my nation of the United States." (White, *Lincoln's Greatest Speech*)

1. FIRST APPEARANCE OF THE TERM "HAPPY HOUR" IN PRINT: 1912

2. FIRST PROMOTION OF A "COCKTAIL HOUR" BY A BAR: 1920s

Sources: **1.** Being drunk used to be referred to as being "happy" by some, hence the origin of the term "happy hour," according to the American Dictionary of Food and Drink. **2.** According to one source, the first "cocktail" or "happy" hour began during Prohibition at a New York establishment on East 53rd Street named Tony's, which, in a tacit arrangement with the police, was allowed to operate between the hours of 4 and 6 P.M. (*Restaurant Hospitality*, 4/92)

1. STATE WITH HIGHEST NUMBER OF BARS PER PERSON: WISCONSIN

2. STATE WITH SECOND HIGHEST NUMBER OF UFO SIGHTINGS: WISCONSIN

Sources: **1.** At last count, Wisconsin had more than 12,000 taverns. (*Milwaukee Journal Sentinel*, 4/16/04) **2.** Coincidence? We don't think so. Incidentally, New Mexico ranks first in UFO sightings. In 1988, a man named Tom Weber led a campaign to raise $25 million to build a welcoming center for aliens in Elmwood, Wisc. Ground has yet to be broken. (*Madison Capital Times*, 10/24/98)

1. TOP-SELLING HARD LIQUOR IN AMERICA: VODKA

2. STATE WITH THE HIGHEST BINGE DRINKING RATE:

WISCONSIN

3. STATE WITH THE LOWEST: TENNESSEE

Sources: **1.** Americans spent $3 billion on vodka in 2003, and $1.3 billion on whiskey, in second place. (*Forbes*, 5/10/04)
2, 3. Over 25% of Wisconsin citizens had engaged in binge drinking (five drinks or more), compared to only 7.4% in Tennessee. San Antonio, Tex., has the highest percentage of binge drinkers of any city in America (23.9%). (*Alcohol and Drug Abuse Weekly*, 4/12/04)

PENALTY FOR DRINKING LIQUOR IN THE KORAN: 80 LASHES

[lash lash lash lash lash lash lash lash lash lash lash lash lash lash lash lash lash lash lash lash lash lash lash lash lash lash lash lash lash lash lash lash lash lash lash lash lash lash lash lash lash lash lash lash lash lash lash lash lash lash lash lash lash lash lash lash lash lash lash lash lash lash lash lash lash lash lash lash lash lash lash lash lash lash lash lash lash lash lash lash lash lash lash lash lash lash lash lash lash lash lash lash lash lash lash lash lash lash]

While many Muslim scholars believe the penalty is discretionary, the penalty is still meted out in several Muslim countries that ban alcohol sale and use. For instance, in January 2003, 11 Iranian boys received 100 lashes—80 for consuming alcohol and 20 for yelling under the influence of alcohol in public. And on July 20, 2001, 45 men were flogged for alcohol use in one of Teheran's main squares. (Xinhua News Agency, 1/25/03; *Washington Post*, 8/16/01)

1. HANGOVERS PER YEAR SUFFERED BY THE AVERAGE DRINKER: 8 TO 12

2. LIQUOR LIKELY TO CAUSE THE WORST HANGOVERS, IN DESCENDING ORDER:

BRANDY, RED WINE, RUM, WHISKEY, WHITE WINE, GIN, VODKA

Sources: **1.** The medical term for a hangover is "veisalgia", which combines a Norwegian term meaning "uneasiness following debauchery" and the Greek word for "pain." (*Seattle Times*, 12/31/03) **2.** Lighter-colored drinks (such as gin and vodka) tend to result in less severe hangovers than dark-colored drinks. (*British Medical Journal*, 1/4/97)

YEAR A WORM FIRST APPEARED IN A BOTTLE OF TEQUILA: 1950

In 1950, a Mexican artist turned liquor producer named Jacobo Lozano Paez began to put worms in his bottles of mezcal (a cousin of tequila) as a marketing gimmick. The rest is history. Incidentally, there are no worms in bottles of tequila, only in mezcal. (*Cheers On-Premise Handbook*, 5/1/03)

Origin of the term "the real McCoy": Bootlegger Bill McCoy, due to the quality of his scotch

Other terms with alcohol origins: "speakeasies" (the illegal bars frequented during Prohibition, called that because a password spoken softly through a peephole gained entrance); "cocktail" (which, depending on the source, emanates either from a New York tavern-keeper who served drinks stirred with rooster feathers, a mispronunciation of the French word "coquetier"—an egg cup that was used as a jigger in New Orleans—or a Mexican leader's daughter named "Coctel"); and "bootleggers" (who got their name because some smuggled whiskey in their boots). (*Chicago Tribune*, 8/24/86; *Charlotte Observer*, 12/26/03; *New Orleans Times-Picayune*, 12/2/02)

1. NUMBER OF BARS IN AMERICA IN THE YEAR BEFORE PROHIBITION: 15,000

2. NUMBER OF ILLEGAL BARS IN AMERICA 8 YEARS LATER: 30,000

Those that enacted Prohibition were some of its biggest violators. Pres. Warren Harding hosted liquor parties. The Senate Library contained a secret bar behind one of its walls. And the cellars of Congress were filled with bottles of liquor. There were some true believers—a Rep. Thomas Blanton tried to have the *Washington Post* prosecuted for printing George Washington's recipe for beer. (Behr, *Prohibition*; *Independent*, 6/15/97; *Washington Post*, 10/4/93)

The first cocktail book was called How to *Mix Drinks, or the Bon Vivant's Companion*, written by Jerry Thomas. Mixed drinks did not begin to become truly popular until Prohibition, when many mixed drinks were invented to hide the taste of bootleg liquor. (*New York Times*, 12/24/03)

Origin of Famous Mixed Drinks

The margarita: After a woman asked for a drink he'd never heard of, a bartender in Ciudad Juarez, Mexico, created this tequila-based concoction on July 4, 1942. But another account claims that the drink was created by Texas socialite Margaret Sames at her Alcapulco home in 1948.

(*Los Angeles Times*, 1/8/97; *Chicago Sun-Times*, 8/13/97)

The martini: Contrary to popular belief, the drink was probably not first made for John Rockefeller by a New York bartender named Martini di Arma di Taggia, but rather emanates from a drink first made in 1862 at San Francisco's Occidental Hotel, named after a California gold rush town called Martinez.

(*Restaurant News*, 4/24/00)

Manhattan: Created at New York's Manhattan Club in 1874 for Jenny Jerome (mother of Winston Churchill), who was hosting a party there celebrating the election of New York governor Samuel J. Tilden.

(*New York Times*, 3/17/04)

Mai tai: In 1944, Victor Bergeron (better known as "Trader Vic") concocted a rum-based drink at his Oakland restaurant for a friend visiting from Tahiti, who, after taking a sip, said, *"Mai tai, roa ae!"*—which means "out of this world" in Tahitian.

(*Atlanta Journal-Constitution*, 4/8/04)

Cosmopolitan: Reinvented by Toby Cecchini in 1987, who was then a bartender at New York's Odeon restaurant, who originally made the drink for the staff.

(Cecchini, *Cosmopolitan*)

Bloody Mary: First made in 1924 at Harry's New York Bar in Paris by bartender Fernand Petiot, the drink was renamed the Red Snapper when Petiot took over bartending duties at the St. Regis in New York in 1934, but the original name stuck.

(*Chicago Tribune*, 7/24/02)

1. NUMBER OF RUSSIANS WHO DIE OF ALCOHOL POISONING EVERY YEAR: 40,000

2. NUMBER OF AMERICANS WHO DIE: 300

This in spite of the fact that the U.S. has more than twice Russia's population. (*Washington Post*, 8/25/01)

ANATOMY (MALE)

0 1 2 3 4 5 6

1. AVERAGE LENGTH OF AN ERECT PENIS, ACCORDING TO

2. AVERAGE LENGTH, ACCORDING TO AMERICAN WOMEN: 4 INCHES

3. SIZE OF THE AVERAGE ERECT PENIS: 5.1 INCHES

4. BIGGEST ERECT PENIS ON

5. SMALLEST: 1.75 INCHES

Sources: **1, 2.** Kanner, *Are You Normal About Sex?* **3.** Based on measurements made by researchers on *60 Minutes.* in San Francisco. (*Los Angeles Times,* 5/2/95) **4, 5.** Kinsey Institute.

Longest sustained erection recorded in medical literature: 7 weeks

According to George Gould and Walter Pyle in their book *Anomalies and Curiosities of Medicine*, "Salzer describes one patient of forty-six who awoke one morning with a strong erection that could not be reduced by any means. . . . Despite all treatment this condition continued for seven weeks."

NUMBER OF ERECTIONS PER NIGHT EXPERIENCED BY THE AVERAGE SLEEPING MALE: 3 TO 5

(*Harvard Medical School Health Letter,* 9/89)

PERSON WHO SAID THE PENIS "HAS A MIND OF ITS OWN": LEONARDO DA VINCI

Da Vinci—the first to discover that the penis fills with blood during an erection—said this about the male organ: "The penis does not obey the order of its master, who tries to erect or shrink it at will, whereas instead the penis erects freely while its master is asleep. The penis must be said to have its own mind, by any stretch of the imagination." (*Alternative Medicine Review,* 3/1/04)

16

| 8 | 9 | 10 | 11 | 12 | 13 |

AMERICAN MEN: 10 INCHES

RECORD: 13.5 INCHES

SPECIES WITH THE LARGEST PENIS: GREAT WHALES (UP TO 10 FEET)

Jackie Kennedy's second husband, Greek shipping magnate Aristotle Onassis, covered the bar stools in his yacht with skin from the whale penis, and is reported to have told Greta Garbo during an onboard visit that she was "sitting on the largest penis in the world." (*Japan Times*, 5/19/02)

President who was most preoccupied with his anatomy: Lyndon Baines Johnson

According to Robert Caro, when Johnson was in the Senate, he would occasionally show off his penis—which he nicknamed "Jumbo"—to shocked colleagues. And when once asked one too many times about why the country had troops in Vietnam, Johnson unzipped his fly, pulled out his penis, and said, "This is why!" (Caro, *Master of the Senate*; Friedman, *A Mind of Its Own*)

1. PERCENTAGE OF MALE BABIES WHO ARE CIRCUMCISED IN THE U.S.: 65%
2. PERCENTAGE WHO ARE CIRCUMCISED IN ENGLAND: 10%

Sources: **1.** *St. Petersburg Times*, 7/5/03. **2.** *Sunday Telegraph*, 8/29/99.

ANNOUNCERS

1. Number of people who watched the first TV broadcast of the World Series in 1947: **3.9 million**

2. Number of those 3.9 million who watched from a bar: **3.5 million**

3. First broadcasting celebrity: **Graham McNamee**

4. Highest amount ever paid to a sports broadcaster: **$8 million per year**

Sources: **1, 2.** *New York Times*, 11/20/95. **3.** McNamee became the first sports broadcaster to go beyond a dry recitation of the facts and offer color. During the 1923 World Series, McNamee's call of the games over the radio prompted writer Ring Lardner to comment, "I don't know which game to write about—the one I saw today, or the one I heard Graham McNamee announce as I sat next to him at the Polo Grounds." (*Newsday*, 7/11/89) **4.** Paid by CBS to John Madden to cover 16 NFL games a year, plus the playoffs. In 2002, Madden jumped to ABC's Monday Night Football, where his salary decreased to $5 million per year. (*Mediaweek*, 2/4/02)

MONTHS CELTICS ANNOUNCER JOHNNY MOST UNKNOWINGLY HAD AN EARPLUG STUCK IN HIS EAR: 18

Most, complaining of hearing loss, went to see the Celtics' team doctor, who discovered the television earplug, which Most had inserted during a broadcast 18 months earlier. (*Los Angeles*, 6/6/87)

FIRST SPORTING EVENT ON RADIO: APRIL 1898

In April 1898, radio pioneer Guglielmo Marconi broadcast the annual Irish regatta over shortwave radio to a crowd that certainly numbered in the tens of . . . tens. England's first sports radio broadcast was of a cricket match between England and Wales on Jan. 15, 1927. The announcer had a blind assistant who—given the newness of the medium—was there "to prompt reasonable questions." (*Irish Times*, 4/24/94; *Times* [London], 1/15/87)

FIRST MAJOR SPORTS BROADCAST: JULY 2, 1921
(BOXING MATCH BETWEEN JACK DEMPSEY AND GEORGES CARPENTIER)

Broadcasting from a stadium in Jersey City, New Jersey, which was hastily elected for the event, one J. Andrew White gave the blow-by-blow over WJY radio station to thousands who had come out to listen to the event in New York's Times Square and theaters broadcasting the event throughout the Northeast. Though generally acknowledged as the first American sports broadcast, there were earlier local broadcasts: in 1912, a Minnesota football game was broadcast by an experimental radio station, and in 1920, radio station WTAM broadcast the Texas A&M–Texas game. (Earlyradiohistory.us; Smith, *Play by Play*)

Longest continuous broadcast by a sports announcer:
16 hours (Jim McKay, Munich Olympics)

On Sept. 5, 1972, Palestinian terrorists broke into the Olympic compound and took 11 Israeli athletes hostage. Americans followed the drama live on ABC, where Jim McKay broadcast for 16 straight hours. After learning that the hostages had been killed at Munich's airport after a botched rescue mission, McKay announced to America: "Our worst fears are realized tonight. They're gone. They're all gone." (*Baltimore Sun*, 1/30/02)

First use of instant replay: Dec. 7, 1963

Instant replay was used for the first time during the 1963 Army-Navy football game when CBS showed Army quarterback Rollie Stichweh scoring a touchdown on a 1-yard run—twice. While the first replay aired, announcer Lindsay Nelson warned the audience: "This is not live, Ladies and gentlemen, Army has not scored again." (NPR, 12/8/03)

MOST FAMOUS EX–BASEBALL ANNOUNCER: RONALD REAGAN

Ronald Reagan's first job out of college was as a baseball announcer with radio station WHO in Des Moines, Iowa, where he became well known under the name Dutch Reagan (a nickname given him by his father). In the year following his presidency, Reagan guest-sat as the color commentator for the first inning of the 1989 All-Star Game. "I've been out of work for six months," Reagan said. "Maybe there's a future here." (AP, 7/12/89)

NAME OF THE "AGONY OF DEFEAT" SKI JUMPER ON ABC'S *WIDE WORLD OF SPORTS*: VINKO BOGATAJ

In one of television's most enduring images, Bogataj, a 22-year-old from Yugoslavia, was seen weekly falling off a ski jump during the opening sequence of ABC's *Wide World of Sports* while an announcer intoned on the "agony of defeat." Says Bogataj's daughter, "When we came to the U.S. for the first time, none of us could believe how everybody wanted to meet my dad. All from that one fall." (*Los Angeles Times*, 2/9/02)

RECORD FOR CONSECUTIVE GAMES BROADCAST BY A SINGLE ANNOUNCER: 7,000 (HARRY CARAY)

Chicago Cubs announcer Harry Caray claimed that he had not missed a ballgame from 1946 until the opening weeks of the 1987 season, when he was recovering from a stroke. Before his death in 2002, Chick Hearn broadcast 3,338 consecutive games for the Los Angeles Lakers from Nov. 21, 1965 (a 104–100 loss to the Philadelphia 76ers) to Dec. 20, 2001, when he underwent surgery to block a torn aortic valve. (*Los Angeles Times*, 12/20/01; 2/27/87)

APOLOGIES

1. ORIGIN OF THE WORD "APOLOGY": FROM THE GREEK *APOLOGIA*, MEANING A SPEECH IN DEFENSE

2. NUMBER OF TIMES THE AVERAGE WOMAN OFFERS SOME TYPE OF APOLOGY EACH DAY: 5.2

3. NUMBER OF TIMES THE AVERAGE MAN APOLOGIZES EACH DAY: 3.6

4. PERCENTAGE OF AMERICAN CATHOLICS WHO REGULARLY GO TO CONFESSION: LESS THAN 25%

5. ODDS THAT A MEDICAL MALPRACTICE PLAINTIFF WOULD NOT HAVE SUED IF THEIR DOCTOR HAD APOLOGIZED: 1 IN 3

Sources: **1.** Thus, while the modern use of the term usually means an acknowledgment of fault, the word originally was used to refer to defense of conduct, such as Plato's "Apology of Socrates," in which Socrates defends himself against accusations of corruption. (*Scotland on Sunday*, 12/15/02) **2, 3.** According to Deborah Tannen, a professor at Georgetown University who's written extensively on the subject, women apologize most to other women. Men also apologize more to women than to other men. Tannen notes that when women say "I'm sorry," however, it's not necessarily to accept blame, but rather to express regret that something happened. (*Dallas Morning News*, 9/15/98; Tannen, *Talking from 9 to 5*) **4.** In 1965, almost 40% of American Catholics went to confession on a monthly basis, according to the National Opinion Research Center. (*Seattle Post-Intelligencer*, 11/21/03) **5.** Based on a 1994 British study. Apologies would go a long way to curb road rage as well—a recent survey found that 66% of drivers with road rage would have been satisfied if the other driver apologized for their recklessness. (*Business Week*, 8/26/02; Orange County Register, 3/9/98)

Amount of time Emperor Henry IV stood barefoot in the snow in order to obtain the pope's forgiveness: 3 days

Holy Roman Emperor Heinrich IV had become involved in a dispute with Pope Gregory VII over which of them had the power to appoint German bishops. In retaliation, the pope excommunicated the emperor who, in A.D. 1077, waited outside in the snow for the pope to grant his forgiveness and rescind the excommunication. (*Columbia Encyclopedia*)

1. Amount charged for conveying an apology by the Apology and Gift Center of Tianjin, China: $2.50

2. Number of people who listen to the Beijing radio program *Apologize in Public Tonight:* 1 million

Sources: **1.** The company, whose motto is "We Say Sorry for You," has 20 employees who deliver the apologies in western business attire. (*New York Times*, 1/3/01) **2.** The call-in show broadcasts apologies from and to listeners. A quarter of the calls involve things that happened during the Chinese Cultural Revolution in the 1960s and early 1970s, when acknowledging any type of wrongdoing meant potential imprisonment, torture, and death. (*Irish Times*, 4/2/01)

Political Apologies

"Indeed I did have a relationship with Ms. Lewinsky that was not appropriate. In fact, it was wrong. It constituted a critical lapse of judgment and personal failure on my part for which I am solely and completely responsible."

President Clinton (1998)

"I hope you all know how very sorry I am that so much attention was brought to the building."

Note from Monica Lewinsky to her neighbors in Washington (1998)

Sports Apologies

"It will never happen again."

Mike Tyson, after biting a piece of Evander Holyfield's ear off during a championship bout (1997)

"Yes, I was wrong, but I didn't kill anybody."

Latrell Sprewell, after choking his coach (1999)

Miscellaneous

"I couldn't stop. I had to do it, see, I had this . . . irresistible impulse."

Lorena Bobbitt, after sexually emasculating her husband (1993)

1. WHAT TELEVANGELIST JIMMY SWAGGERT SAID TO HIS CONGREGATION WHEN HE WAS CAUGHT IN THE COMPANY OF A PROSTITUTE IN 1988:

"I HAVE SINNED AGAINST YOU."

2. WHAT SWAGGART SAID TO HIS CONGREGATION WHEN HE WAS AGAIN CAUGHT WITH A PROSTITUTE IN 1991:

"THE LORD TOLD ME IT'S FLAT NONE OF YOUR BUSINESS."

(*Dallas Morning News*, 9/1/01)

APPARITIONS

1. Percentage of Americans who believe God performs miracles: **84%**

2. Percentage of Americans who say they have witnessed or experienced a miracle themselves: **48%**

3. Amount bid on eBay for a grilled cheese sandwich purportedly bearing the image of the Virgin Mary:

$28,000

Sources: **1, 2.** *Newsweek* poll (quoted in *Christian Century*, 5/24/00) **3.** The sandwich was made by Diana Duyser of Hollywood, Fl., in 1994, who was about to take her second bite when she saw the Virgin Mary staring back at her from the bread. Duyser kept the sandwich on a shelf for 10 years, until she auctioned the sandwich on eBay in November 2004. (*Chicago Tribune*, 11/21/04)

DECEMBER 1996: STAIN RESEMBLING THE VIRGIN MARY APPEARS ON A BUILDING HOUSING THE UGLY DUCKLING USED CAR COMPANY IN CLEARWATER, FLA.

The rainbow-colored stain covers nine panes of glass on the office building's windows on Drew Street in Clearwater, attracting hundreds of thousands of visitors since it was first discovered in December 1996. In the spring of 1997, someone tossed an acidic substance on part of the image. For a few days, the apparition lost its likeness. Then, amazing even scientists, the image of Mary reappeared. (*Dallas Morning News*, 12/20/97)

MAY 1991: IMAGE OF JESUS APPEARS ON A BILLBOARD FOR PIZZA HUT IN STONE MOUNTAIN, GA.

According to the *Associated Press*, "dozens of motorists claimed to have seen Jesus shrouded in spaghetti and tomato sauce on the pizza chain's billboard." A Pizza Hut spokesman disclaimed any intent to put subliminal messages into their ad, stating, "It's total coincidence." (*San Francisco Chronicle*, 5/24/91)

SEPTEMBER 1998: IMAGE OF JESUS APPEARS ON A DONUT SHOP IN CAPE BRETON, CANADA

The image of Jesus appeared on the wall near Tim Horton's drive-through window for 4 nights, drawing the curious and the faithful. Then, as the *Toronto Star* reported, "an employee changed a lightbulb, and Jesus Christ disappeared." (*Toronto Star*, 11/2/02)

DECEMBER 1997: IMAGE OF THE VIRGIN MARY FORMED BY SAP DRIPPING FROM A TREE APPEARS IN COLMA, CALIF.

The image appeared on a portion of a 100-foot California pine tree about 10 to 12 feet off the ground where a branch had been cut off. (*Dallas Morning News*, 12/21/97)

JUNE 1997: IMAGE OF THE VIRGIN MARY APPEARS IN A PUDDLE OF WATER AT A SUBWAY STATION IN MEXICO CITY

At its height, 2,000 people per hour came to witness the image of the so-called Subway Virgin formed in a puddle of water at the Hidalgo metro station in downtown Mexico City. (Reuters, 6/4/97)

ART

1. Things Americans like in a painting, according to a recent poll:
The color blue, clothed people in groups, water, wild animals, and famous people

2. Things Americans don't like in a painting: Abstract images; the colors pink, coral, teal, or gold; and sharp angles

Sources: **1.** A poll commissioned by two Russian American artists on Americans' artistic likes and dislikes led to the creation of *America's Most Wanted,* a painting depicting the top American picks. The painting is a landscape: a mountain lake, with blue skies, two deer and a hippopotamus playing in the water, and three young people walking along the shore near George Washington. (*Washington Post,* 4/6/01) **2.** The same 1994 poll that led to the creation of America's Most Wanted also resulted in America's Least Wanted, an abstract of triangles superimposed on each other, in pastel colors and with mottled, pocked textures. Later polls confirmed that these dislikes were common in most countries. (*Independent,* 1/17/98)

PICASSO'S FULL GIVEN NAME: PABLO DIEGO JOSÉ SANTIAGO FRANCISCO DE PAULA JUAN NEPOMUCENO CRISPÍN CRISPINIANO DE LOS REMEDIOS DE LA SANTÍSIMA TRINIDAD RUIZ BLASCO Y PICASSO LOPÉZ

(*USA Today (Magazine),* 7/1/97)

PEOPLE KILLED BY WORKS OF ART: 1

In 1991, environmental artist Christo installed 1,760 yellow umbrellas on a California hillside. Lori Rae Matthews was killed when one of the 20-foot, 485-pound umbrellas was toppled by 40 mph winds and crushed her against a boulder. (*People,* 11/11/91)

Biggest art thief of all time: Stephane Breitweiser (239 paintings, 174 separate thefts)

Breitweiser, a French waiter, was finally caught in 2001 after stealing 239 paintings valued at more than $1 billion. After learning of her son's arrest, Mireille Breitweiser set about destroying the evidence, shredding 60 to 70 oil paintings and shoving them down her kitchen sink disposal, and dumping 109 other artworks into the nearby Rhine-Rhode Canal. His lawyer blamed Breitweiser's actions on an absent father. "After the break-up of his parents, his father took all the furniture from the family home. As a child Stephane was devastated by this and wanted to reconstruct the ideal world he lost." (*Scotland on Sunday,* 2/2/03; *People,* 6/3/02)

1. BEST-SELLING ART POSTER IN AMERICA: *STARRY NIGHT* (VAN GOGH)

2. SECOND-BEST-SELLING ART POSTER IN THE MIDWEST: *FRIEND IN NEED* (BETTER KNOWN AS DOGS PLAYING POKER)

(*American Artist*, 11/1/99)

Estimate of the percentage of major paintings for sale that are fakes: **10–40%**

Among the forgers: Perhaps the greatest of all time was Hungarian Elmyr de Hory, who created over 1,000 paintings credited to Matisse, Picasso, and others. His creations were displayed alongside original works in respected museums, and fetched over $60 million. The works were authenticated many times, including at least once by the forged artist himself (painter Kees van Dongen). Doubts have even been raised about the authenticity of the *Mona Lisa* in the Louvre. After Italian Vincenzo Perugia returned the painting in 1913 (having stolen it in 1911) some questioned whether the original was returned. Since then, five other versions have been credited as being the original. (*Wilson Quarterly*, 3/22/00; Columbia Encyclopedia, 1/10/04; Quadrant, 12/1/98; *Daily Mail*, 4/7/03)

AMOUNT ENGLAND'S TATE GALLERY RECENTLY PAID FOR ARTIST PIERO MANZONI'S EXCREMENT: APPROXIMATELY $38,000

In 1961, Manzoni used his own waste to fill 90 cans, which were later sealed and circulated to museums around the world. A Tate spokesperson said of the purchase: "What he was doing with this work was looking at a lot of issues that are pertinent to 20th-century art, like authorship and the production of art. It was a seminal work." (*Sunday Telegraph* [London], 6/30/02; Art Journal, 9/22/93)

BABIES

1. BIRTHS IN THE U.S. IN 2003: 4,093,000

2. AVERAGE NUMBER OF BIRTHS PER DAY: 11,213

3. DIAPER CHANGES DAILY PER BABY: 6

4. TIME SPENT CRYING PER DAY, ON AVERAGE: 2.2 HOURS

5. AMOUNT OF SLEEP LOST BY PARENT IN FIRST YEAR: 200 HOURS

Sources: **1, 2.** Report published in June 2004 by the U.S. Department of Health and Human Services. **3.** Studies indicate that while 90% of kids were out of diapers by age 21/2 in the 1960s, not even a quarter are toilet-trained that early now, and 40% remain untrained at age **4.** (Kimberly Clark Consumer Services; *Hamilton Spectator*, 8/20/04) **5.** This is the average amount a newborn infant cries. Crying peaks at about 6 weeks and then declines thereafter to about 1 hour. A 1997 study found that the average baby emits 90 decibels of noise when she cries, 15 decibels less than a power mower. (*American Family Physician*, 8/15/04) According to the National Sleep Foundation. Other estimates put the figure at 400 hours, and some go as high as 700 hours. In a 1999 survey, 48% of new parents said they prefer sleeping to sex. (*People*, 4/23/01; *Arizona Republic*, 1/31/99)

AVERAGE AGE OF AMERICAN WOMEN WHEN THEY GIVE BIRTH FOR THE FIRST TIME: 25.1

(*Kansas City Star*, 5/8/04)

1. Twins born in the U.S. in 2002: 125,134
2. Triplets: 6,898
3. Quadruplets: 434
4. Quintuplets or higher: 69

Sources: **1–4.** (U.S. Newswire, 5/5/04; *Newsday*, 4/26/04)

ODDS OF HAVING FOUR CONSECUTIVE SETS OF TWINS IN A ROW: 1 IN 64 MILLION

This according to the doctor of Elvira Guillen, a 29-year-old Minnesotan who accomplished just that feat. "That's enough, already. No more," the mother of nine said after delivering her most recent pair in 1992. (*Newsday*, 5/25/92)

PERCENTAGE OF MOTHERS WHO ANSWERED "STAYED OUT OF THE WAY" WHEN ASKED WHAT THE FATHER DID BEST DURING THE BABY'S FIRST WEEKS: 21%

(BabyCenter.com survey)

OLDEST MOTHER ON RECORD: ADRIANA ILIESCU, 66 YEARS

Iliescu gave birth to daughter Eliza on Jan. 16, 2005, at the age of 66 years. She underwent 9 years of fertility treatments after delaying motherhood to pursue a career as a profesor. (*Boston Globe*, 1/23/05)

1. MOST POPULAR NAME FOR NEWBORN BOYS IN 2003: JACOB

2. MOST POPULAR NAME FOR NEWBORN GIRLS IN 2003: EMILY

3. MOST POPULAR NAME FOR NEWBORN BOYS IN 1900: JOHN

4. MOST POPULAR NAME FOR NEWBORN GIRLS IN 1900: MARY

Sources: **1.** Followed by Michael, Joshua, Matthew, and Andrew. (Social Security Administration) **2.** Followed by Emma, Madison, Hanna, and Olivia (SSA) **3.** SSA. 4. Mary was the most popular girl name of the 20th century—31 of every 1,000 girls born were named Mary, which was the 61st most popular name in 2003. Other once-popular girl names that have fallen from view: Linda, the most popular American girl name in 1947–52 (now the 412th most popular); Lisa, the most popular name in 1962–69 (now 370th); and Jennifer, the most popular name in 1970–84 (now 31st). (*Milwaukee Journal Sentinel*, 5/28/04)

1. Percentage of Americans who would prefer a boy if they could only have one child: 38%

2. Percentage that would prefer a girl: 28%

Based on a recent Gallup poll, slightly more than a quarter of the respondents said they had no preference and the rest had no opinion. (*Christian Science Monitor*, 10/8/03)

1. RATIO OF BOYS TO GIRLS BORN IN THE U.S.: 104.8 MALES FOR EVERY 100 FEMALES

2. IN CHINA: 117 FOR EVERY 100 FEMALES

Sources: **1.** U.S. Department of Health and Human Services. **2.** *Guardian*, 10/21/03.

BASEBALL

PLACE WHERE BASEBALL WAS DEFINITELY NOT INVENTED: COOPERSTOWN, N.Y.

In 1905, a commission was formed at the urging of Albert G. Spalding, an early sporting goods manufacturer, to determine where baseball began. The committee received evidence, including a letter from an elderly man, Abner Graves, who claimed he had heard Abner Doubleday describing the rules for baseball in 1839. On the basis of Graves's testimony, the committee concluded that "the first scheme for playing baseball, according to the best evidence obtainable to date, was devised by Abner Doubleday at Cooperstown, N.Y. in 1839." As a result, the Hall of Fame was built in the small upstate town, and opened on the 100th anniversary of Doubleday's "discovery." Since then, however, baseball historians acknowledge that there is little evidence Doubleday invented the game, in Cooperstown or otherwise. Indeed, Doubleday's obituary made no mention of baseball, and the first attempt to link Doubleday to the game wasn't made until a decade after his death. (*Sports Illustrated*, 6/12/89)

1. EARLIEST REFERENCE TO "BASEBALL" IN AMERICA: 1791
2. EARLIEST REFERENCE TO "BASEBALL" IN ENGLAND: 1744

1. PERCENTAGE OF AMERICANS IN 2004 WHO SAY BASEBALL IS THEIR FAVORITE SPECTATOR SPORT: 10%
2. PERCENTAGE WHO SAID SO IN 1994: 21%

In a 2003 Gallup poll, only 10% of Americans said that their favorite sport to watch was the national pastime, surpassed by both football (37%) and basketball (14%). (Gallup, 1/30/04)

1. Time it takes a 95 mph fastball to reach home plate: **4/10 second**
2. Batters struck and killed by major league pitches: **1**
3. Record for most times hit by a pitch: **287**
4. Record for most-hit batters: **203**

Sources: **1.** Batters have about .17 seconds to decide to swing. If they swing 7 milliseconds too soon, they'll hit it foul on the third-base side. Seven milliseconds too late, and the ball sails foul to the right of first base. (*Adair, Physics of Baseball*) **2.** On Aug. 16, 1920, Ray Chapman, a short-stop for the Cleveland Indians, was hit in the head by a pitch, the only major leaguer ever killed from a game injury. After Chapman's death, baseball ended the practice of retrieving scruffed-up foul balls from the stands, which hitters found difficult to see. (*Washington Post*, 4/14/2000) **3.** Held by Hughie Jennings, who played in the 1890s. Ron Hunt, who holds the modern record for being leveled 50 times in 1971, said, "Some people give their bodies to science; I gave mine to baseball." (*Sports Illustrated*, 6/15/98) **4.** Walter Johnson plunked 203 batters during his 20-year career with the Washington Senators. (*Daily News*, 6/6/04)

1. INNING IN WHICH THE MOST HOME RUNS ARE HIT: FOURTH
2. DAY IN WHICH THE MOST HOME RUNS ARE HIT: SUNDAY

Sources: **1.** The fourth inning has the most home runs, followed by the sixth inning. (Society for American Baseball Research) **2.** More home runs have been hit on Sundays (followed by Saturdays) than other days of the week, largely due to the now rare practice of scheduling doubleheaders on the weekend. (SABR)

1. Years after Babe Ruth died that Roger Maris broke his home run record: **13**
2. Years after Roger Maris died that Mark McGwire broke his record: **13**

Ruth died in 1948, and Maris broke the record in 1961. Then Maris died in 1985, and McGwire broke his record in 1998. (*St. Louis Post-Dispatch*, 10/4/98)

ONLY NUMBER NEVER AGAIN TO BE WORN IN THE MAJOR LEAGUES: 42

In 1998, every major league team simultaneously retired the number worn by Jackie Robinson throughout his career with the Brooklyn Dodgers. The practice of wearing numbers was begun by the 1929 New York Yankees, who issued numbers based on spots in the batting order, which is why Babe Ruth wore number 3 and Lou Gehrig wore number 4. (*Cincinnati Enquier*, 9/6/04)

BEER

1. AMOUNT OF TOTAL BEER CONSUMPTION ATTRIBUTED TO THE 10% OF HEAVIEST BEER DRINKERS: 43%

2. PERCENTAGE OF BEER IN THE U.S. CONSUMED OUTSIDE THE HOME: 26%

3. STATE WHERE A PARENT CAN BUY A BEER FOR HIS CHILD AT A BAR: WISCONSIN

Sources: **1.** *Brown University Digest of Addiction Theory and Application*, 3/00. **2.** In England, in contrast, about 65% of beer consumption occurs in pubs and other places outside the home. (*Grocery Headquarters*, 1/1/04; *International Herald Tribune*, 8/23/03) **3.** That's right. In Wisconsin, no matter the age, a parent can bring his kid to a bar and order a beer—or indeed any other drink—for him or her. The restaurant industry is opposing any change to the law. Said one lobbyist: "Experiencing the responsible consumption of alcohol with a parent in the type of social environment that an underage person could undoubtedly be exposed to during the course of their life would seem to be an opportunity that cannot be overlooked." (*St. Paul Pioneer Press*, 8/22/03)

TOP FIVE BEER-CONSUMING STATES IN AMERICA, IN ORDER:
NEW HAMPSHIRE, NEVADA, NORTH DAKOTA, MONTANA, WISCONSIN

Source: Beer Institute Study of Per Capita State Consumption.

PERCENTAGE BY WHICH OTHERS INCREASE IN ATTRACTIVENESS AFTER SEVERAL BOTTLES OF BEER, ACCORDING TO A RECENT STUDY: 25%

"We wanted to measure once and for all whether a moderate amount of alcohol increases the judgment of facial attractiveness," said Prof. Barry Jones, the author of the Scottish study. Analyzing the so-called beer goggles effect, subjects were asked to looked at photos of men and women and rate their attractiveness from 1 to 7. The study found that, regardless of sex, subjects who were asked to drink 2 pints of beer beforehand rated the people in the photos as more attractive than those who remained sober. (*Toronto Sun*, 8/20/02)

DATE BEER WAS FIRST SOLD IN CANS: JAN. 24, 1935

While solid food had been successfully sold in tin cans for many years, the wax lining on the inside of the cans affected the flavor of beer. In the early 1930s, can manufacturers came up with another lining, and in January 1935, the Gottfried Krueger brewery in Newark, N.J., became the first to sell canned beer. (*Steel Times*, 5/1/01)

Biggest beer-drinking colleges, according to the *Princeton Review*:

2004: University of Wisconsin
2003: Clemson University
2002: University of Tennessee

(*Princeton Review*, cited in the *Deseret Morning News*, 8/22/03)

AMOUNT A BEER COMPANY PAID NASA TO SEE WHETHER BEER COULD BE BREWED IN SPACE: $130,000

In 1993, Germany's Beck's brewery paid to place a tube with its beer ingredients aboard the space shuttle to determine whether beer produced in a weightless environment fermented faster and was less likely to produce a hangover. In a related study, researchers at Denmark's Delft University of Technology spent a half year devising a way to get beer out of a keg and into astronauts' mouths in space's zero-gravity environment. After adjustments to the keg, beer exited smoothly out of the tap, floating in space in portions the size of Ping-Pong balls. (*Cleveland Plain Dealer*, 5/1/93; Agence France-Presse, 12/20/93)

NUMBER OF BEERS ESTIMATED TO HAVE BEEN DRUNK BY AN ARIZONA MAN ARRESTED FOR DRUNK DRIVING IN 2000: 80

(*Arizona Republic*, 1/4/00)

1. FIRST BEER COMMERCIAL: 1945

2. AMOUNT ANHEUSER-BUSCH SPENT ON BEER ADVERTISING IN 2003: $407 MILLION

Sources: **1.** An old advertising adage says "Sports sell beer," and according to *All About Beer* magazine, New England's Narragansett brewery introduced the first beer commercial when it sponsored broadcasts of Red Sox games in 1945. The first prerecorded beer commercials were probably made by St. Louis's Hyde Park Brewery in February 1947. (BeerHistory.com) **2.** TNS Media Intelligence.

BIRTHDAYS

1. NUMBER OF BIRTHDAY CARDS RECEIVED BY THE AVERAGE AMERICAN: 8

2. NUMBER OF BIRTHDAY GIFTS RECEIVED BY THE AVERAGE AMERICAN: 4

3. PERCENTAGE OF PEOPLE WHO ADMIT TO GIVING UNWANTED PRESENTS TO SOMEONE ELSE: 35%

Sources: **1–2.** Hallmark. **3.** According to a recent poll, the most frequent "regifters" are Southerners, Democrats, and women. (*New York Post*, 12/16/03)

1. MONTH WITH THE MOST BIRTHDAYS: AUGUST

2. MONTH WITH THE FEWEST BIRTHDAYS: FEBRUARY

Sources: **1.** If births were evenly distributed throughout the year, about 8.3% of the population would have a birthday each month. But according to Hallmark, August constitutes 9.14% of American birthdays. July ranks second at 8.82%. (*USA Today*, 5/5/04; Hallmark) **2.** In 2002, 304,000 American children were born in February, followed by November (318,000) and April (324,000). (National Center for Health Statistics)

1. DAY OF THE WEEK ON WHICH THE MOST BABIES ARE BORN: TUESDAY

2. DAY OF THE WEEK ON WHICH THE FEWEST BABIES ARE BORN: SUNDAY

In 2002, there were 14% more babies born on Tuesdays than on the average day, and 66% more than on Sundays. (National Center for Health Statistics)

ONLY TIME "HAPPY BIRTHDAY" HAS BEEN SUNG TO A PRESIDENT BY THE FULL HOUSE AND SENATE: FEB. 6, 1985

On Feb. 6, 1985, at the end of Pres. Ronald Reagan's annual televised State of the Union address to Congress, the president was serenaded with the song by the full House and Senate in honor of his 74th birthday. After the congressional serenade, Reagan said, "Thank you for making the 35th time I have been 39 the happiest of them all." Incidentally, in the days after the performance, lawyers for the copyright owners of "Happy Birthday" criticized Congress for singing the song without permission. (*Los Angeles Times*, 4/5/85)

1. Percentage of women who make birthday wishes: 75%

2. Percentage of men who do so: 17%

According to a survey conducted by Carvel Ice Cream. Of those adults who made wishes, only 2% wished for something good for someone else, while over half of kids did so. The most popular wish of the women surveyed was to spend more time with their husband, while the most popular wish among men was to improve their golf game, with more time with the wife finishing 23rd. (*Albany Times Union*, 5/3/97)

YEAR IN WHICH THE SONG "HAPPY BIRTHDAY" WAS CREATED: 1893

First written as a classroom song in 1893 by a Louisville, Ky., schoolteacher named Mildred Hill, the original lyrics were "Good morning to you, / Good morning to you, / Good morning, dear teacher, / Good morning to you." Though some versions of the story say that after Mildred died, her sister Patty rewrote the lyrics, most attribute the new lyrics to a man named Robert Colman, who wrote the new stanza without the sister's permission. (*Austin American-Statesman*, 3/7/98)

1. YEAR IN WHICH "HAPPY BIRTHDAY" WAS COPYRIGHTED: 1935

2. LAWSUITS INVOLVING ILLEGAL SINGING OF THE SONG: 2

3. PRICE PAID FOR THE RIGHTS TO THE SONG IN 1988: $25 MILLION

Sources: **1.** Which means that it is illegal to sing the song in any public place without paying a royalty, including restaurants. To avoid paying the royalty, some restaurants, like Red Lobster, have come up with their own birthday song. Others pay the royalty, or take the risk of being caught, which is minimal. As a spokesman for ASCAP (the company that enforces musical copyrights) said: "I'm not saying that they wouldn't need permission to do that. But I am saying, generally speaking, we don't have the resources to be going into every restaurant." (*Chicago Tribune*, 3/9/01) **2.** In 1935, Irving Berlin was sued after "Happy Birthday" was sung to a character playing John D. Rockefeller in a performance of a Broadway show called *As Thousands Cheer*. The parties settled out of court. Subsequently, a company called Postal Telegraph was sued for using the song in singing telegrams. (*Los Angeles Times*, 4/5/85) **3.** The copyright runs out in 2030. (*San Jose Mercury News*, 2/22/94)

IMPORTANT PEOPLE WHO CHANGED THEIR BIRTHDAY:

PRESIDENT NGUYEN VAN THIEU (SOUTH VIETNAM)

Changed his birthday from November 1924 to Apr. 5, 1923, at the urging of an astrologer. The gods were not fooled, however, and in a televised resignation speech as Vietnam was crumbling in 1975, Thieu said: "Over the past 10 years, all years, months, days, and hours in my life have been bad, as my horoscope forecast." (*New York Times*, 12/30/01)

GEORGE VI OF ENGLAND

Although he was born on December 14, King George changed the celebration of his birthday to June 9 because he didn't want his birthday to be celebrated in the cold weather or to interfere with Christmas. (Yenne, *Black 41*)

1. NUMBER OF FREE BIRTHDAY MEALS GIVEN OUT BY DENNY'S BEFORE IT ENDED THE PROGRAM ON SEPT. 30, 1993: 10 MILLION

2. WHAT MANERO'S STEAKHOUSE IN GREENWICH, CONN., OFFERS TO ANY BABY BORN IN THE RESTAURANT: FREE MEALS FOR LIFE

Sources: **1.** *San Jose Mercury News*, 2/22/94. **2.** So far, no one has qualified, though one woman's water broke during dinner. (*San Jose Mercury News*, 2/22/94)

BLINDNESS

1. WORLD BLIND POPULATION: 45 MILLION

2. ODDS THAT A BLIND PERSON WATCHES TELEVISION AT LEAST 24 HOURS A WEEK: 9 IN 10

3. ODDS THAT A BLIND PERSON READS BRAILLE: 1 IN 10

Sources: **1.** *Guardian*, 10/9/04. **2.** Actually, the figure was 97%. The shows of choice: news, talk, and the shopping networks. (*Washington Post*, 8/9/98) **3.** In 1963, more than half of blind people read Braille. (NPR's *All Things Considered*, 8/6/01)

NUMBER OF BLIND MOVIE REVIEWERS: 1

According to CNN, Jay Forry's movie reviews are heard on 23 radio stations around the country. Forry, who lost his eyesight to diabetes, gives each movie a letter grade, with an A meaning "So good, blind people like it;" B, "I'm glad I could hear it;" C, "I had one eye open;" D, "It's good I couldn't see it;" and F, "Blindness is a blessing." (CNN.com; *Tampa Tribune*, 9/19/98)

BLIND DOCTORS: 5

In 1972, David Hartman, who lost his sight due to glaucoma at age 8, became the first blind person accepted to medical school, and now practices psychiatry in Virginia. While he wasn't required to interpret X-rays, Hartman was in most other respects treated like other medical students. . . . Jane Poulson, Canada's first blind physician, wrote an autobiography titled *The Doctor Will Not See You Now*. . . . In 1996, the Ohio Supreme Court upheld Case Western Medical School's refusal to admit Cheryl Fischer, saying that sight is essential in a medical student and physician. In a dissenting opinion, one justice called the court's ruling "a case of prejudice, pure and simple." (Reuters, 7/31/96; AP, 3/18/01; 10/31/98; *Braille Monitor*, 2/97)

BLIND BASEBALL RADIO BROADCASTERS: 1

Don Wardlow, born without eyes, became the first blind radio announcer in baseball history in 1991, when he broadcast a game for the appropriately named Miami Miracle. "Sure, he provided a publicity gimmick for our team, but I wouldn't have hired him if he didn't have talent," said Miami owner Mike Veeck. Before each game, Wardlow has statistics and personal information about every player in the league translated into Braille, which he relies on while broadcasting. Now with over 1,500 broadcasts under his belt, Wardlow is considered one of the better color commentators in baseball. Says his play-by-play colleague Jim Lucas: "I'll sometimes look over at Don during a game, and he'll have his back to home plate, announcing into a blank wall, and I'll crack up on the air. Here's a guy born without eyes announcing a baseball game on the radio!" (*Sports Illustrated*, 7/8/96; 8/12/02)

Percentage of people who say they feel "very comfortable" with blind people: 47%

Based on a poll by Louis Harris & Associates. Nineteen percent reported being "very comfortable" when meeting someone with mental illness, 33% with someone who has mental retardation, 39% with a deaf person, and 59% with someone who uses a wheelchair. (*Atlanta Journal-Constitution*, 9/17/91)

What blind people dream about more often than sighted people:
Problems with getting from place to place

Studies show that people frequently dream about waking-life concerns, and blind people are twice as likely to dream about mobility issues than sighted people. For example, one dreamer found himself on his hands and knees with his ear to the ground listening for traffic at a crosswalk. Another dreamed that she and her guide dog were lost, but pretended that she wasn't lost so no one would know. (Hurovitz, *Dreaming*)

YEAR THE FIRST GUIDE DOG CAME TO AMERICA: 1928

Germany was apparently the first country to train dogs as guides for blind veterans. In 1928, Morris S. Frank, a blind insurance salesman of Nashville, Tenn., brought the first guide dog back from Europe and named him Buddy. (*Christian Science Monitor*, 7/6/98)

NUMBER OF COPIES OF *PLAYBOY* PRODUCED MONTHLY IN BRAILLE:
500

The Library of Congress spends about $60,000 each year to print the Braille versions of *Playboy*. They contain no pictures. (Library of Congress)

1. NUMBER OF PRIVATE BOATS IN THE U.S.: 17 MILLION

2. MOST POPULAR BOAT NAMES, IN ORDER:

Happy Hours

Carpe Diem

Reel Time

3. NUMBER OF DAYS SPENT ON THE WATER BY THE AVERAGE BOATER: 20 DAYS PER YEAR

4. PERCENTAGE OF BOATERS WHO ARE WOMEN: 12%

Sources: **1.** Ranging from yachts to kayaks. The average boat costs about $11,000. (*American Demographics*, 5/1/03)
2. A survey by the largest boat owners association in the U.S. found these to be the top three boat names. Rounding out the top ten were: *Sea Biscuit, Freedom, Summer Wind, Aquaholic, Serenity, No Worries,* and *Mental Floss.* Though it stands at #8 now, *Serenity* was the most popular boat name in the 1990s. (*Dallas Morning News*, 2/4/04) 3. *Boat US* magazine, 11/1/00. 4. *Tampa Tribune*, 10/29/00.

1. U.S. STATE WITH THE MOST BOATS PER CAPITA: MINNESOTA

2. CITY WITH THE WORLD'S HIGHEST NUMBER OF BOATS PER CAPITA: AUCKLAND, NEW ZEALAND

Sources: **1.** California recently overtook Michigan as the state with the most registered boats in America (1,051,000), but Minnesota still has the most boats per capita, with about one boat per six residents. (*Detroit Free Press*, 2/12/04) **2.** Also known as the "City of Sails," Auckland has 11 km of waterfronts, and one boat per 11 residents. (*International Herald Tribune*, 9/24/99)

PEOPLE WHO SURVIVED LONG PERIODS ADRIFT IN LIFE RAFTS:

Louis Zamperini (47 days): After his B-24 bomber crashed during World War II, Zamperini survived 47 days on a life raft on rainwater and caught fish, only to be "rescued" by a Japanese enemy patrol; he spent 2 years in prison labor camps before finally being returned home.

(*New York Times*, 2/15/03)

Steven Callahan (76 days): A storm wrecked Callahan's boat in 1982, leaving him stranded on a life raft with only 8 pints of water and little food. He managed to catch fish to survive until he was finally rescued.

(*Christian Science Monitor*, 1/31/86)

Bill and Simone Butler (66 days): In 1989, after an attack by whales, this couple's boat sank; they survived by catching fish and turtles after their food supply ran out midway. Although they spotted 40 ships while drifting, it was only on day 66 that they were finally rescued by the Costa Rican coast guard.

(*Los Angeles Times*, 8/22/89)

Maurice and Maralyn Bailey (117 days): This couple survived for almost 4 months after their boat was capsized by whales in 1973.

(*Bailey and Bailey, 117 Days Adrift*)

---

1. Average toll to pass through the Panama Canal: **$28,000**
2. Lowest toll ever paid to go through the canal: **36¢** (1928)

Sources: **1.** The average toll to pass through the Suez Canal is $120,000. (*Times Higher Education Supplement* [London], 2/20/04) **2.** Paid by Richard Halliburton, who took 10 days to swim the 50-mile-long canal. The highest toll paid yet was $200,000 by a 90,000-ton cruise ship. (*Times Higher Education Supplement* [London], 2/20/04)

NUMBER OF *TITANIC* SURVIVORS STILL LIVING AS OF JULY 2004: 3

The last three survivors are Lillian Gertrude Asplund, 97, of Worcester, Mass.; Barbara West Dainton, 93, of England; and Eliza Gladys Milvina Dean, 93, also of England. Dean was just 2 months old when her family embarked on the *Titanic* for a new life in America. Her father died, but she was rescued along with her mother and brother and returned to England. Asplund was 5 when the boat sank. She was traveling third class, and by the time her family reached the lifeboat deck, most of the boats were gone. Nevertheless, she managed to board one with her mother and brother, leaving her father and three older siblings behind. (Titanic Historical Society; *Guardian*, 4/16/96)

YEAR WILLIAM LEAST HEAT MOON BOATED ACROSS AMERICA: 1995

Over a period of 4 months, Moon (an author) covered 5,222 miles from New York Harbor to the mouth of the Columbia River in a 22-foot dory powered by two 45-horsepower outboard motors, traveling less than 75 miles out of water along the way. The route took Moon up the Hudson River to the Erie Canal, across the canal to Lake Erie, and then into the Allegheny, the Ohio, the Mississippi, the Missouri, the Jefferson, the Beaverhead, the Lehmi, the Salmon, the Snake, and finally the Columbia River. (*Washington Post*, 11/7/99)

Number of pirate attacks in 2003: **445**

Despite its romantic connotation, piracy on the high seas is increasingly dangerous; in the last year, 21 seafarers were killed, 71 went missing, and 359 were taken hostage during ship hijacking. Indonesian waters are the most dangerous in terms of piracy, with 111 attacks occurring off its shores in the past year. (*Traffic World*, 2/2/04)

BOOKS

1. WORLD'S OLDEST BOUND BOOK:
THE BOOK OF PSALMS (1,600 YEARS OLD)

2. WORLD'S OLDEST BOOKSTORE:
MORAVIAN BOOK SHOP IN BETHLEHEM, PENN.

Sources: **1.** Discovered in 1984 in a Christian cemetery 85 miles south of Cairo, Egypt, the 490-page manuscript dates back to the second half of the fourth century A.D. (The Codex Vaticanus in the Vatican Library and the Codex Sinaiticus in the British Museum are thought to be contemporaries.) (*New York Times*, 12/24/88; *Washington Post*, 8/12/01) **2.** Founded in 1745, the store has been owned by the Moravian Church ever since. (*Publishers Weekly*, 8/14/00)

1. FIRST USE OF "ONCE UPON A TIME" IN A STORY: 1595

2. FIRST USE OF "IT WAS A DARK AND STORMY NIGHT" IN A NOVEL: 1830

Sources: **1.** *Oxford Dictionary of Literary Quotations*, Times Newspapers, 10/13/97. **2.** First used by Baron Edward Bulwer-Lytton in the novel *Paul Clifford*, the complete line was, "It was a dark and stormy night; the rain fell in torrents—except at occasional intervals, when it was checked by a violent gust of wind which swept up the streets (for it is in London that our scene lies), rattling along the housetops, and fiercely agitating the scanty flame of the lamps that struggled against the darkness." Widely regarded as one of the worst opening lines of all time, the sentence has spawned the annual Bulwer-Lytton Fiction Contest, in which contestants are required to create the worst opening sentence of an imaginary novel.

1. **Total book sales in the U.S. (2003): 2.22 billion**
2. **Number of books published in the U.S. in 2003: 164,000**
3. **Number of book-length manuscripts written by Americans annually: 750,000**
4. **Percentage of Americans who think they could write a book: 81**

Sources: **1.** Book Industry Study Group, *Atlanta Journal-Constitution*, 5/14/04. **2.** In 1975, 39,000 new books were published; by the year 2000, that number had risen to 122,000. In the same time period, the number of best-selling books sold has also skyrocketed. In 1975, the best-selling novel *Ragtime* by E. L. Doctorow sold 230,000 copies, while in 2000 the best-selling novel *The Brethren* by John Grisham sold 2,875,000 copies. (Bowker's *Books in Print*, reported in *Newsday*, 5/3/04; *New York Times*, 3/1/04) **3.** *American Libraries*, 2/03. **4.** Twenty-eight percent believe they could write a self-help or do-it-yourself book, 27% of 1975 would write fiction, and another 27% would write a historical work, biography, or other piece of nonfiction. (Jenkins Group, cited in *Charlotte Observer*, 1/8/03).

1. PERCENTAGE OF NOVELS SOLD IN THE UNITED STATES THAT ARE ROMANCE NOVELS: 34%

2. MYSTERIES OR THRILLERS: 19%

3. SCIENCE FICTION OR FANTASY: 6%

Thus, novels that have traditionally been viewed as trashy far outsell the category of "general fiction," the name given to works viewed as more literary, which accounts for only 25% of total fiction sales. (Ipsos Book Trends, reported in *Time Magazine*, 11/24/03)

Longest distance ever traveled to buy a book: 3,950 miles

On June 21, 2003, 16-year-old Emerson Spartz flew from Chicago to London for the purpose of buying a copy of *Harry Potter and the Order of the Phoenix*–in Spartz's words, "where the story began." "I want to feel the weight of that book," Spartz told the *Los Angeles Times*. "I want to hug it to my heart." (*Los Angeles Times*, 6/21/03).

FIRST TITLE IN THE CLIFFSNOTES SERIES: *HAMLET* (1958)

The inventor of CliffsNotes, Clifton Keith Hillegass, never wrote any of the study guides that made him wealthy. But he did donate $250,000 to establish a professorship in 19th-century literature at the University of Nebraska, Lincoln. (*Baltimore Sun*, 5/8/01)

1. FASTEST-SELLING BOOK OF ALL TIME: *HARRY POTTER AND THE ORDER OF THE PHOENIX*

2. SECOND-FASTEST-SELLING BOOK: *HARRY POTTER AND THE GOBLET OF FIRE*

3. RANK OF HARRY POTTER AMONG THE MOST FREQUENTLY BANNED BOOKS IN AMERICA: FIRST

4. RANK OF *HUCKLEBERRY FINN* AMONG BANNED BOOKS: SEVENTH

Sources: **1.** In its first 24 hours, J. K. Rowling's fifth installment in the Harry Potter series sold 5 million copies in the U.S. and another 1 million copies in the U.K. After the books went on sale on June 21, 2003, at 12:01 A.M., Barnes and Noble sold the book at the rate of more than 80 copies per second. By midnight on June 22, 1 in every 60 Americans had bought a copy of the book. (*Guardian*, 7/1/03; *Entertainment Weekly*, 12/26/03) **2.** The fourth book in the Harry Potter series sold a mere 3 million copies in its first 48 hours. The Potter franchise has been good to the author Rowling. A single mother "on the dole" when she began the series, she is now richer than Queen Elizabeth II. (Knight Ridder/Tribune Business News, 6/20/03) **3.** Harry Potter books have not only been banned, they've been burned. Jack Brock, pastor of the Christ Community Church in Alamogordo, N.M., called the Potter books "a masterpiece of satanic deception" as his congregation burned them in December 2001. A congregation in Greenville, Mich., relegated Harry Potter books "and other witchcraft items" to a bonfire in August 2003. (*Independent*, 1/1/02; AP Online, 12/31/01; *Detroit Free Press*, 8/6/03) **4.** *South Florida Sun-Sentinel*, 9/21/03.

World's most prolific author: José Carlos Ryoki Inoue of Brazil

After abandoning a medical career in 1986, Inoue has churned out a staggering 1,070 books. Using 39 different pseudonyms, including Tex Taylor and Billy Smart, Inoue specializes in pulp fiction, private eye stories, and westerns. Apart from his public output, Inoue's diary, which stretches over 2 decades, is 38 million words long and growing. He can write a chapter during a trip to the bathroom, and a 195-page novel in one day. According to the man himself, "Truthfully, I haven't even read all the books I've written." (*Wall Street Journal*, 2/5/96; *Akron Journal*, 12/29/96; e-mail to the author)

1. BEST-SELLING COPYRIGHTED BOOK OF ALL TIME: *GUINNESS BOOK OF WORLD RECORDS*

2. BEST-SELLING NONCOPYRIGHTED WORKS, IN ORDER: THE BIBLE, THE KORAN, MAO'S *LITTLE RED BOOK*

Sources: **1.** The Guinness book first won a place in its own pages in 1974, with 23.9 million copies sold, and has since cracked the 100 million sales threshold. The book was originally conceived on a 1951 hunting trip when an argument ensued about what was Europe's fastest bird. No book held the answer, so Norris and Ross McWhirter wrote one. (*New York Times*, 4/21/04) **2.** *Independent*, 4/21/04.

Original titles of famous books:

1. "Catch-18" (*Catch-22*)
2. "Pansy" (*Gone With the Wind*)
3. *1805* (*War and Peace*)
4. "Trimalchio in West Egg" (*The Great Gatsby*)
5. "The Last Man in Europe" (*1984*)

Sources: **1.** Heller's title had to be changed to *Catch-22* because Leon Uris was coming out with *Mila 18* the same year. (*Deseret Morning News*, 6/25/03) **2.** In earlier drafts, Scarlett was named *Pansy* O'Hara, hence Mitchell's aborted title for the book. Prospective titles also included "Tote the Weary Load" and "Tomorrow Is Another Day." **3.** Tolstoy originally meant to call it "1825," then published it as *1805* before changing it to *War and Peace*. (*Independent*, 10/2/99) **4.** Fitzgerald was also considering calling Gatsby "The High Bouncing Lover." (Bernard, *Now All We Need Is a Title*) **5.** Orwell thought "The Last Man" title was too bleak, and instead switched the last two digits of the year it was completed (1948) to come up with the title. (*New York Times*, 12/28/83)

FIRST BOOKS PUBLISHED IN PAPERBACK:

LOST HORIZON (JAMES HILTON) THE GOOD EARTH (PEARL BUCK)

Although rudimentary paperback books had been printed since the 18th century, the first "official" paperbacks were published by Pocket Books in 1939 and sold for 25¢, about an hour's wage at the time (Buck's book was also the first to use the phrase "Complete and Unabridged"). The first paperback to sell 1 million copies was *How to Win Friends and Influence People*, written in 1940 by Dale Carnegie. (*The Great American Paperback*; Columbia (S.C.) *State*, 2/10/02)

1. Most books written about a president:
1,098 (Abe Lincoln)
2. Most books written about a baseball team:
215 (New York Yankees)

Sources: **1.** Washington comes in second (750 books as of 2004), followed by Jefferson (716) and Kennedy (695). (*USA Today*, 2/14/04) **2.** The Red Sox, alas, finish second, with 115 books as of 2004, followed by the Cubs, with 99. (*Bowker's Books in Print*, cited in *USA Today*, 3/3/04)

BOSSES

1. Percentage of Americans who say they would prefer working for a male boss: 48%

2. Percentage who would prefer having a female boss: 22%

3. Odds that a worker will be criticized by their boss on any given day: 1 in 5

Sources: **1, 2.** Interestingly, women are 5% more likely to prefer a male boss than their male colleagues. Only 15% of senior management positions in American companies are held by women. (Gallup poll, December 2000; *Economist*, 6/28/03) **3.** *Fortune*, 3/18/96.

1. NUMBER OF TIMES GEORGE STEINBRENNER HIRED BILLY MARTIN TO BE YANKEES MANAGER: 5

2. NUMBER OF TIMES STEINBRENNER FIRED MARTIN: 5

Martin was also fired by four other teams during his managing career. When Martin died in a car accident in 1989, Steinbrenner said that "it's like losing part of my own family." (*USA Today*, 12/26/89)

NUMBER OF EMPLOYEES TERMINATED BY "NEUTRON" JACK WELCH: 118,000

Welch received the nickname "Neutron Jack" because (like the bomb of the same name), he eliminated people but kept buildings intact. Welch fired about 118,000 employees in his first few years as head of General Electric, but was eventually named Manager of the Century by *Fortune* magazine. (*Baltimore Sun*, 2/8/04)

PERCENTAGE OF A COMPANY'S EMPLOYEES THAT JACK WELCH SAYS SHOULD BE ELIMINATED EVERY YEAR: 10%

At General Electric, Welch created a system (widely imitated since) of employee grading, under which the bottom 10% of employees are laid off. In his book *Jack, Straight from the Gut*, Welch tells a story about going into a tie store on Fifth Avenue. The manager had seen Welch on TV, and asked whether he could have a word with him in the back. Gesturing toward his 20 salesmen, he asked, "Do I really have to let two go?" Welch answered, "You probably do, if you want the best sales staff on Fifth Avenue." (Welch, *Jack, Straight from the Gut*)

Most deceptive euphemism for laying off employees: "Rightsizing"

Originally used by IBM when it layed off 35,000 employees in the early 1990s, the term is now regularly used to refer to the firing of groups of employees. Other euphemisms for getting rid of employees include "reengineering," "outsourcing," and "managing down." (*New York Times*, 11/10/02; *U.S. News and World Report*, 11/25/02)

INCREASED RISK OF HEART ATTACK FACED BY EMPLOYER FIRING AN EMPLOYEE IN THE WEEK AFTER GIVING THE AX: 100%

According to a 1998 study from the Beth Israel Hospital in Boston, managers are twice as likely to have a heart attack in the week after they fire someone. (*Chicago Tribune*, 3/23/98)

FIRST REAL-LIFE EMPLOYER CHARACTERIZED IN THE NEWSPAPERS AS "THE BOSS FROM HELL": LEONA HELMSLEY

Helmsley, the owner of numerous Manhattan hotels with her husband Harry, had a reputation for being a difficult boss, and it came back to haunt her at her 1989 trial for tax fraud. One of her hotel managers testified that when he refused to sign a doctored invoice, she screamed, "You f**k, you're not my partner! You sign what you're told to sign." Another employee testified that when he tried to convince Helmsley to pay a contractor by noting that he had six children to support, she responded, "Why didn't he keep his pants on?" Even her own attorney at the trial characterized her to the jury as a "tough bitch." (*People*, 9/11/89; *Newsday*, 7/14/89)

PERCENTAGE OF WORKERS WHO SAY THEY HAVE TOLD LIES ON BEHALF OF THEIR SUPERVISORS: 88%

Roughly a quarter of secretaries have seen bosses fake expense reports, a fifth have seen information destroyed, and a third have observed time sheets doctored. (*U.S. News and World Report*, 9/28/98)

1. RATIO BETWEEN THE PAY RECEIVED BY THE AVERAGE CEO AND THE AVERAGE AMERICAN WORKER IN 2004: 301 TO 1

2. RATIO BETWEEN THE PAY RECEIVED BY THE AVERAGE JAPANESE CEO AND WORKER IN 2004: 10 TO 1

Sources: **1, 2.** It was only 42 to 1 as recently as 1980. (UPI, 8/6/04)

BOWLING

1. **Number of perfect 300 games rolled in 1952:** 198
2. **Number in 2003:** 48,810
3. **Number of bowling alleys in 1963:** 10,883
4. **Number of bowling alleys in 2002:** 5,973

Sources: **1.** And in 1970, there were 854 perfect games bowled. (*Dayton Daily News*, 4/2/04) **2.** Experts attribute much of the dramatic increase in perfect games to a lane-oiling method called the "house shot," in which a heavier coat of shine is applied to the center of the lane, with the sides left thinner to form "dry boards." (*New York Times*, 1/5/03; ABC) **3.** More alleys than at any time in history. (*Los Angeles Times*, 9/2/03) **4.** *Los Angeles Times*, 9/2/03.

1. HIGHEST SCORE EVER
BOWLED BY A FIRST-TIME BOWLER:

298

(STEVE TUDOR, MAY 23, 2003)

(American Bowling Congress)

HIGHEST BOWLING SCORE EVER ACHIEVED BY A PRESIDENT: 233 RICHARD NIXON

Nixon took up the sport in the 1970s and quickly became an avid player. He had a bowling alley built at Camp David, and could often be found late at night at the White House lanes, bowling alone, his score kept by Joe Taylor, the keeper of the White House lanes. (*Smithsonian*, 1/03; Reeves, *Nixon*)

OLDEST STILL-OPERATING BOWLING ALLEY IN AMERICA: HOLLER HOUSE IN MILWAUKEE, WISC.

Opened in 1908 and still operated by the same family, Holler House occupies 2 lanes in the basement of a tavern in downtown Milwaukee. Score sheets at Holler House are clipped to the wall with wooden clothespins, and pins are still picked up and set by pin boys. The second-oldest bowling alley is Elk's Bowling Lanes, operating 4 lanes in Fond du Lac, Wisconsin since 1909. (American Bowling Congress)

PEOPLE WHO'VE QUIT THEIR JOBS TO BOWL IN EVERY STATE IN AMERICA: MIKE WALSH

Motivated by his late father, who died before completing his own quest to play handball in every state in America, Walsh quit his marketing job and on Sept. 17, 2002, began his own epic bowling trip across America. Walsh logged 25,211 miles as he bowled from Sawmill Lanes in Columbus, Ohio, to Hilo Lanes in Hawaii (he flew there), where he completed his goal on Mar. 5, 2003. His final stats: 65 pairs of bowling shoes rented, and a paltry 132 average. But it was never about the bowling. Says Walsh: "People don't just bowl at bowling alleys. . . . They forget about work, home, tragic news headlines. And they smoke. Man, do they smoke." (*Chicago Sun-Times*, 3/6/03; BowlingRoadTrip.com)

FIRST BOWLING FACILITY IN AMERICA: 1733
(BOWLING GREEN PARK, NEW YORK CITY)

In 1733, the land that is now called Bowling Green in downtown Manhattan was rented to three citizens for one peppercorn a year for the purpose of building a bowling green. The game was more akin to lawn bowling than the sport we know today. (Bosker, *Bowled Over; New York Times*, 3/21/85)

1. Year a bowling alley was installed in the White House: 1947
2. Only president to appear on the cover of a bowling magazine: Harry Truman
3. Year a bowling league began in the White House: 1950

Sources: **1.** In 1947, friends of Harry Truman paid to install a two-lane bowling alley in the White House basement for the president's 63rd birthday. (Williams, *How to Be President*) **2.** A picture of Truman bowling appears on the cover of the June 1947 edition of the *National Kegler*, a magazine devoted to bowling. (*Chicago Tribune*, 9/8/95) **3.** The league—featuring teams from the Secret Service, the secretarial staff, domestic help, gardeners, and secretaries—was the only one in history where every member had to have top security clearance. The league's last game was played on Sept. 10, 2001. After Sept. 11, the league members were refused entry. (*Smithsonian*, 1/03)

NUMBER OF BOWLING INJURIES REQUIRING HOSPITAL EMERGENCY ROOM VISITS IN 2003: 21,514

A significant percentage of these emergency room visits involve bowlers who drop balls onto their foot, or get their fingers caught between two bowling balls in the bowling ball return. (NEISS)

Years that *Bowling for Dollars* ran on television: 10

The syndicated show, in which amateur bowlers introduced themselves and then bowled for prizes, routinely beat out the evening news in many markets. Unlike other sports, bowling has inspired numerous TV game shows including *Celebrity Bowling, Make That Spare, Pinbusters,* and *Strikes and Spares*. (KidScreen, 12/1/97)

BRAINS

1. Weight of the average human male brain: 3.08 pounds

2. Weight of the average female brain: 2.85 pounds

3. Weight of Einstein's brain: 2.71 pounds

4. Percentage by which human brains have shrunk in the past 30,000 years: 10–15%

Sources: **1, 2.** Human male brains contain 22.8 billion neurons, as opposed to 19.3 billion neurons in female brains. However, there is no sex difference in neuronal density, which is thought to be more closely correlated to intelligence. (*Intelligence*, 3/1/99; *Toronto Star*, 8/28/95) **3.** Despite the relatively small size of Einstein's brain, his parietal lobes were 15% larger than average, which is the part of the brain responsible for mathematical reasoning. (*Guardian*, 4/5/04; *Miami Herald*, 8/3/04) **4.** Some theorists attribute the reduction to smaller body mass, while others point out that domesticated mammals like ourselves tend to have smaller brains than those that live in the wild. (*Times* [London], 4/22/03)

NUMBER OF YEARS EINSTEIN'S BRAIN WAS LOST: 23

After his death at Princeton Medical Center on Apr. 18, 1955, Einstein was cremated, but not before his brain was removed by Dr. Thomas Harvey, who was going to have it examined by a nationwide team of experts. Instead, however, Harvey kept the brain himself until 1978, when a reporter researching the brain's whereabouts finally found him in Wichita, Kans., along with two mason jars that contained Einstein's brain. (*Newsweek*, 6/28/99)

1. MAN WHO INVENTED THE FIRST INTELLIGENCE TEST: ALFRED BINET
2. YEAR THE TERM "IQ" WAS COINED: 1916

Sources: **1.** In 1905, French psychologist Alfred Binet devised a test involving analogies and reasoning skills to identify Parisian schoolchildren in need of remedial education. (*Newsweek*, 10/24/94) **2.** In 1912, German psychologist William Stern came up with a means of determining intelligence irrespective of age by dividing a person's so-called mental age by his chronological age, which he called the "intelligence quotient." Four years later, Lewis Terman tweaked Stern's formula and shortened "intelligence quotient" to "IQ," which has become the accepted term. (Black, *War Against the Weak*)

1. AVERAGE AMERICAN IQ: 98
2. NATION WITH THE HIGHEST AVERAGE IQ: HONG KONG (107)

Source: **1.** The United States is tied for 17th in the international IQ standings with Australia, Denmark, France, and Norway, according to a recent study from the University of Vienna Medical School. **2.** South Korea, Singapore, and Japan took places 2, 3, and 4. (*Sunday Times* [London], 12/21/03)

SOMETHING SAID BY AN ANIMAL WITH THE ABILITY TO COMMUNICATE WITH HUMANS:

"I want to buy a pool."
—Spoken on a keyboard voice synthesizer by Chantek,
a 20-year-old orangutan with a sign language vocabulary of 2,000 words.
A heat wave had been making life in its cage unbearable.

(*Sunday Times* [London], 7/25/99)

FARM ANIMALS RANKED BY INTELLIGENCE:
1. DOG 2. PIG 3. HORSE 4. CAT 5. COW
6. SHEEP 7. CHICKEN 8. TURKEY

This ranking is based on a 1997 Oregon State University survey of zoologists, animal science faculty, and students. A letter writer took issue with the chicken's lowly rank, its writer informing the article's author that if he had been taken away from his mother at a young age and confined for life to a small cage, he too would not seem terribly smart. (*Feedstuffs*, 9/17/01)

TWO CONTENDERS FOR THE SMARTEST PERSON EVER:
MICHAEL KEVIN KEARNEY (1984–):

Born nearly 2 months premature, he was supposed to be developmentally slow, but at 4 months, he was already saying "Daddy," "Mama," and "Where's my breast milk?" At 6 months, during a visit to the pediatrician, Michael diagnosed himself when he told the stunned doctor, "I have a left ear infection." By age 6, he had maxed out on his IQ test, which, adjusted for his chronological age, registered at an astonishing 325. He graduated high school at age 6 and received a bachelor's degree in anthropology from the University of South Alabama at age 10. Kearney hopes to become a game show host because, he says, the job pays "quite a lot of money for not a lot of work." (*Saturday Evening Post*, 5/96; *Edmonton Journal*, 3/24/02; *Newsday*, 6/30/94)

WILLIAM JAMES SIDIS (1898–1944):

He could read the newspaper at 18 months of age, completed a treatise on anatomy by age 5, and became the youngest person to attend Harvard at age 11. He eventually learned all the world's major languages and even created one of his own, which he called "Vendergood." At age 11, he lectured on the topic of "four-dimensional bodies" at Harvard's prestigious Mathematical Club. His IQ is believed to have been between 250 and 300. Unfortunately, he was never allowed to be a child, was hounded by the media into adulthood, and died of a stroke, embittered and destitute, at the age of 46. (*Washington Post*, 7/27/86; *New York Times*, 6/13/86)

World's most intelligent couple: Marilyn vos Savant and Dr. Robert Jarvik

According to the *Guinness Book of World Records*, Marilyn vos Savant is the world's most intelligent woman. When she took the Stanford-Binet test at age 10, her IQ was measured at 230. Dr. Jarvik developed the first artificial heart. The couple's wedding rings were crafted by Jarvik out of gold and pyrolitic carbon, the same materials used to make the artificial heart's valves. According to vos Savant, her first conversation with Jarvik was about "how difficult it is to find anyone really to talk to." (*Orlando Sentinel*, 4/5/90; *Syracuse Post-Standard*, 8/26/87)

BREAKFAST

1. Number of breakfasts the average American skips annually: 50

2. Times per year the average American eats cereal for breakfast: 98

3. Times per year the average American eats eggs for breakfast: 33

4. Percentage of those eggs that are scrambled: 45%

5. Times per year the average American eats bacon for breakfast: 13

Sources: **1.** Recent studies indicate that 17% of Americans do not eat breakfast at all. (NPD Group, *USA Today*, 9/26/02; Copley News Service, 9/22/03) **2.** The average American also eats cereal about 2.2 times annually for lunch, 2.3 times for dinner, and 3.2 times as a snack. (*Grocery Headquarters*, 11/1/02) **3.** NPD Group, cited in *USA Today*, 9/26/02 **4.** *Research Alert*, 10/4/02. **5.** The average American eats sausage for breakfast 10 times a year. (*Deseret Morning News*, 10/10/02)

WORLD'S MOST EXPENSIVE OMELET: $1,000 (PARKER MERIDIEN HOTEL, NEW YORK CITY)

The omelet features six eggs, lobster, and 10 ounces of sevruga caviar (the hotel purportedly pays $65 per ounce). Said one diner quoted in New York's *Daily News*, "When I saw '1,000' on the menu, I thought it was the calorie count." As of October 2004, four of the $1,000 omelets had been ordered. (*Daily News*, 5/17/04)

1. FIRST CEREAL TO HAVE A PRIZE INSIDE EACH SPECIALLY MARKED BOX: QUAKER OATS (1891)

2. NUMBER OF DEEDS TO AN INCH OF LAND DISPENSED IN SPECIALLY MARKED POST CEREAL BOXES IN 1955: 21 MILLION

Sources: **1.** In 1891, Quaker offered a piece of chinaware inside every box of its oats. (QuakerOatmeal.com) **2.** In 1955, Quaker paid $1,000 for a 7.7-hectare piece of land in the Canadian Yukon, divided it into 1-inch pieces, and then offered deeds to those pieces in 21 million boxes of puffed wheat and rice. In 1965, the Canadian government seized the land for failure to pay $37.20 in unpaid taxes. Quaker still gets dozens of inquiries a year from people with deeds to the 1-inch parcels. (*Tampa Tribune*, 5/17/04)

FIRST BREAKFAST CEREAL: GRANULA (1863)

It was invented by Dr. James C. Jackson, operator of a spa called our Our Home Hygienic Institute and a believer in "regularity." Granula ("little grain" in Latin) was a graham flour and water mixture that tasted somewhat like Grape Nuts. Though it had to soak in milk overnight before the cereal softened enough to eat, Granula was a commercial success. (*Oxford Companion to Food*)

Strangest reported benefit of eating a breakfast cereal: Aphrodisiac

In 1956, Frank Sinatra told the magazine *Hollywood Confidential* that he ate a bowl of Wheaties before each one of his sexual escapades, which made him "the Tarzan of the boudoir." (*Newsday*, 3/11/02)

1. WORLD'S LARGEST CEREAL CONSUMERS: THE ENGLISH

2. BEST-SELLING CEREAL IN ENGLAND: WEETABIX

3. BEST-SELLING CEREALS IN AMERICA: CHEERIOS, FROSTED FLAKES, HONEY NUT CHEERIOS

Sources: **1.** The British bought $35 worth of breakfast cereal per capita in 1999, while Americans bought $32 per capita. Generally, English-speaking countries are the highest breakfast cereal consumers in the world. In Spain, consumers spend only about $2 per person on cereal, and in Italy, about $3.40. (*Guardian*, 12/19/03; *International Food Ingredients*, 3/00) **2.** Weetabix is similar to Shredded Wheat. (*Marketing*, 5/12/04) **3.** Sales in 2003: 103 million boxes of Cheerios, 88 million boxes of Frosted Flakes, and 73 million boxes of Honey Nut Cheerios. (*Grocery Headquarters*, 4/1/04)

ORIGINAL NAMES OF CEREALS:

WHEATIES: "WASHBURN'S GOLD MEDAL WHOLE WHEAT FLAKES"

CHEERIOS: "CHEERIOATS"

KELLOGG'S CORN FLAKES: "GRANOSE FLAKES"

Source: **1.** *Newsday*, 3/11/02. **2.** Cheerioats debuted in 1941. In 1945, Cheerioats was forced to change its name to Cheerios when Quaker Oats protested the name's use of "oats," which Quaker Oats had trademarked. (*Consumer Reports*, 10/96) **3.** *Oxford Companion to Food*. **4.** When C. W. Post brought out his version of corn flakes in 1906, he called his product Elijah's Manna, after the food that rained down on the Israelites and the biblical prophet. Christian clergy were aghast, and in 1908, he changed the name to Post Toasties. (*Washington Post*, 6/10/81)

CALENDARS

1. **NUMBER OF CALENDARS OWNED BY THE AVERAGE AMERICAN HOUSEHOLD:** 5
2. **PRECISE LENGTH OF A SOLAR YEAR:** 365.2421896698 DAYS
3. **LONGEST YEAR IN HISTORY:** 445 DAYS (45 B.C.)

Sources: **1.** Calendar Marketing Association, *Hartford Courant*, 12/9/99. **2.** Meaning, it takes exactly 365 days, 5 hours, 48 minutes, and 46 seconds for the earth to orbit the sun. (*San Francisco Chronicle*, 11/29/03) **3.** In 46 B.C., Julius Caesar returned home to find that the Roman calendar had gotten ahead of the solar calendar by a full 2 months. To correct this, Caesar ordered that several additional months be added to 46 B.C. between November and December. Known as "the Year of Confusion," the year 46 B.C. thus ended up with a total of 445 days. (Duncan, *Calendar*)

DATE NEW YEAR'S DAY WAS CELEBRATED IN AMERICA UNTIL 1752: MARCH 25

As a British colony, the American colonies adopted the British Empire's rejection of the January 1 New Year's date in the Gregorian calendar, which was followed by most of the rest of the world. Thus, under the British system, March 24, *1740*, would be followed by March 25, *1741*. The year would change, but the month would stay the same. And Dec. 31, 1741, would be followed by Jan. 1 of the same year, with 1742 not arriving until March 25. (Steel, *Marking Time*)

1. **Date George Washington was born:** Feb. 11, 1731
2. **Date George Washington would have been born if our current calendar had been in use:** Feb. 22, 1732

The problem with the Julian calendar (named for Julius Caesar) used by the Americans wasn't limited to its odd date for New Year's. The Julian calendar gave each year an extra 11 minutes and 15 seconds more than the solar year allowed, amounting to an extra day every 128 years. Thus, by the time Washington was born, the American calendar had fallen behind the Gregorian calendar used by the majority of the world by 11 days. (*Chicago Tribune*, 1/1/88)

DATE AFTER WEDNESDAY, SEPT. 2, 1752, IN AMERICA: THURSDAY, SEPT. 14, 1752

In 1751, the British agreed to convert to the Gregorian calendar. To correct for the 11-day difference between the old and new calendars (see above), the authorities essentially eliminated 11 days, saying that Sept. 2 would be followed by Sept. 14. Workers in England protested under banners that said, "Give Us Back Our Eleven Days," and riots erupted, with some calling the calendar change a Catholic plot to deprive workers of their wages. (Duncan, *Calendar*)

NUMBER OF DAYS LATE THE RUSSIAN OLYMPIC TEAM ARRIVED AT THE 1908 LONDON OLYMPICS: 12

The problem arose from the difference in calendars used by Russia and the rest of the world. Russia still used the Julian calendar at the time of the 1908 Olympics, and calculated their date of arrival accordingly. However, since the Julian calendar was at that point over 12 days behind the Gregorian calendar used by most of the rest of the world, the team arrived after the competition had already been completed. Russia did not finally change calendars until 1918, after the "October Revolution" (which actually fell in November under the Gregorian calendar). (Richards, *Mapping Time*)

Meaning of "A.D.": "Anno Domini" (Latin for "in the year of the Lord")

It is unknown why B.C. is an abbreviation of the English phrase "before Christ" while its A.D. counterpart is in Latin. (*New York Times*, 10/20/81)

1. WHAT OUR A.D. YEAR IS ALLEGEDLY CALCULATED FROM: BIRTH OF JESUS
2. NUMBER OF YEARS OUR CALENDAR IS IN ERROR ABOUT JESUS' BIRTHDATE: AT LEAST 4

Sources: **1.** In the sixth century A.D. a monk named Dionysius Exiguus ("Denny the Short") invented the modern calendar by calculating what he believed to be the date of Jesus's birth, and then devised a system whereby the years would be calculated from that date. According to Dionysius, Jesus was born 525 years earlier, and so the present year was 525 A.D. (*Atlantic Monthly*, 7/97) **2.** The general consensus among scholars today is that Jesus was born no later than 4 B.C., though some place his birth as far back as 7 B.C. In any event, our calendar is at least 4 years behind where it should be. (*Atlantic Monthly*, 7/97)

DICTATORS WHO RENAMED MONTHS:
JULIUS CAESAR OF ROME

Renamed the month Quintilis to Julius (July). (*Atlanta Journal-Constitution*, 12/30/02)

AUGUSTUS OF ROME

Successor to Julius Caesar, he renamed Sextilis to Augustus (August), and added an extra day to it so it would be as long as July. (*Guardian*, 8/25/01)

SAPARMURAT NIYAZOVN OF TURKMENISTAN

January became Turkmenbashi (the president's nickname); April is Gurbansoltan Edzhe (the name of his mother); and September became Rukhnama (the name of a book he wrote). (*RIA Novosti*, 8/12/02)

1. YEAR 1 IN THE HEBREW CALENDAR: 3761 B.C.
2. YEAR 1 IN THE MUSLIM CALENDAR: 622 A.D.
3. YEAR 1 IN THE CHINESE CALENDAR: 2637 B.C.

Sources: **1.** Being the year in which traditional Jews believe the world was created. Thus, in the Jewish calendar, the year 2005 A.D. is the year 5766. (*Washington Post*, 1/1/96) **2.** The date of Muhammad's journey from Mecca to Medina. Therefore, in the Muslim calendar, 2005 is the year 1383. (*Financial Times* [London], 1/3/87) **3.** The prevailing belief is that a Chinese emperor named Huangdi introduced the calendar in 2637 B.C., although others attribute the beginning of the Chinese calendar to 1953 B.C. For calculation purposes, however, it makes no difference, since the year on the Chinese calendar in 2005 (4074) bears no relationship to our Gregorian calendar. (Steel, *Marking Time*)

CANDY AND OTHER SNACKS

1. ORIGIN OF THE WORD "CANDY": THE SANSKRIT WORD "KHANDA" (MEANING "PIECE OF CRYSTALLIZED SUGAR")

2. AMOUNT THE AVERAGE AMERICAN SPENDS ANNUALLY ON CANDY: $84

3. AMOUNT OF CANDY CONSUMED ANNUALLY BY THE AVERAGE AMERICAN: 23.9 POUNDS

4. AMOUNT OF THAT WHICH IS CHOCOLATE: 11.6 POUNDS

5. PERCENTAGE OF THE WORLD'S ALMONDS THAT END UP IN CHOCOLATE BARS: 40%

Sources: **1.** Indians were the first people to boil down the sap from sugar cane and make it into a primitive form of sugar. (*Los Angeles Times*, 2/13/92) **2.** *Candy Industry*, 11/1/03. **3.** According to the National Confectioners Association, candy consuming by Americans reached a high of 25.4 pounds a year in 1997. (*Candy Industry*, 10/1/03) **4.** *Candy Industry*, 11/1/03. **5.** Likewise, 20% of the world's peanuts are also combined with chocolate. (*Atlanta Journal-Constitution*, 10/31/02)

YEAR THE FIRST CHOCOLATE BAR WAS INTRODUCED: 1847

In 1847, Fry and Sons, a British concern, mixed some cocoa butter with chocolate, added sugar to create a paste, and made the first commercial chocolate bars, known as Five Boys (after Fry's sons). In 1849, Cadbury Brothers, another British company, came out with its own candy bar. Hershey's, the first American chocolate bar, came out in 1905. (*Times Higher Education Supplement* [London], 5/21/04)

1. Largest per capita candy consumption in the world: Denmark
2. Largest per capita chocolate consumption in the world: Switzerland

The average Dane consumes 35.1 pounds of candy and other sweets per year. The average Swiss citizen consumes 22.4 pounds of chocolate per year. (*Professional Candy Buyer*, 5/02)

PERCENTAGE OF CANDY SALES THAT ARE "IMPULSE BUYS": 55%

A recent study suggests that chocolate can produce opiates—druglike chemicals that cause pleasure sensations in the body. "It's a form of addiction," says University of Michigan professor Adam Drewnowski. "You really can be a chocoholic." (*Confectioner*, 9/03)

YEAR THOUSANDS OF BABY RUTH BARS WERE DROPPED BY PLANE OVER PITTSBURGH: 1923

In a 1923 publicity stunt, Otto Schnering, founder of the Curtiss Candy Company, chartered a plane and dropped thousands of Baby Ruths on Pittsburgh, each of which floated to the ground under a small parachute. The stunt resulted in an enormous traffic jam and headlines for the 3-year-old candy, and Baby Ruth repeated the "bombing" in 40 states. (Brenner, *Emperors of Chocolate*)

1. Average number of M&M's eaten in one sitting by a person with a 1-pound bag of the candy: 112
2. Average number of M&M's eaten by a person with a 2-pound bag: 156

In other words, people eat what they're given, according to Brian Wansink, director of the Food and Brand Research Lab at the University of Illinois, who conducted the study. Similar results occurred with bags of popcorn. (*Minneapolis Star Tribune*, 1/21/00; ABC's *20/20*, 4/2/99)

CRIMINAL DEFENSES BASED ON THE ALLEGED OVERCONSUMPTION OF JUNK FOOD:

TWINKIE DEFENSE (1978)

After San Francisco city supervisor Dan White killed Mayor George Moscone and another elected official, a psychiatrist argued that the perpetrator suffered from temporary insanity due to the overconsumption of Twinkies and other junk food. "There is a substantial body of evidence that in susceptible individuals, large quantities of . . . junk food . . . can precipitate . . . violent behavior," testified Dr. Martin Blinder. The jury absolved White of murder but convicted him of voluntary manslaughter. (AP, 10/17/84)

COTTON CANDY DEFENSE (1995)

On Apr. 7, 1995, Wesley Shaffer broke into a house in Boca Raton. After his subsequent arrest, his lawyer had two psychiatrists testify that Shaffer's consumption of a bag and a half of cotton candy on April 6 prompted a psychotic episode in Shaffer, a diabetic, causing him to commit the burglary. The jury didn't buy it, and found him guilty. (*South Florida Sun-Sentinel*, 11/19/96)

BEST-SELLING COOKIES IN THE U.S.:
1. OREOS
2. CHIPS AHOYS
3. GIRL SCOUT THIN MINTS

In 2003, more than 200 million boxes of Girl Scout Thin Mints were sold in the U.S. (*New York Times*, 3/14/04)

RANK OF HOLIDAYS BY CANDY SALES, FROM MOST TO LEAST:

1. Halloween
2. Easter
3. Christmas
4. Valentine's Day

(National Confectioners Association, *MMR*, 5/31/04)

FIRST COMMERCIALLY SUCCESSFUL COMBO CANDY BAR: CLARK BAR (1917)

Made of both chocolate and peanuts, the candy bar was an instant success with Allied troops, who happily consumed D ration candy bars throughout World Wars I and II. It was originally marketed as a health food, with a wrapper reading: "Try eating a Clark bar every day between 2 and 4 p.m. Drink a glass of water and see how much pep you have when the day is done." (NPR, 10/31/03; Richardson, *Sweets*)

1. AMOUNT OF SUGAR THE AVERAGE AMERICAN CONSUMED ANNUALLY IN 1800: 7 POUNDS

2. SUGAR CONSUMED ANNUALLY IN 2002: 147 POUNDS

(Atlanta Journal-Constitution, 11/17/02)

NUMBER OF NUTS IN EACH SNICKERS BAR: 15

Forrest Mars, the founder of the Mars company, was a perfectionist, and insisted that each Snickers Bar contain exactly 15 peanuts. (*Washington Post*, 7/6/99)

First heart-shaped box of chocolates: 1861

Sometimes attributed to 1868, though there is no dispute that the first heart-shaped box chocolate was made by Richard Cadbury, and featured a picture of his daughter holding a kitten. (*Times Higher Education Supplement* [London], 5/21/04; *San Francisco Chronicle*, 2/10/99)

JELL-O CAPITAL OF THE WORLD: SALT LAKE CITY, UTAH

No place ranks higher than Salt Lake City in per capita Jell-O consumption. That title was briefly lost to Des Moines, Iowa, in 1999, but has again been retaken. Lime is the favorite flavor. (*Salt Lake Tribune*, 2/19/02)

1. NUMBER OF COCOA BEANS IT COST A MAYAN TO PURCHASE A RABBIT IN THE 12TH CENTURY: 8
2. TO PURCHASE A SLAVE: 100

(*Times Higher Educational Supplement*, [London], 5/21/04)

BIRTH OF THE LOLLIPOP: 1892

While sources differ as to the precise date, most agree that the lollipop was invented by Connecticut candy maker George Smith who put candy on a stick and called it a "lollypop" after a popular racehorse of the time. Smith trademarked the word in 1931, but it is now in the public domain, and open to all users. (*Time*, 9/14/98)

PERCENTAGE OF M&M'S THAT ARE BROWN: 30%

Red and yellow each account for 20%; and orange, blue, and green 10% each. Called "the Howard Hughes of candy," Forrest Mars, the man who created M&M's, was such a tightwad that his own children were not allowed to eat his M&M candies—Mars told them there were none to spare. For years, there has been a persistent urban myth that green M&M's are a sexual stimulant. Seeking neither to confirm nor deny the rumor, Mars put out a press release in 1997 stating that "There is no scientific evidence that green is not an aphrodisiac." (*Art Journal*, 2/22/99; *Dallas Morning News*, 1/23/97)

CARS

1. Miles the average American drives each year: 15,000

2. Amount the average American family spends on gasoline: $2,700

3. Percentage of Americans who believe they're above-average drivers: 74%

4. Percentage who believe they're below average: 1%

Sources: **1.** The average parent spends more than twice as much time with their car than with their children. Among things people do in their cars: pick their nose (17%); meditate (33%); drum on the dash (22%); shave (12%); talk to themselves (46%); have sex (8%); and flirt with other motorists (17%). (American Automobile Association; *Toronto Sun*, 5/20/01) **2.** *Newsweek*, 9/6/04. **3, 4.** Eighty-one percent of men say they are above-average drivers, compared to 67% of women. (*Journal of Safety Research* 34, 2003)

1. CARS SOLD IN AMERICA IN 1900: 4,192
2. NUMBER OF CARS IN AMERICA IN 2004: 204 MILLION
3. NUMBER OF DRIVERS IN AMERICA IN 2004: 191 MILLION

Sources: **1.** *Washington Post*, 7/10/96. **2, 3.** Members of the average household journey out about four times a day by car, 45% of the time to shop or run errands. (*Atlanta Journal-Constitution*, 8/29/03; *Boston Globe*, 12/22/03)

NUMBER OF CARS IN CHINA IN 2004: 10 MILLION

A paltry number, considering China's whopping population of 1.3 billion. (*New York Times*, 9/26/04)

HIGHEST RECORDED MILEAGE ON A SINGLE AUTOMOBILE: 2.1 MILLION MILES

The record is held by Irv Gordon's 1966 Volvo P1800 sports car. The car's engine was rebuilt at 680,000 miles, and its transmission was replaced at 2 million miles. Gordon purchased the car for $4,150 on June 30, 1966, and attributes its longevity to (among other things) frequent washing. (*Florida Times-Union*, 5/14/04; *Toronto Star*, 3/11/00)

Worst car of the 20th century: The Yugo

Based on a survey of listeners of *Car Talk*, a syndicated show on NPR. Said one Yugo owner about the car: "At least it had heated rear windows—so your hands would stay warm while you pushed." Other cars in the bottom five: Chevy Vega, Ford Pinto, American Motors Gremlin, and the Chevy Chevette. (*New York Times*, 4/2/00)

First Japanese car imported into the U.S.: Toyopet Crown (1957)

Made by Toyota, the car was a commercial failure in the U.S., selling 1,028 cars at its peak in 1959. (*Autoweek*, 8/3/92)

Odds that a person has given another driver the finger: 4 in 10

The things that piss off drivers the most? Slow drivers in the left lane, abrupt lane-changers, and tailgaters. (*Dallas Morning News*, 9/9/97; NPR, 7/24/97)

1. PRICE OF A GALLON OF GAS IN HONG KONG IN 2004: $5.45
2. PRICE OF A GALLON IN CARACAS, VENEZUELA: 14c

London is next most expensive ($5.23 a gallon), followed by Tokyo ($4.53). (*Kansas City Star*, 5/22/04)

1. AGE AT WHICH THE AVERAGE PERSON'S DRIVING SKILLS BEGIN TO RAPIDLY DECLINE: 65
2. AGE AT WHICH THE AVERAGE PERSON GIVES UP DRIVING: 85

Sources: **1.** Statistics show that drivers older than 65 have the highest accident rates per miles driven. (*Minneapolis Star Tribune*, 11/23/99)
2. Indeed, in a recent study, 55% of men were still driving at 85 or older. (*Men's Health*, 5/1/01; Cox News Service, 7/29/02)

1. ODDS THAT A FEMALE DRIVER WILL CONSULT A MAP WHEN LOST: 8 IN 10
2. ODDS THAT A MALE DRIVER WILL DO SO: 5 IN 10

According to a recent survey by Marketfacts, rather than look at a map, 1 in 2 male drivers will continue driving until they figure out where they are. (PR Newswire, 5/25/04)

REASON WHY THE BRITISH FIRST BEGAN DRIVING ON THE LEFT:
BECAUSE SWORDS WERE WORN ON THE LEFT

In medieval times, English warriors (most of whom were right-handed) wore their swords on their left sides. To prevent injury to pedestrians or horses going the other way, foot and horse traffic in England moved on the left, a practice that continued after the introduction of the automobile. (*Sunday Times* [London], 6/20/04)

PERCENTAGE OF THE WORLD'S COUNTRIES THAT DRIVE ON THE LEFT TODAY: 30%

Out of the world's 206 countries, 62 drive on the left, and 144 on the right. Numerous countries have switched from left to right, while the island of Okinawa made the only recorded switch from right to left, on July 30, 1978. (Shy, *The Economics of Network Industries*)

1. First traffic light: Cleveland, Ohio (1914)
2. First stop sign: Detroit, Mich. (1915)

Sources: **1.** The first electric traffic light was erected on the corner of 105th Street and Euclid in Cleveland on Aug. 5, 1914 (though Salt Lake City claims a rudimentary traffic signal was operating there in 1912). The light in Cleveland had two colors, red and green, and a buzzer to provide a warning for color changes. In 1918, the first three-color light was erected in New York City. (*Quality Progress*, 2/01) **2.** Originally, stop signs were yellow octagons with black letters before they became red and white. (*Boston Globe*, 10/27/02)

DATE ON WHICH THE U.S. GOVERNMENT BANNED ALL PLEASURE DRIVING ON THE EAST COAST: JAN. 6, 1943

Source: To conserve gasoline and rubber for the war effort, easterners either had to walk or take public transportation on family outings, or they couldn't go. (*USA Today*, 6/3/94)

1. NUMBER OF HOURS THE AVERAGE AMERICAN SITS IN TRAFFIC ANNUALLY: 46

2. NUMBER OF HOURS THE AVERAGE AMERICAN WAS STUCK IN TRAFFIC IN 1982: 16

According to the Texas Transportation Institute, Los Angeles had the worst traffic in the country in 2004, followed by San Francisco (73 hours stuck in traffic annually), Washington (67 hours), Dallas (61 hours), and Houston (58 hours). (*Chicago Tribune*, 9/8/04)

FIRST AUTO FATALITY IN THE U.S.: HENRY BLISS (SEPT. 13, 1899)

While stepping off a trolley car at Central Park West and 74th Street, Bliss was run over by a taxicab. Bliss was not the world's first road death, however—in 1896, one Bridget Driscoll was hit by a car on a London street. (*Chicago Tribune*, 9/26/04)

FIRST PERSON TO DRIVE CROSS-COUNTRY: HORATIO JACKSON (1903)

On May 23, 1903, Jackson, a Vermont doctor, set off from San Francisco in a 20-horsepower vehicle after a friend bet him $50 he couldn't complete the trip. There were 150 miles of paved roads in the entire nation, and no gas stations, road maps, or mechanics. Nevertheless, 63 days after starting the trip, Jackson pulled into Manhattan at 4:30 A.M. on July 26, 1903, having driven a total of 5,600 miles. On his way home to Vermont, Jackson got a speeding ticket "for driving the machine more than six miles an hour." (*Boston Globe*, 8/9/03)

1. First American to buy auto insurance: Gilbert Loomic (1897)

2. First car theft: Peugeot (Paris, 1896)

Sources: **1.** Loomis bought the plan from Travelers Property Casualty on Oct. 20, 1897, to cover an automobile that he had built from scratch. He paid a premium of $7.50 for $1,000 in coverage. (*Washington Post*, 7/10/96) **2.** In 1896, a Peugeot owned by a Baron de Zuylen was stolen by a mechanic after the Baron brought it in to the manufacturer for repairs. The first reported car theft in America took place in St. Louis, in 1905. (Berliner, *Book of Answers; St. Louis Post*, 2/5/00)

CATS

1. NUMBER OF CATS IN THE U.S.: 77.7 MILLION
2. AVERAGE LIFE EXPECTANCY: 15 YEARS
3. PERCENTAGE OF LIFETIME SPENT SLEEPING: 62%
4. PERCENTAGE OF LIFETIME SPENT GROOMING: 12%

Sources: **1.** Cats now outnumber both dogs and children in the U.S. Despite this, 73% of Americans still believe that dogs are the "better" pet—even among cat owners, 35% rate dogs as better. The potential reason? As author Mary Bly once noted, "Dogs come when they're called. Cats take a message and get back to you later." (*Tampa Tribune*, 9/4/04, *Dallas Morning News*, 12/1/01) **2.** The oldest cat on record was named Puss, who passed away in 1939, one day after celebrating his 36th birthday (about 157 in human years). (*St. Louis Post-Dispatch*, 11/23/96) **3.** Cats sleep an average 15 hours a day, but only when you're awake and want to bond. Otherwise, cats are nocturnal animals, which is a fancy way of saying that they find it amusing to wake you up at three in the morning. (Coren, *Sleep Thieves*) **4.** Cats spend about one-third of their waking hours grooming. (Neville, *Perfect Kitten*)

Hairballs coughed up during a cat's lifetime: 180

(*Dallas Morning News*, 12/1/01)

PERCENTAGE OF PEOPLE WHO'VE ENDED A ROMANTIC RELATIONSHIP BECAUSE OF THEIR CAT: 11%

More prominent causes of romantic breakdown include poor communication, financial problems, lack of commitment, and infidelity. (*Houston Chronicle*, 2/24/99)

1. Percentage of people who buy their cats Christmas presents: 58%
2. Percentage who hang "kitty stockings" on Christmas: 37%

Dogs get more presents: 63% of dogs receive Christmas presents, and 40% had stockings. (Gallup poll, 1996)

MOST CATS OWNED BY ONE PERSON:
689

Jack Wright of Kingston, Ontario, holds the record. "You don't set out to do something like this," Wright says. "You can visualize a hundred cats. Beyond that, you can't. Two hundred, five hundred, it all looks the same." Says his wife Donna: "To tell you the truth, I get a little depressed sometimes. Sometimes I just say, 'Jack, give me a few bucks,' and I go out and have a beer or two. I sit there for a few hours and it's great. It's peaceful—no cats anywhere." (*Toronto Star*, 4/28/94)

1. PERCENTAGE OF CAT OWNERS WHO ALLOW THEIR CATS IN BED: 30%
2. PERCENTAGE OF CAT OWNERS WHO ARE WOMEN: 84%

Sources: **1.** NPR, 11/9/04. **2.** *Spokesman-Review*, 7/25/04.

1. WEALTHIEST CAT IN THE WORLD: TINKER

2. NET WORTH OF TINKER'S HOLDINGS:

$722,000

A onetime common alley cat, Tinker befriended a well-to-do British widow named Margaret Layne, and when she died at 89, Tinker inherited it all: a swank London home valued at $562,000 and a $160,000 trust fund just to ensure the caviar keeps coming. Two trustees are responsible for Tinker's care and feeding. (*Independent,* 5/11/03)

FIRST COMMERCIAL DESIGNED TO SPECIFICALLY APPEAL TO CATS RATHER THAN THEIR OWNERS: WHISKAS CAT FOOD (1999)

According to the makers of Whiskas, 60% of the cats that saw the commercial—featuring bright colors, motion, and high-pitched sounds—showed some interest in it. When CBS showed it to an audience of cats, a cat therapist gauged their reaction as follows: "Let me see. We have cats who are saying, Hey, this is terrific. Other cats are saying, Well, I think I'll go take a nap. I think we have kind of a mixed reaction here." (*CBS This Morning,* 6/3/99)

NUMBER OF TIMES A CAT RETURNS TO ITS BOWL IN AN AVERAGE DAY: 36 TIMES

(Cooper, *227 Secrets Your Cat Wants You to Know*)

Percentage of cats who escape who are found within three houses of their home: 77%

(*People*, 6/12/00)

NUMBER OF MILES A MINNESOTA CAT WALKED TO GET HOME AFTER BEING LOST BY HER OWNERS IN WISCONSIN:

350

Charmin Sampson lost her orange tabby Skittles in September 2001 while on a family trip to Wisconsin. On Jan. 14, 2002, the cat showed up on the Sampsons' doorstep in Hibbing, Minn., five months later. Skittles was skinny and his paws were raw, but otherwise in good shape after his 350-mile journey. (*Washington Post*, 2/6/02)

Miles Morris the Cat annually traveled on behalf of 9Lives cat food: 200,000

The original Morris was rescued from a Chicago animal shelter by trainer Bob Martwick on the day he was scheduled to be euthanized. He made 58 commercials for 9Lives between 1969 and his death in 1978, was featured on *Lifestyles of the Rich and Famous*, and was so popular that a secretary had to be hired to answer his mail. (*Toronto Star*, 5/28/89)

DURATION OF A CAT'S DREAMS: 2 TO 3 MINUTES

According to Stanley Coren, professor of psychology at the University of British Columbia, an average cat may dream as often as every 12 to 15 minutes. By contrast, large dogs dream only once every 65 minutes or so, while the average dream cycle for people is about 90 minutes. Incidentally, experts say cats dream about what they are genetically programmed to do: pouncing and stalking prey. (*Chicago Tribune*, 4/16/00)

CHARITY

1. **Total charity given by Americans in 2003:** **$240 billion**

2. **Average charitable contribution per American family:** **$1,052**

3. **Average percentage Americans donate of their annual incomes:** **2.2%**

4. **Percentage of income donated by Canadians:** **0.62%**

5. **Percentage donated by Britons:** **0.5%**

Sources: **1.** *Chronicle of Philanthropy*, 6/24/04. **2, 3.** National Center for Charitable Statistics. **4.** *Ottawa Citizen*, 12/12/03. **5.** Times Newspapers, 3/19/04.

Number of libraries donated to towns across America by Andrew Carnegie: 2,509

Over the course of his lifetime, Carnegie (1835–1919) donated over $56 million for the construction of 2,509 library buildings in the U.S. and around the world. Carnegie believed that wealth must be administered for the good of mankind. "To die rich," Carnegie often said, "is to die disgraced." (*American Libraries*, 12/1/99)

1. **LARGEST GIFT EVER GIVEN TO A SINGLE CHARITY:** $1.5 BILLION (SALVATION ARMY)

2. **LARGEST GIFT EVER TO A UNIVERSITY:** $600 MILLION (CAL TECH)

3. **LARGEST GIFT EVER GIVEN TO A MAGAZINE:** $100 MILLION (*POETRY*)

4. **LARGEST GIFT EVER GIVEN TO A RADIO STATION:** $200 MILLION (NPR)

5. **LARGEST GIFT EVER GIVEN TO A DOG:** $80 MILLION (GUNTHER)

Sources: **1.** While Bill Gates of Microsoft gave away $5 billion to his foundation, that money is disseminated to many different individual groups. (*Independent*, 1/22/04) **2.** The largest donation ever pledged to a private institution is the $600 million donated to the California Institute of Technology in 2001 by Gordon Moore, one of the founders of Intel. (*Orange County Register*, 11/12/01) **3.** In November 2002, pharmaceuticals heiress Ruth Lilly shocked the poetry world by giving $100 million to this obscure 91-year-old journal. The gift occurred despite the fact that *Poetry* had rejected each of Lilly's submissions. Following the gift, the magazine tripled the amount it paid for published poems from $2 to $6 a line. (*Ottawa Citizen*, 12/29/03) **4.** In 2003, Joan Kroc, widow of the founder of McDonald's, gave $200 million to National Public Radio. (*Boston Globe*, 11/9/03) **5.** In 1991, a German countess named Carlotta Liebenstein willed her entire $80 million estate to her dog Gunther. In 2001, the *Miami Herald* reported that Gunther had purchased Madonna's home in Miami for $7.5 million. (*New Yorker*, 9/8/03; *Independent*, 11/15/01)

1. MOST CHARITABLE U.S. CITY: SALT LAKE CITY, UTAH
2. LEAST CHARITABLE U.S. CITY: MIAMI, FLA.
3. MOST GENEROUS U.S. STATE: UTAH
4. LEAST GENEROUS U.S. STATE: SOUTH DAKOTA

Sources: **1.** In a study by the *Chronicle of Philanthropy*, residents of Salt Lake City gave an average of 14.9% of their discretionary income to charity. Of the 50 largest cities, Detroit is the most charitable, giving an average 12.1% of their discretionary income to charity. (*Deseret Morning News*, 4/28/03) **2.** According to a recent report, residents of Miami give only 4.6% of their discretionary income to charity. (*Chronicle of Philanthropy*, 5/1/03) **3.** The average Utahn gives 5% of his or her income to charity, more than double the average in the U.S. Residents of Washington, D.C., come in second, giving 3.4% of their income to charity. (National Center for Charitable Statistics) **4.** In 2001, the average South Dakotan only gave 0.4% of their income to charity, amounting to about $144 per taxpayer. South Dakota was followed by West Virginia (1.3% of income). (National Center for Charitable Statistics)

MOST MONEY EVER GIVEN AWAY ANONYMOUSLY: $600 MILLION

Charles Feeney, who made a fortune operating airport duty-free shops, gave away $600 million without announcing it to anyone. None of the recipients of Feeney's generosity knew the source of the money, since donations were always made by cashier's check. Feeney was forced to reveal himself in 1997, when he sold his company for $3.5 billion. Feeney gave away $3.495 billion of that money, keeping $5 million for his family's maintenance. "Money has an attraction for some people," Feeney told the *New York Times*, "but nobody can wear two pairs of shoes at one time." (*New York Times*, 1/23/97)

Number of kidney donations made by Americans to complete strangers through 2004: 228

One of those donors was a wealthy Philadelphian named Zell Kravinsky. On July 22, 2003, after Kravinsky's wife told him she was "adamantly opposed" to his planned donation, Kravinsky snuck out of his house at 6 A.M. and had his right kidney removed and implanted in a stranger some 3 hours later. Later that day, his wife learned what her husband had done after seeing a headline in the *Philadelphia Daily News* at the supermarket. (*Tucson Citizen*, 10/9/04; *New Yorker*, 8/2/04)

CHARITY THAT RAISES THE MOST MONEY IN THE U.S.: SALVATION ARMY ($1.3 BILLION ANNUALLY)

(*Chronicle of Philanthropy*, reported in the *Los Angeles Times*, 10/25/04)

1. KINDEST CITY IN THE WORLD, ACCORDING TO ONE RECENT STUDY: RIO DE JANEIRO, BRAZIL
2. KINDEST CITY IN AMERICA: ROCHESTER, N.Y.

Sources: **1.** Robert Levine conducted three experiments in 22 of the world's great cities to assess kindness: First, the percentage of people who give inadvertently dropped pens back to their owner. Second, the likelihood that a man with an injured leg gets help picking up a dropped magazine. And third, the likelihood that a blind person will be helped across a busy street. Rio scored highest on the assistance scale, while Kuala Lumpur, Malaysia, scored lowest, with New York not far behind. (*Independent*, 7/5/03) **2.** Based on similar experiments conducted by Levine in 36 American cities and recorded in his book *A Geography of Time*.

CHEATING

1. ODDS THAT AN AMERICAN BELIEVES THAT "HONESTY IS THE BEST POLICY": **1 IN 3**

2. PERCENTAGE OF HIGH SCHOOL STUDENTS WHO ADMIT TO CHEATING ON A TEST: **75%**

3. PERCENTAGE WHO ADMITTED DOING SO IN 1950: **20%**

Sources: **1.** According to James Patterson's study of the American psyche, *The Day America Told the Truth*. Incidentally, the phrase "honesty is the best policy" first appeared in Cervantes's *Don Quixote*. (*St. Louis Post-Dispatch*, 9/22/98) **2.** Half of the students surveyed said that they have handed in work written by someone else. Said one student: "If Clinton can do it and get away with it, why can't we?" (*Houston Chronicle*, 3/7/04; *U.S. News and World Report*, 5/21/01) **3.** *U.S. News and World Report*, 5/21/01.

1. ODDS THAT AN AMERICAN AGREED WITH THE STATEMENT "MOST PEOPLE CAN BE TRUSTED" IN 1960: 6 IN 10

2. ODDS THAT AN AMERICAN BELIEVED "MOST PEOPLE CAN BE TRUSTED" IN 1998: 4 IN 10

(Callahan, *The Cheating Culture*)

1. Percentage of business school deans who say they would admit a clearly unqualified student if his parents donated $1 million: 25%

2. Percentage of deans who say they would help a donor to get an improper tax deduction by backdating a $500,000 contribution: 58%

Based on 291 business school deans who were surveyed anonymously by Tammy Hunt, a professor of management and marketing at the University of North Carolina at Wilmington. Nearly half said they'd probably admit an unqualified student if his or her parents were friends of the dean. (*Washington Post*, 9/6/98)

1. NUMBER OF AMERICAN COLLEGE STUDENTS WHO ADMITTED TO PLAGIARIZING FROM THE INTERNET IN 2000: **10%**
2. NUMBER WHO ADMITTED TO DOING SO IN 2002: **41%**

(New York Times, 11/2/02)

PERCENTAGE OF AMERICANS WHO HAVE:

SAID A PAYMENT IS IN THE MAIL WHEN IT WASN'T: 62%
TAKEN COMPANY OFFICE SUPPLIES FOR USE AT HOME: 63%
SWITCHED PRICE TAGS ON AN ITEM: 12%

(Chicago Sun-Times, 1/26/04; Reader's Digest poll, 9/18/98)

PERCENTAGE OF AMERICANS WHO BELIEVE IT IS ALL RIGHT TO CHEAT ON TAXES: **17%**

A 1990 study found that auto dealers, restaurateurs, and clothing store operators fudge the most on their taxes, underreporting nearly 40% of their taxable income; doctors, lawyers, barbers, and accountants understate their income by about 20%; farmers 18%; and real estate operators and insurance agents about 16%. . . . In 1937, banker J. P. Morgan was asked about not having paid any income tax in 1931 or '32, and said, "If [Congress] doesn't know how to collect them, then a man is a fool to pay." (Boston Globe, 4/2/04; Money, 4/1/91, 4/1/01)

1. CHANCE THAT A LOST WALLET WILL BE RETURNED BY A FINDER: **56%**
2. COUNTRY IN WHICH A LOST WALLET IS MOST LIKELY TO BE RETURNED: **NORWAY**
3. COUNTRY IN WHICH A LOST WALLET IS LEAST LIKELY TO BE RETURNED: **MEXICO**

Sources: **1.** In a 2001 study, Reader's Digest "lost" more than 1,100 wallets in 117 cities around the world. Each contained $50 in local currency and the name and phone number of the true "owner." **2.** Every lost wallet was returned in Norway and Denmark; in the U.S., 70% of the lost wallets were returned. Of U.S. cities, Seattle had the highest rate of return and Atlanta the lowest. (USA Today, 5/1/01) **3.** Only 21% of the wallets left in Mexican stores, parking lots, and other public locales were returned to their owners. (Journal of Economic Issues, 9/02)

WHAT THE SOUTH KOREAN JUSTICE MINISTRY DOES TO PREVENT APPLICANTS FROM CHEATING ON THE JUDICIAL EXAM: DOESN'T LET THEM GO TO THE BATHROOM

In lieu of the loo, proctors place "emergency facilities" (i.e., buckets and plastic bags) at the rear of the testing facilities for use during the 3-hour exam. In 2002, long plastic skirtlike receptacles were added in order to accommodate the dignity of the female applicants. (Washington Post, 12/29/02)

CHRISTIANS

1. ESTIMATED NUMBER OF CHURCHES IN THE U.S.: 400,000

2. WORLD'S LARGEST CHURCH: BASILICA OF OUR LADY OF PEACE, IVORY COAST

3. WORLD'S LARGEST CHURCH CONGREGATION: 800,000 MEMBERS

4. LARGEST CHURCH CONGREGATION IN AMERICA: 25,000

5. PERCENTAGE OF AMERICANS WHO DESCRIBE THEMSELVES AS "BORN AGAIN": 39%

Sources: **1.** *Washington Post*, 5/14/04. **2.** Built at an estimated cost of $300 million by President Houphouet Boigny as a monument to his rule, the church's dome reaches 525 feet—about 100 feet higher than St. Peter's in Rome. Though it can comfortably hold 20,000 worshippers, no more than a few hundred attend the church at any one time. (Africa News Service, 4/5/01) **3.** The Yoido Full Gospel Church in Seoul, Korea, has 650 pastors and a main sanctuary and satellite chapels that together can hold 75,000 worshippers. Average Sunday attendance at Yoido is estimated at about 100,000. (*Washington Post*, 5/15/04) **4.** The honor goes to the Lakewood Church in Houston, Tex. A church called World Changers, in College Park, Ga., is ranked second, with 23,093 attendees. (*Charlotte Observer*, 5/29/04) **5.** Barna Research Group; *American Demographics*, 3/03.

NUMBER OF MISSIONARIES KILLED IN AN AVERAGE YEAR: 150

(*World Christian Encyclopedia*)

FIRST BOOK PUBLISHED IN AMERICA:
THE WHOLE BOOKE OF PSALMS FAITHFULLY TRANSLATED INTO ENGLISH METRE

1,700 copies of the hymnal (also known as the *Bay Psalm Book*) were published in 1640. (*Boston Globe*, 6/10/95)

First drive-in church: Whitfield Estates Presbyterian (Florida)

In 1952, Whitfield Estates Presbyterian opened on 10 acres, with parking for 400 cars. While the lot was full in early years, with worshippers listening to the service on speakers, fewer than ten cars take in the service on the average Sunday today. Other drive-in churches have picked up the slack, however. The Daytona Beach Drive-In Christian Church (operating since about 1953) attracts about 700 worshippers each week, who receive a packaged communion kit when they first drive in. (*Bradenton Herald*, 7/14/03; *Seattle Times*, 6/26/04)

FIRST PERSON TO SPEAK IN TONGUES: AGNES OZMAN (JAN. 1, 1901)

In Topeka, Kans., on New Year's Day 1901, Agnes Ozman asked her pastor, the Rev. Charles Parham, to lay hands on her and pray. According to Parham's account of the event, "I had scarcely repeated three sentences when glory fell upon her, a halo seemed to surround her head and face, and she began speaking in the Chinese language, and was unable to speak English for three days." Called the "touch felt around the world," Ozman's experience spawned the Pentecostal movement, which now has over 200 million members. (Synan, *Century of the Holy Spirit*)

NUMBER OF MILES KEITH WHEELER HAS CARRIED A NINE-FOOT WOODEN CROSS: 15,500

As Wheeler relates, he and a friend built the cross after God told him to carry one through the streets of Tulsa, Okla., on Good Friday in 1985. Since then, he has carried the cross 15,500 miles through 133 countries, on annual trips lasting no more than 3 weeks. He has been beaten, chased by wild animals, and thrown in jail some 14 times. In April 2002, he carried the cross to Bethlehem while Israelis and Palestinians traded gunfire outside the Church of the Nativity. (*Southland Times*, 1/23/03; *Tulsa World*, 5/4/02)

Name of the "John 3:16" guy at 1980s sporting events: Rollen Stewart

Stewart gained fame in the 1980s by being shown on television at hundreds of sporting events holding signs reading "John 3:16." ("For God so loved the world, that He gave His only begotten Son. . . .") In 1992, Stewart was arrested on a kidnapping charge, and is currently serving a life sentence in a California prison. (*Seattle Post-Intelligencer*, 2/1/94)

CIGARETTES

1. NUMBER OF CIGARETTES SMOKED ANNUALLY WORLDWIDE: 5.3 TRILLION

2. RATION OF MALE TO FEMALE SMOKERS: 4 TO 1

3. PUFFS TAKEN PER CIGARETTE BY THE AVERAGE SMOKER: 10

Sources: **1.** Worldwide, approximately 1.3 billion people currently smoke cigarettes or other tobacco products. (Kyodo News Service, 5/21/03; *Time International*, 1/13/03) **2.** Approximately 1 billion men and 250 million women smoke. There are only five countries in which more women smoke than men: Norway, Papua New Guinea, Sweden, the Cook Islands, and Nauru. (2003 Tobacco Control Country Profile) **3.** A typical smoker will take 10 puffs on a cigarette over a period of 5 minutes that the cigarette is lit. (*Washington Post*, 2/19/02)

FAMOUS CHAIN SMOKERS:
YVES ST. LAURENT (150 CIGARETTES PER DAY)
PRINCESS MARGARET (60 CIGARETTES PER DAY)

Princess Margaret reportedly cut down after having part of her left lung removed. (NPR, 1/7/02; *Daily Telegraph*, 2/8/99)

Principal use for nicotine other than in cigarettes: Insecticide

An estimated 4,000 ingredients are in a typical cigarette, and at least 60 are suspected carcinogens, such as arsenic, industrial cleaners, tar, insecticides, and embalmers. (*Tampa Tribune*, 7/7/03)

1. COUNTRY WITH THE HIGHEST SMOKING RATE IN THE WORLD:
NAURU (54% OF ADULTS)
2. STATE WITH THE HIGHEST SMOKING RATE: KENTUCKY (31%)
3. STATE WITH THE LOWEST SMOKING RATE: UTAH (12%)

Sources: **1.** According to the World Health Organization's *Tobacco Atlas*, the tiny Pacific nation of Nauru is followed by Guinea (51%), Namibia (50%), Kenya (49%), and Bosnia (48%). (*Tobacco Atlas*) **2, 3.** *USA Today*, 11/11/04.

Ads touting cigarettes' health benefits:

"Not one single case of throat irritation due to smoking Camels!" (1938)

"Many prominent athletes smoke Luckies all day long with no harmful effects." (1929)

(*Review of Health References in Cigarette Advertising 1927–1964*, reported by AP, 5/2/98)

YEAR THE SURGEON GENERAL FIRST WARNED ABOUT THE DANGERS OF CIGARETTES: 1929

As quoted in a June 10, 1929, speech on the Senate floor, Surgeon General Hugh Cumming claimed that cigarettes caused nervousness, insomnia, and other ill effects in women, and warned that smoking could lower the "physical tone" of the nation. In an 1888 article, the *New York Times* put it more bluntly, warning that "if this pernicious practice obtains among adult Americans the ruin of the Republic is at hand." (*Art Journal*, 2/18/02; *Public Health Reports*, 9/19/97)

YEAR A TOBACCO COMPANY PRESIDENT CLAIMED THAT CIGARETTES WERE NO MORE ADDICTIVE THAN GUMMI BEARS: 1997

Said Philip Morris president James Morgan in a sworn deposition, "If [cigarettes] are behaviorally addictive or habit forming, they are much more like . . . Gummi Bears. I love Gummi Bears . . . and I want Gummi Bears, and I like Gummi Bears, and I eat Gummi Bears, and I don't like it when I don't eat my Gummi Bears, but I'm certainly not addicted to them." In the same vein, in testimony before Congress in 1994, the CEO of R. J. Reynolds claimed that smoking was no more addictive than Twinkies. (*Time*, 5/12/97)

WARNING ON JAPANESE CIGARETTES:

Your Health May Suffer, So Take Care Not to Smoke Too Much

WARNING ON FRENCH CIGARETTES:

Smoking May Cause a Slow and Painful Death

(*International Herald Tribune*, 8/11/03; Reuters, 4/12/02)

PERCENTAGE OF DOCTORS IN CHINA WHO SMOKE: 57%

In a 1999 American Medical Association survey, 40% of Chinese people surveyed did not know that smoking can cause cancer. (*Newsweek International*, 11/11/02)

COFFEE, ETC.

1. NUMBER OF AMERICANS WHO DRINK COFFEE: 167.1 MILLION
2. LEGENDARY DISCOVERER OF THE COFFEE BEAN: KALDI, AN ETHIOPIAN GOATHERD
3. ODDS THAT A COFFEE DRINKER TAKES IT BLACK: 4 IN 10
4. CHILDREN UNDER 16 WHO DRANK COFFEE IN THE 1930S: 15%

Sources: **1.** *Financial Times* (London), 3/26/04. **2.** According to legend, in A.D. 850, Kaldi went searching for his flock after they failed to return home after grazing. He discovered his goats acting quite hyper near bushes with red berries. Kaldi tried the berries himself, liked what he felt, and shared his discovery with monks at a nearby monastery, who roasted the berries and added them to water, thus creating the first coffee brew. (*Washington Post*, 2/18/01) **3.** *Restaurant Hospitality*, 11/1/03. **4.** Indeed, surveys indicated that 4% of children under age 6 drank coffee. (Pendergrast, *Uncommon Grounds*)

Invention of the coffee break: 1952

Though defense plant workers were given a break for coffee during World War II, the term "coffee break" was coined in a set of 1952 ads for the Pan American Coffee Bureau (a consortium of coffee producers), which told Americans to "Give yourself a coffee break—and get what coffee gives to you." The "coffee break" spread instantaneously, and by the close of 1952, 80% of American workplaces had introduced a coffee break. (Pendergrast, *Uncommon Grounds*)

1. COFFEE CONSUMED BY THE AVERAGE AMERICAN TODAY: 1.64 CUPS
2. COFFEE CONSUMED BY THE AVERAGE AMERICAN IN 1962: 3.12 CUPS

That year (1962) was the peak year for coffee consumption in America. (*Chicago Sun-Times*, 6/3/00; *Prepared Foods*, 4/1/04)

WORLD'S BIGGEST COFFEE-DRINKING NATION: FINLAND (1,652 CUPS PER PERSON ANNUALLY)

(*International Coffee Organization*)

FIRST PERSON TO DRINK COFFEE IN SPACE: WALLY SCHIRRA

Upon discovering that water could be heated enough to make coffee aboard the space shuttle, Schirra (one of the original NASA astronauts) insisted that coffee be available on his next mission. The flight doctor refused, saying it served no nutritional value, but Schirra convinced him by holding back the coffee during one morning meeting. "The doctor asked me where the coffee was," Schirra said recently. "I said, 'If you can't do without it for one meeting, I sure as hell can't go without it for 11 days.' After that we had coffee on the missions." (*Albuquerque Tribune*, 6/12/2000)

Number of different Starbucks shops visited by John Smith as of July 2004: 4,289

Smith's goal is to drink coffee in every one of the 4,900 Starbucks shops in the world, and has been to 4,122 in North America, 114 in Britain, and 53 in Japan. Smith faces a problem, though, because Starbucks opens 10 new stores a week. (*Fortune,* 7/12/04)

World's first coffee shop: 1475 (Constantinople)

The place was named Kiva Han. (*Melbourne Herald,* 10/24/03)

1. MOST EXPENSIVE COFFEE IN THE WORLD: KOPI LUWAK (UP TO $300 A POUND)
2. PRINCIPAL INGREDIENT: EXCRETED COFFEE BEANS

The palm civet, an Indonesian marsupial that resembles a weasel, likes to eat the ripest coffee berries. Some resourceful Indonesians noticed that the civet excretes them almost completely intact. Connoisseurs say that the animal's stomach enzymes give the beans a unique flavor, and it is advertised as "Good to the last dropping." (*Washington Times,* 3/25/02; *Houston Chronicle,* 4/24/04)

WORLD'S BIGGEST TEA-DRINKING COUNTRIES:

1. TURKEY (1,150 CUPS OF TEA PER PERSON PER YEAR)
2. ENGLAND (1,000 CUPS)

Tea sales in England have fallen from 279 million pounds of tea bags in 1997 to 250 million pounds in 2002. (Datamonitor; *Sunday Times* [London], 6/22/03; *Independent,* 6/16/03)

COLLEGE

1. NUMBER OF HIGH SCHOOL VALEDICTORIANS WHO APPLIED TO HARVARD FOR THE CLASS OF 2006: 3,172

2. NUMBER OF VALEDICTORIANS ACCEPTED: 591

3. RANK OF HARVARD AMONG MOST SELECTIVE COLLEGES IN 2004: SECOND

4. FIRST WORD IN PRINCETON'S ACCEPTANCE LETTER UP UNTIL 2004: YES!

Sources: **1, 2.** In other words, Harvard rejected over 81% of high school valedictorians. (*Miami Herald*, 6/1/03) **3.** Yale was the most selective school in 2004, rejecting 90.1% of applicants, followed by Harvard (89.7%), Columbia (89.5%), and Princeton (88.1%). (*Bergen Record*, 5/3/04) **4.** *Daily Princetonian*, 1/8/04

Schools that lead the nation in sales of licensed apparel:

1. North Carolina   2. Michigan   3. Texas

(Collegiate Licensing Company)

1. AVERAGE SAT SCORE IN 2003: 1026

2. RELIGIOUS AFFILIATION WITH THE HIGHEST AVERAGE SAT SCORES: UNITARIANS

Sources: **1.** Broken down to 508 on the verbal and 518 on the math. (*Wall Street Journal*, 9/1/04) **2.** Clocking in with an average score of 1209, the Unitarians (Universalists) have the highest average among recorded religious affiliations. Judaism comes in second with 1161, followed closely by the Society of Friends (otherwise known as the Quakers) with 1153. (*Dallas Morning News*, 7/13/02)

1. NUMBER OF STUDENTS WHO ACHIEVED A PERFECT 1600 ON THE SAT IN 2004: 778

2. NUMBER WHO ACHIEVED A PERFECT SCORE IN 2001: 587

3. IN 1995: 25

4. 1989: 5

(*Allentown Morning Call*, 5/13/04; *Fort Worth Star-Telegram*, 8/29/01; *Washington Times*, 1/1/96; UPI, 5/9/89)

1. AVERAGE TUITION COST AT AMERICAN PRIVATE UNIVERSITIES:
1984: $5,093   2004: $19,710

2. MOST EXPENSIVE COLLEGE IN AMERICA IN 2004:
LANDMARK COLLEGE, PUTNEY, VT. ($35,300 *WITHOUT ROOM AND BOARD*)

3. MOST EXPENSIVE KINDERGARTEN:
BREARLEY SCHOOL, NEW YORK CITY ($26,200)

4. AVERAGE ANNUAL COST FOR COLLEGE BOOKS: $898

Sources: **1.** At state schools, the average tuition was $4,694 in 2004, up from $1,148 in 1984 (College Board, cited in *U.S. News and World Report*, 4/19/04) **2.** Second on the list is Sarah Lawrence College ($30,824), followed by Kenyon and Trinity. (*Chronicle of Higher Education*) **3.** *New York Post*, 2/24/04. **4.** *Art Journal*, 2/23/04.

1. ODDS THAT AN AMERICAN ADULT HAS A COLLEGE DEGREE: 1 IN 4

2. STATE WITH THE HIGHEST PERCENTAGE OF COLLEGE DEGREE HOLDERS: MASSACHUSETTS

3. CITY WITH THE HIGHEST PERCENTAGE: SEATTLE, WASH. (48.8%)

4. CITY WITH THE HIGHEST PERCENTAGE OF ADVANCED DEGREES: WASHINGTON, D.C. (23.6%)

Sources: **1.** According to census figures released in May 2004, 25.9% of Americans 25 or older have a bachelor degree. (UPI, 5/10/04) **2.** Followed by Colorado, Maryland, and Connecticut. The lowest percentage of people with college degrees is in West Virginia, at 16%. **3.** Followed by Raleigh, N.C. (48%) and San Francisco (47.8%). (*Journal Record*, 5/11/04) **4.** *Atlanta Journal-Constitution*, 4/28/04.

LAST PRESIDENT WITHOUT A COLLEGE DEGREE: HARRY TRUMAN

(*San Francisco Examiner*, 2/15/99)

1. ODDS THAT A GRADE GIVEN AT HARVARD IN 2002 WAS AN A OR A- : 1 IN 2

2. ODDS THAT A GRADE GIVEN AT HARVARD IN 1950 WAS AN A OR A- : 1 IN 5

(*USA Today*, 2/5/03)

1. FIRST COED DORM: UNIVERSITY OF INDIANA (1956)

2. LARGEST DORM IN THE NATION: (4,100 STUDENTS) BANCROFT HALL, U.S. NAVAL ACADEMY

3. FIRST CLOTHING-OPTIONAL DORM: WESLEYAN UNIVERSITY (LATE 1990S)

Sources: **1.** Dykstra Hall at UCLA followed 3 years later. Today, the only state whose universities have no coed dorms is Mississippi. (*Bergen Record*, 5/14/98; University Wire, 6/29/98) **2.** Followed by University of Texas's Jester Hall (1,700 students) and Boston University's Warren Towers (1,700). (*Washington Post*, 8/16/01) **3.** Though officially denied by the school administration, the *New York Times* published a front-page article under the headline "Naked Dorm? That Wasn't in the Brochure," and quoted one resident of the dorm as saying, "There's an exhibitionist part of me. If I feel the need to take off my pants, I take my pants off. It's kind of cool that there is a place you can do that." (*New York Times*, 3/18/00)

MOST HONORARY DEGREES HELD BY ONE PERSON: 150

The record is held by Father Theodore Hesburgh of the University of Notre Dame. The tradition of handing out honorary degrees goes back to 1493, when Cambridge University awarded a degree to poet John Skelton. (*Newhouse News*, 4/29/04)

Four curious accredited college courses:

1. "Pornography: Writing of Prostitutes"

2. "How to Be Gay: Male Homosexuality and Initiation"

3. "American Golf: Aristocratic Pastime or the People's Game?"

4. "Philosophy and *Star Trek*"

Sources: **1.** Offered at Wesleyan University. (*Albany Times Union*, 5/9/02) **2.** Offered at the University of Michigan. (*Seattle Times*, 10/19/03) **3.** Offered at Carnegie-Mellon University. (*Seattle Times*, 10/19/03) **4.** Offered at Georgetown University. (*Chattanooga Times Free Press*, 9/9/02)

1. FIRST INTERCOLLEGIATE SPORTING EVENT: ROWING
2. FIRST COLLEGE FOOTBALL GAME: 1869
3. FIRST COLLEGE BASKETBALL GAME: 1895

Sources: **1.** A crew of rowers from Harvard beat a crew from Yale in the first known intercollegiate sporting event in 1852. (*Chronicle of Higher Education,* 9/19/03) **2.** Held in New Brunswick, N.J., between Queens College (now Rutgers University) and the College of New Jersey (now Princeton). (*Bergen Record,* 5/6/04) **3.** On Feb. 9, 1995, the Minnesota School of Agriculture beat Hamline by a score of 9 to 3 in the first college basketball game. (*Sporting News,* 1/30/95)

AVERAGE SALARY OF A COLLEGE PROFESSOR: $66,475

Harvard's tenured professors are the nation's best paid, averaging $145,000.
(*Chronicle of Higher Education,* 4/23/04; *Times Higher Education Supplement* [London], 11/22/02)

1. ODDS THAT A COLLEGE STUDENT GRADUATES WITHIN FOUR YEARS: 1 IN 3
2. ODDS THAT A STUDENT CHANGES THEIR MAJOR AT LEAST ONCE: 4 IN 10

Sources: **1.** *Cincinnati Enquirer,* 8/13/03. **2.** *New York Times,* 8/3/03.

FIVE PECULIAR ACADEMIC SCHOLARSHIPS

1. "LEFTIES" SCHOLARSHIP
2. THE INTERNATIONAL BOAR SEMEN SCHOLARSHIP
3. BILLY BARTY FOUNDATION DWARFISM SCHOLARSHIP
4. NATIONAL ASSOCIATION TO ADVANCE FAT ACCEPTANCE SCHOLARSHIP
5. THE ZOLP SCHOLARSHIP

Sources: **1.** Available to lefties at Juniata College in Huntingdon, Penn. (*Los Angeles Times,* 6/25/04) **2.** Available for study of pig management in Cleveland, Ohio. (*Seattle Times,* 3/2/03) **3.** Made available by a 3'9" actor to people born with dwarfism. (*Cleveland Plain Dealer,* 2/18/03) **4.** Available to high school seniors who are obese. (*Deseret News,* 10/7/02) **5.** Available at Loyola University to anyone with the name Zolp. (*New York Times,* 11/7/04)

COLORS

1. Pecentage of Americans who say blue is their favorite color: 41%
2. Second most popular color in the U.S.: Red
3. The prophet Muhammad's favorite color: Green

Source: **1.** Pantone, Inc., survey, cited in *American Demographics*, 12/1/03. **2.** *American Demographics*, 12/1/03.
3. Which is why the color of the flag of Saudi Arabia is green. (*Hamilton Spectator*, 6/25/04)

COLOR BOYS WERE DRESSED IN DURING THE EARLY 20TH CENTURY: PINK
COLOR GIRLS WERE DRESSED IN: BLUE

As Michael Kimmel says in his book *Manhood in America*, "boys wore pink or red because they were manly colors indicating strength and determination, and girls wore light blue, an airier color, like the sky, because girls were so flighty."

COLOR PREVIOUSLY CONSIDERED UNLUCKY IN IRELAND: GREEN

According to Irish legend, green was the color associated with fairies who stole children and brides. Since fairies were thought to dress in green clothing, wearing the color was believed to arouse the fairies' anger. (UPI, 3/14/81)

OTHER PEOPLE WHO CONSIDER THE COLOR GREEN UNLUCKY: RACE CAR DRIVERS

It was also traditionally considered unlucky in car-racing circles to have peanuts and women in the garages at the raceway. (*Chicago Tribune*, 2/15/01; *Los Angeles Times*, 1/9/00)

COLOR CONSIDERED UNLUCKY IN CHINA: WHITE

Because white signifies death. (*Washingtonian*, 10/00)

YEAR "THE PRESIDENT'S HOUSE" WAS OFFICIALLY CHANGED TO "THE WHITE HOUSE": 1901

It had previously been officially known as either the President's House or the Executive Mansion, though people had begun to call it the White House soon after John Adams became its first occupant in 1800. (*Chicago Tribune*, 10/31/00)

1. PERCENTAGE OF AMERICAN WOMEN WHO DYED THEIR HAIR IN 1950: 7%

2. PERCENTAGE WHO DO SO TODAY: 55%

Until the mid-1950s, women who colored their hair were viewed as "fast."
(*New York Times*, 6/8/98; *Palm Beach Post*, 6/22/02)

1. PERCENTAGE OF WHITE AMERICAN ADULTS WHO ARE NATURAL BLONDS: 5%

2. AMOUNT PRINCESS DIANA SPENT ANNUALLY ON COLORING HER HAIR: $5,600

Only .001% of adults in the world are natural blonds. (Pitman, *On Blondes*)

PERCENTAGE OF PEOPLE IN SWEDEN WHO ARE BLOND: 50%

(*Independent*, 2/26/03)

Man called the "Father of the Yellow School Bus": Frank Cyr

In 1939, America's first generation of school buses was painted in a mishmash of colors, including red, white, and blue to instill patriotism. Cyr, a Columbia-trained Ph.D., convened a conference of educators to come up with uniform school bus standards. Among other things, Cyr convinced those assembled to adopt yellow buses with black lettering as the industry standard because it was the easiest color to see at dawn and dusk. (*Newsday*, 4/26/89)

Inventor of the Yellow Cab: John D. Hertz (1915)

That's the same Hertz that started Hertz Rent-A-Car. In 1910, Hertz got into the taxi business in Chicago, one of the first Americans to do so. However, with no traffic signals and all manner of vehicles using the road, Hertz's drivers got into numerous accidents, cutting profits. After learning about a university study that said that yellow was the most recognizable color, Hertz opened the Yellow Cab Company in Chicago in 1915. (*Chicago Tribune*, 4/19/99)

YEAR YELLOW TENNIS BALLS WERE FIRST USED AT WIMBLEDON INSTEAD OF WHITE: 1986

Wimbledon was the last bastion of the white tennis ball, which did not show up as well on television. The tournament put out a press release saying, "After lengthy discussions, we believe that the advantages of using yellow tennis balls now outweigh the sentimental attachment to white." (*Times* [London], 11/18/85)

COMPUTERS

1. ESTIMATED NUMBER OF COMPUTERS WORLDWIDE: 825 MILLION

2. ODDS THAT A COMPUTER OWNER ADMITS THAT TECHNICAL PROBLEMS RESULT FROM HIS OWN IGNORANCE: 1 IN 6

3. PEOPLE WHO HAVE CONSIDERED PHYSICALLY ASSAULTING THEIR COMPUTERS: 41%

4. THOSE WHO HAVE ACTUALLY DONE SO: 7%

Sources: **1.** *Computer Industry Almanac.* **2.** Among the classic gripes heard by office computer managers: mice that won't work when users pick them up and point them at the computer screen. Another one: e-mails that can't be sent when addressed to a person's street name, town, and zip code. (M2 PressWIRE, 5/27/99) **3, 4.** *Fortune,* 11/14/94.

ORIGINAL NAME FOR A MOUSE: "X-Y POSITION INDICATOR FOR A DISPLAY"

Before Douglas Engelbart invented the mouse in the early sixties, each command had to be typed into a computer. The first computer to come with a mouse was an early Apple computer called Lisa, a forerunner of the Macintosh. By the way, Engelbart doesn't remember who coined the word "mouse" for his invention. (*Financial Times* [London], 4/24/98)

---

1. WEIGHT OF THE WORLD'S FIRST COMPUTER, ENIAC: 30 TONS

2. POWER OF THE ENIAC: 5,000 CALCULATIONS PER SECOND

3. FASTEST COMPUTER IN 1976: 40 MILLION CALCULATIONS PER SECOND

4. FASTEST COMPUTER TODAY: 41 TRILLION CALCULATIONS PER SECOND

Sources: **1.** Created by the army during World War II after 200,000 hours of work and $3 million, ENIAC (or Electronic Numerical Integrator and Calculator) stood 18 feet high and contained 500 miles of wiring in 80 feet of floor space. (*Daily Telegraph,* 8/30/01) **2.** *Pittsburgh Post-Gazette,* 10/25/00. **3.** The first Cray supercomputer, installed at the Las Alamos Nuclear Research Facility in New Mexico. (*Albuquerque Tribune,* 2/2/02) **4.** The Earth Simulator, built by Japan's NEC Corporation, operates at 41 trillion calculations a second (or "teraflops" in supercomputer lingo). The U.S. hopes to have a computer operating at 100 teraflops per second by 2006. (*Art Journal,* 6/7/04)

Product that has more power than the world's most powerful computer 60 years ago: A musical greeting card

(*Seattle Post-Intelligencer,* 11/3/03)

1. DATE THE FIRST PERSONAL COMPUTER WAS PUT ON SALE:
DEC. 19, 1974 (ALTAIR 8800)
2. COST ASSEMBLED: $498

Sources: **1.** The Altair 8800 was put out by a company called MITS, whose world headquarters was located in an Albuquerque, N.M. strip mall next to a massage parlor. While there were earlier computers available for home use (the Scelbi and Mark-8), they did not come assembled, and required additional searching for parts that did not come with the kit. **2.** Because the wait for assembled machines could last months, many ordered just the parts and manual, which saved them $101, but which virtually assured that something would go wrong. Even if everything was installed correctly, the machine was little more than a box of flashing lights, with no keyboard or terminal, and few practical applications. Nevertheless, while its creators only hoped to sell between 200 and 800 year, they received that many orders the day after the 8800 appeared on the January 1975 cover of *Popular Mechanics*. (Manes, *Gates*)

Percentage of people who call for technical support who report that the English of the person helping them was difficult to understand: 60%

(*Consumer Reports*, 6/04)

AMOUNT RON WAYNE SOLD HIS 10% STAKE IN APPLE FOR IN 1976: $500

In 1976, Wayne, concerned about possibly having to shell out money to keep the company afloat, sold his 10% stake in Apple to Steve Jobs for $500, which today would be worth in excess of $1.3 billion. (Freiberger, *Fire in the Valley*)

1. NUMBER OF COMPUTER VIRUSES REPORTED IN 1988: 6
2. NUMBER IN 2003: 137,529

(*St. Petersburg Times*, 8/16/04)

WHAT THE AVERAGE COMPUTER USER SPENDS MORE TIME TOUCHING THAN THEIR SPOUSE OR PARTNER:
A COMPUTER KEYBOARD

(Microsoft, cited in *Fortune*, 9/17/01)

CONTESTS AND PRIZES

1. FIRST TV GAME SHOW: *TRUTH OR CONSEQUENCES*

2. QUESTION THAT HERBERT STEMPEL DELIBERATELY GOT WRONG, LEADING TO THE 1950S QUIZ SHOW SCANDAL: *"WHICH FILM WON THE OSCAR FOR BEST PICTURE IN 1955?"*

3. CONTESTANTS WHO HAVE BEEN SUED BY GAME SHOWS: 1

4. GAME SHOWS THAT HAVE BEEN SUED BY CONTESTANTS: 2

Sources: **1.** *Truth or Consequences* debuted on WNBT in New York in 1941. (*Toronto Star*, 9/13/03) **2.** In December 1956, Charles Van Doren defeated longtime *Twenty-One* champ Herbert Stempel, a brainy contestant who won almost $100,000 but didn't interest TV audiences. Several years later, Stempel claimed that he'd been told to throw the game by the show's producers, and gave the wrong answer (*On the Waterfront*) though the correct answer to the question—*Marty*—happened to be his favorite movie. After initially denying that the show was rigged, Van Doren appeared before a congressional committee on Oct. 23, 1959, and admitted that he'd been fed questions in advance. (*People*, 10/3/94) **3.** In 2002, the producer of *Survivor* sued Stacey Stillman for claiming that *Survivor* had pressured other contestants to have her thrown off the island. (*New York Post*, 1/30/03) **4.** In 2002, Richard Rosner sued *Who Wants to Be a Millionaire* after incorrectly answering "Katmandu" rather than "Quito" to the question "What capital city is located at the highest altitude above sea level?" Rosner claimed the correct answer was La Paz, Bolivia, which was not one of the choices. The court dismissed Rosner's claim after finding that Quito was higher than Katmandu. (*Los Angeles Business Journal*, 6/7/04)

AMOUNT ANDREW WHITTAKER WON IN THE LARGEST LOTTERY JACKPOT IN HISTORY: $314 MILLION

Whittaker, of Scott Depot, W.V., won the Powerball lottery drawn on Dec. 25, 2002. Rather than taking installments, Whittaker opted for a lump sum payment of $170 million. After taxes, the prize amounted to about $115 million. (Agence France-Presse, 12/27/02)

AMOUNT A VIRGINIA SCHOOLBOY WON FOR CREATING MR. PEANUT IN 1916: $5

Mr. Peanut is based on a drawing done by Anthony Gentile, who won $5 for his "little peanut person" in a contest sponsored by Planters. (*New York Times*, 3/19/04)

MOST CONSECUTIVE WINS ON *JEOPARDY!* BY A SINGLE CONTESTANT: 74

In a span lasting from June 2 to Nov. 30, 2004, Ken Jennings, a mild-mannered Mormon from Utah, won 74 consecutive games and $2.5 million in prize money. The previous record was six consecutive appearances made by Sean Ryan in October 2003. Prior to the summer of 2003, *Jeopardy!* rules limited contestants to five appearances.... In 1993, Harry Eisenberg, *Jeopardy!'s* head writer from 1988 to 1991, wrote a book in which he alleged that *Jeopardy!* producers tailored categories before airtime to help female contestants. (*Kansas City Star*, 12/14/04; *People*; 6/7/93)

CELEBRITIES WHO APPEARED AS CONTESTANTS ON *THE DATING GAME* BEFORE THEY WERE FAMOUS: 5

ARNOLD SCHWARZENEGGER, STEVE MARTIN, SALLY FIELD, TOM SELLECK, AND FARRAH FAWCETT

(*Entertainment Weekly*, 6/19/98)

CONTEST PROBLEMS:

Pepsi Bottle Cap Sweepstakes (1992)

Seeking to increase sales in the Philippines, Pepsi creates a bottle cap sweepstakes awarding 18 prizes of $32,000 to customers with winning bottle caps. However, a computer error results in 750,000 winning bottle caps being distributed, touching off riots that left at least six dead after Pepsi refused to honor the winning bottle caps.

(*Hartford Courant*, 8/4/93)

Kraft Cheese's "Ready to Roll" Sweepstakes (1989)

Involved matching game cards obtained in packages of cheese. Though only one grand prize (a minivan) was supposed to be awarded, a printing error resulted in 2 million packages of cheese with winning game cards. Though Kraft canceled the contest, it was sued and ultimately paid $10 million.

(*New York Times*, 3/31/93)

COSMETIC SURGERY

1. YEAR THE TERM "PLASTIC SURGERY" WAS COINED: 1798

2. NUMBER OF AMERICANS WHO UNDERWENT COSMETIC SURGERY IN 2003: 1.8 MILLION

3. AGE GROUP UNDERGOING THE MOST PLASTIC SURGERY: 35 TO 50

Sources: **1.** In 1798, Pierre Desault proposed the term "plastic surgery" as the label for procedures to repair facial deformities. It has its origins in the Greek word "plastikos," meaning "fit for molding." (Gilman, *Making the Body Beautiful*) **2.** Doctors performed an additional 6.4 million nonsurgical cosmetic procedures in 2003, such as botox injections. (*New York Times*, 4/27/04) **3.** Some 45% of cosmetic surgery procedures are performed on 35- to 50-year-olds, 23% on 51- to 64-year-olds, and only 5% on people over 65. (*Atlanta Journal-Constitution*, 9/22/04)

1. NUMBER OF NIPPLE ENLARGEMENTS PERFORMED IN AMERICA IN 2003: 529
2. NUMBER OF NIPPLE REDUCTIONS: 1,591

(American Society for Aesthetic Surgery)

FIRST WOMAN TO HAVE HER BREASTS ENLARGED: TIMMIE JEAN LINDSEY (1962)

In 1962, Timmie Jean Lindsey was having two tattoos removed at a Houston hospital when her doctors asked her whether she would be interested in being a medical pioneer—the first woman in the world to receive silicone breast implants. After the doctor consented to also pin back Lindsey's ears, she agreed, and the former B-cup left the hospital with firm, round Cs. "When I had them put in, I seemed to get more wolf whistles than before," said the now 73-year-old grandmother. (*Houston Chronicle*, 10/18/03)

MOST POPULAR COSMETIC SURGICAL PROCEDURES IN AMERICA
(AND THEIR AVERAGE COST):

LIPOSUCTION ($2,578): 384,626
BREAST ENLARGEMENT ($3,360): 280,401
EYELID SURGERY ($2,599): 267,627
NOSE JOB ($3,869): 172,429
BREAST REDUCTION ($5,351): 147,173

About 4% of women undergoing breast enhancement surgery in 2003 (some 11,326 women) were under the age of 19. (*Cosmetic Surgery Times*, 5/1/04; *People*, 6/7/04; *Atlanta Journal-Constitution*, 7/11/04)

---

1. Estimate of the number of Americans who have had a sex-change operation: 25,000
2. Sex-change capital of the world: Trinidad, Colo.

Sources: **1.** There are an estimated 50,000 to 75,000 transsexuals worldwide. (*New York Times*, 11/8/98) **2.** With 5,800 operations to date performed by resident Dr. Stanley Biber, the tiny Colorado village boasts more such operations than any other town in the world. At the height of his practice, Dr. Biber was performing about 150 operations a year. (*Rocky Mountain News*, 8/16/04)

CITY WITH THE MOST PLASTIC SURGEONS PER CAPITA IN AMERICA: SAN FRANCISCO

According to figures from the American Society for Plastic Surgeons, San Francisco has 128 plastic surgeons, or one for every 13,525 residents. (ASPS)

MOST POPULAR COSMETIC PROCEDURE IN ASIA: EYELID SURGERY

Approximately half of all Asians and 75% of Koreans are born without a double eyelid crease, which means that no portion of the eyelid is visible when their eyes are open. To remedy this perceived imperfection, many Asians undergo a procedure in which a crease is surgically created above the eye. Doctors estimate that up to 60% of Korean women have had surgery on their eyes. (*Chicago Tribune*, 8/25/04)

---

1. Country with the most cosmetic surgery operations per capita: Brazil
2. Country with the world's highest ratio of breast enlargements: Argentina
3. Country with the highest ratio of plastic surgeons: South Korea

Sources: **1.** Brazilians underwent 500,000 plastic surgery operations in 2003, ranking just behind the U.S. While two-thirds of all plastic surgery in America is performed on accident victims or others seeking to fix a physical deformity, 60% of surgery in Brazil is purely for aesthetic reasons. (*Washington Times*, 8/31/04; *Time*, 7/9/01) **2.** As of 2001, over a million breast enlargements had been performed in Argentina, or about one for every 30 Argentineans. (Gilman, *Body Beautiful*) **3.** As of September 2004, there were 1,287 licensed plastic surgeons in South Korea, one for every 40,000 citizens. A recent survey in Korea found that more than half of all female college students had had plastic surgery, and that 82% of those who hadn't planned to do so. (*Newsweek*, 11/10/03; *Korea Herald*, 5/11/04)

CREMATION

1. **Percentage of bodies that are cremated in the U.S.:** 28%
2. **Percentage of bodies that are cremated in Japan:** 99%
3. **Average weight of cremated remains:** 6 pounds

Sources: **1.** Cremation Association of North America **2.** Japan has the highest cremation rate in the world. (Reuters, 4/4/02) **3.** Crematoriums reach temperatures in excess of 2,000 degrees, consuming everything except bone fragments and any noncombustible material. The remains fit in a shoe box. (*Time*, 8/4/97)

1. **STATE WITH THE HIGHEST NUMBER OF CREMATIONS:** NEVADA
2. **STATE WITH THE LOWEST NUMBER OF CREMATIONS:** ALABAMA

Nevadans are most likely to be cremated (more than 3 in 5), while Alabama has the lowest cremation rate in the U.S. (less than 1 in 20). (*Arizona Republic*, 10/7/03)

MOST UNUSUAL PLACE WHERE ASHES HAVE BEEN SCATTERED: BLOOMINGDALE'S

According to the *New Yorker*, filmmaker Mark Lewis scattered his mother's ashes inside the flagship Bloomingdale's store in New York: "She said she bought a nice cashmere sweater there once. So my brother and I, we walked around the store spreading her ashes." (*New Yorker*, 9/30/02) . . . Churchill Downs gets about a dozen requests a year to have ashes spread over the track. (*Atlanta Journal-Constitution*, 4/28/02) . . . Ernie Banks has been quoted as saying that when he dies, he wants his ashes spread over Wrigley Field—"with the wind blowing out." (*Madison Capital Times*, 2/2/96) . . . Bobby Riggs's remains were spread over a tennis court. (*Newsday*, 10/27/95)

PERCENTAGE OF ASHES THAT ARE NEVER CLAIMED BY NEXT OF KIN: 6%

In 1997, funeral directors were left with in excess of 100 tons of unclaimed remains from 31,000 bodies. For ethical and liability reasons, funeral directors do not throw out unclaimed remains, no matter how old. (*USA Today*, 11/11/98)

YEAR POST OFFICE ADVISED THE PUBLIC THAT CREMATED REMAINS COULD NOT BE SENT BY REGULAR MAIL: 2000

In a postal bulletin issued to employees on Feb. 24, 2000, the U.S. Postal Service advised that cremated remains must be sent Return Receipt Requested, because otherwise the postal service may be "put in the uncomfortable position of losing these items, possibly at the great emotional distress to families of deceased persons." (U.S. Postal Service)

BIZARRE USES FOR CREMATED REMAINS:

Frisbees: When Frisbee inventor Ed Headrick died in August 2002 at age 78, family members had his ashes molded into a flying disc, which, as ABC's Buck Wolf observed, meant that his grandkids could still play catch with Grandpa.

(*USA Today*, 8/30/02)

Ink for comic books: In 1997, the ashes of Mark Gruenwald, an editor at Marvel Comics, were put into the ink of a comic series called Squadron Supreme. "This is something that he really wanted because he really loved comics," said Marvel's editor in chief, Bob Harras."He wanted to be part of his work in a very real sense."

(*International Herald Tribune*, 8/30/97).

NUMBER OF CITIES AROUND THE WORLD IN WHICH VERA ANDERSON'S ASHES WERE SCATTERED: 250

Since the age of 30, Mrs. Anderson had dreamed of travel, but a life plagued by severe health problems kept her confined to her home. So, near death in 2001 at the age of 78, Anderson requested that her son, Ross, mail her ashes to more than 250 cities in all 50 American states and around the world. He did so, mailing them to the head postmaster in each city with a note requesting that they find a nice place to scatter the ashes. (*Washington Times*, 6/3/01)

CRIME

1. WORLD PRISON POPULATION: 9 MILLION

2. PERCENTAGE OF WORLD PRISON POPULATION INCARCERATED IN THE U.S.: 25%

3. CORRECTIONS CAPITAL OF THE WORLD: FLORENCE, COLO.

4. WORLD'S OLDEST BANK ROBBER: 91

5. LONGEST-SERVING AMERICAN INMATE: WILLIAM HEIRENS (INCARCERATED FOR 59 YEARS)

Sources: **1.** In 2004, the U.S. population behind bars numbered about 2.2 million. China has about 1.5 million people incarcerated, and Russia 860,000. Space is at a premium in U.S. prisons; in fact the state of Virginia rents empty prison cells to Michigan and Vermont, which do not have enough room to house their own criminals. (World Prison Population List [5th Ed.]; Hallinan, *Going Up the River*) **2.** The U.S. has just 5% of the world's population, but 25% of those in prison. (*World and I*, 12/1/03) **3.** Florence and surrounding Fremont County have 14 prisons (10 state and 4 federal), including ADX, the nation's only federal supermaximum-security facility, housing the likes of Unabomber Theodore Kaczynski, World Trade Center bomber Ramzi Yousef, and Charles Harrelson (actor Woody's father), convicted of killing a federal judge. Twenty-five percent of the population of Fremont County is made up of incarcerated prisoners. (Hallinan, *Going Up the River*; Knight Ridder/Tribune News Service, 6/17/99) **4.** In August 2003, J. L. "Red" Rountree handed a robbery note to a bank teller in Abilene, Tex. who—after twice asking him whether he was kidding—gave him $2,000. (*Daily Record*, 1/28/04) **5.** In 1946, Heirens was convicted of killing a little girl and two women in a case that transfixed Chicago. A message scrawled in lipstick was found on a mirror in one victim's home: "For heaven's sake, catch me before I kill more. I cannot control myself." (AP, 4/4/02)

HIGHEST MURDER RATE IN THE WORLD: BRAZIL

Brazil has about 45,000 murders a year, according to news sources. Brazil is followed by South Africa and Russia. (UPI, 12/10/03; Xinhua News Agency, 6/20/02)

MONTH IN WHICH THE MOST MURDERS HAPPEN: AUGUST

Based on a U.S. Department of Justice study. (*Washington Times*, 10/5/03)

Most individual murders committed by one American: 48

Gary Leon Ridgeway, known as the "Green River" killer, murdered 48 prostitutes in Washington State over an 18-year period. "Choking is what I did," Ridgeway told investigators, "and I was pretty good at it." Pedro Alonzo Lopez, called the "Monster of the Andes," was convicted of murdering 57 young girls in Ecuador, Colombia, and Peru, but is believed to have murdered more than 300. (*Toronto Star*, 11/6/03; *Washington Post*, 11/16/03)

1. DAY OF THE WEEK MOST BANK ROBBERIES OCCUR: FRIDAY
2. AMOUNT STOLEN IN AVERAGE BANK ROBBERY: $5,000
3. ODDS THAT A BANK ROBBER IS APPREHENDED: 3 IN 4

Sources: **1.** Mondays are the second most frequent day for robberies. Bank robbers also tend to strike in the morning between the hours of 9 and 11 A.M. Los Angeles has long held the title of bank robbery capital of the nation. Metropolitan L.A. averages about 1,000 bank robberies per year; the FBI attributes L.A.'s popularity to the extensive network of freeways, which allows for a fast getaway. (*Credit Union* magazine, 2/04; *Los Angeles Business Journal*, 12/15/03) **2.** AP Online; 10/27/03. **3.** *Christian Science Monitor*, 4/4/00.

1. MONTH IN WHICH MOST HOME BURGLARIES OCCUR: AUGUST
2. ODDS THAT A BURGLARY OCCURS DURING THE DAYTIME: 6 IN 10
3. FIRST PLACE SEARCHED BY BURGLARS: MASTER BEDROOM

Sources: **1.** When many people take vacations. (*Washington Post*, 7/25/02) **2.** *Washington Post*, 7/25/02. **3.** Specifically, the bedroom dresser, according to a recent study of burglars, followed by the bedside table, shoe boxes in the closet, under the mattress, and interestingly, the freezer and refrigerator (based on a belief that people often hide cash there). (Wright, *Burglars on the Job*)

COUNTRY WITH THE WORLD'S HIGHEST NUMBER OF EXECUTIONS: CHINA

Followed by Iran, Saudi Arabia, and the U.S. Among the crimes in China that are punishable by death are "counterrevolutionary sabotage" and the sale of panda skins. In Saudi Arabia, crimes punishable by execution include rape, armed robbery, drug smuggling, witchcraft, and apostasy. Men in Saudi Arabia are beheaded by a public executioner wielding a sword; women are killed with two shots to the head. Incidentally, as of 2004, 108 countries had outlawed capital punishment. (AP, 10/10/03; *Christian Science Monitor*; 6/8/01; *Scotsman*, 2/6/01; *New Yorker*, 1/5/04)

Kidnapping capital of the world: Colombia

Some 2,000 to 3,000 people are abducted in Colombia every year. In 1999, a group burst into a Medellín church and kidnapped the entire congregation, taking them into the mountains as hostages. Kidnapping has become so commonplace in Colombia that there is a weekly radio program called *Voices of Kidnapping*, in which families record messages for their loved ones being held hostage in places unknown. Kidnapping is also rampant in Brazil; in fact, a Brazilian magazine published a "survival guide," which told Brazilians to regularly change the route taken between home and office, and to always carry cash and an ATM card. (*Washington Post*, 3/4/02; *Washington Times*, 12/3/02; *New York Times*, 2/13/02)

YEAR IRAN STOPPED THE STONING TO DEATH OF ADULTERERS: 2002

Under Iranian law, men convicted of adultery were buried up to their waists in a sandpit, and women up to their shoulders. Iran law prohibited the use of stones so large "that a person dies on being hit by one or two of them." If the person to be stoned managed to escape the pit, Iranian law required that the death penalty be commuted. There were two such stonings in Iran in 2000, and one in 2001. (Agence France-Presse, 1/4/03; *Independent*, 11/13/02)

1. LAST EXECUTION BY HANGING IN AMERICA: JAN. 25, 1996
2. LAST USE OF THE ELECTRIC CHAIR: MAY 10, 2002
3. NICKNAMES STATES GAVE THEIR ELECTRIC CHAIRS:

"YELLOW MAMA": ALABAMA
"OLD SMOKEY": NEW JERSEY
"OLD SPARKY": FLORIDA, NEW YORK, TEXAS, OHIO

Sources: **1.** On that day, Bill Bailey was executed in Delaware for killing an elderly couple. Both New Hampshire and Washington still allow for hangings where injection is impractical or where requested by the condemned. According to hanging protocol, on the day before a hanging, a professional hangman weighs the prisoner, then rehearses with a sand bag to gauge the correct "drop" for a fast death. (*Boston Herald*, 1/31/04) **2.** Lynda Lyon Block was executed for the killing of a police officer. Nebraska is the only remaining state that uses the electric chair as its means of execution, though several other states allow inmates to choose the electric chair. Many states had multiple switches for the electric chair operated by several wardens, with only one actually hooked up to the electric current, which was designed to prevent anyone from knowing who actually activated the fatal charge. (Knight Ridder/Tribune News Service, 10/8/01; *Atlanta Journal-Constitution*, 5/9/02) **3.** AP Online, 12/13/02.

MINUTES BEFORE DELMA BANKS WAS SCHEDULED TO DIE THAT THE SUPREME COURT POSTPONED HIS EXECUTION: 10

On Mar. 12, 2003, Banks had finished his last meal and was being strapped to a gurney when Texas corrections officials received word that the Supreme Court wanted the execution stopped so they could review whether the prosecutor at Banks's trial had engaged in misconduct. On Feb. 23, 2004, the court found that prosecutors had withheld crucial information from Banks's attorney, and threw out his conviction. (*Washington Post*, 2/24/04)

Number of people freed from death row as of 2005 following doubts about their guilt:
118

As of January 2005, 946 people had been executed since the Supreme Court found the death penalty constitutional in 1976. While it is impossible to determine whether anyone who has been executed was in fact innocent, the State of Virginia has refused to allow tests on the DNA of Roger Coleman, who was executed in 1992, despite strong evidence indicating that he might have been innocent. Frank Lee Smith was sentenced to death for the 1985 rape and murder of an 8-year-old Florida girl. He was later cleared of these charges through DNA testing, but not before he died of other causes while still on death row. (*Washington Post*, 12/14/03; Death Penalty Information Letter)

COUNTRIES THAT HAVE BROADCAST EXECUTIONS LIVE: 8

In June 2000, the execution of two convicted kidnappers was telecast and repeatedly rebroadcast on every Guatemalan television station. "It's not the kind of thing you want to watch, but you can't stop yourself," said one of the millions of Guatemalans who watched. On Jan. 12, 1928, a photographer for the *New York Daily News* strapped a tiny camera to his ankle and took a picture of the electrocution of Ruth Snyder, the first woman to die in the electric chair. The following day's front page showed a picture of Snyder under the headline "DEAD!" While executions have never been televised in the U.S., a 1995 survey of prisoners on death row found that 50% supported televising executions. (*St. Petersburg Times*, 6/30/00; *Madison Capital Times*, 7/25/01; *Editor and Publisher*, 4/24/00)

Most requested last meal: French fries

The next most popular requests are hamburgers, steak, ice cream, and fried chicken. Before his 1995 execution in Oklahoma, convicted murderer Thomas Grasso told reporters in his final statement: "I did not get my SpaghettiOs. I got spaghetti. I want the press to know this." In Indiana, they do not refer to the condemned's final meal as the "last meal." Instead, according to a spokesperson, "we refer to it as their 'special meal.'" (*Los Angeles Times*, 1/14/04; *Insight on the News*, 5/28/01; *New York Times*, 3/21/95)

PERCENTAGE OF PRISONERS WHO APOLOGIZE FOR THEIR CRIME IN THEIR FINAL WORDS BEFORE BEING EXECUTED: 28%

Based on a study of 138 executions. (*Cornell Law Review*, 1/1/03)

CROSSWORDS

1. NUMBER OF AMERICANS WHO DO CROSSWORD PUZZLES: 50 MILLION

2. FIRST CROSSWORD PUZZLE: DEC. 21, 1913

3. FIRST CLUE: "WHAT BARGAIN HUNTERS ENJOY" (5 LETTERS)

Sources: **1.** *New Yorker*, 3/4/02. **2.** The first crossword puzzle was created by Arthur Wynne and published in the Sunday *New York World* on Dec. 21, 1913. Wynne's puzzle—which he called a "Word Cross"—differed from today's crosswords in that it was diamond-shaped and contained no internal blocked-out squares. In the third week of publication, the paper made a mistake, accidentally switching the two words in the title. The name "Crossword" has been with us ever since. (*Los Angeles Times*, 11/24/88) **3.** The answer: s-a-l-e-s. (*Atlanta Journal-Constitution*, 3/15/02)

Date the *New York Times* dismissed crossword puzzles as "temporary madness" and a "primitive sort of mental exercise": Nov. 17, 1924

On Nov. 17, 1924, the opinion read: "Scarcely recovered from the form of temporary madness that made so many people pay enormous prices for mahjong sets, the same persons now are committing the same sinful waste in the utterly futile finding of words the letters of which will fit into a prearranged pattern. . . . This is not a game at all, and it hardly can be called a sport; it merely is a new utilization of leisure by those from whom it otherwise would be empty and tedious." (*New York Times*, 10/17/24)

Date the *New York Times* published its first crossword: Feb. 15, 1942

The first crossword in the weekday *New York Times* appeared on Sept. 11, 1950. The theme was New York's water supply. (*Atlanta Journal-Constitution*, 3/15/02)

CROSSWORD PUZZLE CREATORS ARRESTED FOR ESPIONAGE: 1

During the planning for the Normandy invasion of June 6, 1944, the Allies used closely guarded code words: *Utah* and *Omaha* for the beaches where the landing would take place; *Mulberry* for the artificial harbor that would be put in place after the landing; *Neptune*, the overall plan for naval operations; *Overlord*, the entire planned invasion itself. Inexplicably, on May 3, 1944, *"Utah"* appeared as an answer in London's *Daily Telegraph* crossword puzzle. When, on May 23, *"Omaha"* appeared, the puzzle's author was placed under surveillance. After *"Mulberry"* appeared on June 1, and *"Neptune"* and *"Overlord"* on June 2, the puzzle's creator was arrested, but was ultimately freed after it was determined that the presence of the words in the puzzle was the product of a series of astounding coincidences. (*National Geographic*, 6/1/02)

NUMBER OF MARRIAGE PROPOSALS HIDDEN IN *NEW YORK TIMES* CROSSWORD PUZZLES:

1

On Jan. 7, 1998, the *New York Times* personalized a crossword for Bill Gottlieb as a means of asking Emily Mindel to marry him. The puzzle included her first name (18 Across: poet Dickinson); Gottlieb's first name (14 Across: Microsoft chief, to some); the words "This Diamond Ring" (38 Across: 1965 Gary Lewis and the Playboys hit); and finally "Will You Marry Me" (56 Across: 1992 Paula Abdul hit, with Stevie Wonder on harmonica). Mindel, who was doing the puzzle next to Gottlieb at the time, said, "In the back of my mind, I thought this has to be for me, but it can't be. It was just too coincidental." (*Dallas Morning News*, 1/9/98)

COUNTRY IN WHICH CROSSWORDS WERE ONCE BANNED: SOVIET UNION

Stalin deemed crossword puzzles bourgeois and degenerate. (*Minneapolis Star Tribune*, 1/9/95)

NUMBER OF MISTAKES ACKNOWLEDGED BY THE *NEW YORK TIMES* CROSSWORD EDITORS OVER A 12-MONTH PERIOD IN 2001: 18

In an Aug. 9, 2001, article, puzzle editor Will Shortz wrote about some of the puzzles' errors, which are often raised in notes like this one from a reader in Middle Village, N.Y.: "I wish to inform you that on Monday you had an error in 6-Down. 'Kitchen whistler' was the clue. The answer was teapot. A teapot does not whistle; a tea kettle does." Shortz said, "To my chagrin, she was right." (*New York Times*, 8/19/01)

1. RECORD FOR SOLVING A NEW YORK TIMES CROSSWORD IN THE LEAST TIME: 2 MINUTES, 14 SECONDS

2. RECORD FOR SOLVING A CROSSWORD PUZZLE IN THE LONGEST TIME: 34 YEARS

Sources: **1.** Held by Stan Newman on a Monday edition puzzle. Perhaps the most famous crossword legend involves David Rosen, a four-time American cross-word puzzle champion, who beat a crossword puzzle creator named Peter Gordon on a puzzle Gordon himself created. (*New York Times*, 3/10/02) **2.** A Fijian woman took 34 years to complete a London *Times* crossword puzzle. (*Times* [London], 1/9/95)

CURSES (SPORTS)

1. NUMBER OF ARTICLES WHICH HAVE BEEN WRITTEN ON THE "*SPORTS ILLUSTRATED* COVER JINX": 534

2. YEAR THE JINX FIRST PURPORTEDLY BEGAN: 1955

3. ODDS THAT A TEAM HAS HAD BAD LUCK WITHIN TWO WEEKS OF APPEARING ON THE COVER OF *SPORTS ILLUSTRATED:* 4 IN 10

Sources: **1.** One of the most well-documented of all sports curses, the "Cover Jinx" posits that anyone who has the misfortune of appearing on the magazine's cover will soon experience misfortune. In 1984, two USC researchers sought to refute the jinx, finding that teams and athletes actually improved their performance 58% of the time after appearing on the cover. At the time of the study, however, several cover appearances seemed to confirm the jinx's viability: Cubs first baseman Leon Durham was injured shortly after he appeared on *SI's* cover and, after Magic Johnson graced the cover, the Boston Celtics came back from a 2–1 deficit against the Lakers to win the NBA Championship. (Lexis Search; AP, 7/11/84) **2.** Most say the jinx began with *Sports Illustrated's* Jan. 31, 1955 issue, featuring American ski champion Jill Kinmont on the cover. On Jan. 30, 1955–four days after the issue went on sale–Kinmont was paralyzed after hitting a tree during a training run. (*Sports Illustrated*, 11/10/03; 1/21/02) **3.** *Sports Illustrated*, 1/21/02.

EXAMPLES OF THE *SPORTS ILLUSTRATED* COVER JINX IN ACTION:

1970: The University of Texas football team fumbled nine times a week after they appear on the cover, ending their 30-game winning streak.

1978: After winning seven straight marathons, Bill Rogers finishes in sixth place in his first race after gracing the *SI* cover.

1984: After starting the season 11–0, the Miami Dolphins lose their next game following the *SI* cover.

(*San Diego Union-Tribune*, 11/6/03)

1. ODDS THAT AN ATHLETE SUFFERS SERIOUS INJURY AFTER APPEARING ON THE *SPORTS ILLUSTRATED* COVER: 1 IN 8

2. ATHLETES WHO DIED SHORTLY AFTER APPEARING ON THE *SPORTS ILLUSTRATED* COVER: 3

LAURENCE OWEN
PAT O'CONNOR
RICARDO RODRIGUEZ

Sources: **1.** *Sports Illustrated.* **2.** Along with the rest of U.S. Figure Skating Team, Laurence Owen died in a plane crash on Feb. 15, 1961, two days after she appeared on the *SI* cover. Featured in *SI's* May 1958 Indy 500 preview, Pat O'Connor crashed and died on the race's first lap. And eight months after appearing on *SI's* cover in 1962, another racedriver named Ricardo Rodriguez died during a practice run for the Mexican Grand Prix. (*San Diego Union-Tribune*, 11/6/03)

NFL TEAM THAT HIRED A VOODOO PRIESTESS TO GET RID OF A CURSE:
NEW ORLEANS SAINTS

The Saints built the Superdome on the site of the old Girod Street Cemetery, which had up to 30,000 graves. As the team went from one miserable season to the next, many attributed the team's misfortunes to its failure to respect the departed. To rid itself of the curse, the team hired Ava Kay Jones, a Voodoo priestess in New Orleans, who performed a pregame ritual before a Dec. 30, 2000, playoff game against the Rams. With a boa constrictor wrapped around her neck, Jones made offerings to the spirits on the 50-yard line as the Superdome crowd watched. Apparently, it worked: New Orleans won its first playoff game that afternoon in its 33-year history. (*New Orleans Times-Picayune*, 2/1/04)

YEAR WITCH DOCTORS WERE BANNED FROM THE FIELD DURING AFRICAN CUP GAMES: 2002

While most teams abhor the practice, several African teams have used witch doctors (called jujumen) to improve their fortunes. At the 2001 African Cup, host Mali would not allow Cameroon to practice the day before a critical semifinal game because of a belief that Cameroon's jujuman intended to cast a spell on the field. Before Senegal's matches, an unidentified man rubbed an ointment on the goalposts defended by Senegal. Subsequently, the team went 448 minutes without allowing a goal. (*San Diego Union-Tribune*, 6/21/02)

Food-related sports curses: Curse of the Colonel — Hanshin Tigers

Afflicted Japan's Hanshin Tiger baseball team from 1985 to 2003. The curse originated in 1985 after the Tigers last won the Japanese World Series, when ecstatic fans took a statue of Colonel Sanders from a Kentucky Fried Chicken and tossed it into an Osaka river where the team had gone to celebrate. After 1985, the team went 18 years without winning again, and fans—attributing the drought to the statue—attempted to dredge it up, with no luck. Twelve articles were written on the curse before 2003, when Hanshin won the Japanese series. (NPR, 9/24/03)

EFFORTS TO BREAK "THE CURSE OF THE BAMBINO" (BEFORE IT WAS BROKEN):

RETRIEVING A PIANO BABE DUMPED IN A LAKE

On several occasions, Red Sox fans hired divers to scour the bottom of a Sudbury, Mass., pond in search of a piano allegedly dumped there by the Babe when he occupied a waterside cabin before being traded to the Yankees. (*Boston Herald*, 4/14/02)

BURNING THE CONTRACT THAT SENT BABE AWAY

In 1994, a Red Sox fan named Allen Feinstein paid $99,000 for the original contract that formalized Ruth's trade to the Yankees and offered to give it to the Red Sox if they would burn it at home plate on Opening Day. (NPR, 7/9/94)

DAYS

1. HOURS OF DAYLIGHT IN FAIRBANKS, ALASKA, ON DECEMBER 21:
3 HOURS 42 MINUTES

2. HOURS OF DAYLIGHT IN FAIRBANKS, ALASKA, ON JUNE 21:
21 HOURS, 42 MINUTES

Sources: **1.** On December 21 in Fairbanks, the sun rises at 10:56 A.M. and sets at 2:42 A.M. (Timeanddate.com) **2.** On June 21 in Fairbanks, the sun sets at 12:44 A.M. and rises at 3:02 A.M., allowing Fairbankers to hold the annual Midnight Sun Baseball Game, now in its 99th year. Outfielders can lose fly balls in the glare of the sun—at midnight. (Timeanddate.com; *New York Times*, 6/25/04)

NUMBER OF STATES THAT DON'T OBSERVE DAYLIGHT SAVINGS TIME: 3

Arizona, Indiana, and Hawaii all observe year-round standard time. In Hawaii, it's because the tropical climate offers plenty of sunlight. In Arizona, after a year of trying out DST, things got so hot that no one wanted an extra hour of sun. Indiana is divided into both central and eastern time zones, which provides some confusion, but as former Indiana House Speaker John Gregg put it, "It's still 24 hours. If you want more daylight, get up earlier." (AP, 4/3/04)

1. Consecutive days of daylight in Barrow, Alaska: 84 days

2. Consecutive days of darkness: 66

Sources: **1.** At 400 miles north of the Arctic Circle, Barrow is America's northernmost town and subject to some of the longest stretches of daylight and darkness in the world. In a typical year, the sun rises on about May 10 and does not set again until August 2. (AP, 5/10/04) **2.** In a typical year, the sun sets in Barrow at about 12:50 P.M. on Nov. 18 and is not seen again untnil Jan. 24. (Alaska State Climate Center)

DATE OF THE U.S. PRESIDENTIAL ELECTION AS REQUIRED BY STATUTE:
TUESDAY AFTER THE FIRST MONDAY IN NOVEMBER

In the early days of the republic, voting often required extensive travel to polling stations; November was chosen because it was the month after harvest and before the onset of winter. Tuesday was chosen for a similar reason—it gave voters a day to travel to the polling stations, without requiring them to travel on Sunday, the Christian day of rest. Saturday was market day, and Thursday was ruled out because it was the traditional date that England held its elections. (*Dallas Morning News*, 11/7/96)

ORIGIN OF THE NAMES OF THE DAYS OF THE WEEK

SUNDAY: FROM *SUNNANDAEG*, SAXON FOR "DAY OF THE SUN"

MONDAY: FROM *MONANDAEG*, SAXON FOR "DAY OF THE MOON"

TUESDAY: NAMED FOR TIW, SAXON GOD OF WAR; *TIWESDAEG* IN SAXON MEANT "DAY OF TIW"

WEDNESDAY: NAMED FOR WODEN, CHIEF GOD OF THE SAXONS (*WODNESDAEG*)

THURSDAY: NAMED FOR THOR, GOD OF THUNDER (*THURSDAEG*)

FRIDAY: NAMED FOR FRIGGA, WODEN'S WIFE AND CHIEF GODDESS (*FRIGEDAEG*)

SATURDAY: NAMED FOR THE ROMAN GOD SATURN (*SAETERDAEG*)

(Panati, *Sacred Origins*)

1. DAY OF THE WEEK WITH THE FEWEST TRIPS BY CAR: SUNDAY
2. DAY WITH THE MOST TRIPS: FRIDAY

Of all trips by car, 12.9% take place on Sunday, compared to 15.6% on Friday. (*Adweek*, 9/15/03)

MOST DANGEROUS DAY TO BE IN NEW YORK CITY: SATURDAY

Police records indicate that Saturday is the most dangerous day to be in New York City, with homicide incidents reaching weekly highs on the day. (*Daily News*, 1/13/04)

PERCENTAGE MORE PEOPLE WHO SUFFER A HEART ATTACK ON A MONDAY: 33%

An American study confirmed that dangerous abnormalities in heart rhythm generally peak on Mondays, with lows on Saturdays and Sundays. (CBS News, 7/19/94; *National Post*, 6/19/04)

PERCENTAGE OF CAR ACCIDENTS THAT OCCUR ON A FRIDAY: 16.4%

More car crashes happen on Fridays than any other day of the week, with the rate peaking between 3 and 6 P.M. (*Wall Street Journal*, 11/7/03)

DEATH

1. Average life expectancy of a human being today: 66.7 years

2. World's longest average life expectancy: 83.50 years (Andorra)

3. Shortest average life expectancy: 30.76 years (Botswana)

4. Average life expectancy in the U.S.: 77.6 years

Sources: **1.** *Ottawa Citizen*, 9/26/03. **2.** The tiny landlocked country between France and Spain has only 69,000 citizens. Andorra is followed in the longevity race by Macau (82.03), San Marino and Singapore (both 81.53), Hong Kong (81.39), and Japan (81.04). (*CIA World Factbook*) **3.** This drastically low life expectancy is due to the prevalence of AIDS, which is ravaging many African countries. Botswana is followed by Zambia (35.18 years), Angola (36.79), Lesotho (36.81), and Mozambique (37.10). (*CIA World Factbook*) **4.** American women live an average of 80.1 years, while American men live 74.8 years. (Centers for Disease Control and Prevention)

TOP FIVE DEADLIEST JOBS:

1. TIMBER CUTTERS: 117.8 DEATHS PER 100,000 WORKERS

2. FISHERMEN: 71.1 DEATHS

3. PILOTS AND NAVIGATORS: 69.8 DEATHS

4. METAL WORKERS: 58.2 DEATHS

5. DELIVERY PEOPLE: 37.9 DEATHS

Rounding out the top ten were roofers, electrical power installers, farm workers, construction workers, and truck drivers. (Bureau of Labor Statistics, cited in the *Indianapolis Star*, 7/16/04)

Odds that an American dies unexpectedly, within hours after the onset of symptoms: 1 in 5

(Nuland, *How We Die*)

1. NUMBER OF AMERICANS WHO DONATE THEIR BODIES TO SCIENCE EACH YEAR: 10,000

2. COST TO BUY VARIOUS BODY PARTS FOR SCIENTIFIC PURPOSES:

HEAD: $500   TORSO: $5,000   KNEE: $650
SKIN (PER SQUARE FOOT): $1,000

Sources: **1.** *New York Times*, 3/12/04. **2.** *San Francisco Chronicle*, 3/10/04; *New York Times*, 3/12/04.

Estimated number of people who died of fright during the 1994 earthquake in Los Angeles: 21

A study by L.A.'s Good Samaritan Hospital found that on the day of the earthquake, there were five times as many sudden cardiac deaths as would normally be expected, which the study concluded were brought on by the intense anxiety associated with the quake. (*New Scientist*, 3/6/99)

Instances of people dying from excitement:

1992: Bob Bittner, a 40-year-old from Taylor, Mich., who had been bowling for 31 years, bowled his first 300 game on Dec. 14, 1992. Minutes later, he suffered a heart attack at the alley and died.

(*Calgary Herald*, 12/17/92)

1994: There have been at least four reported instances of men dying immediately after hitting a hole in one. In 1994, for instance, Emil Kijek hit a hole in one on the sixth hole at Sun Valley Golf Course in Rehoboth, Mass. As Kijek approached his ball at the seventh tee, he stopped, said, "Oh, no," and then toppled over. Peter Sedore died after hitting his 18th hole in one in California. Sedore's son said, "There's no other way he would have wanted it."

(*New York Times*, 11/12/94; *International Herald Tribune*, 12/26/95)

1. U.S. STATE WITH THE HIGHEST LIFE EXPECTANCY: HAWAII (79 YEARS)
2. U.S. STATE WITH THE LOWEST LIFE EXPECTANCY: MISSISSIPPI

Sources: **1.** Followed by Minnesota. (*Minneapolis Star Tribune*, 7/2/03) **2.** CDC.

1. Month with the most deaths: January   2. Month with the fewest deaths: September

According to the National Center for Health Statistics, about 9.5% of all deaths occur in January, while only 7.7% occur in September. After January, the months with the highest mortality rates are March, December, and February. Winter months lead the rest of the year because of influenza, pneumonia, and the added stress of cold weather. Some experts also attribute the January spike to a determination on the part of the sick to put off death until after Christmas. (*Washington Times*, 1/3/01)

DESIRE

1. Time a couple is most likely to engage in sex: 10:34 P.M.
2. Time at which a man's sex drive hits its peak: 8:00 A.M.
3. Month in which the amount of sex peaks: July

Sources: **1.** Based on a study conducted by the Kentucky-based Andrology Institute. (*Financial Times* [London], 6/6/96) **2.** *Cosmopolitan*, 5/1/01. **3.** According to a 1981 study from Indiana's Sex Research Institute. Other studies indicate that June is the most common month for a person to lose their virginity. (UPI, 2/20/81; *Sunday Times* [London,] 6/6/04)

1. PERCENTAGE OF MALE COLLEGE STUDENTS IN A RECENT STUDY WHO ANSWERED YES WHEN AN ATTRACTIVE FEMALE APPROACHED THEM AND ASKED THEM TO HAVE SEX: 75%

2. PERCENTAGE OF FEMALE COLLEGE STUDENTS WHO ANSWERED YES WHEN AN ATTRACTIVE MALE ASKED THEM TO HAVE SEX: 0%

Of the 25% of males who said no, many asked for a rain check. (*New Yorker*, 2/9/98)

TWO FOODS THAT WERE INITIALLY DEVELOPED TO CURB SEXUAL DESIRE:
KELLOGG'S CORN FLAKES
GRAHAM CRACKERS

Both Sylvester Graham (inventor of the Graham cracker) and John Harvey Kellogg (inventor of corn flakes) believed that certain diets promoted untamed sexual desire and masturbation, a problem that could be remedied by the increased consumption of whole wheat. Graham wrote that "high-seasoned food, rich dishes," and the "free use of flesh" increase "excitability of the genital organs." (Haber, *From Hardtack to Homefries;* Davison, *Abnormal Psychology*)

Side effect reported by some users of the antidepressant drug Anafranil: Orgasms from yawning

The drug's unusual side effect was originally reported in a 1983 paper in the *Canadian Journal of Psychiatry*, and reported again 12 years later in the *Washington Post*. Estimates of the number of Anafranil users who experience yawning orgasms range from well below 1% to up to 5%. The *Post* described one man who found the consequences of the condition so embarrassing that he was forced to wear a condom continuously. Several studies have also reported that giving clams Prozac results in increased sexual activity, and several individuals have also reported spontaneous orgasms after their Prozac dosage has been increased. (*Washington Post*, 9/23/95; *New York Times*, 2/17/98)

1. PERCENTAGE OF WOMEN OLDER THAN 75 WHO SAY THEY "WOULD BE QUITE HAPPY TO NEVER HAVE SEX AGAIN": 36%
2. PERCENTAGE OF 75-YEAR-OLD MEN WHO SAY THE SAME: 5%

(*Time*, 8/16/99)

1. Percentage of males who say they would be flattered if a coworker asked them to have sex: 66%

2. Percentage of females who would be insulted if a coworker did the same: 66%

(Buss, *The Evolution of Desire*)

1. NUMBER OF SEXUAL PARTNERS THE AVERAGE MALE WOULD LIKE TO HAVE OVER A LIFETIME: 18
2. NUMBER OF SEXUAL PARTNERS THE AVERAGE FEMALE WOULD LIKE OVER A LIFETIME: 4 TO 5

(Research conducted by psychologist David Buss, reported in the *Guardian*, 1/17/98)

NUMBER OF TIMES THE AVERAGE FRENCH ADULT MAKES LOVE ANNUALLY: 137
ENGLAND: 119 UNITED STATES: 111
CHINA: 132 SWEDEN: 94 JAPAN: 46

In the 2004 Durex Global Sex Survey, the French were the most sexually active nation in the world, followed by Greece (133 lovemaking sessions a year) and Hungary (131).

RECORD FOR MOST FEMALE PARTNERS BY A PROFESSIONAL ATHLETE: 20,000

The late Wilt Chamberlain devoted an entire chapter of his autobiography to sex. "I got the number by going through date books I've kept over the years since 1969, counting the names on a month-to-month basis and coming up with a prorated figure. At my age, that equals out to having sex with 1.2 women a day, every day since I was fifteen years old." Added Wilt the Stilt: "I'm sure plenty who read the numbers will no doubt think my taste is not particularly high or that I am 'easy.' I am a man of distinctive taste and most of the women I have encountered, the average Joe would have proposed marriage to on the first date." Chamberlain also said that of the 20,000 women, none was married: "Even as a single man, infidelity has no place in my life." (*Entertainment Weekly*, 10/25/91)

1. NUMBER OF CONTINUOUS HOURS MAE WEST PURPORTEDLY ONCE MADE LOVE: 15
2. NUMBER OF CONTINUOUS HOURS STICK INSECTS MAKE LOVE: 1,440

Sources: **1.** In her autobiography, Mae West wrote about a sexual liaison between her and a man named Ted that lasted for 15 consecutive hours. "He was," West reportedly said, "26 men in one night." (*Guardian*, 11/21/92) **2.** Stick insects remain in flagrante delicto for months. (*American Scientist*, 5/1/01)

DIAMONDS

1. **NUMBER OF CARATS MINED WORLDWIDE ANNUALLY: 120 MILLION**
2. **AMOUNT CHARGED FOR THESE UNCUT DIAMONDS BY PRODUCERS: $7 BILLION**
3. **VALUE OF THESE DIAMONDS IN FINISHED JEWELRY: $58 BILLION**
4. **ODDS THAT A DIAMOND PASSES THROUGH ANTWERP, BELGIUM: 1 IN 2**

Sources: **1.** This figure totals about 24 tons, which could fit snugly inside the back of a single 18-wheel truck. Only about 50% of these mined diamonds end up as jewelry, however, with the rest serving industrial uses such as drill bits for oil exploration, etc. (*National Geographic*, 3/1/02) **2, 3.** *International Journal*, 9/01. **4.** *Jewelers Circular Keystone*, 4/1/03.

1. **YEAR THE FIRST DIAMOND ENGAGEMENT RING WAS GIVEN: 1477**
2. **AVERAGE SIZE OF AN AMERICAN DIAMOND ENGAGEMENT RING: 0.8 CARATS**
3. **ODDS THAT AN AMERICAN WOMAN RECEIVES A DIAMOND ENGAGEMENT RING: 8 IN 10**

Sources: **1.** Archduke Maximilian of Austria presented Mary of Burgundy with a gold band crowned with a piece of sparkling carbon. The ring was placed on the third finger of Mary's left hand, the finger that ancient Egyptians believed held the vein of love, coursing directly to the heart. (*National Post*, 4/1/00) **2.** *Chicago Tribune*, 8/31/04. **3.** Princess Diana briefly popularized alternatives to the diamond engagement ring when she received a sapphire ring surrounded by diamonds from Prince Charles. (*Vancouver Sun*, 4/23/02)

1. **AVERAGE AMOUNT DE BEERS SUGGESTS BRITISH MEN SPEND ON AN ENGAGEMENT RING: 1 MONTH'S SALARY**
2. **AMERICAN MEN: 2 MONTHS' SALARY**
3. **JAPANESE MEN: 3 MONTHS' SALARY**

(*Economist*, 12/19/98)

1. **Origin of the word "carat": From the carob tree**
2. **Weight of a carat: 0.007 ounces**

Sources: **1.** Because seeds from the fruit of the carob tree have a uniform weight of about one-fifth of a gram, they were used as the unit to measure diamonds. (*Washington Post*, 12/8/02) **2.** A diamond loses about 50% of its weight as it goes through the cutting and polishing process. (*Toronto Star*, 9/4/94)

Celebrity diamond rings:

5 carats: Bruce Willis to Demi Moore

6 carats: Ben Affleck to Jennifer Lopez (returned)

10 carats: Michael Douglas to Catherine Zeta-Jones

16 carats: Victor Luna to Liz Taylor (returned)

22 carats: Howard Marshall to Anna Nicole Smith

29 carats: Mike Todd to Liz Taylor

40 carats: Aristotle to Jackie Kennedy Onassis

69.4 carats: Richard Burton to Liz Taylor

When asked why he bought Taylor a huge 29-carat engagement ring, Todd answered: "Thirty carats would have been vulgar." (*New York Post*, 5/13/00; *CBS This Morning*, 2/30/95; *Entertainment Weekly*, 3/26/04; *Deseret Morning News*, 1/5/01; *Courier-Mail*, 4/25/87; UPI, 8/30/84; *People*, 5/6/96)

1. LARGEST ROUGH DIAMOND EVER FOUND ON EARTH: 3,106 CARATS

2. LARGEST DIAMOND EVER FOUND IN THE UNIVERSE: 10 BILLION TRILLION TRILLION CARATS

Sources: **1.** Called the Cullinan, the 3,106-carat hunk was discovered on Jan. 26, 1905, in the Premier mine of South Africa. It was cut into nine major diamonds and hundreds of smaller ones, including the Great Star of Africa—the largest cut diamond in existence at 530.2 carats, now in the royal scepter of the British Crown Jewels. (*Houston Chronicle*, 4/28/02) **2.** Discovered in February 2004 by scientists at the Harvard-Smithsonian Center for Astrophysics, the diamond is 50 light-years away in the constellation Cetaurus. "It's the mother of all diamonds," said one of the discoverers. At 2,600 miles across, it certainly is. (Deutsche Presse Agentur, 2/23/04)

1. Year a jeweler first lent diamonds to an Oscar nominee: 1943

2. Most expensive piece ever worn to the Oscars: $20 million
(Gloria Stewart, 1998)

3. Most expensive piece ever lost at the Oscars: $6 million
(Whoopi Goldberg, 2002)

Sources: **1.** In 1943, movie producer David O. Selznick asked Harry Winston if he would lend jewelry to Jennifer Jones, who was nominated for best actress that year for her role in *The Song of Bernadette.* Winston agreed, and Jones won. Today, 20% to 30% of the nominees will eventually buy the pieces they borrow. (NPR, 3/1/04; *Los Angeles Times*, 3/19/99) **2.** In 1998, Stewart, nominated for best supporting actress for her role in *Titanic*, wore a 15-carat blue diamond necklace inspired by the fictional "Heart of the Ocean" diamond in the movie. Stewart was flanked by two security guards throughout the ceremonies. (*Palm Beach Post*, 3/19/03) **3.** Whoopi was wearing a $6 million 80-carat yellow diamond on a necklace borrowed from Harry Winston while hosting the Oscars in 2002. During a commercial break, Goldberg noticed that the diamond was gone. After a frantic search, a Winston security man noticed that the diamond was hidden in Whoopi's cleavage. (*Ottawa Citizen*, 4/6/02)

DIETS

1. ORIGIN OF THE WORD "DIET": FROM THE GREEK *DIAITA* (MEANING "WAY OF LIFE")

2. ODDS THAT AN AMERICAN IS OVERWEIGHT: 2 IN 3

3. ODDS THAT AN AMERICAN IS AT LEAST 100 POUNDS OVERWEIGHT: 1 IN 20

4. NUMBER OF OVERWEIGHT PEOPLE WORLDWIDE: 1.1 BILLION

Sources: **1.** Wanjek, *Bad Medicine.* **2.** Although today this fuels a $40 billion diet industry, not too long ago, having a few extra pounds was not considered so bad. In fact, in the 19th century, it was common for women to pad their bodies to look heavier, and until the early 20th century, medicines promising weight gain outnumbered those advertising weight loss. (*Newsday,* 1/12/04; UPI, 1/23/04; *People,* 6/22/90) **3.** *Journal of the American Medical Association,* 2004. **4.** According to the Worldwatch Institute, more than 20% of the world's population have a body mass index of 25 or higher. (*Sunday Telegraph,* 1/12/03)

1. Percentage of American women who are trying to lose weight at any given time: 44%

2. Percentage of American men: 29%

3. Percentage of people in Japan who said they have dieted recently: 37%

4. Percentage of South Korean dieters: 91%

5. Australians: 74%

Sources: **1, 2.** Similar to the figures in Britain, in which 43% of women and 25% of men said they were trying to lose weight in November 2004. (*U.S. News and World Report,* 2/9/04; *Mirror,* 11/5/04) **3–5.** ACNeilsen study, reported by Agence France-Presse, 7/28/04.

1. ODDS THAT A PERSON CLOSELY FOLLOWS A DIET: 1 IN 4

2. ODDS THAT A PERSON COMPLETELY ABANDONS A DIET: 4 IN 10

Sources: **1.** Based on a recent Tufts University study of overweight people who were asked to follow either the Atkins, Weight Watchers, Ornish, or Zone diet. (NPR, 11/10/03) **2.** In the Tufts study, 22% of the dieters had given up after 2 months. After a year, 35% had dropped out of Weight Watchers and the Zone, while 50% had quit Atkins and Ornish. (*San Diego Union-Tribune,* 11/10/03)

WORLD RECORD FOR GREATEST WEIGHT LOSS: 924 POUNDS

In the late 1970s, Jon Minnoch weighed about 1,400 pounds, and required the help of 13 people to roll him over in bed. After being hospitalized in 1978, he reportedly dropped to 476 pounds, but then gained much of it back. Minnoch struggled with his weight until he died at 42 of heart failure (at 800 pounds). (AP, 9/15/83)

1. MOST OBESE STATE IN AMERICA: WEST VIRGINIA
2. SLIMMEST STATE: COLORADO

Sources: **1.** With 28% of its adult population obese, West Virginia has the dubious honor of being the fattest state; Mississippi follows closely behind, with 27% of its adults obese. **2.** Colorado is the slimmest state, with only 15% of adults obese. (*New York Times*, 1/1/04)

MOST OBESE PLACE IN THE WORLD: KOSRAE ISLAND, MICRONESIA (85% OBESE)

Scientists believe that, because their ancestors lived through periods of famine, the residents of these islands possess genes that in effect instruct the body to store as much fat as possible. The introduction of fast food and Spam has, in one generation, created extreme obesity in the majority of the population. (*Sunday Telegraph*, 1/12/03)

1. Number of Americans who had their stomach stapled in 2003: 103,000
2. Number who had their stomach stapled in 1993: 16,000

(*Richmond Times-Dispatch*, 4/5/04)

YEAR FIRST DIET SOFT DRINK INTRODUCED: 1958

Diet Rite began the diet soda phenomenon. Joined in 1963 by Tab, which became the best-selling diet soda but which even devotees admitted had a slightly chemical taste. One "Tabaddict" explained: "It has a taste that's tinny and horrible. That's why I love it." (*Food Processing*, 3/1/03; *Forbes*, 6/17/96)

FIRST DIET BOOK:

The Physiology of Taste (1825): **In this first diet book, and the forebear of the low-carb diet, author Jean-Anthelme Brilliat-Savarin urges people to avoid rolls, potatoes, and cookies. To those who ignore this advice, he writes: "Very well then; eat! Get fat! Become ugly and thick, and asthmatic, finally die in your own melted grease." The book is also the source of the phrase "you are what you eat."**

(*New York Times*, 2/22/04; *Los Angeles Times*, 10/20/94)

DISABILITY

1. Years after Beethoven became deaf that he composed his Ninth Symphony: 20

2. Year a double amputee swam the English Channel: 1997

3. Sale of first electric wheelchair: 1956

Sources: **1.** "How can I, a musician, say to people that I am deaf?" Beethoven wrote. "I shall, if I can, defy this fate." (*Press*, 6/20/01) **2.** Masadur Baidya, who lost both his legs in a boyhood train accident, completed the 21-mile swim in 16 hours and 23 minutes. (Press Trust of India, 2/27/02) **3.** Invented by Herbert Everest and Harry Jennings, who also invented the first folding wheelchair in 1933. (*Popular Mechanics*, 6/1/01)

NUMBER OF PEOPLE MISSING LIMBS WHO'VE PLAYED MAJOR LEAGUE BASEBALL: 3

In 1944, Lt. Bert Shepard lost his right leg when his fighter plane was shot down over Germany. After eight months in a German POW camp, he came home determined to resume his baseball career. He was fitted with an artificial leg and was signed by the Washington Senators. On Aug. 4, 1945, Shepard came into a game against Boston, pitching 5 1/3 innings, allowing three hits and one run. He never pitched again in the majors. . . . Pete Gray lost his right arm in a farming accident at age 6. He taught himself to bat and field with his remaining left arm, and in 1945, played 77 games for the St. Louis Browns, with 13 runs batted in and 162 putouts in the outfield. . . . Jim Abbott, who pitched for the Angels, Yankees, and Brewers in the1990s, was born without a right hand. In 1991, Abbott finished third in Cy Young voting, and in 1993, pitched a no-hitter. Brewers manager Phil Garner said this about Abbott: "The way I look at it we're the ones who are handicapped. It takes us two hands to do what he does with one." (*Toronto Star*, 2/16/91; *Wisconsin State Journal*, 3/23/99)

NUMBER
OF BLIND PEOPLE
WHO'VE CLIMBED
MOUNT EVEREST: 1

On May 18, 2001, Erik Weihenmayer became the first blind person to climb Everest, aided by directions from the other climbers and bells attached to their jackets. Weihenmayer insisted on carrying an equal share of the team's supplies: "I wasn't going to be carried to the top and spiked like a football." (*Time*, 6/18/01)

FIRST ASCENT OF EVEREST BY AN AMPUTEE: MAY 27, 1998

Tom Whittaker, who lost his right foot in a car crash, said his first thought upon reaching the summit was "Who'd have thought it? It's still a mystery to me how a 50-year-old guy with an artificial leg can climb a mountain as big as this." (*Arizona Republic*, 1/4/99)

Year disabled athlete first appeared on a box of Wheaties: 1984

Paralyzed from the waist down since a hunting accident at age 14, George Murray, a wheelchair runner and marathoner, broke the five-minute barrier with a 4:59.7 mile in 1979, and the four-minute mile in 1985. (*Sports Illustrated*, 8/14/95)

FIRST DEAF PERSON TO PLAY IN THE NFL:
BONNIE SLOAN (ST. LOUIS, 1991)

Sloan played a single season. In 1991, Kenny Walker, a college standout at defensive end who lost his hearing at age 2, was relegated to the eighth round of the NFL draft due to his deafness, but was finally picked by Denver. With the aid of an interpreter on the sidelines flashing his coach's instructions, Walker played for two years with the Denver Broncos before being waived in 1993. (*Los Angeles Times*, 9/4/93)

DOGS

1. NUMBER OF DOGS IN THE U.S.: 65 MILLION
2. COST TO RAISE: $4,476
3. HOURS OF SLEEP PER DAY, ON AVERAGE: 14
4. ATTACKS ON MAILMEN PER DAY, ON AVERAGE: 8 1/2

Sources: **1.** Labrador retrievers are the nation's most popular breed. (*Los Angeles Times*, 8/20/04) **2.** Based on an annual expenditure of $373 over a dog's average 12-year lifetime. The estimate does not include the cost of doggie summer camp ($1,000 per week), a doghouse designed by Denver's Petite Maison "with wallpaper options available" (starting at $4,500), an Hermès dog collar ($278), or a proper dog funeral (starting at about $250) at one of America's 600 pet cemeteries. (*Washington Post*, 4/8/04) **3.** *Canadian Press*, 3/9/04. **4.** In 2002, more mailmen were bitten by dogs in Indiana than in any other state. (Cox News Service, 6/6/03)

Ratio of people who consider their dogs "smart" or "geniuses" as opposed to of "average" intelligence: 3 to 1

Cats generally score lower than dogs on IQ tests. (From a survey sponsored by the Animal Hospital Association, cited in the *Dayton Daily News*, 1/16/00)

1. PERCENTAGE OF PEOPLE WHO SAY THEY WOULD RISK THEIR LIFE FOR THEIR DOG: 83%
2. PERCENTAGE WHO BELIEVE THEIR DOG WOULD RISK ITS LIFE FOR THEM: 70%

Sources: **1.** Moreover, 38% of dog owners said they would spend "any amount" to save their pet's life. (*USA Today*, 3/15/99) **2.** Dogs are credited with saving 10,000 American lives in Vietnam through mine detection and alerting troops to ambushes. (Gannett News, 4/29/97; *Minneapolis Star Tribune*, 3/16/97)

AMOUNT PAID BY AN ANONYMOUS TEXAN IN 1999 TO HAVE HIS PET COLLIE MISSY CLONED: $3.7 MILLION

The effort has so far proved unsuccessful, depsite the fact that the same lab cloned the first cat (aptly named Copycat) in February 2002. (*Austin American-Statesman*, 8/8/04)

1. AVERAGE LIFE SPAN OF A DOG TODAY: 12 YEARS

2. AVERAGE LIFE SPAN OF A DOG IN 1930: 7 YEARS

(According to the Senior Dog Project, reported in the *New York Times*, 12/30/03)

1. NUMBER OF DOGS THAT WERE KNOWN TO BE ON BOARD THE *TITANIC*: 9

2. NUMBER THAT SURVIVED: 3

Henry Sleeper Harper was able to get his dog (a Pekingese named Sun Yat-sen) onboard a life raft, as were Margaret Hays and Elizabeth Rothschild (though her husband perished). (*Atlanta Journal-Constitution*, 4/12/98)

1. MOST INTELLIGENT DOG BREEDS, IN ORDER:

BORDER COLLIE, POODLE, GERMAN SHEPHERD

2. LEAST INTELLIGENT DOG BREEDS, IN ORDER:

BULLDOG, BASENJI, AFGHAN HOUND

For his book *The Intelligence of Dogs*, Stanley Coren asked every registered dog judge in North America to rank dog breeds on how easily they can be trained. According to the study, while it took the average border collie only five times to learn a new command, the average chow-chow (just above bulldogs in the study) needed at least 80 to 100 demonstrations before it could begin to respond correctly, leading Coren to conclude that "there is probably furniture out there that is more trainable than chows." (Coren, *The Intelligence of Dogs; Guardian*, 11/13/03)

Sound Chinese dog makes when barking: *"Wung-Wung"*

While most English speakers believe a dog says "ruff-ruff" when barking, to the Spanish it's "*jau-jau*," to the French "*woa-woa*," to the Russians "*gav-gav*," and to Koreans "*mung-mung*." (Reuters, 4/17/00)

ESTIMATE OF THE NUMBER OF AMERICANS WHO MENTION THEIR DOG IN THEIR WILL: 27%

(*Miami Herald*, 1/15/03)

1. Intelligence level of the average dog: Equivalent to a 2-year-old human's

2. Intelligence level of the average cat: Equivalent to a 1 1/2-year-old human's

According to Stanley Coren, the average dog understands about 200 words. (Coren, *Why We Love the Dogs We Do*)

ELVIS

1. WHERE ELVIS WAS WHEN HE DIED: ON THE TOILET AT GRACELAND

2. NUMBER OF TIMES ELVIS WAS BURIED: 2

3. PERCENTAGE OF AMERICANS WHO BELIEVE ELVIS IS STILL ALIVE: 7%

Sources: **1.** At around 2:30 in the morning on Aug. 16, 1977, Elvis was found sprawled on the bathroom floor, his pajamas below his knees, by girlfriend Ginger Alden. He had had a heart attack while on the toilet, reading a book entitled *The Scientific Search for the Face of Jesus.* Doctors found 10 drugs in Elvis's system, including morphine, phenobarbital, methaqualone, Valium, Carbrital, and Demerol, but no cause of death was ever established. (*Entertainment Weekly,* 8/11/95) **2.** Presley was originally laid to rest in Memphis's Forest Hill Cemetery on Aug. 18, 1977, entombed in a large mausoleum. In the early morning hours of August 29, three Memphis men were arrested for trying to steal Elvis's body. As a result, Presley's father had his body disinterred and reburied on the grounds of Graceland on Oct. 2, 1977. (*Entertainment Weekly,* 10/6/00) **3.** On Elvis's grave, his middle name, Aron, is misspelled as Aaron, giving Elvis conspiracy theorists reason to conclude that Elvis Aron Presley is not buried there. In Wright City, Mo., there is an Elvis Is Alive Museum run by Bill Beeny, 71, who has had DNA tests conducted on tissue samples he got from doctors in Memphis The result, says Beany: "No match." (*Time,* 10/10/88; *St. Louis Post-Dispatch,* 7/13/00; *Chicago Tribune,* 8/25/02)

WHAT THE *NEW YORK TIMES* SAID AFTER ELVIS'S FIRST NATIONAL TV PERFORMANCE: "MR. PRESLEY HAS NO SINGING ABILITY"

In addition, the *New York Herald-Tribune* described Elvis as "unspeakably untalented and vulgar," the *Daily News* called him "appalling musically . . . , tinged with the kind of animalism that should be confined to dives and bordellos," and the Rev. Billy Graham said, "I would not let my daughter cross the street to see Elvis Presley." (*Newsday,* 1/8/95)

1. AMOUNT EARNED BY ELVIS ON HIS FIRST RECORD CONTRACT: $5,000

2. WORTH OF ELVIS ESTATE AT THE TIME OF HIS DEATH: $4.9 MILLION

3. AMOUNT EARNED BY ELVIS IN 2004: $40 MILLION

Sources: **1.** In addition to the five grand, Elvis also got a penny and a half for each record sold. (AP Online, 10/9/99) **2.** *People,* 3/18/91. **3.** Most of it goes to his daughter, Lisa Marie, who owns his estate. (Forbes.com)

1. NUMBER OF ELVIS IMPERSONATORS AT THE TIME OF HIS DEATH: 48
2. ESTIMATED NUMBER TODAY: 35,000

Sources: **1.** *Minneapolis Star Tribune,* 12/3/95. **2.** *Seattle Post-Intelligencer,* 1/9/03.

SITE OF WORLD'S LARGEST ELVIS STATUE: ABU GHOSH, ISRAEL

Looming over the Tel Aviv–Jerusalem highway, the 22-foot-high statue of Elvis is the centerpiece of the Elvis Inn, a highway stop whose walls and ceiling are covered with Elvis memorabilia. (*Dallas Morning News,* 9/6/98)

1. ANNUAL VISITORS TO GRACELAND ($27 PER TICKET): 700,000
2. ANNUAL VISITORS TO THE WHITE HOUSE (FREE): 1,250,000

Depending on who's counting, Graceland is either the second or third most visited house in the U.S. after the White House and (maybe) Mount Vernon. (*Chicago Tribune,* 3/2/03)

Number of times Elvis performed outside the U.S.: 3

All in Canada. Elvis played Vancouver, Toronto, and Ottawa in 1957, but never played outside the U.S. again. The only time Elvis ever set foot in England was during a refueling stop on the way back from army service in Germany. Yet as of 2004, Elvis had spent more weeks on the British singles charts than any other artist—including the Beatles and Cliff Richard. (*Chicago Tribune,* 8/15/02; BPI Entertainment News, 7/1/04)

ENDORSEMENTS

1. FIRST ATHLETE TO HAVE A PRODUCT NAMED AFTER HIM: GOLFER HARRY VARDON

2. FIRST ATHLETE TO ENDORSE A SNEAKER: CHARLES "CHUCK" TAYLOR (CONVERSE ALL STARS)

3. FIRST ATHLETE TO SIGN A NIKE ENDORSEMENT DEAL: STEVE PREFONTAINE

Sources: **1.** After Vardon won the British Open in 1898, Spalding named a golf ball after him called the "Vardon Flyer." (*Golf Magazine*, 4/92)
2. Taylor, who barnstormed for four professional teams (with names such as the Buffalo Germans and Akron Firestones) in pre-NBA days, was hired as a salesman for Converse in 1921, and had his name added to the All Stars in 1923 after he suggested a slight restyling to make it more suitable for basketball. During its heyday in the 1960s, 90% of professional and college ballplayers wore All Stars. Over a billion pairs have been sold. (*Deseret Morning News*, 4/8/01; *Boston Globe*, 5/31/02) **3.** Prefontaine, whose most memorable race was a loss at the '72 Olympics in Munich, was paid $5,000 by Nike (then an unknown sneaker maker) in 1974, becoming its first athletic endorser. (*Newsday*, 1/29/97)

FIRST ATHLETE TO APPEAR ON A BOX OF WHEATIES: LOU GEHRIG (1934)

(*Palm Beach Post*, 6/18/03)

AMOUNT VIDEO GAME MAKERS PAY THE NFL EACH YEAR TO USE REAL PLAYERS IN THEIR GAMES: $250 MILLION

(*Street and Smith's Sports Business Journal*, 5/3/04)

1. AMOUNT OF MERCHANDISE SOLD ANNUALLY BY THE NFL: $3.2 BILLION

2. NUMBER OF LEBRON JAMES JERSEYS SOLD DAILY IN THE FIRST YEAR THEY WERE OFFERED: 5,542

1. *Seattle Times*, 4/8/04. 2. *Chicago Tribune*, 4/8/04.

Cigarette endorsements by athletes:

Lou Gehrig:
"For a sense of deep-down contentment,
just give me Camels after a good, man-sized meal."

Joe DiMaggio: "When I need a 'lift' in energy, Camels is the cigarette for me."

Ted Williams: "Chesterfields. The baseball man's cigarette."

(Field and Stream, 3/95; U.S. News and World Report, 3/22/99; Syracuse Post Standard, 1/10/99)

First baseball player to endorse a product:
Honus Wagner for Louisville Sluggers (1905)

In 1905, Wagner signed a contract giving the company the right to use his autograph on Louisville Sluggers, in what was the first product endorsement by an athlete in a team sport. *(Cincinnati Enquirer, 6/29/03)*

First animal to endorse a product: Dan Patch

Over a 9-year harness racing career, Dan Patch won 54 of 56 races and set a record for the mile that stood for 40 years. The horse's image appeared on over 500 products including horse feed, cigars, sheet music, stoves, and cars. *(Chicago Tribune, 7/25/03)*

TOP ATHLETES IN ENDORSEMENT INCOME:

TIGER WOODS (GOLF): $70 MILLION
MICHAEL SCHUMACHER (AUTO RACING): $40 MILLION
LEBRON JAMES (BASKETBALL): $35 MILLION
ANDRE AGASSI (TENNIS): $24 MILLION

(Los Angeles Times, 4/6/04; Sports Illustrated, 5/17/04; Forbes, 4/12/04)

FANS

1. INCREASE IN THE TESTOSTERONE LEVEL OF BRAZILIAN FANS AFTER BRAZIL DEFEATED ITALY IN THE 1994 WORLD CUP: 28%

2. WAITING LIST FOR GREEN BAY PACKERS SEASON TICKETS AS OF OCTOBER 2004: 60,507

3. BANKS ROBBED BY CLAUDE JONES TO PAY FOR TICKETS TO L.A. RAIDERS GAMES: 24

Sources: **1.** A Georgia State University psychologist sampled saliva from Italian and Brazilian fans before and after the 1994 game to reach this conclusion. (UPI, 1/26/04) **2.** It's even worse than the number indicates. Every person on the list can buy up to four seats, and the seats can be passed down to relatives. "We only ask that children actually be born before they're placed on the list," says Packers ticket director Mark Wagner. (*Sports Illustrated*, 10/6/03; AP, 9/22/04) **3.** In 1991, Jones was sentenced to nearly 10 years in federal prison after robbing 24 banks to support his Raiders habit, which included going to away games as well. (*USA Today*, 1/5/01)

DESPONDENT FANS:

Amelia Bolanios (El Salvador)

On June 8, 1969, Honduras defeated El Salvador by the score of 1–0 in a World Cup qualifying match. Amelia Bolanios, who was watching the game on television in her family's apartment, took her father's pistol from a drawer and shot herself in the heart. "She could not bear to see her fatherland brought to its knees," wrote a Salvadorian newspaper the following day. Bolanios was given a televised state funeral, at which the president and soccer team marched behind her flag-draped coffin. She became a national heroine.

(*Independent*, 10/18/90)

1. First rendition of the "wave": oct. 31, 1981

(Stanford–Washington football game)

2. Number of people required to start a wave: 25

Sources: **1.** "The wave"—in which successive sections of fans stand up, raise their arms, and then sit down—is believed to have first occurred in the third quarter of a 1981 game between Washington and Stanford. Former Washington cheerleader Robb Weller and band director Bill Bissell led the historic routine, in which the crowd remained standing until a full circle was completed. (*Washington Post*, 11/4/01; AP Online, 11/3/01) **2.** Researchers at the University of Budapest studied film footage of waves to draw their conclusions, which were originally published in the British journal *Nature*. The research also found that the wave usually proceeds in a clockwise direction around the stadium and typically moves at a speed of about 20 seats per second. (Agence France-Presse , 9/11/02; BBC, 9/12/02)

DEDICATED FANS:

1. GILES PELLERIN: ATTENDED 797 CONSECUTIVE USC FOOTBALL GAMES FROM 1926 TO 1998

2. ANDY NICOLSON: DROVE FROM ENGLAND TO JAPAN TO WATCH ENGLAND PLAY IN THE 2002 WORLD CUP

3. RANDY "ZIP" PIERCE: BLIND SEASON TICKET HOLDER, NEW ENGLAND PATRIOTS

Sources: **1.** Pellerin went to every game, whether home or away, for 71 years, traveling over 650,000 miles and to more than 50 cities (including Tokyo), until he died, fittingly, while attending the 1998 Rose Bowl against crosstown rival UCLA in Pasadena. Pellerin's streak was almost broken in 1949 when he had to have an emergency appendectomy, but the streak remained intact after he sneaked out of the hospital to attend the game. (*Los Angeles Times*, 11/23/98) **2.** The trip covered 11 countries and 23,000 miles (*Miami Herald*, 4/23/02) **3.** Pierce lost his vision in one eye in 1989, and the second eye in 2000. He relies on ticket holders around him to tell him what's happening on the field. (*Boston Herald*, 1/30/04)

INSANE FANS:

Unidentified South Korean soccer fan

Set fire to himself during the 2002 World Cup tournament as a means of spurring the South Korean team on. "I intend to become a ghost and the twelfth player, and will do my best to help Korea win," he said in a note. According to a Japanese newswire, the man kept chanting "Victory to Korea" while he was being taken to the hospital.

(Japanese Economic Newswire, 6/14/02)

Female Japanese David Beckham fans

According to the Japanese daily *Shukan Post,* one fan of the British soccer star checked in to a hotel room where Beckham stayed during the 2002 World Cup and licked the toilet seats. Another woman broke her engagement and became a prostitute to fund a trip to England to take Beckham from his wife.

(*Orlando Sentinel*, 8/29/02)

Yai Yam-Uarn

Killed his wife after she tried to change the channel during a World Cup soccer match between Italy and Mexico.

(*Toronto Star*, 6/16/02)

INCREASE IN NUMBER OF HEART ATTACKS IN BRITAIN AFTER IT LOST TO ARGENTINA IN A PENALTY SHOOTOUT AT THE 1998 WORLD CUP: 25%

According to an article in the *British Medical Journal,* researchers believe that many of those watching the game on television were ultimately stricken by the tension. "The increase in admissions suggests that myocardial infarction can be triggered by emotional upset, such as watching your football team lose an important match," the researchers wrote. The report urged World Cup authorities to find another way to decide a winner, saying that "perhaps the penalty shootout should be abandoned on public health grounds." (AP Online, 12/19/02; *Evening Mail*, 12/20/02)

FARMS

1. NUMBER OF FARMS IN AMERICA: 2.1 MILLION

2. NUMBER OF AMERICAN FARMS IN 1950: 5.4 MILLION

3. AVERAGE SIZE OF A U.S. FARM TODAY: 441 ACRES

4. AVERAGE SIZE OF A U.S. FARM IN 1910: 139 ACRES

Sources: **1.** The official number of farms is somewhat deceiving, since the U.S. government defines a farm as any enterprise selling more than $1,000 in agricultural products. Six in 10 American "farms" sell less than $10,000 worth of goods annually. (*Chicago Tribune*, 6/4/04) **2.** *Sioux Falls Argus Leader*, 6/5/00. **3.** *World* magazine, 6/19/04. **4.** *New York Times*, 4/2/00.

PERCENTAGE OF THE LOWER 48 STATES THAT IS MADE UP OF FARMLAND: 49%

There are 1.9 billion acres in the continental U.S., 938 million of which are made up of farmland. (USDA, 2/04)

PERCENTAGE OF AMERICANS WHO WERE FARMERS

1. IN 1801: 95%

2. IN 1901: 45%

3. IN 2001: 2%

(*Wichita Eagle*, 4/13/04)

1. Average life span of a broiler chicken: 42 days

2. Of a farm-raised pig: 5 1/2 months

3. Of a farm-raised lamb: Under 12 months

Sources: **1.** Ricketts, *Introduction to Agribusiness*. **2.** *Wichita Eagle*, 6/30/02. **3.** *Atlanta Journal-Constitution*, 4/17/03.

1. NUMBER OF EGGS LAID ANNUALLY BY THE AVERAGE HEN IN 1900: 30

2. AVERAGE LAID ANNUALLY TODAY: 275

Sources: **1.** *Arkansas Democrat-Gazette*, 1/21/98. **2.** *Kansas City Star*, 4/19/03.

1. STATE WITH THE MOST FARMS: TEXAS (229,000)

2. STATE WITH THE FEWEST FARMS: ALASKA (610)

3. STATE WITH THE LEAST LAND UNDER CULTIVATION: RHODE ISLAND (60,000 ACRES)

Sources: **1.** Followed by Missouri (106,000), Iowa (90,000), and Tennessee and Kentucky (each with 87,000). (USDA, 2/04)
2. Followed by Rhode Island (850), Delaware (2,300), Nevada (3,000), and New Hampshire (3,400). (USDA, 2/04) **3.** USDA, 2/04.

Largest ranch in America:
King Ranch, Tex. (825,000 acres)

About the size of the state of Rhode Island, the King Ranch was founded by a former steamboat captain in 1853, and has 60,000 head of cattle, 1,000 registered quarter horses, and 424 separate wells. The largest ranch within one fence in the country is the Waggoner Ranch, spreading over 500,000 acres about 200 miles west of Dallas. (*Boston Globe*, 3/23/03; *Dallas Morning News*, 8/3/03)

Number of cows and calves slaughtered annually in the U.S.: 36 million

According to the USDA, 70% of the cow carcass ends up as meat. (*New York Times*, 1/20/04)

Countries in which it's illegal to kill cows: 2 (Nepal and India)

Cows are considered holy in both Hindu-dominated countries. However, it is not illegal to eat beef in either.
When the Indian prime minister was recently accused of eating cows by political opponents, he said: "I prefer to die rather than eat beef."
(*Hinduism Today*, 12/31/96; AP, 3/14/03; AP, 6/13/03)

LAST PRESIDENT TO KEEP A COW AT THE WHITE HOUSE:
WILLIAM HOWARD TAFT

The cow's name was Pauline Wayne, and she spent her days grazing on the White House lawn. (*Chicago Tribune*, 12/15/97)

FASHION

1. PAIRS OF JEANS OWNED BY THE AVERAGE AMERICAN: 9

2. NUMBER OF THOSE WORN ON A REGULAR BASIS: 5

3. NUMBER OF T-SHIRTS OWNED BY THE AVERAGE AMERICAN: 25

4. ODDS THAT AN AMERICAN MAN OWNS A PAIR OF KHAKI PANTS: 3 IN 4

Sources: **1.** They also own four pairs of denim shorts and two denim shirts. (*Women's Wear Daily*, 5/27/04; *Wichita Eagle*, 6/7/04)
2. *Women's Wear Daily*, 5/27/04. **3.** *Wearables Business*, 4/1/03. **4.** *New York Times*, 1/14/03.

FIRST DESIGNER LABEL: CHARLES FREDERICK WORTH

Called the "King of Dress" before his death in 1895, Worth founded modern couture: the first designer to create a collection of gowns from which his clients could choose rather than producing only according to their wishes, the first designer to use models and mannequins, and the first to put his name on the label. Worth dressed many of Europe's female nobility in the mid19th century, including Eugenie Bonaparte, wife of Napoleon III, who reportedly had duplicates of all her ball gowns so that she could change during a party and look fresh. (*Montreal Gazette*, 7/8/98; *Independent*, 4/1/04)

PRICE AT WHICH THE FIRST PAIR OF LEVI'S 501s SOLD FOR IN THE 1890s: $1.25

Strauss called his first pairs of jeans "Waist-High Overalls." This was to distinguish them from bib overalls, until then the norm. The first Levi's had no back pockets or belt loops. Belt loops were added in 1922. Strauss's jeans were so durable that when they finally wore out, miners used them to hold up small rockslides. (*Denver Post*, 9/3/98)

1. BIRTH DATE OF THE T-SHIRT: 1899
2. FIRST COLLEGE T-SHIRT: UNIVERSITY OF MICHIGAN (1920s)
3. FIRST PROMOTIONAL T-SHIRT: *THE WIZARD OF OZ* (1939)
4. FIRST POLITICAL MESSAGE ON A T-SHIRT: "DO IT WITH DEWEY" (1948)

Sources: **1.** Crew-neck T-shirts first entered the American consciousness as navy regulation uniforms, first meant to be worn as undershirts, but eventually worn alone. In 1913, the U.S. Navy officially adopted the short-sleeved crew-neck T-shirt as regulation military wear. (*Chicago Tribune*, 12/5/96) **2.** UCLA followed suit with theirs in 1931. (*Guardian*, 1/17/02) **3.** *Los Angeles Times*, 10/10/93. **4.** Thomas E. Dewey lost the 1948 presidential race to Harry Truman, likely because people didn't want to do it with him. (*Australian Magazine*, 8/3/02)

WHAT THE GAP'S FOUNDER ORIGINALLY INTENDED TO CALL THE STORE: "PANTS AND DISCS"

Donald Fisher's original concept involved selling pants and records in the same store, hence the name "Pants and Discs." The night before he had to finalize the name for the sign painter, his wife convinced him to name the store the Gap, after the alleged generation gap. The first Gap opened in San Francisco in 1969. (*Denver Post*, 9/3/98)

1. DIMENSIONS OF THE AVERAGE FASHION MODEL: 5'11", 117 POUNDS
2. DIMENSIONS OF THE AVERAGE AMERICAN WOMEN: 5'4", 140 POUNDS

(*Women's Health Weekly*, 1/15/04)

First American fashion show:
Chicago Dressmaker's Club Show, 1911

Papers reported every seat in the house filled, with the boxes replete with society women and aristocrats. The first fashion runway appeared at another Chicago show in 1914, where "100 shapely women" strutted 250 American-made styles. (*Women's Wear Daily*, 7/16/01; Gross, *Model*)

FIRST WIDE-CIRCULATION AMERICAN FASHION MAGAZINE: *HARPER'S BAZAAR*

The magazine launched in 1867, taking much of its tone and format from a German fashion magazine, *Der Bazar*. The debut of *Vogue*, with its lofty target market of New York City elite, came in 1892. (*London Free Press*, 4/15/01)

FAST FOOD

1. ODDS THAT AN AMERICAN EATS AT A FAST-FOOD RESTAURANT ON ANY GIVEN DAY: 1 IN 4

2. ODDS THAT AN AMERICAN KID EATS AT McDONALD'S IN ANY GIVEN MONTH: 9 IN 10

3. AMOUNT OF MONEY AMERICANS SPENT ON FAST FOOD IN THE YEAR 2003: $119 BILLIO I

4. YEAR THE TERM "FAST FOOD" WAS INTRODUCED: 1951

Sources: **1, 2.** Schlasser, *Fast Food Nation*, cited in *U.S. News and World Report*, 1/22/01. **3.** That is more than Americans spend on higher education; books, movies, magazines, newspapers, videos, and music combined. Americans spent about $6 billion on fast food in 1970. (Research Alert, 5/7/04) **4.** *Dallas Morning News*, 1/26/01.

MINUTES THE AVERAGE AMERICAN SPENDS EATING LUNCH: 23

(*Washington Times*, 8/24/00)

1. NUMBER OF HAMBURGERS THE AVERAGE AMERICAN CONSUMES EACH WEEK: 3

2. AMOUNT OF FROZEN FRENCH FRIES CONSUMED BY THE AVERAGE AMERICAN IN 1960: 4 POUNDS

3. AMOUNT OF FROZEN FRENCH FRIES CONSUMED TODAY: 30 POUNDS

(Schlosser, *Fast Food Nation*)

First fast-food chain: White Castle (1921)

In 1921, the first White Castle opened in Wichita, Kan., with hamburgers for a nickel each. As part of a study to determine the nutritional value of its hamburgers, White Castle paid a University of Minnesota medical student in 1930 to eat nothing but White Castle hamburgers and water for 3 months. White Castle is famous for the holes in its hamburgers, which were rumored to be where the ketchup was supposed to go, but which actually help the burgers to cook more evenly. (Eberts, *Opportunities in Fast Food Careers*)

First hot dog chain: Nathan's (1916)

When it first opened, Nathan's had workers wearing physicians' white smocks eating hot dogs out in front of the store to show people they were safe to eat. Also in 1916 was the inauguration of Nathan's hot dog–eating contest, which for the past 4 years has been won by a 132-pound Japanese man named Takeru Kobayashi, who bested rivals weighing as much as 400 pounds by eating 53 1/2 hot dogs in 12 minutes. (Jackle, *Fast Food*; Daily News, 7/5/04)

1. YEAR McDONALD'S SOLD ITS 100-MILLIONTH HAMBURGER: 1958
2. ITS BILLIONTH BURGER: 1963
3. ITS 50-BILLIONTH BURGER: 1984

(Milwaukee Journal, 2/2/03; AP, 11/19/84)

Year McDonald's finally allowed women to work in its restaurants: 1968

Because of a fear that female employees would attract young men hanging around the parking lots, McDonald's had an unwritten rule prohibiting female employees. In the late 1960s, however, a franchisee in Elkhart, Ind., had problems finding men to fill positions at his restaurant, and hired the first female McDonald's restaurant employee—the wife of a preacher. Nevertheless, when McDonald's corporate managers found out, they threatened to terminate the franchise unless she was fired. When the franchisee refused, the company eventually backed down, and formally rescinded the restriction against women in 1968. (Love, *McDonald's: Behind the Arches*)

INVENTION OF THE DRIVE-THROUGH WINDOW: 1931

The Pig Stand restaurant in Los Angeles had a side door where someone would come out and hand people their food while they were in their cars. Jack in the Box introduced the drive-through window at its stores in 1951. (Jackle, *Fast Food*)

1. AVERAGE AMOUNT OF TIME IT TAKES TO GO THROUGH A McDONALD'S DRIVE-THROUGH WINDOW, ACCORDING TO A RECENT STUDY: 157 SECONDS
2. AMOUNT OF TIME IT TAKES TO GO THROUGH A WENDY'S DRIVE-THROUGH: 116 SECONDS

(Forbes, 3/29/04)

TERMS TRADEMARKED OR SOUGHT TO BE TRADEMARKED BY McDONALD'S:

McFAMILY McKIDS McTV McHOAGIE
McMUSIC McRECYCLE McWORLD
McMEMORIES McTIME McFOLKS
McMOM McMATH McREAD McHOLIDAY
McMILLIONS McSTOP

(Harper's Magazine, 5/1/01; Rocky Mountain News, 8/4/04)

NUMBER OF McDONALD'S RESTAURANTS EATEN AT BY PETER HOLDEN: 11,620

Holden first started visiting McDonald's while on vacation in the 1960s. His record is 45 McDonald's restaurants in a single day—and he doesn't count one unless he actually eats at it. In 2000, a former Denny's waiter named Jason Vanderford-Pfaff ended his quest to eat at every one of the 1,500 Denny's restaurants around the world after visiting only 250 of them. (*Washington Times*, 1/2/3/03; *East Bay Express*, 1/22/03)

1. **First McDonald's:** San Bernadino, Calif. (1948)
2. **First Kentucky Fried Chicken:** Salt Lake City, Utah (1952)
3. **First Burger King:** Miami, Fla. (1954)
4. **First IHOP:** Toluca Lake, Calif. (1958)
5. **First Wendy's:** Columbus, Ohio (1969)

Sources: **1.** *New York Times*, 7/25/99. **2.** In 1952, Harland Sanders persuaded a Utah restaurant owner named Pete Harman to put his chicken recipe on the menu. Trying to drum up interest in the item, Harmon put up a sign on his restaurant's window that said "Kentucky Fried Chicken." The poultry proved more popular than anything else Harmon offered, and the first KFC franchise was born. A 14-piece bucket, five dinner rolls, and a pint of gravy sold for $3.50. (*Louisville Courier*, 8/4/02) **3.** Burger King's original name was "Instaburger King." (*Restaurant News*, 8/19/96) **4.** *Rocky Mountain News*, 6/25/04. **5.** Founder Dave Thomas named the franchise after the nickname of his daughter Melinda Lou. (*Akron Beacon Journal*, 10/3/03)

1. PRICE OF A BIG MAC WHEN IT WAS INTRODUCED IN 1968: **45¢**

2. CHEAPEST PLACE TO BUY A BIG MAC IN 2004: **PHILIPPINES ($1.23)**

3. MOST EXPENSIVE PLACE TO BUY A BIG MAC: **SWITZERLAND ($4.90)**

4. MOST BIG MACS CONSUMED BY ONE PERSON: **20,000**

Sources: **1.** The Big Mac was invented in Pittsburgh by a McDonald's franchisee named Jim Delligatti. (*Toronto Star*, 5/4/93) **2.** According to the Big Mac Index, a chart put out annually by the *Economist*, China came in a close second at $1.26. (*Seattle Times*, 7/18/04) **3.** *Seattle Times*, 7/18/04. **4.** An American named Donald Gorske started eating at least one Big Mac per day on May 17, 1972, and has averaged about 600 per year since. (*St. Paul Pioneer Press*, 7/21/04)

FIRST RONALD McDONALD:
WEATHERMAN WILLARD SCOTT

McDonald's was originally going to name its new clown mascot "Archie McDonald," in reference to the "Golden Arches"; the name was changed to Ronald because there was a baseball broadcaster named Arch McDonald. (Love, *McDonald's: Behind the Arches*)

1. RANK OF RONALD McDONALD AMONG MOST RECOGNIZABLE PUBLIC FIGURES FOR AMERICAN SCHOOLCHILDREN: SECOND
2. PUBLIC FIGURE RANKED FIRST: SANTA CLAUS

In *The Lexus and the Olive Tree*, Thomas Friedman relates a story about Martin Indyk, the U.S. ambassador to Israel, while presiding over a ceremony marking the opening of the first McDonald's in Jerusalem. A young boy with a McDonald's hat approached him, requested his autograph, and asked how it felt to be an ambassador from McDonald's opening restaurants around the world. When Indyk told him that he was not the McDonald's but the American ambassador, the boy no longer wanted his autograph. (*Atlanta Journal-Constitution*, 8/8/02)

RANK OF THE GOLDEN ARCHES AMONG THE MOST RECOGNIZABLE SYMBOLS IN THE WORLD: **SECOND**

According to the book *McLibel* by John Vidal, "Only the five rings of the Olympic Games are better known." (*Sunday Star Times* [New Zealand], 6/22/97)

FBI

1. DAY THE FBI WAS FOUNDED: JULY 26, 1908
2. NUMBER OF FBI AGENTS IN 1909: 9
3. NUMBER OF AGENTS IN 2004: 11,900

Sources: **1.** *Newsday*, 4/13/04. **2.** The agency debuted with nine detectives, 13 civil rights investigators, and 12 accountants. (*St. Louis Post-Dispatch*, 5/27/00) **3.** *Washington Times*, 1/12/04.

FAMOUS PEOPLE WHOM THE FBI KEPT FILES ON:

Mickey Mantle
Albert Einstein (1,800 pages)
Charlie Chaplin (2,063 pages)
Frank Sinatra (1,275 pages)
Lucille Ball
Groucho Marx
Martin Luther King, Jr. (17,000 pages)
Elvis Presley (663 pages)
Eleanor Roosevelt (3,000 pages)
Bud Abbott (14 pages)
Sammy Davis, Jr.
Jackie Robinson (131 pages)

The Mantle file was once delivered to the White House, though who requested it has never been revealed. (*Minneapolis Star Tribune*, 5/5/98). . . . As a part of the FBI's surveillance of Dr. King, the agency routinely bugged his hotel rooms, occasionally picking up episodes of sexual activity. The FBI sent a tape of one of those episodes to King's office in 1964, attaching an anonymous note that said: "You are done. There is but one way out for you. You better take it before your filthy, abnormal fraudulent self is bared to the nation." (*Dallas Morning News*, 1/9/00). . . . Presley's reveals that Elvis offered to spy on the Beatles and other "subversive" musical groups for the FBI (ABC's *Good Morning America*, 8/11/97). . . . Robinson's file noted that he was on the NAACP board of directors and was New York chairman of the United Negro and Allied Veterans of America, which was labeled a "communist front" that sought to "provoke racial friction." (*Cincinnati Post*, 5/6/03)

Official casting director for early films about the FBI: J. Edgar Hoover

During his tenure over the FBI (1924–1972), Hoover had all public operations on lockdown, including the casting of Hollywood films. Hoover allegedly personally auditioned Jimmy Stewart for *The FBI Story*, and once told James Cagney to, at the end of the film, "Make sure you're dead, because I don't want to see any crooks living." (NBC News Transcripts, 4/11/04)

1. TOTAL NUMBER OF CRIMINALS ON THE 10 MOST WANTED LIST SINCE 1950: 478
2. NUMBER OF THOSE WHO WERE WOMEN: 7

The list came into being after a newspaper reporter asked the FBI for a list of the "toughest guys" it wanted to apprehend. The agency supplied a list of the 10 fugitives it considered the most dangerous, which was then circulated in newspapers. Director J. Edgar Hoover was so delighted with the interest that he made the list a permanent feature. (FBI; *Chattanooga Times Free Press*, 3/26/00)

FIRST PERSON ON 10 MOST WANTED LIST:
THOMAS JAMES "TOUGH TOMMY" HOLDEN

In 1949, Holden shot his wife and her two brothers to death in Chicago after a night of heavy drinking and disappeared. Placed on the list on Mar. 14, 1950, Holden was apprehended on June 23, 1951, after a man in Beaverton, Ore., recognized him from a picture in a newspaper article. (*Oregonian*, 3/14/00)

1. LONGEST APPEARANCE ON THE LIST: 24 YEARS
(DONALD EUGENE WEBB)

2. SHORTEST APPEARANCE: 2 HOURS
(BILLY AUSTIN BRYANT)

Sources: **1.** On Dec. 4, 1980, Webb allegedly killed Police Chief Gregory B. Adams of Saxonburg, Penn., with two shots at close range. Webb was first added to the list on May 4, 1981, and has been on the run ever since. The name "Don" is tattooed on the back of Webb's right hand and the name "Ann" is tattooed on his chest. (FBI) **2.** On Jan. 8, 1969, Bryant was placed on the list at 5 A.M. after he killed two FBI agents. By 7 A.M., he had been captured. (*Dallas Morning News*, 3/10/95)

QUESTIONS FROM THE FBI EMPLOYMENT APPLICATION:

"HAVE YOU ENGAGED IN ACTS OR ACTIVITIES DESIGNED TO OVERTHROW THE UNITED STATES GOVERNMENT BY FORCE? IF YES, PROVIDE DETAILS."

"HAVE YOU USED MARIJUANA MORE THAN 15 TIMES?"

"HAVE YOU EVER SOLD ILLEGAL DRUGS? IF YES, PROVIDE DETAILS."

FIRST WOMEN

1. FIRST FEMALE LAWYER IN AMERICA: ARABELLA MANSFIELD (1869)

2. FIRST FEMALE DOCTOR: ELIZABETH BLACKWELL (1849)

3. FIRST FEMALE TENNIS PRO TO PLAY WITHOUT STOCKINGS: RUTH TAPSCOTT (1927)

Sources: **1.** Arabella Mansfield was the first woman in America actually licensed to practice law, admitted to the Iowa Bar in September 1869. Myra Bradwell sought admission to the Illinois Bar before Mansfield, but was rejected because of her gender. In upholding that decision, Justice Bradley of the Supreme Court wrote that "The paramount destiny and mission of women are to fulfill the noble and benign offices of wife and mother." (*Columbia Journal of Gender*, 9/03) **2.** Blackwell was rejected by at least 15 medical schools before Geneva Medical College finally accepted her after the faculty required a unanimous vote from the male students who, as a practical joke, voted her in. The joke was on them, however—Blackwell ended up at the top of her class. (NPR, 7/3/94) **3.** South African Ruth Tapscott caused a stir when she went bare-legged at Wimbledon. In 1931, Lili de Alvarez became the first woman to play in shorts. (*Seattle Post-Intelligencer*, 6/26/98)

First female film director: Alice Guy (1896)

Ms. Guy—initially a secretary—was allowed to direct as long as it "didn't interfere" with her secretarial work. In 1896, she became the first woman to write and direct a fiction film, *La fee aux choux* (The Cabbage Fairy), and ended up making some 800 films. She also reputedly was the first director to use the close-up shot. (*Daily Variety*, 11/12/03)

1. FIRST FEMALE POLICE OFFICERS:
LOLA BALDWIN (1905) ALICE WELLS (1910)

2. NUMBER OF FEMALE POLICE OFFICERS TODAY: 78,000

Sources: **1.** In 1905, Baldwin was sworn in as an officer on the Portland, Ore., police force, and in 1910, Wells joined the Los Angeles Police Department. Few people at the time accepted the idea of a woman police officer; indeed, when Wells showed her badge, she was often accused of borrowing her husband's. In the decades thereafter, female officers served mostly in desk jobs such as radio dispatching. It wasn't until 1968 that Indianapolis became the first force in the country to assign a woman to full-time street patrol. (*Independent*, 9/9/90; *USA Today*, 4/26/04) **2.** U.S. Newswire, 2/13/04.

FIRST FEMALE TO APPEAR ON A WHEATIES BOX: ELINOR SMITH (1934)

Actually, Smith, who set the women's endurance record for airplane flight (26 hours, 23 minutes), appeared on the back of a Wheaties box. The first woman to appear on the front of the box was gymnast Mary Lou Retton, in 1984. (*Houston Chronicle*, 11/18/03)

FIRST FEMALE COMBAT PILOT: SABIHA GOKCEN (1937)

Born in Turkey and orphaned at an early age, Sabiha earned her pilot's wings in 1937 and, that same year, flew bombing raids that helped crush a rebellion in eastern Turkey. In 2001, one of the two airports in Istanbul was named after her. The first American female fighter pilot to see action was Lt. Andrea Quy, who bombed a target in Iraq from her F-14 Tomcat on Dec. 18, 1998. (*Independent*, 3/24/01; *Chicago Tribune*, 12/21/98)

FIRST FEMALE SUBMARINE COMMANDER: SOLVEIG KREY (1995)

Lt. Solveig Krey of the Norwegian navy became the world's first female submarine commander in 1995. "I've been accepted by the crew as one of them," says Krey, 32. "Mostly I'm just 'the boss.'" (*Time*, 12/18/95)

First female prime minister: Sirimavo Bandaranaike (1960)

Known affectionately in Sri Lanka as "Mrs. B," Sirimavo served 12 years as prime minister in two separate terms, 1960–65 and 1970–77. (*Time*, 4/13/98)

FIRST FEMALE VICE-PRESIDENTIAL CANDIDATE: GERALDINE FERRARO (1984)

Ferraro was Walter Mondale's running mate in his unsuccessful quest for the presidency in 1984. In her acceptance speech, Ferraro said that "by choosing an American woman to run for our nation's second highest office, you send a powerful signal to all Americans. There are no doors we cannot unlock. If we can do this, we can do anything." (*Washington Post*, 7/20/99)

FIRST WOMAN TO PLAY IN AN NHL HOCKEY GAME:
MANON RHEAUME (1992)

On Sept. 23, 1992, in a preseason game against the St. Louis Blues, Rheaume allowed two goals and made seven saves for the Tampa Bay Lightning. "Honestly, I didn't care why I was invited to try out," said Rheaume recently. "So many times growing up I'd been told 'no' because I was a girl that I was happy to play." (*London Free Press*, 4/30/01)

1. FIRST WOMAN TO BREAK A MEN'S WORLD RECORD: SYBIL BAUER (1924)

2. FIRST WOMAN TO PITCH IN A PROFESSIONAL BASEBALL GAME: JACKIE MITCHELL (1931)

Sources: **1.** On a trip to Bermuda in 1922, Bauer became the first woman to break an existing men's world record—Stubby Kruger's 440-yard backstroke, which she lowered by 4 seconds to 6:24. Tragically, she died of cancer at the age of 22, with some pointing to her death as proof that women were not meant to compete in vigorous athletic competition. (Swimming Hall of Fame) **2.** In 1931, Jackie Mitchell, pitching for the Chattanooga Lookouts, struck out Babe Ruth and Lou Gehrig back-to-back in an exhibition game against the Yankees. Ruth was reported to have thrown his bat against the dugout in disgust. The following day, baseball commissioner Kenesaw Landis voided Jackie's contract on the grounds that baseball was "too strenuous" for a woman. (Berlage, *Women in Baseball*)

FIRST FEMALE BULLFIGHTER:
JUANITA CRUZ (1933)

Hiding behind a mask and going by the name Senorita X to prevent her parents from discovering, Cruz displayed enormous courage, refusing to run even when cornered by a bull. "If I were a man, I would run," she said." But if I run, someone in the audience will yell that I am running because I am a woman and I am scared—so I will not run." (*Sports Illustrated*, 3/9/92)

FIRST FEMALE IN SPACE: VALENTINA TERESHKOVA (1963)

On June 16, 1963, Tereshkova, a former textile worker and amateur parachutist, was launched into orbit by the Soviet Union. Another woman (Tatyana Morozycheva) had initially been chosen to be the first woman in space, but Tereshkova (code-named Seagull) moved ahead of her after Morozycheva became pregnant. Despite her cheery messages from space, the flight was a nightmare for Tereshkova, who was so sick when the spacecraft landed that the event had to be restaged for the media the following day.... It wasn't until 1983 that America launched Sally Ride, its first woman, into space. (*Russian Life*, 5/03)

1. FIRST FEMALE FIREFIGHTER: JUDY BREWER (1974)
2. NUMBER OF FEMALE FIREFIGHTERS TODAY: 8,500

Sources: **1.** The Arlington, Va., Fire Department made U.S. history in 1974 when it hired Brewer as the nation's first female firefighter. Brewer retired in 1999 as a battalion chief. (*USA Today*, 10/12/89) **2.** U.S. Newswire, 2/13/04.

First girl to play Little League baseball: Katheryn Johnston (1950)

Johnston played for the King's Dairy team in Corning, N.Y., in 1950. Afraid a girl wouldn't be allowed to try out, Katheryn cut her hair short and tucked it under her cap. It wasn't until 2 weeks into the season that her coach found out Katheryn's secret. He didn't care, but the league did, and the following year, the Little League added a rule barring participation by girls. It wasn't until 23 years later that the second girl took the field, after a court forced a team in New Jersey to allow 9-year-old Liz Osder to play. (AP, 8/23/01)

FIRST WOMAN TO RUN THE BOSTON MARATHON: ROBERTA GIBB (1966)

When Gibb wrote for an application, race officials refused, saying women couldn't run such long distances. "That was the first time somebody told me I couldn't be who I am because I'm a woman. To me, that was all the more reason to run." Forbidden to officially run in the marathon, Gibb hid in the bushes at the start of the race and just jumped in, finishing in 3 hours, 20 minutes. (RunnersWorld.com)

1. FIRST WOMAN TO TRY OUT FOR AN NBA TEAM: ANNE MEYERS (1979)

2. FIRST WOMAN TO DUNK IN A BASKETBALL GAME: GEORGEANN WELLS (1984)

Sources: **1.** In September 1979, the Indiana Pacers signed the 24-year-old Meyers to a $50,000 contract and invited her to try out for the team during a rookie–free agent camp. "Some people were really concerned about where I would shower," she said. Meyers was cut after six practice sessions. (WNBA.com) **2.** On Dec. 21, 1984, Wells, a 6'7" center playing for West Virginia, became the first female rim rocker during a rout against the University of Charleston. "It's not so much that the women's game needs dunking," she said recently. "My thing is, 'Why not slam? Do it because you can.'" (*Newsday*, 3/31/00)

FISH

1. MOST POPULAR SEAFOOD IN AMERICA: SHRIMP
2. NUMBER OF FISHERMEN IN AMERICA: 34.1 MILLION
3. NUMBER OF PET FISH IN AMERICA: 192 MILLION

Sources: **1.** Americans eat an average of more than 3.4 pounds per person annually, more than they do canned tuna, which was the previous most popular seafood up until 2002. Japan leads the world in per capita shrimp consumption. (*Progressive Grocer*, 5/1/04) **2.** U.S. Fish and Wildlife Service. **3.** Comprising 185 million freshwater and 7 million saltwater pet fish, living in 13.9 million American households. (*Sacramento Bee*, 3/5/04; *New York Times*, 5/2/04)

FISH WITH THE LONGEST NAME IN THE WORLD:

HUMUHUMUNU-KUNUKUAPUAA

The Humuhumunukunukuapuaa (also known as the Queen Triggerfish) is Hawaii's state fish. The literal translation of the Hawaiian word is "the trigger fish that grunts like a pig." (*Ken Schultz's Fishing Encyclopedia*)

1. NUMBER OF DAYS THE AVERAGE ANGLER FISHES ANNUALLY: 16
2. PERCENTAGE OF FRESHWATER ANGLERS WHO FISH FOR BLACK BASS: 38%
3. FOR TROUT: 28%
4. FOR CATFISH: 27%

The most popular fish sought by oceangoing fishermen are flatfish (flounder, halibut), followed by striped bass. (U.S. Fish and Wildlife Service)

Number of states with an official state fish: 42

Brook trout are the most common state fish. (*Hartford Courant*, 4/8/03)

ONLY STATE WITHOUT BASS: ALASKA

(*New Orleans Times-Picayune*, 8/1/03)

DATE A FISH ALLEGEDLY SPOKE TO WORKERS AT A SUBURBAN NEW YORK FISH STORE: JAN. 28, 2003

The incident took place at the New Square Fish Market, located in a fervently orthodox Jewish community some 30 miles outside of Manhattan. According to two employees who witnessed it, at about 4 P.M., they were about to kill a carp when the fish started talking in Hebrew, telling them to repent because the end was near, and identifying itself as the soul of a man who used to frequent the store. As one of the fish cutters later told the *New York Times*, "I don't believe any of this Jewish stuff. But I heard that fish talk." (*New York Times*, 3/15/03)

Price that a single Atlantic bluefin tuna sold for in a Japanese market in 2001: $175,000

The fish, weighing 444 pounds, was considered an average specimen when it sold at a Tokyo central seafood market auction at roughly $400 a pound; some Atlantic bluefin—the largest of the bluefin species—can grow to 1,500 pounds. (*San Francisco Chronicle*, 8/17/01)

FISHERMEN KILLED BY FISH:

In 2000, an Acapulco fisherman was killed when the blue marlin he was wrangling leaped out of the water and impaled him on its nose.

In 1997, a Taiwanese fisherman bled to death after his throat was slit by a spearfish he'd hauled aboard.

In 1998, a fisherman in Australia was dragged out to sea by a giant fish he had just snagged after becoming tangled in his own line.

(*Orange County Register*, 1/11/01; Deutsche Presse Agentur, 5/20/97; *Courier-Mail*, 5/30/98)

Longest battle with a fish: 23 hours

On Aug. 24, 1990, Ron Smothers hooked a giant marlin estimated at 1,100 pounds during a fishing tournament off the Hawaiian coast. The marlin hit at 8:30 A.M., and because tournament rules prohibited anyone from helping, Smothers was on his own. For 23 hours, Smothers fought the fish to a stalemate, but at 7:30 A.M. the following morning, with waves breaking over the boat and Smothers near collapse from exhaustion, the line snapped. (*Los Angeles Times*, 9/1/93)

LARGEST FISH EVER CAUGHT ON A ROD AND REEL:
2,664-POUND GREAT WHITE SHARK

Alfred Dean caught the shark (which measured in at 16' 10" long and 9' 6" in girth) off of Denial Bay, Australia, on Apr. 21, 1959. For bait, he used a whole porpoise. (*Palm Beach Post*, 1/6/00; *Sports Afield*, 8/1/01)

ESTIMATED NUMBER OF VETERINARIANS WHO TREAT PET FISH IN THE U.S.: 100

Fish veterinarians can do anything from a basic checkup (about $40), to resetting broken fish bones, to giving enemas for digestive problems, to plastic surgery. Perhaps the most common fish condition is what is known as a "buoyancy disorder," usually caused by an infection in the digestive tract that prevents the fish from swimming or floating upright. Doctors have found that surgically inserting a small pebble into the fish's abdomen cures the problem, or (for as-yet unknown reasons) feeding a fish a green pea daily. (*Journal of the American Veterinary Medical Association*, 12/15/02; *New York Times*, 5/2/04)

Number of rescuers in England who recently attempted to save a goldfish poured down the drain: 11

On Apr. 14, 2004, rescuers from the Royal Society for the Prevention of Cruelty to Animals rushed to a sewer grate in Newcastle, England, after a concerned resident noticed a fishbowl and decorative pebbles lying at its side. Six goldfish didn't make it, but one (nicknamed William by his rescuers) was safely removed from the sewer after a nearly 3-hour rescue. Said an RSPCA spokesperson: "Goldfish may not be as cute as cats or dogs, but they still deserve our respect and the chance to live out their lives." (Press Association, 4/16/04)

1. ESTIMATED NUMBER OF FISH SPECIES IN THE WORLD: 23,000

2. NUMBER OF NEW SPECIES OF FISH THAT ARE BEING DISCOVERED EACH YEAR: 160

Sources: **1.** According to *Ken Schultz's Fish Encyclopedia,* 40% are freshwater fish, 60% saltwater. (*Pittsburgh Post-Gazette*, 2/20/00) **2.** Because 95% of the ocean bottom remains unexplored, scientists are currently conducting a massive 10-year Census of Marine Life, expected to lead to the discovery of another 5,000 species of fish that were previously unknown. Newfound species include the Hairy Angler, which has a soccer-ball-sized body covered with antennas that alert it to passing prey, and the Rasta Sponge, a bright red sponge discovered off the Florida Keys. (*U.S. News and World Report*, 2/23/04; 8/16/04)

YEAR SCIENTISTS DETERMINED THAT FISH FEEL PAIN: 2003

In 2003, a study conducted at the University of Edinburgh revealed that fish possess a basic nervous system that responds to painful stimuli. Experiments in which trout were exposed to bee venom and acid revealed increased respiratory rates in the fish, as well as a pronounced rocking motion comparable to human responses to pain. (Agence France-Presse, 4/30/03)

SADDAM HUSSEIN'S FAVORITE BAIT FOR CATCHING FISH: GRENADES

Instead of a rod, Saddam would throw a grenade into the water and then have a scuba diver retrieve the dead fish from the water. (Agence France-Presse, 4/20/03)

ONLY STATES IN WHICH FISH SHOOTING IS PERMITTED: VERMONT AND VIRGINIA

Though there have been several efforts to ban the pastime as "unsportsmanlike," Virginians and Vermonters head out every year with hand pistols, shotguns, and even AK-47s to shoot fish. The object is to shoot just in front of the fish, causing a concussion that brings the dead (but intact) fish to the surface. (*New York Times*, 5/11/04)

NUMBER OF FISH NAMES CHANGED BECAUSE THEY WERE POLITICALLY INCORRECT: 2

In 1998, the Squawfish was renamed the Pike Minnow after complaints from Native Americans. In 2001, the Jewfish had its name changed to Goliath Grouper. (*Baltimore Sun*, 6/1/01)

CITY WITH THE HIGHEST PERCENTAGE OF ANGLERS IN THE U.S.: MINNEAPOLIS

Some 38% of adults in Minneapolis fish. (*American Demographics*, 10/03)

1. WORLD'S RAREST FISH: OARFISH
2. MOST RECENT OARFISH SIGHTING: 2003 (VAL FLETCHER)

Sources: **1.** The bright metallic fish swims vertically and can grow up to 45 feet in length. It has been seen only about 25 times since the 1700s, usually washed up onshore, where it is frequently mistaken for a sea monster. In 1963, an 18-foot specimen washed ashore in Malibu, Calif., causing temporary panic among beachgoers. (*Washington Post*, 7/9/97) **2.** While fishing for codfish near her home on England's northeast coast, novice angler Val Fletcher hooked an 11-foot oarfish. Scientists hoping to examine the fish were disappointed when they learned it had been cut up and put in Mrs. Fletcher's freezer. (*Daily Telegraph*, 2/21/03)

FOOTBALL

1. NUMBER OF FOOTBALLS THE HOME TEAM IS REQUIRED TO HAVE ON HAND FOR EACH NFL GAME: 36

2. POINTS AWARDED FOR A TOUCHDOWN UP UNTIL 1912: 5

3. ODDS THAT AN NFL GAME FROM 1920 TO 1932 WAS A SHUTOUT: 2 IN 3

4. LARGEST STADIUM IN THE NFL: FedExField (91,665)

5. LARGEST COLLEGE FOOTBALL STADIUM: MICHIGAN STADIUM (107,501)

Sources: **1.** NFL teams that play in outdoor stadiums are required to have 36 new balls on hand, while those in indoor stadiums must only have 24. Twelve balls are set aside, marked with a K, that are used only by kickers. (*Kansas City Star*, 1/10/04) **2.** Other differences between the early game and the one played now: fields were 110 yards long (and still are in Canadian football) with two 50-yard lines; there was no forward passing; teams had three downs rather than four to make 10 yards; and they received four points for a field goal until 1909. (Whittingham, *Rites of Autumn*) **3.** In its first season, 90% of the games in the NFL were shutouts. (*New Orleans Times-Picayune*, 9/2/94) **4.** *Washington Post*, 9/12/04. **5.** *Wall Street Journal*, 9/20/04.

NAMES OF THE 14 ORIGINAL NFL TEAMS:

AKRON PROS BUFFALO ALL-AMERICANS CANTON BULLDOGS CHICAGO CARDINALS CHICAGO TIGERS CLEVELAND TIGERS COLUMBUS PANHANDLES DAYTON TRIANGLES DECATUR STALEYS DETROIT HERALDS HAMMOND (IND.) PROS MUNCIE (IND.) FLYERS ROCHESTER JEFFERSONS ROCK ISLAND (ILL.) INDEPENDENTS

The NFL debuted as the American Professional Football League in 1920. The Akron Professionals were the first league champions. (*New Orleans Times-Picayune*, 9/2/94)

1. Cost of an NFL franchise in 1920: $100

2. Cost of an NFL franchise in 1999: $700 million

3. Highest price ever paid for an NFL team: $800 million

Sources: **1.** Two years later, Curley Lambeau paid $50 to buy what became the Green Bay Packers. In 1925, a New York bookmaker named Tim Mara paid $500 for the right to start the New York Giants with money he reportedly won at the track that morning. (*New Orleans Times-Picayune, 9/2/94; Sports Illustrated, 3/10/86*) **2.** The price Robert McNair paid for the expansion Houston Texans. (*Wall Street Journal, 9/20/04*) **3.** The price paid by Dan Snyder for the Washington Redskins, which included the team's stadium. (*Wall Street Journal, 9/20/04*)

NUMBER OF NFL PLAYERS WHO WEIGHED 300 POUNDS

1. IN 1980: 1
2. IN 1990: 39
3. IN 2004: 339

Sources: **1, 2.** The NFL's first 300-pound player was Les Bingaman, who played both offensive guard and defensive tackle for the Detroit Lions from 1948 to 1954. (*San Diego Union-Tribune, 1/23/03*) **3.** *Toronto Star, 9/20/04.*

1. FINAL SCORE OF FIRST ROSE BOWL ON JAN. 1, 1902: MICHIGAN 49, STANFORD 0

2. NUMBER OF YARDS ROY RIEGELS RAN THE WRONG WAY DURING THE 1929 ROSE BOWL: 60

Sources: **1.** The game ended with 8 minutes to go when Stanford, embarrassed by the deficit, walked off the field. The game's promoters were embarrassed as well, and for the next 13 years, replaced the football game with polo matches and then chariot races until football returned in 1916. (*USA Today, 1/4/99*) **2.** On Jan. 1, 1929, Riegels, a linebacker for the University of California, picked up a fumble by a Georgia Tech player on the Tech 40-yard line, ran a few yards toward the right end zone, but then reversed course and inadvertently started running toward his own. Riegel was stopped by one of his own teammates on the 1-yard line to prevent him from scoring for the other team. On the next play, Cal's punt was blocked for a safety, giving Georgia Tech an 8–7 win. For the rest of his life, Riegels was known throughout America by the nickname "Wrong Way." (*International Herald Tribune, 12/27/03*)

MOST CONCUSSIONS SUFFERED BY AN NFL PLAYER OVER A CAREER: 13 (AL TOON, NEW YORK JETS)

Toon played 8 years for the Jets. Sixty percent of NFL players suffer at least one concussion during their career, and 1 in 4 suffer two or more. (*Baltimore Sun*, 8/13/00; *San Francisco Chronicle*, 9/1/02)

1. ODDS THAT AN NFL PLAYER SUFFERS A MAJOR INJURY OVER THE COURSE OF HIS CAREER: 7 IN 10

2. NFL PLAYERS WHO HAVE DIED AS A DIRECT RESULT OF AN ON-FIELD INJURY: 1 (STONE JOHNSON, KANSAS CITY CHIEFS, 1963)

Sources: **1.** According to a 1990 NFL Players Association study. According to another study, 45% of players retire as a direct result of injury. (*San Diego Union-Tribune*, 1/23/03; *San Francisco Chronicle*, 9/1/02) **2.** Johnson, an Olympic sprinter at the Rome Olympics, was blocking on a kickoff return in the Chiefs' final exhibition game against the Houston Texans when he collided headfirst with a Houston player. The hit paralyzed Johnson from the chest down, and he died in the hospital 10 days later. On Oct. 24, 1971, Detroit Lions wide receiver Chuck Hughes collapsed after catching a pass against the Bears. He died an hour later at the hospital of what was later found to be degenerative heart disease. (*Dallas Morning News*, 9/27/01)

AMOUNT AMERICAN NETWORKS LOSE ANNUALLY TELEVISING NFL FOOTBALL: $325 MILLION

In 1998, CBS, Fox, ABC, and ESPN paid a combined $17.6 billion for the right to televise NFL games through 2005. Each team receives roughly $85 million annually from these contracts. (*Wall Street Journal*, 9/20/04)

MOST OPERATIONS DURING A FOOTBALL CAREER: 29
MARK SCHLERETH, DENVER BRONCOS
DAN HAMPTON, CHICAGO BEARS

Before he even got to the NFL, Schlereth had already had six football-related operations. Over the course of a 12-year career as an offensive lineman with the Denver Broncos, which ended in 2002, Schlereth underwent 23 more operations, including 15 alone on his left knee. In 1996, Schlereth had six operations between the start of training camp and the end of the season—but missed only two games. "For seven seconds, during each play, I'm able to forget about it and put it on the back burner," he said. "As soon as the play ends, I start limping back to the huddle in pain." Hampton, a defensive lineman for the Bears, not only endured 29 operations, but had 400 stitches during his 12-year career. "That's what's great about this game," Hampton said during his induction ceremony into the Hall of Fame. "It says a lot about us, the willingness to destroy your body, to sacrifice for the team." (*Los Angeles Times*, 1/22/03; *Fort Worth Star-Telegram*, 8/4/02)

1. LARGEST PRO FOOTBALL PLAYER EVER:
AARON GIBSON (6'6", 410 POUNDS)

2. SMALLEST PLAYER: REGGIE "SUPER GNAT" SMITH (5'4", 160 POUNDS)

Sources: **1.** Gibson, an offensive lineman for the Chicago Bears in 2004, is 6'6" tall and fluctuates between 382 and a whopping 410 pounds. (*Montreal Gazette*, 8/17/04) **2.** Smith returned kickoffs and punts for the Atlanta Falcons in 1980 and '81. Mark McMillian, a 5'7" cornerback for the Chiefs and Eagles in the 1990s, was listed as low as 140 pounds by some newspapers. (*Kansas City Star*, 12/21/98; *Washington Post*, 2/4/83)

NFL coach whom both parties considered nominating for vice president in 1968: Vince Lombardi

Impressed with the legendary leadership skills of the coach of the Green Bay Packers, Richard Nixon had a background check done on Lombardi, and found out he was a Kennedy Democrat, though his wife was a conservative Republican. (Maraniss, *When Pride Still Mattered*)

INVENTOR OF THE "HUDDLE": PAUL HUBBARD (1894)

Up until the 1890s, plays were called at the line of scrimmage through hand signals given by the quarterback. In 1894, Hubbard was the quarterback for Gallaudet University, a school for the deaf in Washington, D.C. During practice one day, he noticed that the Gallaudet defense was intercepting his signals, and thus started gathering the offense several yards off the line of scrimmage to convey the plays in secret. Though Hubbard reportedly used the huddle in several games in 1894, the huddle did not gain wider popularity until it was used by the University of Illinois in early 1921. (*Washington Post*, 10/6/00; *Newsweek*, 11/8/99)

The last NFL player to . . . :

Throw an interception and intercept a pass in the same game: Tony Dungy (1977)

Start at both offense and defense in a game:
Deion Sanders (1996)

Sources: **1.** Dungy, now the Colts' coach but then a safety for the Steelers, subbed at quarterback in the fourth quarter for quarterback Terry Bradshaw (injured in the first quarter) and his backup Mike Kruczek (injured in the third). (*Indianapolis Star*, 9/19/04) **2.** In 1996, Sanders, a cornerback for the Dallas Cowboys, also started eight games as wide receiver, catching 36 passes for 475 yards. The last player to play the full game on both offense and defense was Chuck Bednarik, a center and linebacker with the Eagles, who once said about Sanders, "This guy couldn't tackle my wife Emma." (*San Francisco Chronicle*, 9/10/96)

1. LAST NFL PLAYER TO PLAY WITHOUT A HELMET: DICK PLASMAN (1940)
2. LAST NFL PLAYER TO GO WITHOUT A FACE MASK: TOMMY MCDONALD (1969)

Sources: **1.** Plasman played without a helmet in the 1940 championship game for the Chicago Bears before donning a helmet in 1941. By the time the NFL made helmet wearing mandatory in 1943, everyone was wearing one. Incidentally, former president Gerald Ford played 3 years of college football for Michigan before helmets became standard, causing Lyndon Johnson to once remark that "Jerry played too many football games without a helmet." (*NFL Encyclopedia of Football*) **2.** McDonald, a 5' 9", 175-pound wide receiver, played for 12 years without a face mask for the Eagles, Cowboys, and Rams, and never once lost a tooth or suffered a broken nose. He did suffer a broken jaw in the 1959 season opener, however, but continued playing through the season without a face mask after doctors wired his jaw shut. (*Dallas Morning News*, 7/24/98)

FOUR-LETTER WORDS

1. PERCENTAGE OF CONVERSATION AMONG COLLEGE STUDENTS THAT INCLUDES CURSE WORDS: 8.1%

2. PERCENTAGE OF ADULT CONVERSATION INVOLVING CURSING: 13%

3. FIRST USE OF THE WORD "GODDAMN" ON NETWORK TELEVISION: DEC. 1, 1988 (L.A. LAW)

Sources: **1.** Sixty-four percent of people use curse words to express anger or frustration, 14% to provide descriptions ("I have to take a sh*t"), 12% in jokes, 5% to express surprise ("Holy sh*t!"), and the remaining 5% to express sarcasm ("No sh*t, Sherlock") (Jay, *Cursing in America*) **2.** Jay, *Cursing in America*. **3.** *Washington Post*, 6/25/89.

1. Earliest printed example of the F word in English: 1475
2. Year it was removed from mainstream English dictionaries: 1795
3. Year it was first openly printed in the U.S.: 1926

Sources: **1.** Sheidlower, *The F Word*. **2.** *U.S. News and World Report*, 10/16/95. **3.** It appeared once in a book called *Wine, Women and War*, a diary of author Howard O'Brien's experiences during World War I. It appeared again in James Joyce's *Ulysses*, which was finally admitted into the U.S. in 1933 after a long court battle. Then there was a dry spell of almost 2 decades, during which novelists like Norman Mailer were forced to use invented alternatives like "fug," as he did in *The Naked and the Dead*. Finally, in 1951, James Jones wrote *From Here to Eternity*, which—despite the presence of 50 F words—won the 1952 National Book Award. (*Chicago Tribune*, 10/13/95)

AMOUNT MAKERS OF *GONE WITH THE WIND* WERE FINED FOR USING THE WORD "DAMN": $5,000

Indeed, Rhett Butler's immortal line ("Frankly, my dear, I don't give a damn.") almost ended up on the cutting-room floor. Because of the threat of censorship, the script included an alternative: "Frankly, my dear, I just don't care." (*Washington Post*, 6/1/99)

YEAR THE TERM "SUCKS" WAS FIRST USED IN A NETWORK PRIME-TIME SERIES: 1990

In 1990, CBS caused an uproar when a 6-year old character on a sitcom called *Uncle Buck* said to her brother, "Miles, you suck!" And in an NBC medical series that same year called *Life Stories*, a doctor said to a cancer patient, "So, life sucks?" after which the patient replied, "Life has never so totally sucked." (*Washington Post*, 9/4/90)

WORD THAT COMEDIAN LENNY BRUCE WAS ARRESTED FOR SAYING ON OCT. 10, 1961, IN SAN FRANCISCO:

C*CKS*CK*R

Bruce was arrested after performing at a place called the Jazz Workshop in San Francisco. He was booked, then released on $367 bail in time for the 1 A.M. show, at which he told the audience, "Better keep my coat on. I may have to go out again." Bruce was acquitted of obscenity charges for using the word, as he was after subsequent arrests in New York and Chicago for using similar language. However, in 1964, Bruce was convicted by a New York court of "word crimes" for a stand-up routine that made fun of former first ladies Jacqueline Kennedy Onassis and Eleanor Roosevelt. He served 4 months at Rikers Island prison. (*Newsweek*, 7/20/64; CNN.com, 12/24/03)

MOST CURSES IN A SINGLE MOVIE: 411 (*PULP FICTION*)

However, *South Park: Bigger, Longer and Uncut*, at 399 curses in 80 minutes, has more profanity per minute. Other notables: the 1984 movie *Scarface* had 299 cusswords and the 1990 gangster film *GoodFellas* contained 246 F words alone. (*Minneapolis Star Tribune*, 7/22/99; *Newsday*, 5/13/93)

WORDS USED IN THE SEPT. 21, 1993, SERIES PREMIERE OF *NYPD BLUE*:

"PISSY," "BITCH," "DICKHEAD," AND "ASSHOLE"

(*Entertainment Weekly*, 4/14/00)

YEAR THE F WORD MADE IT TO THE SUPREME COURT: 1971

In April 1968, Paul Cohen entered a Los Angeles courthouse wearing a jacket with the words "F**k the Draft" emblazoned on the back. Cohen was promptly arrested for disturbing the peace. He appealed his conviction all the way to the Supreme Court, which overturned his conviction on the grounds that the vulgarity on his jacket was protected by the First Amendment. The Court said that "while the particular vulgarity being litigated here is perhaps more distasteful than others of its genre, it is nevertheless often true that one man's vulgarity is another's lyric." (Bollinger, *The Tolerant Society*)

GAMBLING

1. POPULATION OF LAS VEGAS: 535,000
2. RATIO OF VEGAS RESIDENTS TO SLOT MACHINES: 3.5 TO 1
3. AMOUNT THE AVERAGE AMERICAN ADULT LOSES GAMBLING EACH YEAR: $350

Sources: **1.** Not including surrounding Clark County, which adds 1 million additional residents. (*American City and County*, 7/1/03) **2.** There are about 150,000 slot machines in Las Vegas. (*Washington Post*, 7/18/04) **3.** People who live near casinos lose far more; indeed, the average Nevada resident loses more than $1,000 a year. (*Washington Post*, 7/18/04)

1. FIRST CASINO IN THE U.S.: 1827 (NEW ORLEANS)
2. FIRST CASINO IN LAS VEGAS: 1931

Sources: **1.** John Davis opened America's first full-fledged casino in 1827 at the corner of Orleans and Bourbon Streets, and kept it open 24 hours a day for betting. In 1832, a casino called the Palace of Fortune opened on Pennsylvania Avenue a short distance from the U.S. Capitol. The Palace was patronized by numerous federal officials; when its owner died, Pres. James Buchanan attended the funeral, and several Congressmen served as pallbearers. (*Scarne's New Complete Guide to Gambling*) **2.** The first casino in Las Vegas was the Northern Club, opening in 1931 with one dice table, two blackjack tables, and one table for poker. Vegas's first casino hotel and resort was the El Rancho Vegas, which opened in April 1941 with 63 hotel rooms, a casino, and a 250-seat showroom. (*San Antonio Express*, 6/18/00; *Las Vegas Review*, 10/14/01)

1. MOST SUCCESSIVE WINS ON A SINGLE NUMBER IN ROULETTE: 6
2. MOST SUCCESSIVE LANDINGS ON RED IN ROULETTE: 32

Sources: **1.** According to *Scarne's New Complete Guide to Gambling*, the number 10 came out six times in a row at a roulette table at Puerto Rico's El San Juan Hotel on July 9, 1959. The odds of this happening are 1 in 133,448,704. **2.** In August 1943, the ball landed on a red number 32 consecutive times at the Arrowhead Casino in Saratoga, N.Y. (*Scarne's New Complete Guide to Gambling*)

Number of clocks and windows you'll see in casinos: 0

The absence of windows and clocks make players lose all sense of time and play longer, which increases the odds of the casino winning. (Bellin, *Poker Nation*)

1. Year the slot machine was invented: 1900
2. Times the average slot machine player tries his luck each minute: 10
3. Amount the average slot machine makes each year after subtracting payouts: $100,000

Sources: **1.** The slot machine was invented in San Francisco by a mechanic named Charles Fey. The first machine featured playing cards and the Liberty Bell. Three bells paid the largest jackpot—20 nickels. (*Baltimore Sun*, 3/8/03) **2.** The typical slot player starts a new round every 6 seconds. (*New York Times*, 5/9/04) **3.** *Washington Post*, 7/18/04.

1. GAMBLING BUDGET OF THE AVERAGE VISITOR TO VEGAS: $480

2. PERCENTAGE OF PEOPLE WHO GAMBLE TO WIN "A REALLY LARGE AMOUNT OF MONEY": 75%

3. AMOUNT LOST EVERY HOUR OF EVERY DAY AT VEGAS CASINOS: $696,000

Sources: **1.** *Las Vegas Review Journal*, 2/10/04. **2.** *American Demographics*, 5/1/97.
3. Gamblers lost $6.1 billion at Vegas casinos in 2003. (*New York Times*, 6/27/04)

BIGGEST JACKPOT EVER WON:
$39,718,982.25

On Mar. 21, 2003, a 25-year-old software designer from L.A. hit the jackpot at Las Vegas's Excalibur Hotel and Casino. He had put about $100 into the machine before the magic numbers hit. The largest slot jackpot ever won in Atlantic City was $8.5 million, in 1994. (*Daily News*, 4/6/04; AP, 7/16/04)

CRAZY GAMBLERS:

William Lee Bergstrom (1980)

Testing a policy at Binion's Horseshoe Casino which purportedly allowed gamblers to bet up to $1 million, Bergstrom asked the casino staff whether he could do so, and when they answered yes, came back with a suitcase filled with $777,000 in cash which was reportedly lent to him by a bank to buy gold. Bergstrom put the suitcase on a craps table without even bothering to change the cash into chips, and bet the entire sum on a woman's roll. He won. On Nov. 16, 1984, however, Bergstrom bet $1 million on a single roll of the dice and lost. In 1985, he was found dead of a drug overdose.

(*Los Angeles Times*, 2/5/85)

Chris Boyd (1994)

After saving $220,000 from his job as a computer programmer over 3 years, Boyd sat down at the roulette table at Binion's and bet the entire amount on the red. Red hit, and Boyd left the casino with $440,000.

(*Daily Mail*, 1/28/04)

GAMES

TOP-SELLING BOARD GAMES IN THE U.S.:

1. TRIVIAL PURSUIT
2. CRANIUM
3. MONOPOLY
4. SCRABBLE
5. THE GAME OF LIFE

At 22 years of age, Trivial Pursuit is still the leader of a $400-million-a-year industry, selling over 1 million copies in 2002 alone. (*USA Today*, 12/15/04)

FIRST BOARD GAME IN THE U.S.:
A TRAVELER'S TOUR THROUGH THE UNITED STATES (1822)

The 1822 game attracted little interest, and the first really successful game didn't come out until Mansion of Happiness in 1843. Early games emphasized moral instruction more than fun: landing on spaces marked "Virtue" or "Justice" in Mansion of Happiness moved a player forward, while spaces marked "Laziness" or "Drunkenness" sent them back. Dice were banned as "instruments of the devil," and players won when they reached the space marked "Heaven." (*Country Living*, 12/97)

Most frequently landed-on spaces in Monopoly, in order:
1. Illinois Avenue 2. Go 3. B&O Railroad

(CBS News, 10/19/03)

FIRST GAME USING PEOPLE AS PLAYING PIECES: TWISTER

Originally called Pretzel when it was first introduced as a beach game, Twister didn't actually catch on until May 3, 1966 when Johnny Carson played the game on *The Tonight Show* with Eva Gabor. (*Toronto Sun*, 5/31/96)

1. NUMBER OF CORRECT ALIGNMENTS OF A RUBIK'S CUBE: 1

2. NUMBER OF INCORRECT ALIGNMENTS: 43 QUINTILLION

Created by Hungarian Erno Rubik in 1974 to demonstrate geometric principles, there were 250 million Rubik's Cubes sold between 1980 and 1985. There is an annual World Rubik's Cube Game Championship, in which contestants use silicone and sandpaper on their cubes to gain a competitive edge. (*New York Times*, 11/16/03)

1. NUMBER OF PING-PONG INJURIES FOR WHICH AMERICANS SOUGHT HOSPITAL TREATMENT IN 2003: 1,440

2. NUMBER OF SHUFFLEBOARD INJURIES: AT LEAST 4

Sources: **1.** The Consumer Product Safety Commission database lists injuries in which patients went to the hospital, including: "Hit in face with a Ping-Pong ball"; "Patient lives in a retirement home and was playing Ping-Pong and ran into a wall"; "Jail inmate, playing table tennis and fell onto concrete floor." **2.** "Splinter in buttock"; "Hit on forehead w/ a shuffleboard puck"; "Visual disturbances—got hit w/a shuffleboard stick in the head."

GAME ORIGINS:

Battleship:

Inaugurated by Milton Bradley in 1967, the game may have been inspired from a similar game called Salvo invented in 1935 by a man named Paul Cowdrey. Cowdrey patented his game in 1940, and went to Milton Bradley, who declined the game, saying it "wasn't adaptable to its line." Ten years after Cowdrey's patent expired, the company came out with the virtually identical Battleship.

(*State Journal-Register*, 12/31/00)

Trivial Pursuit:

The game was spawned by a Scrabble game Chris Haney and Scott Abbott tried to play on a rainy Montreal Saturday in 1979. One news source says that they couldn't find the board, and thus started throwing trivia questions at each other, while another says that they just found Scrabble to be exceptionally boring and thought they could do better.

(UPI, 11/29/83)

Though the playground was little more than piles of sand placed in the yard of a children's mission, it was the first time a public play area was set aside for young children. (*Parks and Recreation*, 5/1/01)

FORMER SIMON SAYS CAPITAL OF THE WORLD: CATSKILL MOUNTAINS, NEW YORK

In the 1940 and '50s, hotels in New York's famed "Borscht Belt" employed tummlers, whose name means "the maker of noise and merriment." Many tummlers prided themselves on their calling of the game Simon Says, with fierce rivalries and competitions erupting between the various hosts. One hotel even offered $10,000 to any contestant who could stay in their Simon Says game for longer than 3 minutes. (*New York Times*, 6/10/98)

MURDERS BLAMED ON THE GAME DUNGEONS & DRAGONS:

June 1983:

Ronald Lampasi, a Laguna Beach teenager and avid D&D player, shot both of his parents in the head. Friends testified that he may have been at a point in the game where he had to kill something to move ahead.

(*Los Angeles Times*, 5/9/85)

November 1985:

A 16-year-old boy shot the 11-year-old companion with whom he played Dungeons & Dragons. The boy told a psychologist that the victim played an evil role in the game and it was his job to extinguish evil.

(*Syracuse Post-Standard*, 12/6/86)

May 1987:

A 20-year-old shot and killed his parents in their sleep. In his closing argument, the defense attorney contends that the defendant believed he was under the control of a character in Dungeons & Dragons called "Mind Flyer" when he shot his parents. The jury didn't buy it, and convicted him of murder.

(*New York Times*, 6/30/88)

USES OF THE GAME
MONOPOLY IN WARTIME:

To calm generals:

According to Philip Orbanes in *The Game Makers,* Gen. Dwight Eisenhower was an avid Monopoly fan, and played the game hours before he led the Allied invasion of North Africa in World War II.

To help POWs escape:

During World War II, British intelligence formed an alliance with the makers of Monopoly to hide maps, compasses, and small saws under the playing board in certain editions of the game shipped to soldiers interned in German POW camps. A map of northern France, for example, was printed on silk and concealed beneath the Free Parking space.

(*Times* [London], 6/12/97)

COUNTRIES IN WHICH MONOPOLY WAS OR REMAINS BANNED: 5

According to the *Oxford History of Board Games,* Monopoly remains officially banned in China, North Korea, and Cuba, and was once banned in East Germany and Russia. Castro called the game "symbolic of an imperialistic and capitalistic system," and Russia called it "a decadent instrument of capitalism." (*Advertiser,* 1/4/86; AP, 11/6/89)

1. NUMBER OF YEARS PINBALL WAS OUTLAWED IN NEW YORK: 35
2. FIRST PINBALL MACHINE WITH FLIPPERS: HUMPTY DUMPTY (1947)

Sources: **1.** Believed to lead children toward delinquency, pinball was banned in New York in 1941, with Mayor Fiorello La Guardia smashing machines with a sledgehammer and dumping them into the East River. The ban wasn't lifted in New York until 1976. (*Newsday,* 2/3/95) **2.** With flippers, what had been a game of almost pure chance became one of skill. Other pinball innovations: the invention of the tilt mechanism in 1932 (originally called a "stool pigeon") and the bumper, introduced on a Bally machine named "Bumper" in 1937. (*Chicago Tribune,* 8/8/93)

GARBAGE

1. AMOUNT OF GARBAGE THROWN OUT
DAILY BY THE AVERAGE AMERICAN: **4.6 POUNDS**

2. PERCENTAGE OF FOOD BROUGHT INTO AN AMERICAN HOUSE THAT IS THROWN OUT: **14%**

3. PERCENTAGE OF FOOD AMERICANS THROW AWAY THAT IS UNOPENED: **15%**

Sources: **1.** This is two to three times as much as the typical western European throws away. According to studies, paper makes up around 45% of the average landfill; glass, metals, and wood 21%; food wastes 8%; plastic 16%; disposal diapers 1.2%; Styrofoam cups 0.8%; and fast-food packaging 0.5%. (*Chicago Tribune*, 11/6/01; *Washington Post*, 4/22/02, 1/23/94) **2.** Americans throw away 470 pounds of food a year. According to a study conducted by Prof. Brian Wansink of the University of Illinois, people keep unwanted food products in their cabinets for 2.7 years before throwing them out. The most commonly discarded item is salad dressing. (CBS News, 11/28/03; Brian Wansink) **3.** Prof. Timothy Jones of the University of Arizona estimates that the average household throws away $590 worth of food a year. (UANews.org, 11/18/04)

LARGEST MAN-MADE STRUCTURE IN THE WORLD: FRESH KILLS GARBAGE LANDFILL, NEW YORK

Before it closed in March 2001, New York deposited 2 billion tons of garbage at the Fresh Kills landfill on Staten Island. The landfill is 20 times the size of the Great Pyramid at Giza, Egypt, and rises to a height of 155 feet, the highest point on the Eastern Seaboard south of Maine. In 1991, it overtook the Great Wall of China as the largest man-made object on earth. Though no longer used, it still is the source of 2% of the world's man-made methane. (NPR's *All Things Considered*, 3/23/01; *Newsday*, 9/30/03)

Number of American universities that award degrees in garbage studies: 1 (University of Arizona)

(University of Arizona)

**Year the word "garbologist"
(a person who studies refuse)
first appeared in the dictionary: 1995**

According to the *Oxford English Dictionary*, the term was coined by Dr. William Rathje, but its use probably originated with one A. J. Weberman, who sifted through Bob Dylan's garbage as a means of analyzing his life and music. (*Independent*, 8/10/01)

1. RECENT INSTANCES IN WHICH LOTTERY WINNERS ACCIDENTALLY THREW AWAY THEIR WINNING TICKETS: 3

2. AMOUNT LOST BY DISCARDING THOSE TICKETS: $6.5 MILLION

Sources: **1.** In December 2001, Tom McDonald, an Australian mechanic, accidentally threw away a winning $1.5 million ticket. McDonald spent weeks searching for the ticket in the local dump, without luck. . . . New Yorker Howard Reid purchased several tickets for the $70 million Lotto drawing of May 31, 1997, but tore them up after seeing the winning numbers and concluding they weren't his. The next day he learned one winning ticket had been sold at the store where he bought his tickets, and after again scanning the numbers, realized he'd thrown out a $7.4 million winner. He rushed home, but his wife had already taken out the garbage, and the truck had picked it up. . . . In September 1996, Irishman Padraic O Tuairisc threw away a winning $3 million lottery ticket before learning the numbers. After realizing his mistake, he began a desperate search of the local rubbish dump (along with crowds of other treasure-hunters) in search of the winning ticket. Although he found the remains of some chicken noodles he had thrown away at the same time, there was no trace of the ticket. (Reuters, 9/9/96; *Newsday*, 9/1/99; AAP General News, 4/24/02). **2.** McDonald and O Tuairisc got no money. As for Reid, he finally was awarded $2.8 million after spending $2 million in attorney's fees attempting to prove that he had thrown away a winning ticket. "It's a hell of a story," he said. "Win. Lose. Win again. I wouldn't want to go through it again." (*Newsday*, 4/10/00)

AMOUNT OF CHANGE PEOPLE THREW OUT EACH DAY IN A RECENT STUDY OF ONE MASSACHUSETTS COMMUNITY: $8,000

Dr. William Rathje studied a Massachusetts incinerator that serves about a million people, and found that they were leaving about $8,000 worth of coins in their garbage every day. "I think it tells us that we're pretty well off," says Rathje, and "pretty careless about the way that we handle money." (AP, 2/23/02)

1. LARGEST GARBAGE-EXPORTING STATE IN THE U.S.: NEW YORK
2. LARGEST GARBAGE-IMPORTING STATE: PENNSYLVANIA

Sources: **1.** New Jersey ranks second in sending its garbage to other states. (*Waste Age*, 3/1/02) **2.** When Virginia politicians objected to New York's attempts to export more trash to their state in 1999, New York's Mayor Giuliani stated that "people in Virginia like to utilize New York, because we're a cultural center. This is a reciprocal relationship." Virginia's Governor Gilmore wrote back, "I am offended by your suggestion that New York's substantial cultural achievements, such as they are, obligate Virginia and other states to accept your garbage." (*Waste Age*, 3/1/03; *Newsday*, 1/22/99)

GAYS

1. PERCENTAGE OF THE U.S. POPULATION WHO IDENTIFY THEMSELVES AS GAY OR LESBIAN: 7%

2. ESTIMATES OF THE NUMBER OF CHILDREN IN AMERICA BEING RAISED BY GAY PARENTS: 1.25 MILLION

3. TOWN WITH THE HIGHEST PERCENTAGE OF GAY RESIDENTS IN AMERICA: PROVINCETOWN, MASS. (39%)

4. EXECUTIONS FOR SODOMY IN ENGLAND BETWEEN 1810 AND 1835: 46

Sources: **1.** Despite the widely touted figure that 10% of the population is gay, current studies indicate a somewhat lower figure. A 2003 study by Witeck-Combs put the figure at 6–7%, or about 14–16 million adults, while a 1993 study indicated that only 1.1% of American males had been exclusively gay all their lives. (*Patriot Ledger*, 10/18/03; *Vancouver Sun*, 6/25/04) **2.** Recent census data indicate that 250,000 children are being raised in households with two gay parents, while an estimated 1 million more are being raised in single-parent gay households. (*U.S. News and World Report*, 5/24/04) **3.** Other facts: Vermont has the highest percentage of same-sex households of any state, and North Dakota has the highest percentage of gay seniors. (*Gay and Lesbian Atlas; Boston Globe*, 5/23/04) **4.** Robb, *Strangers*.

NUMBER OF ANIMAL SPECIES THAT EXHIBIT SOME FORM OF GAY BEHAVIOR: 450

The list includes grizzly bears, gorillas, bighorn sheep, beetles, bottlenose dolphins, bonobo chimpanzees, flamingos, owls, several species of salmon and bees, red and gray squirrels, gray seals, mute swans, and mallard ducks. (Bagemihl, *Biological Exuberance*)

NUMBER OF YEARS TWO GAY MALE PENGUINS HAVE BEEN TOGETHER AT THE NEW YORK AQUARIUM: 8

Wendell and Cass live in the same nest, and regularly engage in intimate relations. "Sometimes they lie on the rocks together," says one of their keepers. "They're one of the few couples that like to hang out together outside their nest." The Central Park Zoo has its own longstanding gay penguin couple, Roy and Silo, who have been in an exclusive relationship for 4 years. When zookeepers tried to separate several other gay penguins in 1997, they soon commenced new same-sex relationships with other partners. (*Pittsburgh Post-Gazette*, 2/22/04)

1. Average age Americans came out of the closet in 2003: 16 for males 17 for females

2. Average age Americans came out in the 1970s: Their early to mid 20s

(*Newsweek*, 6/9/03)

FIRST PERSON IN HISTORY TO COME OUT IN PUBLIC: KARL HEINRICH ULRICHS (1867)

Ulrichs, a German scholar and lawyer, appeared before the Congress of German Jurists in August 1867 and said this about the gay inclination: "You will have to get used to it, like crabs to slow cooking. Hopefully, it will not be detrimental to your health." (*Independent*, 11/23/03)

1. FIRST USE OF THE TERM "HOMOSEXUAL": 1868

2. TERM USED BY MANY HOMOSEXUALS TO DESCRIBE THEMSELVES IN THE MID 1800S: URANIANS

Sources: **1.** Coined by Hungarian writer Karl Maria Benkert. (*Independent*, 11/23/03) **2.** After the muse of same-sex love in Plato's "Symposium." Among the terms used by straight people to describe gays were "lavender aunts," "musical" young men, "green carnations," "crooked fingers," "mollies," "ganymedes," "chestnut-gatherers," and "buggers." (*Nation*, 10/19/92; Robb, *Strangers*)

FIRST OPENLY GAY MOVIE STAR: BILLY HAINES

MGM's #1 box office draw of 1930, Haines was one of the studio's first stars to make the transition to sound. He remained out-loud as well about his gay lover, Jimmie Shields. In 1933, studio heads threatened to tear up the star's contract if he remained with Shields. Billy gave them the go-ahead, remaining true to Shields for a total of 47 years. (*Newsday*, 2/8/98)

FIRST MODERN USAGE OF THE WORD "GAY" IN A MOVIE:
BRINGING UP BABY (1938)

In the scene, Cary Grant's character tries to explain why he's wearing a frilly woman's robe to answer the door:

MR. GRANT: I've lost my clothes.

MS. ROBSON: Well, why are you wearing these clothes?

MR. GRANT: Because I just went gay all of a sudden.

(*Washington Post*, 6/15/96)

FIRST MAINSTREAM COMMERCIAL TO FEATURE A GAY COUPLE: IKEA, 1994

The spot featured a 40-something gay couple shopping at their local Ikea outlet for "a serious dining-room table." In 2000, John Hancock Insurance aired what was arguably the first mainstream lesbian television ad, which featured two women fussing over a new baby, with one saying, "We're a family." (*San Francisco Chronicle*, 6/6/01; *Philadelphia Inquirer*, 9/19/00)

OLDEST CONTINUOUSLY OPERATING GAY BAR IN THE NATION: DOUBLEHEADERS, SEATTLE, WASH.

Opened in Seattle in 1934, the bar has served a principally gay clientele since World War II. (*Seattle Times*, 10/3/99; AP, 5/9/01; *Boston Herald*, 6/14/98)

FIRST GAYS TO TAKE LEGAL MARRIAGE VOWS: AXEL AXGIL AND EIGIL AXGIL (DENMARK, 1989)

On Oct. 1, 1989, Denmark became the first country in the world to legalize gay marriage. That day, Axel Axgil and Eigil Axgil tied the knot at Copenhagen Town Hall. "We decided to get officially 'married' because we have the same feelings for each other as heterosexual couples," explained Axel Axgil, 74, who was dismissed from his job when he first came out in 1980. (*Chicago Tribune*, 10/3/89)

DATE THE *NEW YORK TIMES* RAN ITS FIRST WEDDING ANNOUNCEMENT OF A GAY COUPLE: SEPT. 1, 2002

On Aug. 18, 2002, the *New York Times* announced that it would begin covering gay commitment ceremonies on its wedding pages. On Sept. 1, 2002, the paper published the first such announcement about the union of Daniel Gross, a Fulbright scholar, and Steven Goldstein, owner of a political consulting firm. (*New York Times*, 9/1/02)

First member of Congress to announce he was gay:
Gerry Studds (July 14, 1983)

On July 14, 1983, Rep. Gerry Studds of Massachusetts gave a speech on the floor of the House in which he announced he was gay, in response to accusations that he had had an affair with a congressional page 10 years earlier. As of November 2004, there were three openly gay members of the U.S. Congress. (UPI, 7/14/83)

YEAR AARON FRICKE WENT TO COURT TO BE ALLOWED TO TAKE A MALE DATE TO THE SENIOR PROM: 1980

After Fricke was told by the principal at Rhode Island's Cumberland High School that he could not bring a male date to the prom, Fricke sued and won the right to attend with the date of his choice. Six officers protected the gay couple at the event. (*Washington Post*, 5/31/80)

Number of male bordellos operated by the FBI during World War II: 1

According to the *New York Times*, the FBI operated a male bordello in New York during World War II staffed with gay agents whose responsibility was getting intelligence information from foreign sailors. (*New York Times*, 5/22/03)

GERMS

1. ODDS THAT A PERSON HAS A CLOSE FRIEND OR FAMILY MEMBER WHO IS OBSESSED WITH GERMS: 1 IN 5

2. PERCENTAGE OF PEOPLE IN A POLL WHO SAID THAT, TO AVOID GERMS, THEY DON'T TOUCH PUBLIC TELEPHONES OR AIRPLANE HEADRESTS: 50%

(*New Republic*, 11/10/97)

1. Number of bacteria on the average office desk: 21,000 per square inch
2. Number of bacteria on the average phone receiver: 25,000 per square inch
3. Number of bacteria on the average toilet seat: 50 per square inch

Sources: **1.** According to a recent study, Tucson has the cleanest desks; New York, the dirtiest, probably because office workers there are more likely to eat at their desks. (*U.S. News and World Report*, 4/22/02) **2.** *Palm Beach Post*, 5/16/00. **3.** "People use disinfectant to clean that," explains Charles Gerba, a professor of microbiology at the University of Arizona who conducted the study. (*BusinessWeek*, 6/3/02)

KITCHEN UTENSIL THAT HAS 200 TIMES MORE FECAL BACTERIA THAN A TOILET SEAT: CUTTING BOARD

The five worst spots for germs in descending order are kitchen sponges and dishcloths; the kitchen sink; kitchen faucet handles; cutting boards; and refrigerator handles. (*Palm Beach Post*, 5/16/00; *Arizona Republic*, 7/18/98)

RATIO OF HARMFUL BACTERIA IN THE AVERAGE WOMEN'S REST ROOM COMPARED TO THE AVERAGE MEN'S ROOM: 2 TO 1

Probably because of the presence of discarded sanitary napkins and diaper-changing done inside. (*Newsweek*, 6/2/97)

MOST POPULAR CONTRACEPTIVE USED BY AMERICAN WOMEN IN THE 1930s: LYSOL

The popular home disinfectant was widely touted as a reliable contraceptive douche in the 1930s, and its product guidelines at the time informed women that they could gargle with it, use it to clean their toilet, or as a contraceptive douche. Lysol remained the leading feminine hygiene product in America through the early 1960s, though women who used it this way often suffered burns. (Tone, cited in the *New York Times*, 6/12/01)

LIKELIHOOD THAT A DOLLAR BILL CONTAINS TRACES OF COCAINE: 80%

When a rolled bill used to sniff cocaine or handled by a dealer gets into circulation, the cocaine contaminates ATMs and counting machines, and they, in turn, contaminate the money passing through them. (*Arizona Republic*, 7/3/03)

1. Year the word "cold" was first used to refer to an illness: **1537**
2. Number of colds suffered yearly by the average adult: **2 to 4**
3. Number contracted by the average school kid: **5 to 8**

Sources: **1.** The word "cold" was first used in the state papers of Henry VIII to refer to the common virus that afflicts tens of millions. Despite its name, there is no scientific evidence that being cold increases the risk of getting a cold. (*Sunday Telegraph*, 11/2/03) **2, 3.** On a yearly basis, the common cold results in approximately 20 million absences from work and 22 million absences from school. (*Chest*, 5/1/03; *ADA Journal*, 9/1/04)

NUMBER OF TISSUES USED BY THE AVERAGE AMERICAN EACH YEAR: 743

(*U.S. News and World Report*, 9/15/97)

ORIGIN OF THE CUSTOM OF SAYING "GOD BLESS YOU" AFTER A SNEEZE: ANCIENT ISRAEL

According to Gabrielle Glaser's book *The Nose*, Jewish tradition says that sickness was unknown in the world until the prophet Isaac became ill in Genesis. Alarmed by his father's condition, Jacob asked God to give man a warning of when the end was near, so that he had some time to repent. The sneeze was interpreted as that warning, prompting those within earshot to bless the person afflicted. In the 14th century, in the midst of the Black Plague, Pope Gregory VII decreed that people who heard a sneeze should say "God bless you." (Glaser, *The Nose*)

GHOSTS

1. PERCENTAGE OF AMERICANS WHO BELIEVE IN THE EXISTENCE OF GHOSTS: 34%

2. PERCENTAGE OF PEOPLE IN ENGLAND WHO REPORT HAVING EXPERIENCED GHOSTS PERSONALLY: 13%

3. MOST HAUNTED CITY IN THE WORLD: YORK, ENGLAND

Sources: **1.** 2003 Fox News poll. A 2001 Gallup poll put the number of believers at 38%, up from 25% in 1990. (*Christian Science Monitor*, 10/31/02) **2.** *British Journal of Psychology*, 5/1/03. **3.** According to an organization called Ghost Research Foundation International, over 504 incidents of ghost activity have been documented in York, a city in northern England that was conquered by the Vikings, the Saxons, and the Romans. One hundred forty ghosts are said to haunt York's historic Old City. (*Los Angeles Times*, 10/5/03; *Yorkshire Post*, 9/6/04)

1. What one New York court told a home buyer who tried to end a deal because the seller didn't say the house was haunted: "Too bad"

2. What the buyer's attorney said in saying he would appeal: "Would you want to bump into George Washington in the middle of the night?"

3. What a higher New York court said in concluding the buyer could break the deal: "The house is haunted"

Sources: **1.** In 1989, Helen Ackley put her 18-room Victorian home in Nyack, N.Y., up for sale. It was immediately snatched up by Jeffrey and Patrice Stambovsky, a young Manhattan couple. After making the down payment on the $650,000 purchase, the Stambovskys learned that Ackley had been keeping something from them—the house was haunted, a fact Ackley had written about in a 1977 article in *Reader's Digest*. When the Stambovskys tried to terminate the deal, Ackley refused, though she admitted that the house was occupied by several friendly ghosts, one of whom (according to court documents) "wore a blue suit with ruffles at the wrist, and black patent leather shoes with silver buckles." In ruling against the Strambovskys, however, a trial court found that the seller "had no duty to reveal her beliefs with respect to supernatural inhabitants." (*Newsday*, 3/16/90) **2.** *Newsday*, 3/16/90. **3.** The Appellate Court ruled that since the seller told everyone else the house was haunted, she was required to tell the buyers. The court also noted that the seller had failed to deliver the house vacant as required by the contract. (*Los Angeles Times*, 7/28/91)

STATES THAT DON'T REQUIRE HOME SELLERS TO TELL BUYERS THAT A HOUSE HAS GHOSTS: 4

Following the New York case (see above), Massachusetts, Virginia, Maryland, and New York each passed laws saying that while information about physical defects like leaky roofs must be disclosed, ghosts (or murders in the house) do not. According to real estate brokers, nor should a seller reveal the information voluntarily. "Never, never, never tell anyone you have a ghost," said one broker quoted in the *Washington Post*. (*Washington Post*, 10/26/02)

TOP FIVE MOST HAUNTED STATES:

1. CALIFORNIA
(274 HAUNTED LOCATIONS)
2. VIRGINIA (141)

3. PENNSYLVANIA (99)
4. NEW YORK (92)
5. TEXAS (73)

(Hauck, *Haunted Places*)

EX-PRESIDENT MOST FREQUENTLY SAID TO HAUNT THE WHITE HOUSE: ABE LINCOLN

Among those who professed to see ghosts in Lincoln's bedroom were Winston Churchill, Harry Truman, and President Reagan's daughter Maureen. In August 1945, Truman wrote to his wife Bess (who was at home in Independence, Mo.) about one such late-night encounter: "Night before last I went to bed at nine o'clock after shutting my doors. At four o'clock I was awakened by three distinct knocks on my bedroom door. I jumped up and put on my bathrobe, opened the door, and no one there. Went out and looked up and down the hall, looked into your room and Margie's. Still no one. Went back to bed after locking the doors and there were footsteps in your room whose door I'd left open. Jumped up and looked and no one there! Damn place is haunted sure as shootin'." (*Washington Post*, 10/25/92)

NUMBER OF YEARS JAPANESE PRIME MINISTERS REFUSED TO LIVE IN THE OFFICIAL RESIDENCE BECAUSE OF A BELIEF IT WAS HAUNTED: 20

After several bloody coup attempts at the residence in 1932 left hundreds dead, Japanese premiers abandoned the house for two decades. As recently as 2000, Prime Minister Mori reported strange crawling sounds at night and doorknobs that turned on their own. Mori's wife refused to live in the house. (Agence France-Presse, 5/9/01)

FAMILIES THAT HAVE BEEN DRIVEN OUT OF THEIR HOMES BY GHOSTS: 1

In 1986, Allen Tallman and his family moved into a 4-year-old house in Horican, Wis. Their problems began in the summer of 1987. Shortly after they purchased a secondhand bunk bed for their two baby daughters, furniture in the house started moving on its own, and radios began to change stations wildly. In January 1988, Tallman was putting his girls to sleep when a gassy apparition rose out of the floor and said "You're dead" before disappearing. Immediately thereafter, he moved his family out of the home and signed over his interest to the bank. While another family in Amityville, Long Island, claimed to have been driven out of their home by ghosts in 1975 (the inspiration for the movie *The Amityville Horror*), no paranormal activity has occurred at the home since, and their claims have been widely questioned in the media. (*American Banker*, 2/26/88; ABC News, 10/31/02)

Amount the creators of Casper the Friendly Ghost received for their work: $200

Seymour Reit came up with the idea for the shy, friendly ghost in 1940, and worked with animator Joe Oriolo to flesh out the character. Reit then went off to World War II, and on his return, learned that Oriolo had sold all rights to Casper to Paramount Studios for $200. (*Variety*, 12/24/01)

GOLF

1. PERCENTAGE OF PLAYERS IN RECENT SURVEY WHO SAY THEY PREFER GOLF TO SEX: 11

2. PERCENTAGE OF SPOUSES WHO SAY THAT GOLF IS A SOURCE OF STRESS IN THEIR MARRIAGE: 20%

3. LONGEST DRIVE IN GOLF: 473 YARDS

4. LONGEST DRIVE TO GOLF: BJORKLIDEN GOLF CLUB, SWEDEN (150 MILES NORTH OF THE ARCTIC CIRCLE)

Sources: **1.** *Seattle Times*, 7/5/02. **2.** *Sports Illustrated*, 9/7/98. **3.** On July 20, 1993, Jack Hamm set the record at Highlands Ranch near Denver, Colo. Hamm also holds the record for longest drive at sea level (422 yards), and once hit a ball 1,012 yards (with roll) down a runway at Denver's Stapleton Airport. (*Rocky Mountain News*, 6/28/03) **4.** Reindeer serve as caddies on this course, which includes several unique rules, including: "If a reindeer eats your ball, drop a new one where the incident occurred." (*Sports Illustrated*, 8/4/97)

1. PERCENTAGE OF BUSINESS EXECUTIVES WHO AGREE THAT "THE WAY A PERSON PLAYS GOLF IS SIMILAR TO HOW HE OR SHE CONDUCTS BUSINESS": 59

2. PERCENTAGE OF SAME EXECUTIVES WHO ADMIT TO CHEATING AT GOLF: 82

(*The Seattle Times*, 7/5/02)

RECENT ACCIDENTAL BOMBINGS OF ARIZONA GOLF COURSES: 1

On Dec. 15, 1999, an F-16 fighter jet from Luke Air Force Base near Phoenix accidentally dropped a practice bomb on the Pueblo El Mirage Golf and Country Club. The bomb landed not far from a group of golfers on the 17th fairway, leaving a crater. No one was injured. (*Golf Digest*, 4/1/00)

Highest single-hole score ever in a major tournament: 19

On the par 4 16th hole in the 1938 U.S. Open, Ray Ainsley hooked his drive into the rough, then sent his second shot into a small stream. Ainsley thought the ball was playable, and tried to hit the ball out, but each time it moved further downstream. Asked later why he didn't just take a one-stroke penalty, Ainsley said he thought he had to play the ball. Not true, said a USGA official. (*Newsday*, 6/11/95)

NUMBER OF SHOTS IT TOOK FLOYD ROOD TO HIT A GOLF BALL ACROSS THE UNITED STATES: 114,737

Rood's odyssey began in September 1963 at the Pacific Ocean and ended at the Atlantic 13 months later. Rood lost 3,511 golf balls along the way. (*Orange County Register*, 2/11/99)

NUMBER OF GOLF BALLS ON THE MOON: 2

On Feb. 6, 1971, Apollo 14 astronaut Alan Shepard used a 6-iron to whack two balls on the lunar surface. "He lived every golfer's dream, taking his 6-iron and hitting the ball, in his words, for 'miles and miles,'" Pres. Bill Clinton said upon Shepard's death in 1998. Shepard's tee-off on the moon was a duff. "It got more dirt than ball," Shepard told Mission Control. (*Toronto Star*, 7/24/98)

Most unplayable lie in history: A PGA spectator's bra

In the 1973 Sea Pines Heritage Classic in Hilton Head, S.C., a shot off of Hale Irwin's club landed in a women's bra. Irwin, who had no idea where the ball landed, was searching for it when the woman came forward with the ball still lodged in the cup. She removed the ball and Irwin took a drop. (*Chicago Sun-Times*, 4/28/96)

NUMBER OF JAPANESE GOLFERS WHO CARRY HOLE-IN-ONE INSURANCE: 4 MILLION

The Japanese call a hole in one an *arubatorosu*—an albatross—because those who hit one are required by custom to buy drinks, dinner, and presents for club members and friends, which often adds up to well over $10,000. (*Sunday Times* [London], 4/7/02; *Washington Post*, 5/23/99)

GUM

1. PIECES OF GUM CHEWED ANNUALLY BY THE AVERAGE AMERICAN: 300

2. NAME OF FIRST CHEWING GUM SOLD IN AMERICA: STATE OF MAINE PURE SPRUCE GUM

3. PERCENTAGE OF U.S. GUM SALES THAT ARE SUGARLESS: 65%

4. YEAR THAT WRIGLEY MAILED OUT FREE GUM TO EVERY AMERICAN WITH A PHONE: 1915

Sources: **1.** The figure comes from the Census Bureau; Trident gum's Web site, however, puts the figure at 175 pieces per person. (U.S. Census Bureau Feature, 4/29/04) **2.** In 1848, John Curtis brewed up a batch of the gum by using pulp from a spruce tree. Sales were minimal, apparently because the spruce gum tasted a bit too much like the tree. (Adams, *The Straight Dope*) **3.** Americans spent $2.9 billion on chewing gum in 2002 (*Confectioner*, 3/04; *Research Alert*, 2/21/03) **4.** In 1915, Wrigley mailed out gum to every person listed in a U.S. phone directory (some 1.5 million homes); it did the same thing again in 1919 to 7 million households. (*FSB*, 3/04)

1. FIRST FLAVORED GUM: BLACK JACK (1872)
2. FIRST BUBBLE GUM: BLIBBER-BLUBBER (1906)

Sources: **1.** Black Jack was also the first gum to be sold in sticks. **2.** Invented by Frank Fleer in 1906, the first bubble gum produced largely unsatisfactory bubbles that, once affixed to a chewer's face, required turpentine to remove. (*Austin American-Statesman*, 5/23/04)

INVENTOR OF BUBBLE GUM AS WE KNOW IT: WALTER DIEMER (1928)

In August 1928, Diemer, an accountant with the Fleer gum company who'd been conducting gum experiments on the side, put one of his concoctions into his mouth and blew a large bubble that (unlike Blibber-Blubber) easily peeled off of his face. As Diemer described the day decades later, "We were blowing bubbles and dancing all over the office." Diemer's discovery became Dubble Bubble Gum, first sold on Dec. 26, 1928. Incidentally, pink is the predominant bubble gum color because that's the only food coloring Diemer had around when he first invented the chew. (*Chicago Tribune*, 8/30/90)

COUNTRY WHERE YOU CAN'T BUY GUM UNLESS YOU GIVE YOUR NAME AND ID NUMBER: SINGAPORE

Concerned about litter, Singapore outlawed the sale of gum in 1992, with violators facing jail time. Under U.S. pressure, the government lifted the ban in 2004, but now only allows the sale of gum for medicinal purposes from drugstores. (*Edmonton Journal*, 5/26/04)

UNUSUAL CHEWING GUMS:

Bible Gum:

Instead of comics, has biblical verses inside the wrapper. According to one satisfied customer, "I don't know how many times this gum has been helpful in children receiving Christ as their savior, but it is a goodly number."

Viagra Gum:

Wrigley recently took out a patent on a gum to treat erectile disfunction, but has to wait until the Viagra patent expires in 2011.

(*U.S. Catholic*, 12/98; *Family Practice News*, 8/15/03)

Wrigley's original product: Soap

For Wrigley, gum was an afterthought. In April 1891, William Wrigley began selling Wrigley's Scouring Soap, and offered baking powder as a bonus. When consumers cared more about the baking powder, Wrigley started selling that as his principal product, offering chewing gum as a bonus. Again, the gum proved more popular than what he was trying to sell, and Wrigley went into the gum business. (*Candy Industry*, 8/94)

1. MUSEUMS EXHIBITING CHEWED GUM: 1

2. OTHER CHEWED-GUM-RELATED TOURIST ATTRACTIONS: CHEWING GUM ALLEY, SAN LUIS OBISPO, CALIF.

3. HIGHEST PRICE EVER PAID FOR A PIECE OF USED CHEWING GUM: $10,000

Sources: **1.** Gangster John Dillinger was a big gum chewer, and when he was captured in a Tucson hotel, a pharmacist collected his used gum and provided it to the University of Arizona dental museum, where it now sits. (*Edmonton Journal*, 2/15/04)
2. Chewing Gum Alley is an alley in which two facing walls have been redecorated with hundreds of thousands of wads of used chewing gum deposited by passersby over several decades. The site attracts about 300 visitors on a typical day. (*Edmonton Journal*, 10/22/00)
3. In 2002, a man paid $10,000 for gum that was reportedly chewed and spit out by baseball all-star Luis Gonzalez. (*Time*, 5/27/02)

HAIR

1. AVERAGE NUMBER OF HAIRS ON A MAN'S SCALP: 100,000

2. ANIMAL WITH THE MOST HAIR ON EARTH: SEA OTTER (170,000 TO 1 MILLION HAIRS PER SQUARE INCH)

3. LIFETIME GROWTH OF HAIR: 25 FEET

Sources: **1.** Redheads tend to have less—about 90,000 hairs, whereas blonds typically have about 140,000 hairs, with brunettes falling somewhere in between. About 100 hairs fall out every day, to be replaced by 100 new sprouts. (*Newsweek*, 6/16/03; *Independent*, 2/12/99) **2.** Humans seem bald in comparison—we have only about 1,000 hairs per square inch. (*Los Angeles Times*, 6/17/99) **3.** *Independent*, 4/11/96.

Recent auctions of strands of celebrity hair:

Abe Lincoln (2004): $3,750 (for 40 strands)

King Louis XIV (1998): $5,636

Mickey Mantle (1997): $6,900

Beethoven (1994): $7,300 (578 strands)

Napoleon (1998): $9,200

Marilyn Monroe (2004): $11,500

(*U.S. News and World Report*, 5/10/04; *USA Today*, 11/12/03; *Sacramento Bee*, 9/15/03; *International Herald Tribune*, 10/6/98; *Providence Journal*, 5/2/04)

1. NUMBER OF BARBERSHOPS IN THE U.S.: 45,000

2. NUMBER IN 1963: 106,000

(*Omaha World-Herald*, 10/21/01; *Forbes FYI*, 9/17/00)

1. AVERAGE COST OF A WOMEN'S HAIRCUT IN THE U.S. IN 2004: $21
2. AVERAGE COST OF A MEN'S HAIRCUT: $16
3. WORLD'S MOST EXPENSIVE REGULAR HAIRCUT: $800

Sources: **1.** The average women's haircut costs $21 in a salon with up to six chairs, and goes up to $44 for a cut in parlor with more than 13 chairs. (*American Salon*) **2.** *American Salon*. **3.** Sally Hershberger set the going rate when she raised her price to $600 at her Manhattan salon in 2003, but was soon outpriced by Orlo, a new salon opened by Orlando Pita in New York's Meatpacking District, which charges $800 for an 80-minute cut. Pita defended the price to the *New York Times*: "You can spend a lot on clothes, but you wear your hair every day." (*New York Times*, 11/21/04)

PROFESSION THAT BARBERS TRADITIONALLY PRACTICED IN ADDITION TO CUTTING HAIR: SURGERY

Barbers began performing surgery in 1163 because monks, who had traditionally done so, had to relinquish any bloody duties (deemed unholy) to secular citizens. Since barbers were already adept at wielding sharp instruments, they were the natural choice. The red stripes on the modern-day barber pole come from the bandages that were aired out to dry. (*FDA Consumer*, 3/1/00; *Providence Journal*, 9/30/02)

BEST TIME FOR A HAIRCUT, ACCORDING TO SOME ITALIANS: DURING A FULL MOON

According to ancient superstitions that still hold sway with some Italians, cutting hair during a full moon will make it grow back faster and fuller. (*New York Times*, 6/18/00)

ONE THEORY BEHIND THE DEFEAT OF PRESIDENTIAL CANDIDATE AL GORE: THE RIGHT-SIDE PART IN HIS HAIR

According to anthropologist John Walter, a right part draws attention to the right brain hemisphere, which is correlated with feminine features, whereas a left part brings to mind characteristics traditionally associated with men, like strength and resolve. Although the theory is controversial, few presidents have had right parts, and Pres. Jimmy Carter changed his part from right to left in 1979 after getting a letter from Walter (though he's never acknowledged the link). (*New York Post*, 1/30/04; *New Yorker*, 1/29/01

BEST PREVENTIVE MEASURE AGAINST BALDNESS: CASTRATION

Because testosterone is required to trigger the hair-loss process of male-pattern baldness, if a boy is castrated before puberty, he will maintain a full head of hair. (*U.S. News and World Report*, 8/04/97)

1. TEMPERATURE OF HELL, ACCORDING TO A 1998 STUDY:
833° FAHRENHEIT
2. TEMPERATURE OF HEAVEN: 448°

Sources: **1.** Two physicists from the University of Santiago in Spain started with the passage in the New Testament reporting that "the fearful, and unbelieving . . . shall have their part in the lake which burneth with fire and brimstone." (Revelation 21:8) For such a lake to exist, the temperature must be below the boiling point of sulphur, or just under 833° Fahrenheit. If the temperature was any higher than 833°, the brimstone would vaporize into gas and hence, there would be no lake. (*Minneapolis Star Tribune*, 9/24/98) **2.** In 1972, an article in the journal *Applied Optics* concluded that heaven was actually hotter than hell, reaching a temperature of 976°. A 1998 study, however, determined that the previous study was faulty, and the real temperature of heaven is 448.43°, still very hot, but cooler than hell. "It's good that the bad know that hell is hotter than heaven," said physicist Jorge Mira Perez, the author of the 1998 study. (*Minneapolis Star Tribune*, 8/12/98)

NUMBER OF EXORCISMS PERFORMED IN THE NEW YORK ARCHDIOCESE IN AN AVERAGE YEAR: 10 TO 15

According to traditional Roman Catholic belief, Beelzebub, the leader of the angels who rebelled against God, is incapable of overcoming the Almighty but is capable of possessing individual souls. That is when an exorcist is called in, and the Vatican has had a how-to guide for exorcists since 1614, recently updated in 1999. According to the guide ("De Exorcismis et supplicationibus quibusdam"), signs that a person is under the influence of the devil include "speaking in unknown languages and displaying a physical strength that is at odds with the possessed person's age or state of health." (*Time*, 10/2/00; *Washington Times*, 2/6/99)

1. Percentage of Americans who believe in heaven: 81%
2. Percentage of Americans who believe in hell: 70%
3. Percentage of Americans who believe they have a good chance of ending up in hell: 4%

Sources: **1.** Gallup poll, 5/04. **2.** Twelve percent aren't sure whether hell exists and 17% don't believe in hell. (Gallup, 5/04) **3.** The answer Americans gave when Gallup last asked this question in 1990. In 1965, 31% of those who believed in hell thought they might end up there. (Gallup)

YEAR THE NEW MEXICO LEGISLATURE SOUGHT TO HAVE THE NAME OF U.S. ROUTE 666 CHANGED TO 393: 2003

The number 666 is referred to in the Book of Revelation as "the number of the beast." According to the *Washington Post*, the road, which starts in Gallup, N.M., and runs north into Colorado and Utah, has an extremely high accident rate. (*Washington Post*, 3/30/03)

GREETING THAT THE COMMISSIONERS IN KLEBERG COUNTY, TEXAS, VOTED TO REPLACE "HELLO" WITH: "HEAVEN-O"

The reason: "Hello" contains the word "Hell." The new official county greeting, according to the county resolution, is a "symbol of peace, friendship and welcome" in this "age of anxiety." Kleberg County employees now answer the phones, "Heaven-o." (*Dallas Morning News*, 1/17/97)

PLACES IN THE WORLD NAMED HELL: 3

HELL, MICHIGAN
HELL, NORWAY
HELL, GRAND CAYMAN ISLANDS

A Hell, Mich., resident described how it got its name to CBS News: "There was a family which owned a flour and grain mill on the river, and they used to make moonshine. So at night the wagons would come home without the drivers, because they'd be drunk from the moonshine, and when people would ask the wives where their husbands were, they'd say, 'Oh, they're in hell.' So when it came time to name the town, Reese said, 'Why don't you call it Hell? Everyone else does.' And so it's named Hell." (CBS News, 12/13/99; *Independent*, 4/25/98)

HOMES

1. NUMBER OF TIMES THE AVERAGE AMERICAN MOVES IN A LIFETIME: 12

2. SIZE OF THE AVERAGE AMERICAN HOME IN 1975: 1,500 SQUARE FEET

3. SIZE OF THE AVERAGE AMERICAN HOME TODAY: 2,330 SQUARE FEET

4. AVERAGE NUMBER OF WINDOWS IN A HOUSE: 16

Sources: **1.** Seventeen percent of Americans move each year, more than in any other country. Australia ranks second, with 10.4% of its citizens moving annually. (*Charleston Post and Courier*, 6/5/03) **2, 3.** This while the size of the average American family has decreased from 3.1 to to 2.69 people per household. (*Chicago Tribune*, 5/14/04) **4.** *Washington Post*, 1/21/03.

1. Amount the average American household spends annually on household furnishings: $2,339

2. State where people spend the most on household furnishings: Connecticut

3. State where people spend the least: West Virginia

(ESRI Business Solutions, cited in the *Chicago Tribune*, 4/19/03)

MEANING OF THE TERM "CUL-DE-SAC": "BOTTOM OF THE BAG"

(*San Antonio Express*, 10/16/02)

1. PERCENTAGE OF HOMES BUILT IN AMERICA IN 1950 THAT WERE RANCHES: 86%
2. PERCENTAGE OF RANCH HOMES BUILT TODAY: 47%
3. PERCENTAGE OF NEW HOMES BUILT TODAY THAT ARE AT LEAST TWO STORIES: 52%
4. PERCENTAGE OF HOMES BUILT 30 YEARS AGO THAT WERE TWO STORIES: 17%

Sources: **1, 2.** National Association of Home Builders, cited in the *Chicago Tribune*, 5/25/02. **3, 4.** *Washington Post*, 1/24/04.

AMERICA'S LARGEST HOME CLOSET:
CANDY SPELLING'S (3,500 SQUARE FEET)

The wife of TV producer Aaron Spelling, Candy's Beverly Hills home boasts an entire floor of closets where each piece of clothing is allegedly color-coordinated. However, Spelling says that her closets house mostly casual wear. "I think it's an extravagance," she says of couture fashion, opting instead to fill her closets with "run-around things." (*W*, 10/1/00)

STATE WITH THE HIGHEST PERCENTAGE OF PEOPLE WHO HAVE LIVED
IN THE SAME HOME FOR 30 YEARS: PENNSYLVANIA

Seventeen percent of Pennsylvanians have lived in the same house for 3 decades. West Virginia is second on the list for longtime homeowners, followed by Connecticut, Massachusetts, and New York. (*New York Times*, 11/21/03)

1. Number of people in America who own two homes: 6.4 million
2. Number who owned two homes in 1970: 2.8 million

(*Builder*, 10/1/03)

HIGHEST PRICE EVER PAID FOR AN APARTMENT: $44 MILLION

In July 2003, British financier David Martinez purchased 12,000 square feet of empty raw space on the 76th and 77th floors of the AOL Time Warner Building in Manhattan. In December 2004, however, Rupert Murdoch agreed to buy the late Lawrence Rockfeller's 8,000 square foot penthouse on Fifth Avenue for $44 million. Monthly maintinance on the apartment is over $21,000. (*New York Times*, 12/17/04)

REALLY BIG HOUSES:

Sagaponick, N.Y.:

Estimated at anywhere from 66,000 to 100,000 square feet, Ira Rennert's second home in the Hamptons is the largest private residence in America, featuring 29 bedrooms, 40 bathrooms, three side-by-side swimming pools, a 164-seat theater, and an indoor basketball court, gym, and bowling alley.

(*New York Times*, 7/4/04; *Vanity Fair*, 7/03)

Palm Beach, Fla.:

Built at a reported cost of $50 million, Terry Allen Kramer's 44,000-square-feet Italian Renaissance mansion named La Follia ("the Folly") features a 4,500-foot master bedroom. "People were saying, 'My God, what is that monstrous thing?'" Kramer says. "But when they come inside, people love it and say, 'I can't believe how cozy it is.'"

(*Vanity Fair*, 2/04; *Chicago Tribune*, 5/23/98)

HORSES

1. **Year horses were introduced in America:** 1493
2. **Number of horses in the U.S. today:** 6.9 million
3. **Horses in the U.S. in 1915:** 27 million

Sources: **1.** Christopher Columbus brought 35 horses when he landed on the island of Hispaniola in 1493, reintroducing an animal that had been absent in the New World for around 10,000 years. According to the Smithsonian's Herman Viola, having never seen a horse, the Indians believed that the animal and the man riding it were physically attached. (*Los Angeles Times*, 2/24/95; CBS News, 5/7/90) **2.** According to the American Horse Council, about 1.2 million of these are working horses. (*Rocky Mountain News*, 10/11/03) **3.** Or about one horse for every four people. (*Chicago Tribune*, 9/19/93)

GALLONS OF SALIVA SECRETED DAILY BY AN AVERAGE HORSE: 7

(*Deseret Morning News*, 8/31/03)

1. **COUNTRY WITH THE MOST HORSES PER CAPITA:** MONGOLIA
2. **STATE WITH THE MOST HORSES PER CAPITA:** OKLAHOMA
3. **STATE WITH THE MOST HORSES:** TEXAS (687,000)

Sources: **1.** As of 2002, it had one for every resident. (*Washington Post*, 6/16/02) **2.** Oklahoma has one horse for every 12 people. Oklahoma also has the highest number of horse owners per capita, at one for every 46 residents. (*Daily Oklahoman*, 6/30/03) **3.** *Los Angeles Times*, 5/22/99.

SIDE ROUTINELY USED TO MOUNT HORSES: THE LEFT

Traditionally, warriors would carry their swords on their left leg, so mounting from the left was natural to avoid throwing the sword over the horse while mounting. However, American Indians would usually mount horses from the right side, since they carried their bows in the left hand. (AP, 5/4/84; *Times* [London], 2/19/02)

INVENTOR OF THE TERM "HORSEPOWER": JAMES WATT

Watt, an inventor who refined the steam engine, thought up this measurement to demonstrate the number of horses his device could replace. In the U.S., 1 horsepower is defined as the ability to lift 33,000 pounds 1 foot in 1 minute, or 550 pounds 1 foot in 1 second. Coincidentally, the prolific inventor is also the namesake of another measurement, the "watt." (*Washington Times*, 12/5/03)

1. NUMBER OF HORSES THAT TOOK PART IN WORLD WAR I: 1.5 MILLION
2. NUMBER KILLED: HALF A MILLION

Sources: **1, 2.** Most of the surviving horses were slaughtered after the war for food. (*New York Times*, 9/21/97)

1. HORSE WITH THE MOST EXPENSIVE SPERM IN THE WORLD: STORM CAT
2. STORM CAT'S "STUD FEE": $500,000

Dubbed "the World's No. 1 Stud," Storm Cat earns $23 million a year to breed future racehorses. His income doesn't sound so unreasonable when you take into consideration the fact that his offspring earn about $12 million a year at the track. Since thoroughbreds may not be artificially inseminated, Storm Cat must perform in person, which he does about 115 times a year. After a teaser stallion goes in to make sure the mare is willing, Storm Cat makes his entrance. Typically, the deed is over in about 30 seconds. (*Forbes*, 6/7/04; *New Yorker*, 8/7/00)

NUMBER OF CONSECUTIVE RACES LOST BY GLORIOUS SPRING: 113 AS OF DECEMBER 2004

Though she has never won a race, the lovable also-ran (known as Haru-Urara in Japanese) is the most popular racehorse in Japan. A movie is being developed about Glorious Spring's life, and her image can be found all over mugs, T-shirts, and other tourist souvenirs. (*Nikkei Weekly*, 4/29/04)

NUMBER OF FULL-TIME FARRIERS (HORSE SHOERS) IN THE U.S.: 15,000

(*Modesto Bee*, 5/4/04)

HOTELS

1. NUMBER OF HOTEL ROOMS IN THE U.S.: 4.4 MILLION

2. NUMBER THAT ARE SLEPT IN ON THE AVERAGE NIGHT: 2.5 MILLION

3. WORLD'S MOST EXPENSIVE HOTEL ROOM: $33,000 A NIGHT
(PRESIDENT WILSON HOTEL, GENEVA)

4. COST OF A ROOM AT THE WORLD'S FIRST MOTEL: $1.25

Sources: **1, 2.** Greenberg, *Hotel Secrets from the Travel Detective*. **3.** The Imperial Suite at the President Wilson Hotel takes up the whole top floor of the hotel, and has its own elevator, five bathrooms, and security complete with bulletproof windows and doors. Runners-up are the Royal Suite, Grand Resort Lagonissi in Athens ($25,600) and the Bridge Suite at the Atlantis Resort on Paradise Island, which has 10 rooms, a bar, and a theater, and is decorated with gold throughout. (Forbes.com 2003; *Sunday Age*, 4/27/03) **4.** The first motel was the Milestone Motel in San Luis Obispo, Calif., which opened in December 1925. Arthur Heineman designed the place, and coined the word "motel," which was a combination of "motor" and "hotel." (Copley News Service, 3/8/04)

First American hotel: City Hotel, New York City (1794)

Located on Broadway in what is now downtown Manhattan, the hotel had 73 rooms. (*Appraisal Journal*, 4/1/92)

NUMBER OF TOWELS STOLEN FROM HOLIDAY INNS EACH YEAR:

590,000

A towel is the most likely item to be taken from a hotel room, according to a survey of hotel housekeeping departments. Soap was the #2 item taken, followed by shampoo, bathrobes, and hangers. Removing batteries from TV remote controls is not uncommon, nor is filling an empty minibar bottle of vodka with water. Then there are the inventive lifters, like the couple at the Delano Hotel in Miami Beach who tore a $150 metal angel off the wall and used toothpaste to attempt to hide the resulting hole. (*Minneapolis Star Tribune*, 9/2/96; *USA Today*, 12/7/99; *Washington Post*, 6/3/01; Greenberg, *Hotel Secrets from the Travel Detective*)

Smallest full-service hotel rooms in the world: Washington Jefferson Hotel, Manhattan

The rooms at this New York hotel are about the size of your average bathroom, measuring 7 by 11 feet. The TV is raised so suitcases can fit underneath it. (*USA Today*, 9/17/03)

YEAR A HOTEL FIRST OFFERED FREE SOAP IN EVERY ROOM: 1829
(TREMONT HOUSE, BOSTON)

The Tremont was also the first hotel that had locks on every door, and in which all rooms were private. Other hotel firsts: the Ritz in Paris was the world's first hotel to have a private bathroom in every room (1898; the Statler Hotel in Buffalo became the first American hotel to offer private baths in 1907); both New York's Prospect Mountain Hotel and San Diego's Hotel del Coronado became the first hotels wired for electricity in 1888; the Hotel Statler in Detroit was the first hotel to have central air-conditioning (1934); and New York's Roosevelt Hotel was the first to install televisions in all guest rooms (1947). (*Cleveland Plain Dealer*, 12/18/94; *Public Utilities*, 1/1/94)

NUMBER OF UNDERWATER HOTELS: 2

To check into your room at Jules Undersea Lodge in Key West, Fla., you have to put on scuba gear, swim out to the middle of a lagoon, and then dive 30 feet down. There's no other way in or out. Bellhops swim guests' luggage down to the hotel, and a chef dives down to prepare meals. Over 10,000 people have stayed at the Undersea Lodge, and one guy stayed for 69 nights. . . .The Utter Inn in Sweden is a one-room underwater hotel under Lake Malaren, reached by a hatch leading to an underwater tank. (NPR's *All Things Considered*, 5/17/98; *Toronto Star*, 1/15/00)

ODDS THAT A PERSON LEAVES SOMETHING IN THE ROOM AT CHECKOUT: 1 IN 3

While the most common items forgotten are clothes, underwear, and the like, a recent survey found that 50% of Chicago hotels reported that guests had left behind "sexual items." Guests have also forgotten: a prosthetic leg left at the Fontainebleau Hilton in Miami; human eyes at the Essex House in New York; a live pig at the Fontainebleau in Miami; and a body left under a bed at a Travelodge in Pasadena, Calif. (*USA Today*, 12/7/99; *Washington Post*, 6/3/01)

1. PERCENTAGE OF PEOPLE WHO HAVE BEEN CAUGHT UNDRESSING BY THE MAID: 7%
2. ODDS THAT A MOVIE RENTED IN A HOTEL ROOM IS AN ADULT FILM: 6 IN 10

Sources: **1.** *Dallas Morning News*, 4/4/97. **2.** Greenberg, *Hotel Secrets from the Travel Detective*.

INSECTS AND OTHER PESTS

1. WORLD INSECT POPULATION: 1 BILLION BILLION

2. PERCENTAGE OF THE WORLD'S 1.2 MILLION KNOWN ANIMAL SPECIES THAT ARE INSECTS: 75%

3. PERCENTAGE OF INSECT SPECIES THAT ARE BEETLES: 27%

4. NUMBER OF INSECT FRAGMENTS THE FDA ALLOWS IN 3.5 OUNCES OF PEANUT BUTTER: 30

Sources: **1.** *Houston Chronicle*, 5/23/03. **2, 3.** Scientists estimate that there are 30,000 different types of insect in a single square yard of forest soil. (*Washington Post*, 10/22/00) **4.** Ground cinnamon can contain up to 400 insect fragments per 50 grams, macaroni 225 insect fragments per 225 grams (and up to 4.5 rodent hairs), and certain tomato sauces up to 14 fly eggs and one maggot per 100 grams. (*Boston Globe*, 7/20/03; FDA)

MOST UNUSUAL WEAPON CONSIDERED DURING WORLD WAR II: BAT BOMBS

Dubbed Project X-Ray, the plan involved dropping thousands of Mexican long-tail bats from B-29 bombers over Japanese cities before dawn, each bat with a small incendiary explosive attached to its body with a time-delay fuse. The bats would be roosting in buildings at the time the incendiary devices went off, sending Japanese cities up in flames. Though tests of the "bat bombs" were successful, the project was scrapped in 1944 in favor of the atomic bomb. (Couffer, *Bat Bomb*; *Independent on Sunday*, 7/1/01)

LARGEST LOCUST SWARM:
124 SQUARE MILES
(KENYA, 1954)

Scientists estimated that there were approximately 10 billion locusts in the swarm. (*University of Florida Book of Insect Records*)

LOUDEST INSECT ON EARTH:
AFRICAN CICADA

According to the *University of Florida Book of Insect Records*, sounds from the cicada have been measured at 106.7 decibels at 20 inches away. (*Baltimore Sun*, 9/1/03)

Most recent instance of a rat coming out of a home toilet:
Boston, Mass., Oct. 15, 2004

On Oct. 15, 2004, a woman about to use her bathroom in the Dorchester area of Boston encountered a rat that was trying to exit the bowl. When her husband called the city for help, they told him he might be ticketed for having rats, to which he replied, "This is your rat. It came out of the toilet." (*Boston Globe*, 10/31/04)

LARGEST HOME BEE INFESTATION: 700,000 BEES

In 2004, beekeepers were called in to remove a bee colony consisting of 700,000 bees above the kitchen of Norm Gitzen's Lake Worth, Fla., home. They also removed four 65-pound buckets of honey. (*Orlando Sentinel*, 6/10/04)

1. NUMBER OF TIMES PER DAY A RAT WILL HAVE SEX: 20
2. RATS' FAVORITE FOODS: SCRAMBLED EGGS AND MACARONI AND CHEESE
3. PERCENTAGE OF PHONE DISRUPTIONS THAT ARE CAUSED BY RATS GNAWING THROUGH CABLES: 25%

Sources: **1.** Sullivan, *Rats.* **2.** Rats' least favorite foods are raw beets, peaches, and celery. (Sullivan, *Rats*) **3.** Sullivan, *Rats.*

Top speed of an American cockroach: 3.4 mph

(*University of Florida Book of Insect Records*)

THE INTERNET

1. NUMBER OF SEARCHES PERFORMED ON GOOGLE EACH DAY: 200 MILLION

2. PEAK TIME FOR SEARCHES ON THE WORLD WIDE WEB: 5 P.M.

3. PEAK TIME FOR SEX-RELATED SEARCHES: 11 P.M.

4. ODDS THAT AN INTERNET SEARCH INCLUDES THE WORD "SEX": 1 IN 300

Sources: **1.** Agence France-Presse, 8/19/04. **2.** In Japan, Internet usage is highest after midnight, when phone rates drop. (*New York Times*, 11/28/02) **3.** *New York Times*, 11/28/02. **4.** It is widely agreed that "sex" is the most searched-for word on the internet, with other terms such as "porn," "nude," and "xxx" also in the top 20. (*Research Alert*, 3/2/01)

1. BIRTH OF THE INTERNET: SEPT. 2, 1969

2. FIRST COMMUNICATION BETWEEN COMPUTERS: OCT. 29, 1969

Sources: **1.** On that day, several grad students at UCLA hooked up an Internet Message Processer with a computer in the school's Boelter Hall, the first instance of data being sent back and forth through a central processor. The school put out a press release announcing: "UCLA to be first station in nationwide computer network." Not one newspaper thought it important enough to cover. (*Baltimore Sun*, 9/5/99) **2.** On Oct. 29, 1969, a computer at Stanford was hooked up to the Internet Message Processer at UCLA. The word "L-O-G-I-N" was typed at UCLA; Stanford received "L-O-G" before it's computer crashed, ending the first message sent across cyberspace. (*Baltimore Sun*, 9/5/99)

1. FIRST E-MAIL: 1971

2. SPEED AT WHICH AN E-MAIL TRAVELS FROM SAN FRANCISCO TO NEW YORK: 30,000 MILES PER SECOND

Sources: **1.** Ray Tomlinson devised a program that allowed users on one of four soda-machine-sized computers in a Cambridge, Mass., lab to send messages to the other computers in the lab. While the *Guinness Book of World Records* says the first e-mail message was "QWERTYUIOP," Tomlinson doesn't remember what he wrote, only that he was afraid of being caught by his boss. Tomlinson also invented the "@" sign to indicate an e-mail recipient's network address. (*Forbes*, 10/5/98) **2.** According to *Forbes*, international e-mail travels at about 10,000 miles per second. (*Forbes*, 5/28/01)

1. **TOTAL NUMBER OF WEB PAGES IN 1995:** 1.3 MILLION
2. **WEB PAGES AS OF DECEMBER 2004:** 8 BILLION

Sources: **1.** *New York Times*, 6/29/00. **2.** Google.

LIBRARIAN WHO COINED THE PHRASE "SURFING THE INTERNET": JEAN ARMOR POLLY (1992)

Polly, a librarian in Liverpool, N.Y., wrote a 1992 article in a publication called the *Wilson Library Bulletin* titled "Surfing the Internet: An Introduction," setting one of the most prevalent phrases of the late 20th century in motion. (*Syracuse Post-Standard*, 12/26/97)

HIGHEST AMOUNT EVER PAID FOR A DOMAIN NAME: $7.5 MILLION (BUSINESS.COM)

(*Forbes*, 5/28/01)

ODDS THAT A PERSON'S COMPUTER PASSWORD IS "PASSWORD," ACCORDING TO A RECENT SURVEY: 1 IN 8

Another survey of British workers showed that 47% used passwords relating to their family (such as names or birthdays), and 32% used passwords based on entertainment themes such as the names of sports teams or celebrities. (*Sunday Times* [London], 10/12/03; *New York Times*, 12/27/01)

1. FIRST UNSOLICITED MASS E-MAIL: MAY 3, 1978
2. DATE THE WORD "SPAM" WAS COINED: APR. 12, 1994

Sources: **1.** On May 3, 1978, Gary Thuerk, a marketing manager for Digital Equipment Corp., sent out an unsolicited e-mail to some 600 individuals on the ArpaNet (the predecessor to the Internet), announcing an event at which the company's newest computer would be showcased. (*Los Angeles Times*, 5/11/03) **2.** On Apr. 12, 1994, Laurence Canter, a lawyer in Phoenix, Ariz., sent out an unsolicited e-mail touting his firm to thousands of readers of online message boards. One anonymous Usenet user posted this suggested response: "Send coconuts and cans of Spam to Canter and Company." "Spam" apparently resonated more than "coconuts," and the term has been used ever since. (UPI, 4/12/04)

INVENTIONS

1. ODDS THAT AN AMERICAN BELIEVES THEY HAVE A GOOD IDEA FOR AN INVENTION: 1 IN 3

2. HOLDER OF FIRST PATENT: SAMUEL HOPKINS

3. MOST PATENTS HELD BY A SINGLE INVENTOR: 1,093 (THOMAS EDISON)

4. MOST PATENTS HELD BY A COMPANY: 50,837 (GENERAL ELECTRIC)

Sources: **1.** *Akron Beacon Journal*, 9/6/01. **2.** The first U.S. patent was issued July 31, 1790, for a new process of concocting potash (used in fertilizers and soaps). The patent was signed by "G. Washington." (*Rocky Mountain News*, 7/31/02) **3.** "I find out what the world needs, then I go ahead and try to invent it," Edison once said. Among other inventions, Edison gave the world the lightbulb, the motion picture camera, the phonograph, the electric chair, and the first talking doll. (*Houston Chronicle*, 3/29/98) **4.** As of 2000, among the company's inventions: the electric fan (1902); X-ray tube (1913); jet engine (1941); CAT scanner (1970). IBM holds second place with 32,498 patents, Westinghouse Electric has 28,005, and AT&T is fourth with 24,578. (*Time*, 12/4/00)

ORIGINAL NAMES FOR OTHER INVENTED PRODUCTS:

1. ESCALATOR: "RENO INCLINED ELEVATOR"

2. BLUE JEANS: "WAIST OVERALLS"

3. BALLPOINT PEN: "NONLEAKING WRITING STICK"

4. POPSICLE: "EPSICLE"

5. ALKA-SELTZER: "ASPIR-VESS"

Sources: **1.** Named after Jesse W. Reno, who invented the first escalator, a 6-foot conveyorlike contraption that was installed as a ride at Coney Island in 1891. The Otis Elevator Company coined the term "escalator" in 1900 for the moving stairs it built for the Paris Exhibition. (*New York Times*, 2/4/03) **2.** Jacob Davis invented the pants, which were called waist overalls because they were originally designed to be worn by miners over their clothing. In 1960, Levi's began to officially refer to its "overalls" by the word "jeans," which is supposedly derived from the fact that sailors from Genoa, Italy, wore similar pants in the 18th century. (*Esquire*, 6/01) **3.** Bryson, *Made in America*. **4.** Invented by an 11-year-old named Frank Epperson, who accidentally left his mom's stirring stick inside a cup of fruit punch on his porch overnight. Epperson originally called his creation the "Epsicle," but after obtaining the patent in 1923, changed the name to "Popsicle" because his children reportedly referred to the treat as "Pop's sicle." (*Newsday*, 7/30/03) **5.** *Brand Strategy*, 1/27/95.

MOST PATENTED DEVICE IN U.S. HISTORY: MOUSETRAP

According to Prof. John H. Lienhard of the University of Houston, the Patent Office had issued over 4,400 mousetrap patents as of 1996, and some 400 people apply for mousetrap patents each year. The patent office has 39 categories for mouse-killing devices (including "Impaling," "Choking or Squeezing," "Constricting Noose," and "Electrocuting and Explosive"). The prototypical mousetrap remains the Victor, however, the snapping mousetrap invented in 1899 by John Mast and made famous in cartoons, still manufactured by the Woodstream Corporation of Lilitz, Penn., the world's largest mousetrap manufacturer. (*Time*, 12/4/00; *American Heritage*, 10/96)

1. WHAT THE DIRECTOR OF THE U.S. PATENT OFFICE SAID IN 1899: "EVERYTHING THAT CAN BE INVENTED HAS BEEN INVENTED"
2. NUMBER OF U.S. PATENTS ISSUED IN 2003: 175,000

Sources: **1.** *Washington Post*, 1/4/04. **2.** More than 600,000 patents were issued during the 19th century, among them odd inventions such as a combination "gun/plowshare" (No. 35,600), and a "combined grocer's package, grater, slicer, and mouse and fly trap" patented in 1899. About 6 million patents were issued during the 20th century. (*Washington Post*, 1/4/04)

ORIGINAL NAME FOR THE ZIPPER: "HOOKLESS FASTENER"

The original patent for a "clasp locker for shoes" was obtained by Whitcomb Judson in 1893. Swedish-born inventor Gideon Sundback tweaked Judson's device, and was awarded a patent in 1917 for his "hookless fastener." BF Goodrich was an early purchaser of the fasteners for its shoes, and to its president Bertram Work, the term "hookless fastener" just didn't convey the beauty or speed of the device. At a 1923 sales meeting, some of Goodrich's salesmen were raising similar complaints when Work was reported to have said: "What we need is an action word—something that dramatizes the way the thing zips." Then—taking in the sound of the word—Work added, "Why don't we call it the 'zipper'?" Thus, in 1923, Goodrich trademarked the term "zipper" for its "Zipper Boot." (Petroski, *Evolution of Useful Things*)

Only U.S. president to obtain a patent: Lincoln

On May 22, 1849, Lincoln received Patent No. 6469 for a system of bellows and pulleys used to float boats over shallow waters. The invention never took off in Lincoln's day, though the same principle was later used to float submarines. (*New Scientist*, 3/21/98)

PERSON WHO INVENTED THE PULL-TAB CAN: ERMAL CLEON FRAZE

In 1959, Mr. Fraze went on a family picnic but forgot a can opener, forcing him to use his car bumper to open his beer. Seeking a more convenient way to open beverages, Fraze worked for several years before receiving a patent for a ring that pulled off the entire top. In 1965, he received a second patent for the pop-top can opener, which used a ring to pull a small prepunctured tab. (Petroski, *Evolution of Useful Things*)

Invention of the drinking straw: 1888

In 1888, Marvin Stone wrapped paper around a pencil and secured it with glue, creating the world's first manufactured straw. Prior to Stone's invention, people sipped drinks through hollowed-out blades of rye grass, which tended to affect the drink's taste. (*Christian Science Monitor*, 4/2/02)

1. OCCUPATION OF OTTO ROHWEDDER, THE MAN WHO INVENTED SLICED BREAD: JEWELER

2. NUMBER OF MONTHS THE GOVERNMENT PROHIBITED THE SALE OF SLICED BREAD DURING WORLD WAR II: 3

Sources: **1.** Otto Rohwedder, an Iowa jeweler, began work on his bread-slicing machine in 1912. It took him 16 years to perfect the machine, and in 1928, he introduced a 10-foot machine that both sliced and wrapped. Presliced bread was first sold in Chillicothe, Miss., home of the Chillicothe Baking Company. Within 5 years, 80% of the bread bought in America was presliced. (*Times Higher Education Supplement* [London], 5/31/02) **2.** The government's rationale was that since there was a shortage of steel, it could be put to better use in planes than in bread-slicing machines. The government rescinded the ban in March 1943 after a public outcry. (*Miami Herald*, 8/21/03)

1. DATE OF 1-MILLIONTH PATENT: 1911
2. 2-MILLIONTH PATENT: 1935
3. 3-MILLIONTH PATENT: 1960
4. 4-MILLIONTH PATENT: 1976
5. 5-MILLIONTH PATENT: MARCH 1991
6. 6-MILLIONTH PATENT: DECEMBER 1999

Sources: **1.** Francis N. Holton's solid rubber tire, which he'd hoped would replace air-filled tires. (AP, 3/19/91) **2.** Joseph Ledwinka's automobile wheel rim, which secured tires more thoroughly. (AP, 3/19/91) **3.** Kenneth R. Eldredge's automatic reading device, now widely used by banks to read checks. (AP, 3/19/91) **4.** Robert L. Mendenhall's asphalt recycling system. (AP, 3/19/91) **5.** The University of Florida's genetically engineered microbe that helps convert trash to ethanol fuel. (*New York Times*, 3/23/91) **6.** Palm Pilot device that allows users to synchronize the data on their handheld with the data on their computer. (*Ventura County Star*, 12/30/99)

INVENTIONS NAMED AFTER PEOPLE:

JACUZZI (1968): ROY JACUZZI

ZAMBONI ICE-CLEANING MACHINE (1949): FRANK ZAMBONI

TUPPERWARE (1945): EARL TUPPER

PHILLIPS SCREW (1933): HENRY PHILLIPS

GORE-TEX (1969): WILBERT GORE

(Time, 12/4/00)

INVENTIONS THAT WERE NEVER PATENTED BY THEIR CREATORS:

MOOD RING: Invented in 1975 by Josh Reynolds, who neglected to patent it until the billion-dollar market for the novelty had dried up.

(Forbes, 12/15/75)

ICE CREAM MAKER: Nancy Johnson invented the first modern ice cream churn in 1846; apart from the absence of electricity, hers is not much different than those in use today. But Johnson failed to patent her invention, and in 1848, William Young patented the machine, adding insult to injury by calling it the Johnson Patent Ice Cream Freezer.

(New York Times, 8/27/80)

X-RAYS: Wilhelm Roentgen received the first Nobel Prize in Physics for discovering X-rays in 1895, but refused to patent or profit from it, believing that it belonged to all humanity.

(U.S. News and World Report, 11/6/95)

KARAOKE MACHINE: Daisuke Inoue, a drummer in a lackluster Japanese bar band, invented the first karaoke machine in 1971 after listeners regularly asked if they could get up and sing with the band. Inoue never considered patenting the invention, which made over $7 billion in 2002 in Japan alone.

(Japan, Inc., 6/1/03)

JEWS

1. PERCENTAGE OF WORLD POPULATION THAT IS JEWISH: 0.2%

2. PERCENTAGE OF NOBEL PRIZE WINNERS WHO HAVE BEEN JEWISH: 18%

3. ODDS THAT AN AMERICAN COMEDIAN WAS JEWISH IN 1979: 80%

4. PERCENTAGE OF AMERICAN JEWS WHO BELONG TO SYNAGOGUES: 46%

Sources: **1.** As of 1999, there were 13,866,000 Jews in the world. At the beginning of the 20th century the Jewish population stood at over 15 million and immediately before World War II, there were 18 million Jews in the world, the highest Jewish population in history. (*New York Times Almanac*) **2.** Between 1901 and 2002, 720 Nobel Prizes were handed out. Of these, 130 have gone to Jews or people of Jewish descent, three times the number won by Germany and France, and 10 times the number won by Japan. (*Jerusalem Post,* 10/18/02) **3.** Mel Brooks provides a reason why Jews were so prominent in comedy: "I may be angry at G-d or at the world, and I'm sure that a lot of my comedy is based on anger and hostility. . . . It comes from a feeling that as a Jew and as a person, I don't fit into the mainstream of American society." (*Washington Post*, 11/18/01) **4.** Of these, 39% are Reform, 33% are Conservative, 21% are Orthodox, and 3% are Reconstructionist. (*Jewish Week*, 9/12/03)

1. Percentage of the U.S. population that is Jewish: 2%

2. Percentage of the U.S. population the average American believes is Jewish: 18%

Sources: **1.** There are 5.2 million Jews in the U.S. (*Canadian Jewish News*, 9/18/03) **2.** According to a 1990 Gallup poll, which also revealed gross overestimations of the percentage of America that is made up of African Americans and Hispanics. One in four Americans surveyed believed that Jews comprised more than 30% of the U.S. population, with 12% believing that Jews formed a majority of Americans. (Gallup)

RECENT ARRESTS OF DRUNK CIRCUMCISERS: 1

On June 18, 2002, a mohel was charged with drunk driving after being stopped on his way to circumcise a boy in suburban Detroit. He told police he was en route from another circumcision, at which he had a couple of glasses of wine, but believed that he was sober enough to wield the scalpel. Commenting on the national attention the arrest received, the boy's father said, "Yeah, it was on Leno. It was hysterical. Unless you were my son." (*Detroit Free Press*, 8/23/02)

YEAR IN WHICH EUROPEAN JEWS WERE FIRST REQUIRED TO TAKE LAST NAMES: 1787

In 1787, Hapsburg ruler Joseph the Tolerant issued a decree that required Jews to adopt last names, and the rest of Europe soon followed. Jews were little interested in new names, which were arrived at almost haphazardly. Some were based on their father's name (Jacobson), some based on membership in a particular tribe (Cohen); some by professions (Becker [baker], Kaufman [merchant], and Farber [painter]). In some parts of Hungary, Jews were simply divided into four groups and arbitrarily dubbed black (Schwartz), white (Weiss), big (Gross), or small (Klein). Jews were forbidden to adopt the names of many towns (like Berlin), and so named themselves after mountains, which explains why many Jewish names end in "berg." (*Minneapolis Star Tribune*, 9/21/96)

Most common name in Israel: Moshe Cohen

As of 1997, there were 123,431 Cohens (or Kohens) in Israel. The second most common last name is Levy, with 73,687, then Mizrahi, with 23,897 namesakes. Among first names, Moshe is followed by Ya'acov, Yosef, Avraham, and David. (*Jerusalem Post*, 6/23/97)

ONLY PLACE IN THE WORLD WHERE JEWS ARE CALLED GENTILES: UTAH

All non-Mormons are referred to as Gentiles by Mormons. (*Washington Post*, 12/23/02)

1. PERCENTAGE OF ISRAELIS WHO KEEP KOSHER: 58%
2. PERCENTAGE OF KOSHER FOOD SOLD IN AMERICA THAT IS BOUGHT BY JEWS: 20%

Sources: **1.** *Portrait of Israeli Jewry*, 2000. **2.** Since Kosher food clearly delineates between products containing milk and meat, Muslims, Seventh-Day Adventists, vegetarians, and lactose-intolerant people now are 80% of the kosher market. (*Minneapolis Star Tribune*, 1/29/00; AP, 12/10/04)

HIGHEST PERCENTAGE OF JEWISH VOTES EVER WON BY A REPUBLICAN PRESIDENTIAL CANDIDATE: 38% (RONALD REAGAN, 1984)

It has frequently been said that "Jews live like Episcopalians and vote like Puerto Ricans." No Republican presidential candidate has ever come close to garnering a majority of Jewish votes, and only 16% of American Jews characterize themselves as Republicans, compared to 30% of Catholics and 39% of Protestants. (*Slate*, 2/10/04; Gallup, 5/25/04)

JOKES AND HUMOR

1. NUMBER OF TIMES THE AVERAGE ADULT LAUGHS EACH DAY: 15

2. PERCENTAGE OF ADULT LAUGHTER THAT DOES NOT OCCUR IN RESPONSE TO JOKES OR FUNNY SITUATIONS: 80%

3. PERCENTAGE BY WHICH PEOPLE WHO ARE TELLING A JOKE LAUGH MORE THAN THE PEOPLE THEY ARE TELLING IT TO: 46%

Sources: **1.** Statistics are all over the place on this point: some studies indicate adults laugh an average of 60 times a day, but most newspapers put the number at 15. (Newhouse News Service, 5/30/00) **2.** In a study of over 1,200 episodes of laughter, Robert Provine found that most laughter was not the result of deliberate attempts at humor, but rather innocuous statements such as "I'll see you guys later," "Look, it's Bob," or "Can I join you?" (*Independent*, 2/2/94) **3.** Female speakers laugh 127% more than their male audience. In contrast, male speakers laugh about 7% less than their female audience. (*U.S. News and World Report*, 4/26/99)

1. GROUP THAT TELLS THE MOST JOKES ABOUT THEMSELVES: JEWS

2. GROUP THAT TELLS THE FEWEST JOKES: JAPANESE

Sources: **1.** Says Prof. Christie Davies, "Americans are more obsessed than the French and British with cleanliness, so more of their jokes are about being physically dirty. The British like irony and jokes about social class." Germans enjoy toilet humor the most "because they're potty-trained earlier than anyone else." (*Mirror*, 7/13/01; Davies, *The Mirth of Nations*) **2.** Davies, *The Mirth of Nations*.

GROUPS MOST LIKELY TO LAUGH AT SLAPSTICK:
CHILDREN, PEOPLE WITH BRAIN DAMAGE, AND MEN

Studies of gender differences in humor show that women are more likely to enjoy jokes that brain-damaged patients cannot understand, involving longer narratives and personal anecdotes. In contrast, men are more likely to enjoy jokes involving men in drag or flatulence. Says humor expert Regina Berreca, "I would hate to say that male humor is the humor of the impaired or the infantile, but since science seems to indicate this is true, how can we argue against it?" (*Dallas Morning News*, 4/1/99)

First use of laugh track on television: Sept. 9, 1950

The Hank McCune Show, a comedy about "a likeable blunderer, a devilish fellow who tries to cut corners only to find himself the sucker," was the first. Even shows filmed before a live studio audience are "sweetened" with extra laughs before airing. (*American Scientist*, 2/96)

DURATION OF 1962 AFRICAN LAUGHTER EPIDEMIC: 6 MONTHS

It happened in Tanzania, when a group of schoolgirls were convulsed by a fit of laughter. As the girls' classmates saw them laughing, the laughter spread from school to school and to the surrounding villages. The laughter epidemic lasted 6 months and affected over 1,000 people before it eventually petered out. (Provine, *Laughter*)

TOP JOKE TARGETS OF LATE-NIGHT TALK SHOW HOSTS IN 2004:

1. GEORGE BUSH (1,170 JOKES)
2. JOHN KERRY (505)
3. BILL CLINTON (320)

Leno on Bush: "I guess the President's trip to England is going well. There was one embarrassing moment when the Prime Minister said to President Bush, he said, 'Would you like to see the English Channel?' And Bush said, 'Oh, you gotta get satellite dish. You get 500 channels.'" Letterman on Kerry: "John Kerry went duck hunting. Kerry did pretty well; he came back with four ducks and three Purple Hearts." Letterman on Clinton: "President Clinton had quadruple bypass surgery and is recovering nicely. You know, it really surprised me. Who would have thought his heart would be the first organ to give out?" (Center for Media and Public Affairs)

NUMBER OF JOKES MILTON BERLE KEPT ON COMPUTER: 6 1/2 MILLION

(*The Larry King Show*, 11/2/93)

INSPIRATION FOR RODNEY DANGERFIELD'S "I DON'T GET NO RESPECT" ROUTINE: *THE GODFATHER*

As Dangerfield said in an interview shortly before he died, "When *The Godfather* came out, all you heard was, 'When she's with me, you show her respect. . . . I want respect. . . . I'm with him. OK? Respect.' So I wrote a joke about respect to see what the reaction would be. It was the first joke I wrote. The first time I said 'I don't get no respect,' I said, 'When I was a kid, they played hide-and-seek; they wouldn't even look for me, you know.' And all of a sudden, I found an image." (NPR's *Fresh Air*, 7/6/04)

KIDS

1. Number of kids produced by the average woman on earth in 1900: 6

2. Number of kids produced by the average woman today: 2.7

3. Number of kids in the United States: 73,044,000

4. State with the most kids per capita: Utah

Sources: **1, 2.** While global fertility rates have decreased dramatically, even the current level is unsustainable. If the current fertility rate continues, world population will increase to 134 trillion in 2300. (*Washington Post*, 12/9/03). **3.** Statistical Abstract. **4.** Large families are the result of the prevalent Mormon influence in the state. (AP, 1/28/00).

TOTAL COST OF RAISING ONE AMERICAN CHILD TO AGE 17:

HOUSING:	$97,590
FOOD:	$38,280
TRANSPORTATION:	$33,690
CLOTHING:	$12,840
HEALTH CARE:	$15,210
CHILD CARE AND EDUCATION:	$31,740
MISCELLANEOUS:	$31,920

TOTAL: $261,270

Based on a family making more than $68,000 per year. Families making less than $40,000 spend an average $130,000 raising a child to age seventeen. Families making between $40,000 and $68,000 spend an average $178,500. (USDA Expenditures on Children by Families, 2003)

Average number of times a kid will nag his parents to get something they refuse to purchase: 9

According to a study of twelve- to seventeen-year-olds. (*Washington Post*, 4/6/03)

1. Medical name for compulsive nose-picking: **Rhinotillexomania**

2. Percentage of people (including kids) who admit to picking their nose: **91%**

3. Odds that a nose-picker uses his index finger: **2 in 3**

Sources: **1.** In February 1995, the *Journal of Clinical Psychiatry* published a study on nose-picking called "Rhinotillexomania: Psychiatric Disorder or Habit?" The study arose from a questionnaire sent out to 1,000 Wisconsin residents asking them about their nose-picking habits. **2.** Nine percent said they picked their noses "more than average," and 43% admitted to picking their noses in public, usually in their car or at the office. (*Wisconsin State Journal*, 3/27/95) **3.** However, 16% of people reported using their thumb. Moreover, the journal reported that "once removed, nasal debris was examined, at least some of the time, by most respondents." (*Wisconsin State Journal*, 3/27/95)

ODDS THAT NAGGING BY KIDS CONVINCES PARENTS TO GO TO A FAST-FOOD RESTAURANT OR BUY CLOTHES: 1 IN 3

In a study called "The Nag Factor," Western International Media found that only 31% of parents are not influenced by children's nagging and pleading. (*Toronto Star*, 8/24/98)

1. Amount of time per week that the average kid watches television: **1,680 minutes**

2. Amount of time per week that the average parent spends in meaningful conversation with their kids: **38.5 minutes**

According to widely reported figures put out by a group called the TV Turnoff Network. (*Boston Globe*, 4/29/01)

LOS ANGELES

1. NICKNAMES: LA-LA LAND, CITY OF ANGELS, SOUTHLAND, DIGITAL COAST
2. SUNNY DAYS PER YEAR, ON AVERAGE: 329
3. EARTHQUAKES PER DAY, ON AVERAGE: 1.2

Sources: **1.** Along with Lost Angeles. (*Los Angeles Almanac*) **2.** *USA Today,* 4/16/04. **3.** Most of them undetectable tremors, but collectively they bring L.A. a quarter inch closer to San Francisco every year.... In 1999, geologists discovered a previously unknown fault directly under downtown L.A.... The largest artificial earthquake in the world (8.3 on the Richter scale) takes place 200 times a day at Universal Studios Hollywood.... 1.1 million Californians have earthquake insurance. (Southern California Earthquake Data Center; *Los Angeles Times,* 11/28/04)

1. Annual rainfall: 15 inches
2. Water used per person per day: 140 gallons

Sources: **1.** *Los Angeles Times,* 10/27/04. **2.** According to numbers compiled by the American Water Works Association, the average resident of Los Angeles uses 140 gallons per day, compared to 228 gallons in Denver, 284 in Salt Lake City, and 307 in Las Vegas.

PERCENTAGE OF THEIR TIME THAT LOS ANGELES POLICE OFFICERS SPEND RESPONDING TO FALSE BURGLAR ALARMS: 15%

L.A. police get an average of about 106,000 burglar alarm calls a year, 95% of which turn out to be false. In November 2004, the city began assessing fines of $115 for false alarms. (*New York Times,* 1/17/03; City News Service, 11/8/04)

NUMBER OF MOVIES AND BOOKS FEATURING THE DESTRUCTION OF L.A.: 139

Directors and authors have destroyed L.A. 49 times by nuclear weapons (*Miracle Mile*), 28 times by earthquakes (*Escape from L.A.*), 10 times by evil space aliens (*Independence Day*), seven times by pollution (*Blade Runner*), two times by fire (*The Day of the Locust*), once by global warming (*The Day After Tomorrow*), and one time by giant ants (*Them*). (Davis, *Ecology of Fear*; IMDB.com)

Appearance of first colony of killer bees: 1999

In April 2001, a swarm of bees caused a 9-minute delay in the start of the Dodgers–Padres game. Experts advise people attacked by killer bees to run in a zigzag pattern. Don't go underwater because the bees wait for their victim to resurface. (UPI, 3/16/99; *Newsday,* 4/16/01; *Time,* 9/7/98)

GREAT THINGS PURPORTEDLY INVENTED IN L.A.: 33

Hot fudge sundaes, cafeterias, Cobb salads, Baskin-Robbins, cheeseburgers, double burgers, French dip sandwiches, fortune cookies, California rolls, chili dogs, gas stations, go-go dancers, the Internet, Mickey Mouse, Barbie, the DC-3, the Space Shuttle, gospel music, disc jockeys, "power yoga," the Zamboni ice-cleaning machine, drive-through banks, drive-in churches, self-service gas stations, freeways, Pentecostal churches, TV news helicopters, traffic lights, skateboards, spinning classes, low-rider roadsters, air-soled sneakers, and wheat-grass juice bars. (*Pittsburgh Post-Gazette*, 3/7/02; *Nation's Restaurant News*, 2/5/01; ABC News, 7/21/00)

RANK AMONG CITIES IN NUMBER OF PLASTIC SURGEONS: SECOND

New York takes the top slot with 250 plastic surgeons in residence, beating out L.A.'s 206 by a hair. (American Society of Plastic Surgeons)

AMOUNT OF TIME RESIDENTS WASTE IN TRAFFIC JAMS OVER A LIFETIME: 291 DAYS

That's 93 hours a year stuck in traffic (the worst in the nation), projected over a 75-year life span. . . . According to a ranking by State Farm Insurance, the intersection of Wilshire and Santa Monica Boulevard is the fourth most dangerous in the United States. (*Governing* magazine, 10/04)

NUMBER OF LANES ON THE SANTA ANA FREEWAY: 26

At the intersection of the San Diego and Santa Ana Freeways, the I-5 expands into a confluence of 26 lanes including special collector roads, all manner of car-pool lane connections, and flyover ramps. The stretch is known as the El Toro Y, and for some time was believed to be the widest in the world. (*Orange County Register*, 5/1/00)

LATE-NIGHT TV

1. NUMBER OF AMERICANS WHO WATCHED JAY LENO NIGHTLY IN 2003: 5.8 MILLION

2. NUMBER WHO WATCHED DAVID LETTERMAN: 4.2 MILLION

3. NUMBER WHO WATCHED JOHNNY CARSON IN 1992: 12 MILLION

Sources: **1, 2.** *Baltimore Sun*, 9/28/04. **3.** *Los Angeles Times*, 5/11/92.

Date of first late-night network talk show: Sept. 27, 1954

At 11:30 P.M. eastern time on this date, an NBC announcer began a late-night institution with the words "Live, from New York City, the National Broadcasting Company presents *Tonight*, starring Steve Allen." Allen started the very first late-night monologue like this: "This is *Tonight*. I can't think of too much to tell you about it except I want to give you the bad news first. This program is going to go on forever. Boy, you think you're tired now—wait until one o'clock rolls around. We especially selected this theater—it's a New York theater called the Hudson—and we selected it because I think it sleeps about 800 people." (*Television Week*, 9/27/04)

DATE THE *TONIGHT SHOW*'S FIRST HOST QUIT ON THE AIR: FEB. 11, 1960

Angry because network censors had removed a joke because of its use of the term "water-closet," Jack Paar came out to open the show on Feb. 11, 1960, then told the audience, "I am leaving *The Tonight Show*. There must be a better way of making a living than this." Paar then walked off the set, leaving his startled sidekick Hugh Downs to host the rest of the 90-minute show. Three weeks later, Paar returned to the show. His first words were, "As I was saying before I was interrupted." (NBC, *Brought to You in Living Color*)

1. Amount David Letterman reportedly makes per year to host *The Late Show*: $31 million

2. Amount Jay Leno makes on *The Tonight Show*: $25 million

3. Amount Conan O'Brien makes: $8 million

4. Johnny Carson's salary in 1962: $100,000

5. Salary Carson ended with in 1992: $25 million

Sources: **1.** *Miami Herald*, 3/31/04. **2, 3.** *New York Times*, 9/29/04. **4, 5.** *People*, 5/25/92.

1. NUMBER OF EPISODES OF *THE TONIGHT SHOW* HOSTED BY JOHNNY CARSON: **4,531**

2. FIRST SHOW HOSTED BY CARSON: **OCT. 1, 1962**

3. LAST SHOW: **MAY 22, 1992**

Sources: **1.** *People*, 5/25/92. **2.** Following an intro by Groucho Marx, who said that Carson couldn't come out yet because he sent his suit out to be pressed and it hadn't come back, the 36-year-old Nebraska comic came out and told America, "I want my na-na." In addition to Groucho, guests that first night were Mel Brooks, Rudy Vallee, Joan Crawford, Tony Bennett, and the Phoenix Singers. (Cox, *Here's Johnny*) **3.** In contrast to his star-studded guest list 30 years earlier, Carson was all alone on his last show. After a monologue punctuated by jokes about Dan Quayle, he introduced his family, showed clips from past shows, and then ended with, "And so it has come to this. I am one of the lucky people in the world. I found something that I always wanted to do and I have enjoyed every single minute of it. I bid you a very heartfelt good night." (*Houston Chronicle*, 5/23/92)

THE TONIGHT SHOW'S MOST FREQUENT GUEST: **BOB HOPE** (132 APPEARANCES)

(*People*, 5/25/92)

SECOND HIGHEST RATED EPISODE OF THE TONIGHT SHOW: MARRIAGE OF TINY TIM TO MISS VICKI (1969)

Forty-five million viewers tuned in on Dec. 17, 1969, to see *Tonight Show* regular Tiny Tim (whose "Tiptoe through the Tulips" reached 17 on the pop charts in 1968) wed his 17-year-old bride, Vicki Bundinger, on the air. The highest rated episode was Carson's last show. (*Entertainment Weekly*, 2/19/99)

1. First episode of *Saturday Night Live*: Oct. 11, 1975

2. First person to host *Saturday Night Live*: George Carlin

3. First *SNL* musical guest: Janis Ian

Sources: **1, 2.** The first show in which the stars abhorred the medium, as epitomized by John Belushi, who once told Lorne Michaels: "My television has spit all over it." Controversy erupted before the first show was even aired, with first host Carlin arguing backstage with NBC executives about whether he could take the stage in his undershirt. They eventually settled for a tasteful blazer over a T-shirt. (*Atlanta Journal-Constitution*, 10/4/02) **3.** Ian sang her semiautobiographical hit "At Seventeen." (*Birmingham News*, 9/10/04)

MOST FREQUENT *SNL* GUEST HOST: STEVE MARTIN

Steve Martin has hosted *SNL* 13 times, John Goodman 12 times, and Alec Baldwin 11. (NBC's *Today Show*, 11/17/03)

LAWNS

1. Total acres of lawns planted in the U.S.: 30 million
2. Hours per year the average American spends watering his lawn: 40 hours
3. Size of the average American lawn: 5,500 square feet

Sources: **1.** If all the lawns were patched together into one giant quilt of lawn, it would blanket a landmass the size of Mississippi. (*Christian Science Monitor*, 5/20/04) **2.** *Christian Science Monitor*, 5/20/04. **3.** *New York Times*, 5/9/04.

FIRST SUBURBS THAT FEATURED HOUSES WITH FRONT LAWNS: LLEWELLYN PARK, N.J. (1853) RIVERSIDE, ILL. (1869)

(*Kansas City Star*, 11/2/95)

NUMBER OF HOURS IT TAKES TO CUT THE WHITE HOUSE GRASS: 8

Though the lawn is meticulously maintained—mowed twice a week and kept at a height of 3 inches—when Miracle-Gro founder Horace Hagedorn was treated to a tour of the grounds, he emerged unimpressed. "They could actually use a little more fertilizer," Hagedorn said, then added, "Republicans tend to be better at lawns than Democrats." (*Deseret Morning News*, 7/13/03; *Washington Post*, 3/16/00)

1. FIRST WRITTEN USE OF THE WORD "BACKYARD": 1659
2. FIRST WRITTEN USE OF THE WORD "LAWN": 1733

The word "lawn" comes from *launde*, a French word referring to an open area in the woods. (Askoxford.com)

ORIGIN OF THE LAWN JOCKEY: GEORGE WASHINGTON

Historians believe that the much-derided lawn jockey has its origins in a statue Gen. George Washington commissioned to honor the service of a slave named Tom Graves whose job it was to carry a lantern for troops during the Battle of Trenton, and who died in the line of duty. In the 19th century, the figures were appropriated by plantation owners as a symbol of their slaves' obedience, and in the mid 20th century, lawn jockeys were a fixture of suburban American lawns. (*Washington Post*, 1/9/98)

1. INVENTION OF THE LAWN MOWER: 1830
2. NUMBER OF LAWN MOWERS IN AMERICA IN 1880: 50,000
3. NUMBER OF LAWN MOWERS IN THE U.S. TODAY: 66 MILLION

Sources: **1.** Invented by Edwin Budding, the first lawn mower was a converted carpet-trimming machine that made the necessity of keeping sheep—the original lawnmower—a strictly ornamental business. "Country gentlemen may find in using my machine themselves an amusing, useful and healthy exercise," Budding said in his patent documents. Two people were needed to operate the original lawnmower—one to push the device, and the other to pull. (*Grounds Maintenance*, 5/00) **2.** Ford, *The Space Between Buildings*. **3.** *Wichita Eagle*, 3/15/03.

NUMBER OF PINK FLAMINGOS SOLD IN THE U.S.: 40 MILLION

Designed by artist Dan Featherstone in 1957 based on a bird he saw in *National Geographic*, the flamingo is frequently derided as a symbol of bad taste, and is banned in many towns, including Celebration, Fla., a town built by Disney. (*Washington Post*, 4/26/98; *Modern Plastics*, 11/1/00)

Percentage of residents of Newport, Me., who voted against a proposed ordinance banning topless lawn mowing: 70%

The controversy was precipitated by Shirley Davis's neighbor complaining that Davis's daughter was mowing her lawn topless. After it was determined that town law did not prohibit topless mowing, the question of banning it was put on the ballot, where it was resoundingly defeated by voters in the town of 3,500. (*Boston Globe*, 11/15/98)

NUMBER OF STATE CAPITAL LAWNS MOWED BY RYAN TRIPP: 50

To publicize the plight of Americans who require organ transplants, in 1999 Tripp mowed the lawns of 47 state capitals (and three governors' mansions in states whose capitals don't have lawns), earning the name "Lawnmower Boy" from David Letterman. (*Ottawa Citizen*, 12/31/99)

LAWYERS

1. NUMBER OF LAWYERS IN THE U.S.: 1,084,000
2. STATE WITH THE MOST LAWYERS: NEW YORK (140,000)
3. STATE WITH THE FEWEST LAWYERS: NORTH DAKOTA (1,297)
4. RATIO OF LAWYERS TO RESIDENTS IN ARKANSAS: 1 FOR EVERY 539 RESIDENTS
5. RATIO OF LAWYERS TO RESIDENTS IN WASHINGTON, D.C.: 1 FOR EVERY 14

Sources: **1.** American Bar Association. **2.** In terms of percentages, however, Massachusetts has the highest ratio of lawyers of any state. (ABA; *Boston Business Journal*, 1/23/04) **3.** ABA. **4, 5.** AP, 2/19/02.

1. MOST HOURS BILLED BY ONE LAWYER IN A SINGLE YEAR: 5,471
2. MOST HOURS BILLED BY ONE LAWYER IN A SINGLE DAY: 1,000

Sources: **1.** Called "the hardest-working lawyer in America" by his colleagues, James Spiotto, a partner at Chicago's Chapman & Cutler, billed 15 hours a day, every day, in 1993, and pulled 52 all-nighters. (*Washington Post*, 3/22/98) **2.** The attorney (since disciplined) performed one task and had his secretary bill it at two-tenths of an hour to each of 5,000 cases in a massive asbestos litigation. Incidentally, John McCloy, a founding member of the venerable old-line New York firm of Milbank, Tweed, once said: "If a client doesn't complain about a bill, it isn't high enough." (*New York Times*, 3/20/92)

1. Percentage of lawyers who believe that their colleagues pad hours: 92%
2. Estimate of the legal work done in large cases that is actually necessary: 50%

Sources: **1.** Ross, "The Ethics of Hourly Billing by Attorneys," in *Rutgers Law Review*, 1991. **2.** *ABA Journal*, 8/94.

1. LAWYERS IN AMERICA NAMED "CROOK," ACCORDING TO MARTINDALE-HUBBELL: 42
2. LAWYERS NAMED "TRUTH": 0

There are also three "Schmucks" and two "Putzes." (Martindale-Hubbell)

RATIO OF LAWYERS TO POPULATION IN . . . :

CHINA: 1 LAWYER FOR EVERY 12,745 PEOPLE

JAPAN: 1 FOR EVERY 6,737 PEOPLE

U.S.: 1 FOR EVERY 274 PEOPLE

ISRAEL: 1 FOR EVERY 225 PEOPLE

(*Milwaukee Journal Sentinel*, 5/11/04; *Hamilton Spectator*, 7/16/03; *Los Angeles Times*, 12/13/02; *Jerusalem Post*, 11/29/02)

1. CASES IN WHICH JUDGES DECIDED GUILT OR INNOCENCE BY FLIPPING A COIN: 2
2. BY A SHOW-OF-HANDS VOTE OF COURTROOM SPECTATORS: 1
3. BY THROWING DARTS: 1

Sources: **1.** In re Daniels, 340 So.2d 300, 305 (La. 1976). **2.** When brought before the Judicial Disciplinary Committee, the judge characterized his actions as "innovative" and "creative." (*Matter of Friess*) **3.** *Matter of Meyers.*

Only jobs ranking below lawyers in a survey measuring public perception of honesty in 23 professions:

STOCKBROKING ADVERTISING INSURANCE SALES
HMO MANAGEMENT   CAR SALES

(Gallup poll, 12/1/03)

LEFTIES

1. PERCENTAGE OF PEOPLE WHO ARE LEFT-HANDED: 10%
2. PERCENTAGE OF PEOPLE WHO ARE LEFT-FOOTED: 19%
3. PERCENTAGE OF PEOPLE WHO ARE LEFT-EARED: 41%
4. PERCENTAGE OF PEOPLE WHO ARE LEFT-EYED: 29%

Sources: **1.** Though reports vary, most surveys indicate an average of 10%. (*Syracuse Post-Standard*, 8/10/02) **2.** Handedness and footedness apparently have no correlation, with half of all right-handers being left-footers. (Coren, *The Left-Hander Syndrome*) **3.** Most people hear language with the right ear, and background noise and music with the left; in left-earedness, it's the other way around. (*Arizona Republic*, 5/24/03; Coren, *The Left-Hander Syndrome*) **4.** Coren, *The Left-Hander Syndrome.*

FIRST LEFT-HANDED U.S. PRESIDENT: JAMES A. GARFIELD

He could also write with his right, and used to amuse guests by writing Latin with one hand and Greek with the other. (*Arizona Republic*, 8/13/98)

NUMBER OF LEFT-HANDED PRESIDENTS: 6

James A. Garfield, Herbert Hoover, Gerald Ford, Ronald Reagan, George H. W. Bush, and Bill Clinton. Truman was ambidextrous, and was the first president to throw an opening pitch from the presidential box with his left hand. (*Atlanta Journal-Constitution*, 2/3/04)

RATIO OF MALE TO FEMALE LEFT-HANDERS: 2 TO 1

(*Fort Worth Star-Telegram*, 8/13/02)

Number of discriminatory references to the left hand in the Bible: 100

For instance, in Matthew 25:34–35, it says that on judgment day, Jesus "will say to those at his right hand, 'Come, you that are blessed by my Father, inherit the kingdom' . . . Then he will say to those at his left hand, 'You that are accursed, depart from me into the eternal fire.'" (*Economist*, 12/20/86)

COUNTRY WHERE IT IS FORBIDDEN TO SHOW PEOPLE USING THEIR LEFT HAND IN BOOKS, ADVERTISEMENTS, OR ON TELEVISION: SAUDI ARABIA

In Muslim countries, the left hand was often used for wiping, and is considered unclean. The Koran casts negative inferences on the left hand: on the day of judgment, G-d will present his decree to people in either their right or left hands. Those who receive the decree in their right hand will enter eternal paradise, while those receiving it in the left hand enter hell. (*Journal of Comparative Family Studies*, 4/1/04)

LEFTIES AROUND THE WORLD
U.K.: 11.5%
IVORY COAST: 7.9%
UNITED ARAB EMIRATES: 7.5%
INDIA: 5.8%
CHINA: 5.5%
JAPAN: 4.0%

The different percentages probably have more to do with attempts to persuade or compel lefties to become right-handed than to any differences in the number of actual left-handers in these countries. (McManus, *Right Hand, Left Hand*; *Lab Business Week*, 5/30/04)

PERCENTAGE OF AMERICANS WHO THOUGHT IT WAS A DISADVANTAGE TO BE LEFT-HANDED IN 1948: 24%

Up to the early 1950s, many psychiatrists and educators sought to actively persuade left-handed children to use their right hand. An article that appeared on Nov. 20, 1922, in an Elizabeth, N.J., newspaper (headlined "Left-handedness Cured Among Pupils") reported that "An intensive campaign to cure left-handedness among pupils in local schools here has resulted in a reduction from 250 to 66 since 1919." (Gallup, 9/48; Coren, *The Left-Hander Syndrome*)

WORDS INCLUDED IN THE *AMERICAN HERITAGE COLLEGE DICTIONARY'S* DEFINITION OF "LEFT-HANDED": "AWKWARD" "OF DOUBTFUL SINCERITY" "DUBIOUS"

(*American Heritage Dictionary*)

Sport that cannot be played left-handed: Polo

(*Tampa Tribune*, 6/15/04)

LITERACY

1. ODDS THAT AN AMERICAN IS UNABLE TO NAME A SINGLE MEMBER OF THE SUPREME COURT: 6 IN 10

2. ODDS THAT AN AMERICAN IS ABLE TO NAME THE THREE RICE KRISPIES CHARACTERS: 2 IN 3

3. PERCENTAGE OF YOUNG ADULTS IN THE U.S. WHO CAN'T LOCATE ENGLAND ON A MAP: 69%

4. PERCENTAGE WHO CAN'T LOCATE THE U.S.: 11%

Sources: **1.** For the record, as of November 2004, the Supreme Court justices were William Rehnquist, Antonin Scalia, John Paul Stevens, Clarence Thomas, Ruth Bader Ginsberg, Sandra Day O'Connor, David Souter, Stephen Breyer, and Anthony Kennedy. Only 32% of Americans know that there are nine justices. (*Chicago Sun-Times*, 4/26/02) **2.** Snap, Crackle, and Pop. (*Chicago Sun-Times*, 4/26/02) **3.** From a 2002 survey of Americans aged 18 to 24. Twenty-nine percent couldn't locate the Pacific Ocean, 58% couldn't locate Japan, 65% had no idea where France was, and only 15% could identify Iraq. (*Contra Costa Times*, 10/6/04) **4.** From a survey of Americans aged 18 to 24, half can't point out New York State on a map either. (*Washington Post*, 5/22/03)

NUMBER OF PEOPLE WHO CALLED THE *WASHINGTON POST* AFTER IT PRINTED AN ALLEGEDLY UPSIDE-DOWN PHOTO OF THE EARTH: 1

The person who called? Vice President Al Gore. As the *Post* pointed out in a subsequent article on the VP's complaint, however, there is no upside down in space. (*Washington Post*, 3/16/98)

1. YEAR THE WORD "DIS" FIRST ENTERED THE DICTIONARY: 1995
2. FIRST DICTIONARY APPEARANCE OF "BOOTYLICIOUS": 2003

Sources: **1.** Meaning to disrespect. New words in the 2000 edition of *Webster's College Dictionary*: "my bad" (my mistake), "24/7" (continually, constantly), "jiggy" (wonderful and exciting), and "candy" (something that is excellent, pleasing, or pleasurable). (*Financial Post*, 8/14/96; *Washington Times*, 8/8/00)
2. Meaning sexually attractive, the word was first defined in the 2003 *Oxford English Dictionary*, along with other words like "bitch-slap" ("to deliver a stinging blow to [someone]"), and "bada bing" ("used to emphasize that something will happen effortlessly and predictably"). (*Sacramento Bee*, 8/29/03)

LIKELIHOOD THAT AN ADULT BELIEVES HUMANS AND DINOSAURS ONCE COEXISTED: 1 IN 2

(CBS News, 5/1/02)

PERCENTAGE OF AMERICANS WHO DON'T KNOW WHETHER AN ATOMIC BOMB HAS EVER BEEN DROPPED: 22%

On Aug. 6, 1945, the U.S. dropped an atomic weapon on Hiroshima, Japan, killing 80,000 people. On Aug. 9, 1945, the U.S. dropped a second atomic weapon over Nagasaki, Japan, killing 73,000 people. (*Washington Times*, 5/3/00)

PERCENTAGE OF AMERICANS WHO CAN'T NAME THEIR REPRESENTATIVE IN CONGRESS: 53%

(*San Diego Union-Tribune*, 11/3/02)

ODDS THAT AN AMERICAN DOESN'T KNOW THE EARTH REVOLVES AROUND THE SUN: 1 IN 5

(According to a 1999 Gallup poll, cited in the *Washington Post*, 7/11/99)

LOST AND FOUND

1. AMOUNT OF TIME THE AVERAGE AMERICAN SPENDS EACH DAY SEARCHING FOR LOST THINGS: 4 MINUTES

2. SUNGLASSES HANDED IN TO DISNEY WORLD'S LOST AND FOUND SINCE 1971: 1.5 MILLION

3. NUMBER OF VOTES LOST AND NEVER COUNTED IN THE 2000 PRESIDENTIAL ELECTION: 4 MILLION

Sources: **1.** *American Demographics*, 4/1/03. **2.** Themeparks.com. **3.** *Christian Science Monitor*, 7/17/01.

NUMBER OF RECENT INSTANCES IN WHICH MUSICIANS HAVE LEFT PRICELESS CELLOS IN NEW YORK CITY TAXIS: 2

In May 2001, cellist Lynn Harrell left his $4 million 1673 Stradivarius in the trunk of a taxi. "As soon as I got upstairs, I realized that I had forgotten my cello. My heart dropped," Harrell said. "Not even when I was 7 years old did I ever lose my cello." Harrell located the taxi the following day after tracing it through the receipt from the cab driver. On Oct. 16, 1999, Yo-Yo Ma left his $2.5 million 1733 Montagnana in a cab, which he got back several anxious hours just in time to make it to a performance. "I was in such a rush, I was so exhausted, I'd given a concert at Carnegie Hall last night. I just forgot," Ma said after he got the instrument back.... Not all such instances end so quickly. In August 1967, David Margetts momentarily put a vintage Stradivarius owned by the UCLA Department of Music on his car roof, then drove off without removing it. The violin did not resurface until 1994. (*New York Times*, 10/6/02; *Daily News*, 5/12/04)

AMOUNT OF MONEY THAT FELL OUT OF AN ARMORED CAR IN MIAMI AND WAS TAKEN BY PASSERSBY: $550,000

On Jan. 8, 1997, a Brink's truck overturned on a highway overpass, spilling money onto the streets of Overtown, one of Miami's poorest neighborhoods. Dozens of passersby stuffed money into pockets and shopping bags, calling the loot "pennies from heaven." In a similar episode in Columbus, Ohio, in 1988, only $100,000 out of $2 million was ever returned. (*Time*, 4/4/88; *Miami Herald*, 1/11/97)

Number of pairs of Nike sneakers that fell off a container ship and washed up on the Oregon coast: 40,000

The shoes fell off a ship bound from South Korea to Seattle during an ocean storm. (*Time*, 6/17/91)

Years after Alan Bradley lost his wallet that it was returned to him by Ernie Putt: 30

In 1967, Putt found Bradley's wallet in a Delaware phone booth with $78 inside. For the father of six kids, money was short at the time, so he kept it. As the years went on, he felt increasingly guilty, and in 1997, he located Bradley and mailed him back his wallet with $200 and an apology. The wallet contained a 1967 Elvis Presley calendar, photographs of his then-girlfriend, and a 30-year-old condom. (*Rocky Mountain News*, 3/23/97)

YEARS AFTER *THE COMPLETE HISTORY OF ENGLAND* WAS CHECKED OUT OF THE HARVARD LIBRARY THAT IT WAS RETURNED: 233

"It's remarkable that it's come back," said Roger Stoddard, curator of rare books in the Harvard College Library. No one from Harvard was able to determine where the book had been before it was seen by a rare book dealer in 1997. (*Chicago Sun-Times*, 5/10/97)

NUMBER OF PIECES OF LUGGAGE THAT ARE LOST OR MISDIRECTED EACH DAY BY U.S. AIRLINES: 27,000

Of these, 98% are located by the airlines within five days. When an airline loses your bag, international treaties limit recovery to $1,400 per passenger, no matter how valuable what was inside. (*Boston Globe*, 12/7/03; *Washington Times*, 10/17/01)

LOST IN TRANSLATION

1. NUMBER OF STATES THAT RESTRICTED FOREIGN LANGUAGE STUDY BEFORE SUCH RESTRICTIONS WERE RULED UNCONSTITUTIONAL IN 1923: 22

2. NUMBER OF AMERICAN COLLEGE STUDENTS CURRENTLY TAKING ARABIC: 10,596

3. DATE A NATIONAL SECURITY AGENCY WIRETAP RECORDED COMMENTS MADE IN ARABIC FROM AL-QAEDA OPERATIVES SAYING, "TOMORROW IS ZERO HOUR": SEPT. 10, 2001

4. DATE THOSE COMMENTS WERE ACTUALLY TRANSLATED: SEPT. 12, 2001

Sources: **1.** As Texas's first female governor, Miriam "Ma" Ferguson, purportedly said, "If English was good enough for Jesus Christ, it's good enough for us." (*Government Executive*, 5/1/02) **2.** The American Council on the Teaching of Foreign Languages states that more than 4 million high school students took Spanish in 2000, 1 million studied French, 283,000 took German, 177,000 took Latin, 64,000 studied Italian, and 50,000 studied Japanese. (Knight Ridder/Tribune Business News, 1/27/03; 11/6/03) **3, 4.** Because of the shortage of Arabic translators, 35% of security wiretaps on Arabic speakers went untranslated before 9/11. (*Newsweek*, 10/27/03)

MOVIES:

ENGLISH TITLE:	WHAT IT WAS CALLED IN... :
1. *Dumb and Dumber*	Spain: *Two Stupid, Stupid People*
2. *Annie Hall*	Germany: *The Urban Neurotic*
3. *The Blair Witch Project*	China: *Night in the Cramped Forest*
4. *Texas Chainsaw Massacre*	Greece: *The Schizophrenic Murderer with the Chainsaw*
5. *Austin Powers: The Spy Who Shagged Me*	Spain: *The Spy Who Hugged Me* Iceland: *The Spy Who Nailed Me* Singapore: *The Spy Who Treated Me Nicely*
6. *Boogie Nights*	China: *His Powerful Device Makes Him Famous*
7. *Pretty Woman*	Germany: *I'm Rich but I Like Cheap Prostitutes*
8. *Harry Potter and the Sorcerer's Stone*	England: *Harry Potter and Philosopher's Stone*

Sources: **1–3.** *Daily Record* (Glasgow), 9/17/02. **4.** Fearing a backlash from schizophrenics and kin, distributors in Greece tried to tone down the title of this classic a bit. Though changes could not be made, the film was preceded by a brief reminder that explained that "schizophrenics are not necessarily killers." (Agence France-Presse, 1/29/04) **5.** Countries had problems translating "shag." (*Irish Examiner;* 9/6/99) **6, 7.** *Daily Mail* (London), 9/18/02 **8.** American distributors changed the title from "Philosopher" to "Sorcerer," fearing Americans might not know what a philosopher was. (*Daily Mail* [London], 9/18/02)

PRODUCTS AND SLOGANS:

PRODUCT NAME IN ENGLISH:	TRANSLATION IN . . . :
1. The Buick Lacrosse	Quebec: "Buick Masturbator"
2. Coca-Cola	China: "Bite the wax tadpole"
3. Dristan nasal decongestant	Slavic: "Stomach pain, excessive gas"
4. Kentucky Fried Chicken's "Finger Lickin' Good"	China: "Eat fingers"
5. Pepsi's "Come Alive with the Pepsi Generation"	China: "Bring your ancestors back from the dead"
6. Ford Pinto	Brazil: "Male with Small Genitals"
7. Coors's "Turn It Loose"	Mexico: "Suffer from diarrhea"

Sources: **1.** In French Canadian slang, *lacrosse* means to masturbate. When the car's name was tested out in a focus group of teenage Quebequois, participants giggled, and the name was changed. (*Vancover Sun*, 10/28/03) **2.** After making the discovery that KeKou Cola meant "Bite the wax tadpole," Coca-Cola officials composed a new Chinese equivalent name. The new name meant "Make man mouth happy." (*Communication World*, 10/20/97) **4, 5.** *Newsday*, 6/20/94. **6, 7.** *Mirror*, 4/6/02.

POLITICIANS:

POLITICIAN:	WHAT HE MEANT TO SAY:	WHAT HE ACTUALLY SAID:
1. Dan Quayle	P-o-t-a-t-o	P-o-t-a-t-o-e
2. John F. Kennedy	"I am a citizen of Berlin."	"I am a doughnut."
3. Jimmy Carter	"I hope to have closer relations with Poland."	"I lust for Poles."
4. Ronald Reagan	"I am a citizen of Berlin."	"I am a doughnut."

Sources: **1.** *Christian Science Monitor*, 11/26/99. **2.** Hoping to ease Soviet pressure in Eastern Europe, Pres. John F. Kennedy made a trip to the Berlin Wall in 1963, where he made his famous announcement, "*Ich bin ein Berliner.*" He had meant to say "I am a citizen of Berlin," which would be *Ich bin Berliner*, without *ein. Ein Berliner* is a popular jelly doughnut. (*New York Public Library Book of Popular Americana*) **3.** In a trip to Poland after the fall of the Soviet empire, Carter offered aid to the Poles, saying that he wanted to know their desires, but the translator used the word for "lust" instead. (*Wisconsin State Journal*, 5/12/98) **4.** In 1989, repeating Kennedy's words nearly 30 years later. (*New York Public Library Book of Popular Americana*)

LUCK

1. NUMBER OF AMERICANS AFFLICTED WITH TRISKAIDEKAPHOBIA, OR FEAR OF THE NUMBER 13: 17 MILLION

2. TIME THE ILL-FATED APOLLO 13 SPACE MISSION WAS LAUNCHED FROM THE KENNEDY SPACE CENTER: 2:13 P.M.

3. DATE AND TIME HENRY SEAGRAVE WAS KILLED TRYING TO BREAK THE WORLD WATER SPEED RECORD IN 1930: FRIDAY, JUNE 13, 1:13 P.M.

Sources: **1.** The number 13 became unlucky because of Jesus's Last Supper, attended by 13 people. In the 19th century, Lloyd's of London refused to insure ships sailing on Friday the 13th. The U.S. Navy still will not launch a ship on that date. (*Fort Worth Star-Telegram*, 9/13/02; AP Online, 3/13/98; *Columbian*, 10/13/00) **2.** It was 1:13 P.M. at Mission Control in Houston, or 13:13 military time. Other coincidences: Apollo 13 was launched on Apr. 11, 1970, or 4/11/70—four plus one plus one plus seven plus zero equals 13. No mission since then has been numbered 13. "NASA officially claims that they're not superstitious about 13," says Apollo 13 commander Jim Lovell. "But I dare you to go back in the logs and look at any other manned spacecraft after Apollo 13 that ever had the number 13. There is not another—and most of them were shuttles—there's not one shuttle that had 13." (*Austin American-Statesman*, 4/13/95) **3.** Or 13 minutes past the 13th hour. In 1927, Seagrave became the first person to exceed 200 mph in a car.... Napoleon, Herbert Hoover, and Franklin D. Roosevelt wouldn't allow meals comprising 13 people. Up until the 20th century, the French had the custom of a professional 14th guest who would be called to prevent having 13 diners. (*Washington Post*, 10/13/00; *Atlanta Journal-Constitution*, 3/4/02)

ODDS THAT AN AMERICAN CONSIDERS THEMSELVES SUPERSTITIOUS: 1 IN 4

According to a Gallup poll, the things Americans are most superstitious about are: knocking on wood (27% of Americans say they do it); black cats crossing your path meaning bad luck (13%); and avoiding walking under a ladder (12%). (Gallup, 10/13/00)

1. Percentage of people in Western countries who consider themselves lucky: 12%

2. Percentage who consider themselves unlucky: 9%

The vast majority don't consider themselves to be either, according to a recent British study conducted at the University of Hertfordshire. The same study found that self-called "lucky" people did no better at the lottery than the "unlucky." (*San Diego Union-Tribune*, 5/25/03)

YEAR MURPHY'S LAW WAS FIRST STATED: 1949

The origin of Murphy's Law is ascribed to Capt. Ed Murphy, an engineer who was conducting tests for the air force on how many g-forces a pilot could withstand. After a test pilot had completed a particularly harrowing ride in a primitive rocket, it was discovered that the devices measuring g-forces had not been attached properly, and thus that the entire experiment would have to be repeated. In a fit of exasperation Murphy remarked, "If there's more than one way to do a job and one of those ways will end in disaster, then somebody will do it that way." At a press conference a few weeks later, the test pilot referred to "Ed Murphy's Law," which he said was "If something can go wrong, it will." (*People*, 1/31/83)

NUMBER CONSIDERED THE MOST UNLUCKY IN ITALY: 17

High-rises in Palermo, Sicily, have no 17th floor. Italians (particularly Sicilians) often leave out 17 when counting. (*Washington Post*, 6/11/00; *USA Today*, 1/28/00)

UNLUCKY NUMBERS IN OTHER COUNTRIES:
4 (CHINA, JAPAN, KOREA)
9 (JAPAN)

The word for four sounds like the word for death in the Chinese, Japanese, and Korean languages, and therefore the custom is to invite guests in parties or multiples of five. In China, many buildings have a 13th floor but not a fourth. The Chinese air force does not assign the number 4 to planes, and *The Simpsons* was a flop because the characters have only four fingers. In Japan, nine, pronounced "ku," signifies pain and suffering. (*International Herald Tribune*, 3/28/98; *Atlanta Journal-Constitution*, 3/4/02)

INCREASE IN THE DEATH RATE OF CHINESE AND JAPANESE AMERICANS ON THE FOURTH DAY OF EVERY MONTH: 7%

Researchers believe that the increased death risk is linked to the psychological stress brought about by fear of the number 4 itself. (*Atlanta Journal-Constitution*, 3/4/02; *Chemistry and Industry*, 2/4/02

ORIGINS OF POPULAR SUPERSTITIONS:

Crossing one's fingers:

Originated as a way for Christians to secretly make the sign of the cross when Christianity was still an underground religion.

(Fenton, *Book of Spells*)

Carrying a rabbit's foot:

There are two explanations for why these are believed lucky. First, because rabbits are allegedly born with their eyes open, they can see evil and ward it off and, second, because rabbits live underground, they are presumed to have good relations with the spirits believed to lurk therein.

(*Good Housekeeping*, 3/98)

Walking under a ladder:

May have taken rise from the English tradition of making a condemned man walk under a ladder before being hanged at the gallows. Others look as far back as ancient Egypt, where great power was accorded to the shape of a pyramid; walking through a triangle was said to ruin that power. Still others attribute it to the belief that a ladder was leaning against the cross at the time of Jesus's Crucifixion.

(*Daily Mail*, 3/25/03; *Western Mail*, 3/7/03)

NUMBER OF FORTUNE-TELLERS SADDAM HUSSEIN CONSULTED WITH: 7

According to Saddam's chief wizard, throughout his tenure Saddam frequently consulted with magicians and sorcerers from Iraq, Turkey, India, and Morocco. (AP, 8/14/03)

Number of times Pasquale Benenati has won the California Lottery jackpot: 5

Benenati has taken home five California lottery jackpots totaling $5.18 million. Benenati says his good luck comes from "faith in myself." (Salon.com, 11/22/99)

NUMBER OF TIMES ROY SULLIVAN WAS STRUCK BY LIGHTNING: 7

A park ranger in Virginia, Sullivan was struck by lightning seven times between 1942 and 1977. Sullivan survived each, only to commit suicide in 1983, reportedly after being dumped by a woman. (*Los Angeles Times*, 4/27/04; *Daily Mail*, 4/7/04, 7/7/04)

SUPERSTITIOUS ATHLETES:

Art (Tappy) Larsen:

Winner of the U.S. tennis title in 1950, Larsen got his nickname based on his practice of tapping everything on the court (including his opponent) a set number of times based on the first number that came into his head when he woke up.

(*Sports Illustrated*, 2/8/88)

Wade Boggs:

Perhaps the most superstitious baseball player of all time, among the future Hall of Famer's routines was fielding exactly 150 ground balls during fielding practice before a game, taking batting practice at 5:17 A.M. before night games, and doing wind sprints at 7:17 A.M., drawing the Hebrew word *chai* (life) each time he entered the batting box, and eating only chicken before games.

(*Albany Times Union*, 9/5/04)

Kevin Greene:

Steelers linebacker Greene would meet his wife 30 minutes before kickoff at her usual seat at the 30-yard line for her to give him a quick beating—fists only—and her usual fight talk: "Rack 'em, sack 'em, crack 'em, frack 'em!" The ritual was performed before every home game from 1992 to 1996.

(*Sporting News*, 9/16/96)

RECORD OF THE PHILADELPHIA FLYERS FROM 1969 TO 2004 WHEN THEY PLAY KATE SMITH'S "GOD BLESS AMERICA" BEFORE GAMES: 67 WINS, 17 LOSSES, 3 TIES

On Dec. 11, 1969, the song was played for the first time at a Flyers home game, a 6–3 victory over the Maple Leafs. The singer and the song became the team's good-luck charm, and a recording is often played when the Flyers face a must-win. (*St. Petersburg Times*, 5/7/04)

MAIL

1. **PIECES OF MAIL SENT ANNUALLY AROUND THE WORLD: 425 BILLION**
2. **ANNUAL NUMBER OF LETTERS SENT PER PERSON GLOBALLY: 71**
3. **ANNUAL NUMBER OF LETTERS SENT PER PERSON IN THE U.S.: 660**
4. **ANNUAL NUMBER OF LETTERS SENT PER RESIDENT OF VATICAN CITY: 7,200**

Sources: **1.** CNN, 3/15/04. **2.** *Moscow Times*, 4/1/02. **3.** *New York Times*, 6/27/04. **4.** Because of the sorry state of the Italian postal system, Italians regularly go into Vatican City to send letters. As a result of this and the constant influx of tourists, the Vatican sends out more mail per individual resident than any other place in the world. (*New York Times*, 6/27/04)

America's first stamp: 1847

Before stamps were introduced, mailing a letter cost about 25¢ at a time when the average salary was $1 a day. In 1847, the post office introduced a 5¢ stamp featuring Benjamin Franklin and a 10¢ stamp with George Washington. A 5¢ letter could be mailed 300 miles; 10¢ got you across the U.S. (*New York Times*, 10/14/03)

FIRST STREET CORNER MAILBOX: 1852

Once stamps allowed postage to be paid beforehand, street corner mailboxes became possible, and at the suggestion of a novelist and postal employee named Anthony Trollope, the first four were installed on the Isle of Jersey on November 23, 1852. (*Times* [London], 10/24/02)

1. PIECES OF JUNK MAIL THE AVERAGE AMERICAN RECEIVES ANNUALLY: 572

2. PERCENTAGE OF JUNK MAIL THAT IS THROWN OUT WITHOUT BEING READ: 44%

Sources: **1.** *USA Today*, 10/15/03. **2.** *Washington Post*, 2/17/00.

1. **Number of post offices in the U.S.:** 38,000
2. **Number of post offices in India:** 154,000

Sources: **1.** U.S. Postal Service. **2.** India has the world's largest postal system, with 154,000 post offices and 60,000 postmen delivering 53 million pieces of mail each day. China has the second largest postal service, with 57,000 post offices. (*Economic Times* [India], 12/6/02)

PEOPLE SENT THROUGH THE MAIL: 2

On Feb. 19, 1914, the parents of 5-year-old May Pierstorff paid 50¢ to have her mailed from Grangeville to Lewiston, Idaho, to avoid the higher train fare. And the *Chicago Tribune* reports that a 28-year-old midget once mailed himself from New York to L.A., paying $68.15 in postage. (AP, 10/11/00; *Chicago Tribune*, 11/17/88)

LARGEST OBJECT EVER SENT THROUGH THE MAIL: A BANK BUILDING

In 1916, a merchant named W. H. Coltharp mailed an entire bank building in individual pieces from Salt Lake City to Vernal, Utah. At the time, there was no road between the two cities, and Coltharp figured he'd save money by mailing all 80,000 of the building's bricks over the 427-mile route. That's 40 tons of bank. Shortly after, the post office put out an advisory saying that "it is not the intent of the U.S. Postal Service that buildings be shipped through the mail," and banned the practice. (*Los Angeles Times*, 9/13/99)

LATE-ARRIVING MAIL:

58 YEARS: Bearing a 3¢ stamp and a Feb. 17, 1936, postmark, the letter was from a grandmother in Weirton, Penn., promising to come see her newborn grandchildren in West Virginia. The letter was delivered in 1994.

(*Philadelphia Inquirer*, 12/5/94)

94 YEARS: Postmarked Feb. 6, 1908, a black-and-white postcard addressed to Fanny Myers of Jersey Shore, Penn., asked her to send a cashmere sweater to her sister. On Oct. 22, 2001, the postcard was found in a batch of letters to be delivered at the Jersey Shore Post Office.

(*Buffalo News*, 11/11/01)

66 YEARS: A Valentine card posted in 1932 reached a young couple living in the former addressee's house in 1998. Coincidentally, they were to be married the next day.

(Press Association, 4/11/98)

MARRIAGE AND DIVORCE

1. AGE OF THE AVERAGE AMERICAN MAN WHEN HE FIRST GETS MARRIED: 26.8

2. AGE OF THE AVERAGE WOMAN IN KEBBI STATE, NIGERIA, WHEN SHE GETS MARRIED: 11

3. YEAR IRAN RAISED THE LEGAL AGE FOR GIRLS TO GET MARRIED FROM 9 TO 13: 2002

Sources: **1.** The average American woman first ties the knot at 25.1 years, French women at 28, Indians at 19, and Nigerians at 17. (AP, 2/6/02; Salon.com, 10/13/03; Press Trust of India, 5/16/02) **2.** Other places where child marriages are rampant: 40% of Nepalese women marry before they are 15; 17% of the girls in the Indian state of Rajasthan are married before the age of 10, and 3% before the age of 5. Indeed, though child marriage is illegal in India, it is not unheard of for women in certain rural areas to be mothers at 13, grandmothers in their 20s, and great-grandmothers in their late 30s or early 40s. (*U.S. News and World Report*, 3/19/01; *Times Literary Supplement* [London], 11/16/01) **3.** *Deseret Morning News*, 6/24/02.

1. Number of spouses women are permitted under Islamic law: 1
2. Number of spouses Islamic law permits men: 4

(*Time*, 12/3/01)

1. AVERAGE DURATION OF AN AMERICAN MARRIAGE: 7.2 YEARS

2. YEAR FOLLOWING MARRIAGE IN WHICH MOST DIVORCES OCCUR: FOURTH

3. STATE WITH THE HIGHEST DIVORCE RATE IN AMERICA: NEVADA

4. STATE WITH THE LOWEST DIVORCE RATE: MASSACHUSETTS

5. COUNTRIES WHERE DIVORCE IS ILLEGAL: MALTA AND THE PHILIPPINES

Sources: **1.** Fifty percent of first marriages and 60% of second marriages end in divorce. (*National Review*, 10/27/03; *Los Angeles Times*, 2/9/03) **2.** In a study of divorces around the world, anthropologist Helen Fisher concluded that human beings are subject to a "four year itch"—a biological need to stray that causes divorces worldwide to peak around the fourth year of marriage (and the third year in the U.S.). (ABC, 11/5/04) **3.** Followed by Arkansas. (*Hartford Courant*, 2/22/04) **4.** Actually, according to the National Center for Health Statistics, the District of Columbia had the lowest divorce rate of any place in the United States as of 2001. (*Hartford Courant*, 2/22/04) **5.** Ireland legalized divorce in 1997, and Chile in 2004. (*Washington Post*, 3/30/04)

SHORTEST CELEBRITY MARRIAGES:

RUDOLF VALENTINO AND JEAN ACKER: 6 HOURS

Wed in Hollywood on the evening of Nov. 5, 1919, the marriage unofficially ended when Acker (a lesbian) would not allow the Great Lover into the honeymoon suite, though the official breakup occurred later. (*Toronto Star*, 1/5/04)

ROBIN GIVENS AND SVETOZAR MARINKOVIC: 1 DAY

Givens married and separated from her tennis instructor on the same day, Aug. 22, 1997. Marinkovic told reporters that the couple decided things were wrong after 7 minutes. (*Los Angeles Times*, 7/10/03)

BRITNEY SPEARS AND JASON ALEXANDER: 55 HOURS

Spears and her childhood friend Jason Alexander tied the knot at the Little White Wedding Chapel in Las Vegas. The marriage was over 2 days and 7 hours later because, according to her lawyer, Spears "lacked understanding for her actions." (Times Newspapers, 1/10/04)

DENNIS HOPPER AND MICHELLE PHILLIPS: 8 DAYS

Said Hopper about his short-lived marriage to the singer for the Mamas and the Papas: "Seven of those days were pretty good. The eighth day was the bad one." (*Irish Times*, 1/10/04)

NUMBER OF DIVORCED PRESIDENTS: 1 (RONALD REAGAN)

Reagan married Jane Wyman on Jan. 24, 1940, and divorced her on July 19, 1949, long before he got to the White House. (*Atlanta Journal-Constitution*, 8/21/98)

1. Percentage of men who've cheated on their wives: 22%

2. Percentage of women who've cheated on their husbands: 15%

3. Odds that a married man would cheat with a beautiful woman if he knew he wouldn't get caught: 4 in 10

4. States in which adultery is still a crime: 32

Sources: **1, 2.** National Opinion Research Center, 2002. **3.** *Men's Health*, 9/1/01. **4.** In October 2003, John Raymond Bushey was convicted of adultery in Virginia for having sex outside of marriage. After he paid a $125 fine and performed community service, Bushey appealed the conviction, and the charges were eventually dropped. (*Richmond Times-Dispatch*, 8/27/04)

MASCOTS

1. STARTING MASCOT SALARY: $25,000

2. HIGHEST REPORTED MASCOT SALARY: $150,000

3. AVERAGE WEIGHT OF A MASCOT'S COSTUME: 21 POUNDS

4. PERCENTAGE OF MASCOTS WHO SUFFER FROM CHRONIC LOWER BACK PAIN: 45%

5. MASCOTS WITH THE HIGHEST RATE OF INJURY: NBA TEAM MASCOTS

Sources: **1.** CNNMoney.com, 3/16/04. **2.** The highest paid mascot reportedly is the Phoenix Suns Gorilla, who pioneered a high-flying aerial routine that has since spawned many imitators. (*Deseret Morning News*, 6/11/97) **3.** Based on a 2001 study of 49 NBA, NFL, and major league baseball mascots conducted by Dr. Edward McFarland, director of sports medicine and shoulder surgery at Johns Hopkins. The study found that mascots lose an average 3.8 pounds per game. (*Washington Times*, 6/19/02) **4.** *Washington Times*, 6/19/02. **5.** NBA mascots are generally considered the most daring in professional sports, resulting in more injuries. In April 2001, the New Jersey Nets mascot, Sly the Silver Fox, blew out his knee after participating in a limbo contest during a time-out. And Bear, the mascot for the Utah Jazz, suffered a similar fate after attempting to ski down the stairs at a Jazz home game. "Goes with the territory," he said after the mishap. (*New York Times*, 3/17/96)

First mascot in any sport: Yale Bulldog

In 1892, a Yale student purchased a smoke-sooted bulldog for $5 from a New Haven blacksmith, giving him the name "Handsome Dan." The dog accompanied his owner to school sporting events, barking at Yale's successes and menacing the school's opponents. As the *Hartford Courant* wrote when Dan died in 1898: "He was always taken to games on a leash, and for years the Harvard football team owed its continued existence to the fact that the rope held." So attached were Yalies to their historic mascot that they had him stuffed and placed in a trophy case in the school gym, where he remains to this day. (*Sports Illustrated*, 10/18/91)

FIRST PROFESSIONAL SPORTS MASCOT: SAN DIEGO PADRES CHICKEN (1974)

The Chicken's slapstick antics and gentle mockery of umpires, fans, and members of the opposing team led to income from appearances and promotional endorsements which approached $1 million annually. According to Ted Giannoulas, the original Chicken, the bird's most memorable moment came on June 29, 1979, when, after being delivered to the infield in an armored truck, the Chicken emerged to thunderous cheers out of a giant Styrofoam egg. (*National Post*, 1/16/04; *Los Angeles Times*, 8/18/96)

LONGEST MASCOT KIDNAPPING: 41 DAYS

In 1972, army cadets (aided by intelligence from a West Point student whose father was a naval officer) kidnapped the navy goat and spirited it off to New York. For 41 days, the goat was moved from house to house across New York State, eluding the efforts of midshipmen to locate her. To compound the insult, army cadets took out a full-page ad in the *New York Times*, which (under a picture of the missing goat) asked: "HEY NAVY! Do you know where your 'kid' is today? The Army does." (*Sports Illustrated*, 10/18/91)

FIRST MASCOT TO BE THROWN OUT OF A BASEBALL GAME: PITTSBURGH PIRATE PARROT (MAY 1987)

In May 1987, the Pittsburgh Pirate Parrot drew a one-game suspension after throwing a plastic ball at umpire Fred Brocklander following a controversial call. "I shouldn't have done it," the Parrot said later. "It was dumb." (*New York Times*, 5/1/87)

INSTANCES WHERE BASEBALL MANAGERS DISGUISED THEMSELVES AS MASCOTS AFTER BEING EJECTED BY UMPIRES: 2

According to the *Encyclopedia of Minor League Baseball*, on June 29, 1989, Mal Fichman, the manager for Boise, reappeared on the field in the Boise Hawks mascot suit after being thrown out of a game by the umpires, led the fans in cheers, and continued to manage the team. And in 1984 Ed Nottle, manager of the Tacoma Tigers, donned a Tiger uniform after being ejected by umpires, then was thrown out again after he was revealed. (*Los Angeles Times*, 6/24/97; *St. Louis Post-Dispatch*, 5/22/89)

RECENT ALTERCATIONS BETWEEN MASCOTS:

February 1995: The Tree, of Stanford University, and Oski the Bear, of the University of California, came to blows after Oski gestured mockingly to the Stanford student section. The two mascots had to be pulled apart by police.

March 2003: During a basketball game between Oregon and Utah, the Oregon Duck and Utah Red-Tailed Hawk got into a fight after the Hawk knocked the Duck's head off, a mascot no-no. Afterward, the Hawk apologized. "Sorry, dude," news sources reported the Hawk telling the Duck later. "I swear to God I didn't mean to take it off."

(*Seattle Post-Intelligencer*, 3/22/03)

MEDICINE

1. AVERAGE ANNUAL DOCTOR'S SALARY: $187,000

2. AVERAGE SALARY OF A HOSPITAL CHIEF EXECUTIVE: $268,400

3. RANK OF DOCTORS IN A SURVEY OF THE MOST PRESTIGIOUS PROFESSIONS: FIRST

4. RANK OF DOCTORS IN A STUDY OF HANDWRITING LEGIBILITY: LAST

Source: **1.** Specialists earn more ($219,000 on average), while primary care physicians earn less ($138,000). Meanwhile, doctors in Romania earn $200 a month, in Afghanistan about $80 a month, in Soviet Georgia about $50 a month, and in Cuba about $20 per month. (*Medical Economics,* 5/9/03; *New Statesman,* 10/13/03; *MacLean's,* 12/22/03; *Los Angeles Times,* 10/19/01) **2.** In the late 1990s, the CEOs of the seven largest for-profit HMOs each received an average of $7.9 million in compensation. (*Boston Globe,* 9/28/03) **3.** Bringing up the rear were businessmen, bankers, and accountants, with only 15% rating these professions as "highly prestigious." (Harris poll, 9/00) **4.** According to the September 1998 *British Medical Journal,* "the study suggests that doctors, even when asked to be as neat as possible, produce writing that is worse than that of other professions." A 1987 American Medical Association study found that 1 in 6 doctors has handwriting no one can read. (*Pittsburgh Post-Gazette,* 11/19/02)

1. TREATMENT FOR ASTHMA, ACCORDING TO AN 1899 MEDICAL REFERENCE BOOK: CIGARETTES

2. TREATMENT FOR ACNE: ARSENIC

The 1899 *Merck Manual* also prescribed arsenic as a treatment for baldness, sucking an orange to treat alcoholism, coffee for insomnia, asparagus for rabies, tobacco for bronchitis and nymphomania, mercury for malaria, turpentine oil for impotence, morphine suppositories for vomiting during pregnancy, formaldehyde for a cold, and 139 different treatments for diarrhea. (*Time,* 5/3/99)

1. Average time a primary doctor spends with each patient, according to a recent study: 21 minutes

2. Average time a doctor spends with each patient, according to a different recent study: 6 minutes

The first of these two wildly divergent studies comes from the *Journal of the American Medical Association,* which found that the average male physician spends 21 minutes with each patient while the average female physician spends 23 minutes. The second study, conducted at Vanderbilt Medical School, found that the average primary physician sees 38 patients a day for an average of 6 minutes apiece. Incidentally, studies indicate that the average doctor gives patients only 23 seconds to explain what's wrong before they interrupt. (*Chicago Tribune,* 8/21/02; *Biotech Week,* 1/21/04; *New York Times,* 6/1/04)

NUMBER OF INTERNET HITS FOR "DOCTOR JOKES": 68,800

According to British scientists, this gem was found to be the *second funniest joke* in England (we're not kidding): "A man goes to the doctor and says, 'Doctor, there's a piece of lettuce sticking out of my bottom.' The doctor asks him to drop his trousers and examines him. The man asks, 'Is it serious, doctor?' The doctor replies, 'I'm sorry to tell you but this is just the tip of the iceberg.'" (*New York Times*, 1/27/02)

WORDS ATTRIBUTED TO BUT NOT FOUND IN THE HIPPOCRATIC OATH: "FIRST, DO NO HARM"

While the oath says nothing about "doing no harm," it does require doctors to share their salary with their medical school teachers and the teachers' offspring, and to refrain from sexual relations with slaves. (*Science*, 10/29/99)

ANNUAL NUMBER OF TIMES SURGICAL EQUIPMENT IS ACCIDENTALLY LEFT INSIDE A PATIENT'S BODY AFTER SURGERY: 1,500

A study published in the *New England Journal of Medicine* found that larger-bodied patients were more likely to have things left in them. Fifty-four percent of the surgical tools were left in the abdomen or pelvis, 22% in vaginas, 7% in the chest, and the rest elsewhere. (*Boston Globe*, 1/16/03)

RECENT INSTANCES OF SURGICAL INSTRUMENTS LEFT INSIDE PATIENTS' BODIES:

Sydney, Australia: Doctors left a 6.7-inch pair of scissors in a patient's body after colon surgery until X-ray discovered them one year later.

Detroit, Mich.: Doctors performing surgery on a patient discovered a medical instrument that withdraws fluid left during surgery 2 years earlier.

Seattle, Wash.: Surgeons removing a tumor accidentally left a 13 inch-long, 2-inch-wide instrument in the patient's body.

Boston, Mass.: Surgeons accidentally left five sponges inside a patient's body following gastric bypass surgery.

(*Newsday*, 4/20/4; AP, 6/12/02; *San Antonio Express-News*, 12/6/01; *Patriot Ledger*, 1/15/04)

MEMORY

1. MAXIMUM NUMBER OF UNRELATED NUMBERS THE AVERAGE PERSON CAN STORE IN SHORT-TERM MEMORY: 7

2. AMOUNT OF TIME SHORT-TERM MEMORY RETAINS THIS INFORMATION: 15 TO 30 SECONDS

3. EASIEST NUMBER TO REMEMBER: 8

Sources: **1.** In 1956, a psychologist named George Miller wrote a landmark paper called "The Magical Number Seven, Plus or Minus Two." In it, Miller stated that the average person can store no more than seven unrelated things in short-term memory (give or take two). Miller's conclusion was similar to the results of research conducted by AT&T, which is why basic phone numbers are seven numbers (*Chicago Tribune*, 6/28/98) **2.** Humans have three types of memory: immediate, short-term, and long-term. Immediate memory retains information for just a second or two—long enough to accomplish tasks such as understanding what someone talking to you is saying, or for typists to transfer a word they read to their fingertips. Long-term memories, in contrast, are believed to be retained forever, although they can't always be retrieved. (Hunt's *Story of Psychology*) **3.** This according to Thomas Landauer of the Institute of Cognitive Research at the University of Colorado. Landauer was involved in the research leading to the decision to employ an "888" toll-free prefix for phone numbers after the "800" prefix was exhausted. (*Chicago Tribune*, 6/28/98)

1. PERCENTAGE OF NEWLY LEARNED MATERIAL THAT IS FORGOTTEN IMMEDIATELY: 56%

2. AMOUNT THAT IS FORGOTTEN WITHIN A DAY: 66%

3. AMOUNT THAT IS FORGOTTEN WITHIN A MONTH: 80%

According to 19th-century German psychologist Hermann Ebbinghaus, who developed what is now known as the Ebbinghaus Curve of Forgetting. (*Seattle Times*, 7/7/00)

PERCENTAGE BY WHICH CHEWING GUM REPORTEDLY IMPROVES YOUR MEMORY: 35%

Though researchers aren't sure why, test groups that chewed gum recalled more and performed better on exams than control groups that didn't chew. One theory is that chewing releases insulin, a natural chemical that stimulates the part of the brain related to memory. (*Washington Times*, 3/15/02)

AVERAGE AMOUNT OF MEMORIZATION ABILITY LOST AFTER AGE 55: 1/10 OF A WORD PER YEAR

The results were gleaned from a test group of people over 55 who were given a list of 20 words to memorize. As the subjects aged over 16 years, they exhibited an average memory loss rate of about 1/10 of a word per year. (*Boston Globe*, 12/22/03)

FIVE ITEMS PEOPLE MOST OFTEN FORGET TO PACK WHEN GOING ON VACATION:

1. TOOTHBRUSH (FORGOTTEN 42% OF THE TIME)
2. UNDERWEAR (22%)
3. FILM (11%)
4. SUNSCREEN (11%)
5. CONTRACEPTIVES (6%)

(Study conducted for Celebrity Cruises, cited in the *Houston Chronicle*, 5/9/04)

ONE WAY MEDIEVAL COMMUNITIES SOUGHT TO ENSURE THAT IMPORTANT EVENTS WERE REMEMBERED: BY THROWING A CHILD INTO A RIVER

In his book *Memory and Emotion*, James McGaugh writes: "in medieval times, before writing was used to keep historical records, a young child was sometimes chosen to observe important proceedings carefully, then thrown into a river. In this way, it was said, the memory of the event would be impressed on the child and the record of the event maintained for the child's lifetime." (*Guardian*, 8/9/03)

MOST UNUSUAL RECENT CASE OF AMNESIA:

Krickitt Carpenter: Less than 10 weeks after getting married in September 1993, Carpenter was badly injured in a car accident that left her comatose for 21 days. Though she survived, the trauma erased all memories of the previous 18 months, including of the man she had courted and married. So she and her husband began dating, and eventually fell in love all over again. They were remarried on May 25, 1996.

(*People*, 6/24/96)

POPULAR MNEMONICS:

"My Very Educated Mother Just Served Us Nine Pizzas"
correlates to the sequence of the nine planets of our solar system:
Mercury, Venus, Earth, Mars, Jupiter, Saturn, Uranus, Neptune, and Pluto

(Record, 3/11/01)

"Marilyn Monroe Never Vomits Royal Crown"
the states in New England
(Maine, Massachusetts, New Hampshire, Vermont, Rhode Island, and Connecticut)

(*Austin American-Statesman*, 9/9/01)

MICHAEL JACKSON

1. **HEIGHT AND WEIGHT, ACCORDING TO A 2003 MUG SHOT:** 5'11" 120 POUNDS
2. **ESTIMATED CURRENT NET WORTH:** $350 MILLION
3. **ESTIMATED NET WORTH AT THE HEIGHT OF HIS CAREER:** $750 MILLION
4. **AMOUNT JACKSON ALLEGEDLY SPENDS PER MONTH:** $2 MILLION

Sources: **1.** MSNBC, 11/20/03. **2.** *USA Today*, 4/28/04. **3.** *Newsweek*, 12/1/03. **4.** *USA Today*, 4/28/04.

AMOUNT OF MONEY RAISED FOR AFRICAN HUNGER RELIEF BY THE SONG "WE ARE THE WORLD," WRITTEN BY JACKSON: $60 MILLION

The song—cowritten with Lionel Richie—was the #1 single for 4 weeks in 1985. On April 5, 1985 (Good Friday), at 10:50 A.M. EST, some 6,000 to 8,000 radio stations worldwide played the song simultaneously, including some 75–90% of the radio stations in the U.S. Even President Reagan participated, with the song being broadcast to him aboard a cross-country flight on Air Force One. (*Chicago Tribune*, 4/16/85; *Orlando Sentinel*, 4/17/90)

AMOUNT OF MONEY JACKSON ALLEGEDLY PAID A WITCH DOCTOR IN 2000 TO PUT A CURSE ON STEVEN SPIELBERG AND DAVID GEFFEN: $150,000

According to an April 2003 article in *Vanity Fair*, Jackson was reportedly angry at Spielberg for failing to cast him in the role of Peter Pan in *Hook*. The article reported that some 42 cows were sacrificed for the ceremony. (*Vanity Fair*, 4/03)

1. Size of Jackson's Neverland estate: 2,700 acres
2. Number of Ferris wheels at Neverland: 3
3. Amount Neverland costs monthly to maintain: $333,000

Sources: **1.** The property includes a theme park with 16 rides and a zoo. (*People*, 12/8/03) **2.** Half of the amusement rides at Jackson's complex were constructed without the proper permits or permission, sparking a 2003 lawsuit centered on zoning violations. (*Columbus Dispatch*, 11/25/03) **3.** *New York Times*, 11/20/03.

1. NUMBER OF PLASTIC SURGERY OPERATIONS JACKSON ADMITS TO UNDERGOING: 2

2. ACTUAL NUMBER OF PLASTIC SURGERY PROCEDURES JACKSON HAS REPORTEDLY UNDERGONE: ABOUT 50

The second figure comes from Dr. Wallace Goodstein, a Beverly Hills plastic surgeon who from 1991 to 1993 shared a practice with Jackson's primary specialist, and who gave the information to NBC News. (*Chicago Tribune*, 2/17/03)

Year Jackson reportedly sought a knighthood for his work with little children: 1995

According to news reports, in 1995, Jackson's manager Sandy Gallin contacted Sir Robin Renwick, the British ambassador to the U.S., and requested a knighting for Jackson's work with kids. Jackson was informed that knights do not usually nominate themselves. (*Entertainment Weekly*, July 14, 1995; *Newsday*, 6/23/95)

JACKSON'S EARNINGS PER RECORD (IN MILLIONS):

THRILLER (1982): $115
BAD (1987): $58
DANGEROUS (1992): $58
OFF THE WALL (1979): $37
HISTORY (1995): $35
INVINCIBLE (2001): $15
BLOOD ON THE DANCE FLOOR (1997): $10

(*Forbes*, All Music Guide, 2002)

NUMBER OF LAWSUITS JACKSON HAS BEEN INVOLVED IN OVER THE COURSE OF HIS CAREER: 1,500

His lawyer Brian Oxman says: "He doesn't like lawsuits, and it makes him ill to have to cope with litigation that people seem to heap on him. . . . This is the kind of life that Michael leads. No one wants to be reasonable. Everyone wants to be crazy. He is tired of being sued." (*Guardian*, 5/28/03)

MONEY

1. NUMBER OF MILLIONAIRES IN AMERICA: 2.27 MILLION
2. NUMBER OF MILLIONAIRES IN THE WORLD: 7.7 MILLION
3. NUMBER OF BILLIONAIRES IN THE WORLD: 691
4. NUMBER OF COUNTRIES WHOSE GDP IS LOWER THAN BILL GATES'S NET WORTH: 132

Sources: **1.** If only liquid investable assets are measured, then there are 2.27 million millionaires in the U.S. If the value of homes is taken into account, the number of millionaires jumps as high as 7.78 million. In an effort to reclaim the exclusivity of the title, terms like pentamillion-aire (for people worth more than $5 million) and decamillionaire ($10 million plus) have come into usage amongst the nation's elite. There are about 600,000 pentamillionaires in America. (CBS, 5/13/04 , *Funds International*, 6/30/04) **2.** *Financial Times* [London], 7/7/04. **3.** The total net worth of all the world's billionaires was estimated to be $2.2 trillion dollars in 2005. (*Forbes*, 3/10/05) **4.** Sitting between Ukraine (55) and Morrocco (56) in the World Bank's gross domestic product rankings of the world's 192 countries, Gates's own net worth—$46.5 billion—makes him richer than 132 of the world's nations. Though a far cry from the U.S. GDP of $10.8 trillion, Gates could afford to give $7.50 to every person in the world. (*Forbes*; World Bank)

AVERAGE SAT SCORE OF AN AMERICAN MILLIONAIRE: 1190

According to a study involving 1,300 American millionaires, the average millionaire lives in a $300,000 house, drives a 4-year-old American car, is 54 years old, lives in an upper-middle-class neighborhood, and has never spent more than $38 on a haircut. (Stanley, *The Millionaire Next Door*)

FIRST USE OF THE TERM "MILLIONAIRE": 1719

First used to describe investors who bought public shares in the Mississippi Company, which had the exclusive right to engage in trade between France and its Louisiana colonies. Before the boom went bust, shares in the Mississippi Company went from 500 to 10,000 livres in about 5 months, making paper millionaires out of thousands of individuals who flocked to Paris to buy the shares. The first use of the term in print was in an 1826 novel called *Vivian Grey* by Benjamin Disraeli, Britain's future prime minister. (*Slate*, 6/3/02; *Art Journal*, 7/31/00)

1. First millionaire: John Law
2. First American millionaire: Pierre Lorillard

Sources: **1.** Law was the head of the Mississippi Company, which had the exclusive right to trade between France and its American colonies in the early 18th century. At the height of his wealth, he owned 15 French country estates, much of the city of Paris, most of what is now Arkansas, and millions upon millions in cash. However, he died penniless after investors panicked and tried to sell shares of his company en masse, rendering them worthless. (*Daily Mail*, 11/9/99) **2.** In 1843, the tobacco magnate was the first person identified in writing as a millionaire. (*Chattanooga Times Free Press*, 5/25/95; 4/10/04)

First billionaire: John D. Rockefeller

In 1863, Rockefeller began his business career as an accounting clerk in Cleveland. In 1863, he invested much of his saved earnings in oil as just "a little side issue." That investment eventually became Standard Oil, and Rockefeller was worth $900 million in 1913, which amounted to 1/44th of America's gross national product at the time. Indeed, in relative terms, Rockefeller is the richest American of all time. (*Forbes*, 11/12/99; *Inc.*, 5/99)

CITY WITH THE HIGHEST PERCENTAGE OF MILLIONAIRES IN AMERICA: SAN FRANCISCO

San Francisco has 31,000 millionaires, representing about 4.4% of its households. (Claritas, in *St. Louis Business Journal*, 7/9/04)

CITY WITH THE MOST BILLIONAIRES: NEW YORK

New York has 34, with Moscow a surprise runner up with 20 billionaires. (*Forbes*, 3/10/05)

NUMBER OF MILLIONAIRES AROUND THE WORLD:

ENGLAND: 383,000
CHINA: 236,000
RUSSIA: 84,000
INDIA: 61,000
ISRAEL: 6,000
BULGARIA: 60

(Merrill Lynch/Cap Gemini World Wealth Report; UPI, 6/22/04)

1. Total U.S. paper currency circulating around the globe: $733 billion

2. Odds that a particular bill is counterfeit: 1 in 10,000

Sources: **1.** Of that, two-thirds are in circulation overseas: $500 billion of that is in $100 bills, $105 billion in twenties, and almost $8 billion in ones. (8/8/04 conversation with U.S. Department of Treasury) **2.** *Chicago Sun-Times*, 10/8/03.

WORLD'S WEALTHIEST WOMAN: ALICE WALTON

Worth $18 billion, this Wal-Mart heiress at 56 ranks as the world's wealthiest woman. Generally reported to be an affable and modest billionaire, Walton has nonetheless landed herself in several auto accidents, the most recent of which while drunk. She took the case to court and lost, an officer allegedly reporting that she demanded of him, "Do you know who I am? Do you know my last name?" (*USA Today*, 5/10/02)

1. NUMBER OF BILLIONAIRES WHO ARE SELF-MADE: 388

2. NUMBER OF BILLIONAIRES WHO WERE HIGH SCHOOL DROPOUTS: 18

Sources: **1.** One of the most recent additions to *Forbes*'s billionaire ranking is J. K. Rowling, whose induction distinguishes her as the first billionaire novelist. In only a few years, Rowling's Harry Potter series has seen her go from a penniless single mother to her present status. (Agence France-Presse, 3/10/05) **2.** Including Richard Branson, head of Virgin Airways; venture capitalist Kirk Kerkorian; and David Murdock, head of Dole Food Corporation (*Forbes*, 3/10/05)

SHARE OF WEALTH HELD BY THE TOP 10% OF U.S. HOUSEHOLDS: 70%

(*Kiplinger's Personal Finance*, 1/04)

AMOUNT OF MONEY FOUND IN A FRENCH MAN'S STOMACH: $650

X-rays revealed a solid 12-pound mass of 350 coins swallowed over the course of a decade. The 62-year-old man suffered from a rare condition known as pica, characterized by a compulsion to eat inedible things. (*Bergen Record*, 2/19/04)

WORLD'S CURRENT HIGHEST CURRENCY DENOMINATION: 20,000,000 TURKISH LIRA NOTE (WORTH $15)

(*Financial Times* [London], 1/22/04)

Highest currency denominations of all time:

1. Hungarian 10,000,000,000,000,000,000,000 pengo note (1946) (worth pennies)

2. 100,000 billion German mark (1924) (worth less than a dollar)

(*Independent*, 3/27/04, 8/5/97)

MOVIES

1. NUMBER OF MOVIES THE AVERAGE AMERICAN GOES TO EACH YEAR: 5.5

2. MOST FREQUENT MOVIEGOING NATION IN THE WORLD: ICELAND

3. NUMBER OF MOVIE TICKETS SOLD WORLDWIDE IN 2003: 8.6 BILLION

4. BIGGEST FILM-PRODUCING CITY IN THE WORLD: BOMBAY, INDIA

Sources: **1.** Down from about 40 movies a year in the 1920s. (*Variety*, 1/6/03; *Screen Digest*, 7/1/04) **2.** The average Icelander sees about 5.7 movies per year, slightly ahead of the U.S. (*Screen Digest*, 7/1/04) **3.** Some 1.57 billion movie tickets were bought in the U.S. in 2003, second behind India, where 2.8 billion tickets were sold. (*Variety*, 4/2/04; *Hollywood Reporter*, 3/2/04) **4.** Known as Bollywood, India's film industry, centered in Bombay, produces 1,000 films a year, twice Hollywood's output. Twice as many tickets are sold in India as in the U.S., and 10 times as many as in third-place Indonesia. A typical Bollywood film runs 3 1/2 hours, in a squeaky clean formula that rarely if ever strays—boy meets girl. And invariably, five or six times per movie, the main characters will suddenly break into song and dance. One more difference: filmmakers in Bollywood rarely show kissing on screen. Instead, kissing is depicted by pairs of cooing doves or roses swaying in the wind. (*Washington Times*, 5/21/02; UPI, 4/13/01)

FIRST PUBLICLY SHOWN U.S. FILM: *BLACKSMITHING SCENE* (1893)

The 1-minute film, which showed a blacksmith and two helpers forging a piece of iron and passing around a beer, was made by Thomas Edison's Edison Manufacturing Company, and shown in Brooklyn on May 9, 1893. Also on the bill was another short film called *Horseshoeing*. (Grieveson, *Silent Cinema Reader*)

Opening of the first movie theater: Apr. 14, 1894

On Apr. 14, 1894, the first movie parlor opened at 1155 Broadway in New York City in what had been a former shoe store. Customers paid 25 cents for the opportunity to watch films on one of ten individual Kinetoscope viewing machines. By the end of the day, the theater had grossed $120. (Robinson, *From Peepshow to Palace*)

1. YEAR HIGHEST NUMBER OF MOVIE TICKETS WERE SOLD IN AMERICA: 1946 (4 BILLION)

2. YEAR FEWEST MOVIE TICKETS WERE SOLD: 1971 (820 MILLION)

(*Los Angeles Times*, 12/26/02)

BIGGEST BOX OFFICE FLOPS IN MOVIE HISTORY:

Cutthroat Island (1995):

Directed by Renny Harlin and starring his (soon to be ex-) wife Geena Davis and Matthew Modine after Michael Douglas pulled out, *Cutthroat* bankrupted its studio, Carolco. Reviews were mediocre to scathing: *Newsday* called the movie a "weary rehash of every pirate movie under the sun," and *Entertainment Weekly* said, "Somewhere, Errol Flynn is wincing." The film, which cost about $100 million to make, was pulled from theaters after only 2 weeks, and took in only $9.9 million.

(Entertainment Weekly, 5/1/98; 5/15/98)

Adventures of Pluto Nash (2002):

Featuring Eddie Murphy as a nightclub owner on the moon, the *Washington Post* called it "1 1/2 hours of pure blankness" and the *Boston Globe* said, "you'd have to go as far out as Pluto itself for a read of the distance separating *Pluto Nash* from 'good.'" The film cost $90 million to make, and took in just $4.4 million domestically.

(Pittsburgh Post-Gazette, 9/1/03)

FIRST WORDS SPOKEN ON FILM:

"WAIT A MINUTE! WAIT A MINUTE! YOU AIN'T HEARD NOTHING YET."
–AL JOLSON, *THE JAZZ SINGER*

(Entertainment Weekly, 1/10/92)

MOST MEMORABLE LINES IN FILM HISTORY, ACCORDING TO TWO RECENT STUDIES:

"BOND. JAMES BOND."
–SEAN CONNERY, *DR. NO* (1962)

"I'LL BE BACK."
–ARNOLD SCHWARZENEGGER, *THE TERMINATOR* (1984)

According to a 1999 California State University study, Schwarzenegger's line was #1. According to a 2001 English study, it's Connery's. Other memorable lines on the American list include "Frankly, my dear, I don't give a damn" (*Gone With the Wind*, voted #2); "Show me the money" (*Jerry Maguire*, #3), and "Go ahead, make my day" (Clint Eastwood, *Sudden Impact*, #4). (*USA Today*, 8/11/00)

1. Most animals in a single film: 8,552
(*Around the World in Eighty Days* (1956))

2. Most midgets in a single film: 124 (*The Wizard of Oz*)

Sources: **1.** The 1956 original film employed 3,800 sheep, 2,448 buffalo, 950 donkeys, 800 horses, 512 monkeys, 17 bulls, 15 elephants, 6 skunks, and 4 ostriches. (IMDB.com) **2.** The Munchkins were not even credited by name in the film, and were paid about $100 a week. Toto got $125. . . . In a 1967 interview, Judy Garland said this about the Munchkins: "They were little drunks. They all got smashed every night, and they picked them up in butterfly nets." Responded Mickey Carroll, one of the Munchkins, "Some people had a few drinks, but I certainly never saw anybody swinging from the rafters." (*Washington Post*, 6/20/01; *Daily Telegraph*, 11/1/97)

MOST MOVIES MADE FROM A SINGLE STORY: 87 (*CINDERELLA*)

Cinderella has inspired 87 movies from 1898 to 2002, including animated, operatic, balletic, pornographic, and Jerry Lewis sendups. (IMDB.com)

SHORTEST DIALOGUE SCRIPT: 1 WORD
(MEL BROOKS'S *SILENT MOVIE*)

"*Non*," said by mime Marcel Marceau. (*Entertainment Weekly*, 5/1/98)

LONGEST MOVIE EVER: *DIE ZWEITE HEIMAT*
(25 HOURS, 30 MINUTES; GERMANY, 1992)

The movie traces German history from 1960 through 1970 through the eyes of one German man. (*Entertainment Weekly*, 5/1/98)

MOVIE TICKET PRICES
AROUND THE WORLD:

$19.00—LONDON
$16.80—TOKYO
$10.25—NEW YORK
$1.00—CHINA
$0.20—INDIA

An average movie ticket in the U.S. costs $6.04, while an average movie ticket in Japan is $10.80, the highest in the world. (*New York Times*, 1/11/04; *Los Angeles Times*, 6/25/04)

PERCENTAGE OF MOVIEGOERS WHO BUY FROM THE CONCESSION STAND: 87%

Seventy-eight percent buy a drink, 68% buy popcorn, and 43% purchase candy. (*Minneapolis Star Tribune*, 11/10/02)

First X-rated movie by a major studio:
Midnight Cowboy

The 1969 picture was also the only X-rated film to win the best picture Oscar. (*Chicago Tribune*, 5/20/94)

MUSIC

1. MOST PLAYED SONG IN HISTORY: "YOU'VE LOST THAT LOVIN' FEELING" (RIGHTEOUS BROTHERS)

2. BIGGEST-SELLING SINGLE OF ALL TIME: "CANDLE IN THE WIND" (ELTON JOHN)

3. FIRST ROCK AND ROLL SONG TO REACH #1: "ROCK AROUND THE CLOCK" (JULY 9, 1955)

Sources: **1.** Written by Barry Mann, Phil Spector, and Cynthia Weil and originally recorded by the Righteous Brothers, it received its 8-millionth airing in late 1999. The second-, third-, and fourth-place songs on the list have all received more than 7 million airplays: "Never My Love," "Yesterday," and "Stand by Me." Rounding out the top 10: "Can't Take My Eyes Off of You," "Sitting on the Dock of the Bay," "Mrs. Robinson," "Baby, I Need Your Loving," "Rhythm of the Rain," and "Georgia on My Mind." (*Daily Variety*, 11/22/04; *Dallas Morning News*, 12/25/03) **2.** John's 1997 tribute to Princess Di blew away the previous record holder, the late Bing Crosby's perennial "White Christmas," which since its release in 1942 has sold an estimated 30 million copies. (*Entertainment Weekly*, 5/1/98) **3.** *Christian Science Monitor*, 1/15/04.

Inventor of the term "rock and roll": Alan Freed

The term derives from its original usage as an African American street slang expression for sex during the 1920s and 1930s. "Rock and roll" was first used in reference to music by Cleveland disc jockey Alan Freed in the 1950s, although a group called the Boswell Sisters recorded a song called "Rock and Roll" in 1934. (*Billboard*, 10/25/03; NPR's *All Things Considered*, 3/21/02)

FIRST ROCK AND ROLL SONG: "ROCK AND ROLL" (1949)

In 1949, Modern Records released the R&B 78 rpm single by Wild Bill Moore, the first song to use the term "rock and roll" and sound like it too. Others consider the first true rock and roll song to have been "Rocket 88," recorded by Ike Turner in 1951. (*Entertainment Weekly*, 1/10/92; *Christian Science Monitor*, 1/15/04)

FIRST ROCK AND ROLL CONCERT:
"THE MOONDOG CORONATION BALL"
MAR. 21, 1952

Held in Cleveland, the event was organized by deejay Alan Freed and promised performances from the Dominoes, saxophonist Paul Williams, and guitarist Tiny Grimes, among others. The initial printing of 7,000 tickets sold out in a week, and a riot erupted after the police shut down the concert due to extreme overcrowding. (*Cleveland Plain Dealer*, 3/21/02)

Length of FBI investigation of the song "Louie Louie": 2 years

After the Kingsmen's version of "Louie Louie" made the charts in 1963, rumors circulated that the song contained dirty words that were intelligible only when the record was played at a slower speed. After complaints from parents, the FBI launched a 2-year investigation. On Apr. 17, 1964, the FBI lab audiologists wrote a memo that stated: "The record was played at various speeds, but none of the speeds assisted in determining the words of the song on the record." Thus, the FBI concluded, "Louie Louie" was "unintelligible at any speed." (*Independent*, 7/19/02; NPR, 7/21/93)

SONGS THAT SUPPOSEDLY HAD HIDDEN MEANING PROMOTING DRUG USE:

"Puff the Magic Dragon" (Peter, Paul and Mary)
Supposedly a euphemism for a marijuana high, the song was one of hundreds on a list compiled by the U.S. Army on President Nixon's orders. Radio stations were warned not to play these songs at the risk of losing their license.

(NPR's *All Things Considered*, 6/7/01)

"Lucy in the Sky with Diamonds" (The Beatles)
Because the initials of the song are LSD, people speculated that the song was about drugs, and it was banned from the airwaves by the BBC, though the Beatles insisted it was inspired by a drawing Julian Lennon had done of a friend named Lucy.

(*Guardian*, 4/12/02)

1. NUMBER OF BIRTHS AT WOODSTOCK: 2
2. NUMBER OF DEATHS: 3

Sources: **1.** Billed as "Three Days of Peace and Music," the Woodstock promoters expected 50,000 people max, but 500,000 showed up. The concert wasn't even held in the town of its namesake—Woodstock, N.Y.—but a few miles away on milk farmer Max Yasgur's farm in Bethel, N.Y. (*Daily Telegraph*, 11/24/01) **2.** From a heroin overdose, a ruptured appendix, and being run over by a tractor (*Daily Telegraph*, 11/24/01; Woodstock69.com)

FIRST RAP RECORD:
"RAPPER'S DELIGHT"
(1979; SUGARHILL GANG)

(*U.S. News and World Report,* 7/8/02)

FIRST VIDEO ON MTV:
"VIDEO KILLED THE RADIO STAR"
(AUG. 1, 1981)

The video by a band named the Buggles, aired on Aug. 1, 1981, at 12:01 A.M. when MTV first signed on the air. The first music video was "Bohemian Rhapsody" by Queen, which was first shown on the British show *Top of the Pops* in 1975. (*International Herald Tribune,* 4/16/03; *Christian Science Monitor,* 7/27/01)

YEAR THE FIRST GUITAR WAS SMASHED DURING A CONCERT: 1964

In the summer of 1964, at the Railway Hotel in Harrow, England, the stage ceiling was so low that Pete Townshend often bumped his guitar against it. Losing his cool one night, Townshend went ahead and smashed the guitar to pieces. (McMichael, *The Who Concert File*)

SONGS THAT ARE MOST FREQUENTLY STUCK IN PEOPLE'S HEADS, ACCORDING TO RECENT RESEARCH:

1. "WHO LET THE DOGS OUT"

2. "WE WILL ROCK YOU"

3. KIT-KAT CANDY BAR JINGLE ("GIMME A BREAK . . .")

4. *MISSION: IMPOSSIBLE* THEME

5. "THE LION SLEEPS TONIGHT"

Songs with lyrics are reported as most frequently stuck (74%), followed by advertising jingles (15%). According to the research, singing the song aloud can sometimes erase it. (Kellaris, "Dissecting Earworms," presentation to Society for Consumer Psychology, 2/22/03)

Bizarre onstage behavior by musicians:

The Who:

On *The Smothers Brothers Comedy Hour* in September 1967, an attempt at pyrotechnics went awry. Keith Moon's base drum exploded, and Pete Townshend was left with only partial hearing.

(McMichael, *The Who Concert File*)

Ozzie Osborne:

Thinking it was fake, Ozzie bit the head off a live bat thrown onstage during a 1982 concert, forcing him to undergo a painful round of rabies shots.

(*Daily Record*, 7/29/03)

Alice Cooper:

Unaware that chickens can't fly, Cooper threw a live chicken into the audience at a 1969 Detroit concert, whereupon the crowd tore the animal to pieces.

(*Independent*, 6/19/03)

FIRST BAND TO BE CONVICTED FOR HAVING
OBSCENE LYRICS ON A RECORD: 2 LIVE CREW (1990)

Following the group's arrest in Florida, a federal court found the record "obscene" on the basis of the 80-minute LP's 226 uses of the word f**k, 87 descriptions of oral sex, and many "references to female and male genitalia, human sexual excretion, oral-anal contact, fellatio . . . sadomasochism, the turgid state of the male sexual organ . . . and the sound of moaning." However, the conviction was overturned on appeal. (*People*, 7/2/90)

WORST SONG OF ALL TIME:
"WE BUILT THIS CITY ON ROCK AND ROLL"

The 1985 rock anthem was chosen by both *Blender* magazine and VH1 as the worst song ever. Other songs on the *Blender* list include "Achy Breaky Heart" and "Everybody Have Fun Tonight." According to *Dave Barry's Book of Bad Songs*, the three worst songs of all time are "MacArthur Park" (Richard Harris), "Yummy, Yummy, Yummy, I Got Love in My Tummy" (Ohio Express), and "You're Having My Baby" (Paul Anka). (*Kansas City Star*, 5/11/04)

MUSLIMS

1. NUMBER OF MUSLIMS WORLDWIDE: 1.3 BILLION
2. NUMBER OF MUSLIMS IN AMERICA: 5–7 MILLION
3. NUMBER OF DIFFERENT NAMES FOR GOD IN THE KORAN: 99

Sources: **1.** BBC, 1/29/04. **2.** *New York Times*, 10/22/04. **3.** The 99 names comprise a catalog of God's characteristics, for example: the Merciful, the Compassionate, the Light, the First, the Last, the Exalter, the Abaser, and the Creator, to name a few. By memorizing all the names—an act known in Arabic as *dhikr*—Muslims are better able to see him in all aspects of the world around. (*Fort Worth Star-Telegram*, 1/16/99)

1. PERCENTAGE OF MUSLIMS WORLDWIDE WHO ARE ARABS: 12%
2. COUNTRY WITH THE LARGEST MUSLIM POPULATION: INDONESIA (200 MILLION)
3. COUNTRY WITH THE SECOND LARGEST MUSLIM POPULATION: INDIA (140 MILLION)

Sources: **1.** *Milwaukee Journal Sentinel*, 12/9/01. **2.** *Time International*, 9/13/04. **3.** *New York Times*, 9/15/03.

First mosque built in America: Cedar Rapids, Iowa (1934)

In the 1870s, Muslim immigrants started coming to the area around Cedar Rapids to farm. In 1934, the Muslim community built a mosque in Cedar Rapids, considered the first in the U.S. and called the Mother Mosque of America; it is now used as a museum of the history of Islam in Iowa. Cedar Rapids is also home to the Muslim National Cemetery, the first Muslim cemetery in the U.S. (*Des Moines Register*, 10/20/01)

ESTIMATE OF THE NUMBER OF PEOPLE AROUND THE WORLD WHO CAN RECITE THE ENTIRE KORAN BY HEART: 15 MILLION

To be admitted into Cairo's Al Azhar University, the oldest and largest institution of higher learning in the world, all applicants must be able to recite the Koran by heart, even if they are studying to become doctors or engineers. (*National Post* [Canada], 9/14/02)

1. NUMBER OF MUSLIMS WHO MADE THE PILGRIMAGE TO MECCA IN 1945: 37,630

2. NUMBER WHO MADE THE PILGRIMAGE IN 2004: 2 MILLION

Sources: **1.** Lippman, *Understanding Islam*. **2.** The Saudis provide 20,000 buses to transport this mass of humanity and 44,000 air-conditioned tents at a campsite that can hold 1.5 million people. In the mid 1980s, King Fahd of Saudi Arabia changed his official title from "His Majesty" to "Custodian of the Two Holy Mosques," which is how he is regularly addressed in the Arab and Muslim press. (Agence France-Presse, 2/1/04; 2/20/02)

NUMBER OF PILGRIMS WHO WERE TRAMPLED TO DEATH DURING THE 2004 HAJJ: 251

The pilgrims were trampled to death while stoning three pillars representing Satan. Due to the number of pilgrims, such catastrophies are far from uncommon. Fourteen pilgrims were trampled in 2003, 35 in 2001, 118 in 1998, and 340 in 1997. Commenting on the most recent deaths, the Saudi interior minister said the pilgrims "met their fate because their place and time of death has been decided the moment they were born." (Agence France-Presse, 2/4/04)

1. MUSLIM COUNTRIES WHERE WOMEN ARE REQUIRED TO COVER THEMSELVES: IRAN, SAUDI ARABIA

2. MUSLIM COUNTRIES THAT PLACE RESTRICTIONS ON WOMEN COVERING THEMSELVES: SINGAPORE, TURKEY, TUNISIA

Sources: **1.** *Toronto Star*, 8/5/03. **2.** Singapore banned the head scarf, but not Sikh turbans, in 2002. Tunisia banned the head scarf in schools and public offices in 1981, and Turkey did the same in 1997. Up until 2004, women wearing veils were prohibited from holding certain government jobs in Bahrain. (Pakistan Press, 11/4/04)

NEWSPAPERS

1. PERCENTAGE OF HOUSEHOLDS THAT BUY ONE OR MORE DAILY NEWSPAPERS: 43%

2. PERCENTAGE OF THE ADULTS WHO GET A DAILY PAPER WHO READ THE NEWS SECTION: 87%

3. WHO READ SPORTS: 60%

4. WHO READ THE COMICS: 58%

Sources: **1.** In 1995, 63% of households bought one or more newspapers. Between 1995 and 2001, that figure dove 20 points, reflecting the rise of the Internet. On average, Americans under 50 spend approximately 11 minutes reading a newspaper daily, while people over 50 spend an average of approximately 23 minutes. (*American Demographics*, 7/1/03; Pew Research Center) **2–4.** Newspaper Association of America's Facts about Newspapers study, 2003.

First American newspaper:
Publick Occurrences Both Foreign and Domestick (1690)

Published on Sept. 25, 1690, *Publick Occurrences* was intended to be "furnished once a month (or if any Glut of Occurrences happen, oftener)." However, the colonial government immediately shut the paper down, claiming it had been published without authority. . . . The world's first daily newspaper was London's *Daily Courant*, first published in 1702. The oldest daily newspaper still in print in England is the *Berrow's Worcester Journal*, publishing since 1709. (*Marketing*, 6/23/04; *Editor and Publisher*, 10/11/97)

AMERICA'S OLDEST CONTINUOUSLY PUBLISHED DAILY NEWSPAPER:
NEW YORK POST (FIRST PUBLISHED NOV. 16, 1801)

The *Charleston Post and Courier* is the nation's second oldest newspaper, originally published in January 1803. (AP, 1/10/03, 11/19/01)

FIRST NEWSPAPER AD:
MAY 1704 IN THE *BOSTON NEWSLETTER*

The ad said the following: "This News-Letter is to be continued Weekly, and all persons who have any lands, houses, tenements, farms, ships, vessels, goods, wares or merchandise to be sold or lett; or servants runaway, or goods Stoll [sic], or lost, may have the same inserted at a reasonable rate." (*Houston Chronicle*, 6/22/97)

NUMBER OF DAYS A NEW YORK MAN SPENT TRAPPED UNDER AN AVALANCHE OF OLD NEWSPAPERS IN HIS APARTMENT: 2 DAYS

Patrice Moore was buried when a mountain of unread newspapers collapsed in his Bronx apartment. Moore said he yelled for help repeatedly but that no one answered. Eventually he was freed by the fire department. "I didn't think I was gonna get out," he told the *New York Post*. (*Newsday*, 12/30/03)

MOST FAMOUS NEWSPAPER ERROR OF ALL TIME:

DEWEY DEFEATS TRUMAN

(Headline in the *Chicago Tribune*, Nov. 3, 1948)

(*Washington Post*, 12/1/02)

OTHER MONUMENTAL ERRORS:

ALL TITANIC PASSENGERS ARE SAFE; TRANSFERRED IN LIFEBOATS AT SEA

(Headline in the *Baltimore Sun*, Apr. 15, 1912)

The *Wall Street Journal* also reported the *Titanic* safe, saying that "the gravity of the damage to the *Titanic* is apparent, but the important point is that she did not sink." (*Columbia Journalism Review*, 1/1/99)

NEWSPAPER CORRECTIONS:

"An item in Thursday's Nation Digest about the Massachusetts budget crisis made reference to new taxes that will help put Massachusetts 'back in the African American.' The item should have said 'back in the black.' "
—from the *Sacramento Bee*

"Due to a printing error, Sunday's column for fishballs included 'one cup Vaseline.' "
—from the *Minneapolis Star Tribune*

"An article on Page E4 last Saturday incorrectly said Augie Ratner was married four times to strippers. He was married three times; none of his wives were strippers."
—from the *Minneapolis Star Tribune*

(*Washington Post*, 4/23/01, 4/8/02; *Minneapolis Star Tribune*, 6/2/00)

NEW YORK CITY

1. POPULATION: 8.1 MILLION

2. ESTIMATE OF THE RATIO OF RATS TO RESIDENTS: 1 TO 1

3. ODDS OF BEING BITTEN BY A RAT VERSUS BEING BITTEN BY A RESIDENT: 1 TO 11

Sources: **1.** *Crain's New York Business*, 3/29/04. **2.** Estimates of the number of rats in New York are all over the map, with numbers ranging from 250,000 (a recent book called *Rats*) to 8 million (a 1996 health department estimate) all the way up to 56 million (*New York Daily News*). (Sullivan, *Rats*; *Daily News*, 8/6/03; *New York Times*, 7/21/96) **3.** Based on 2001 data from the New York City Department of Health.

ORIGIN OF NEW YORK NICKNAMES:

Big Apple:

First used by John J. Fitzgerald in his horse racing column in the *New York Morning Telegraph*, who heard it used by New Orleans stable hands in referring to tracks where big money could be made. On Feb. 18, 1924, Fitzgerald wrote: "There's only one Big Apple. That's New York."

(*New York Times*, 9/17/00; 8/29/04)

Gotham:

Anglo-Saxon name meaning "goat town." In the original Gotham, near Nottingham, England, residents were called "wise fools" because they avoided King John's taxes by acting insane. Around 1807, Washington Irving used the term to refer to New York, which he saw as a place of self-important but foolish people.

(*Encyclopedia of New York*)

1. ODDS THAT A NEW YORK CITY TAXI DRIVER WAS BORN IN THE U.S.: 1 IN 10

2. LANGUAGES SPOKEN BY TAXI DRIVERS: 60

3. PERCENTAGE OF TAXI DRIVERS WHO FAIL ENGLISH TEST ON FIRST TRY: 15%

Sources: **1.** One in four New York cab drivers were born in either Pakistan, Bangladesh, or India. (*Daily News*, 7/7/04) **2.** On an average day, drivers serve 30 fares, travel 141 miles, and take home $115 in fares and tips. The fare for the average trip in 2004 was $8.65. Manhattanites hail a cab an average of 100 times per year. (*N.Y.C. Taxi Cab Fact Book*) **3.** Actually, the test only requires drivers to show a minimum ability to read—not speak—English. If they pass, drivers take classes in geography and etiquette, where they are taught phrases such as: *"Please forgive me for not having change of $20. Please let me run to the store right here and get you the correct change"*; *"I'd be happy to take you to Brooklyn"*; and *"I'm sorry if you think I'm driving too fast. I will slow down immediately."* (*Chicago Tribune*, 5/7/96)

Year alligators were found in New York sewers: 1935

That's right, one of the widest known urban myths has a ring of truth. According to a book called *There Are Alligators in Our Sewers*, several alligators were found by inspectors in the New York sewer system in 1935, and were eliminated with rifles and poison. According to city records, another alligator was discovered in the sewer system in the 1960s. (*New York Times*, 2/17/83; AP, 6/19/01)

New Yorkers arrested for trying to sell the Brooklyn Bridge: 2

Two men were arrested and served prison time for "selling" the Brooklyn Bridge to gullible strangers. On Dec. 18, 1928, the *New York Times* told of the arrest of George C. Parker, who had sold the bridge to a visitor from out West for $50,000. He went to Sing Sing for the crime. And in 1901, another con artist, William McCloundy of Asbury Park, N.J., also served prison time for allegedly selling the bridge. (*New York Times*, 10/27/02; 7/11/04)

1. PERCENTAGE OF AMERICANS WHO OWN CARS: 91%
2. PERCENTAGE OF NEW YORKERS WHO OWN CARS: 47%

(*New York Times*, 8/29/04)

1. AVERAGE PRICE OF A MANHATTAN APARTMENT IN 2004: $1,004,232
2. RENT ON THE AVERAGE MANHATTAN APARTMENT: $2,707

Sources: **1.** For the period from April through June 2004, the average price of a Manhattan apartment breached the $1 million mark for the first time. (*New York Times*, 2/23/05) **2.** *New York Times*, 10/31/04.

1. RANK AMONG 36 CITIES IN STUDY OF KINDNESS: 36TH
2. RANK AMONG CITIES IN FREQUENCY OF OBSESSIVE DISORDERS: FIRST

Sources: **1.** Experimenters in various cities inadvertently dropped pens, feigned blindness or injury, or asked for change in order to test the response of residents. Rochester, N.Y., was found to be the kindest. (Provine, *Geography of Time*) **2.** According to a study conducted at the Mount Sinai School of Medicine. (*Chicago Tribune*, 5/2/96)

1. Percentage of Americans who speak English at home: 83%
2. Percentage of New Yorkers who speak English at home: 52%

(*New York Times*, 8/29/04)

PARKING AND SPEEDING

1. TOTAL NUMBER OF PARKING SPACES IN THE U.S.: 105,200,000

2. AVERAGE TIME IT TAKES SOMEONE TO PULL OUT OF A PARKING SPACE: 32 SECONDS

3. TIME IT TAKES TO PULL OUT IF SOMEONE IS WAITING FOR THE SPACE: 39 SECONDS

Sources: **1.** There are also 5 million parking meters. (*Kansas City Star*, 7/16/04) **2, 3.** Barry Ruback, a Penn State sociologist, studied 400 drivers at an Atlanta area mall. Ruback found that drivers took 4 more seconds to pull out if the waiting driver blew his horn. Men, but not women, were influenced by the make of the car waiting for the spot: men pulled out for a luxury sedan in 30 seconds, but took 39 seconds if the waiting car was an old station wagon. (*International Herald Tribune*, 5/15/97)

1. YEAR FIRST SPEEDING TICKET ISSUED: 1899

2. SPEED AT WHICH SAMUEL TILLEY WAS CLOCKED AT WHEN HE WAS PULLED OVER ON SEPT. 18, 2004: 205 MPH

Sources: **1.** On May 20, 1899, a New York City policeman arrested Jacob German, alleging that his electric-powered taxi was going 12 mph in an 8 mph zone. (*Atlanta Journal-Constitution*, 5/31/99) **2.** Tilley was driving his 2003 Honda RC51 sport motorcycle on a stretch of U.S. 61 near Wabasha, Minn., when he was pulled over after driving 140 miles over the posted speed limit. (*St. Paul Pioneer Press*, 9/21/04)

1. NUMBER OF AMERICANS ANNUALLY PULLED OVER FOR SPEEDING: 9.9 MILLION

2. PERCENTAGE BY WHICH MEN ARE MORE LIKELY TO BE STOPPED FOR SPEEDING THAN WOMEN: 41%

Sources: **1.** Or about 5% of all licensed drivers. Based on figures for 1999, the most recent year for which data is available. (*American Demographics*, 7/1/03) **2.** *American Demographics*, 7/1/03.

AMOUNT NEW YORK CITY COLLECTS ANNUALLY IN PARKING FINES:
$300 MILLION

(International Parking Institute)

COST OF SPEEDING TICKET A FINNISH MAN RECEIVED FOR GOING 50 MPH IN A 25 MPH ZONE: $217,000

In February 2004, Jussi Salonoja, heir to a Finnish sausage fortune, was stopped in Helsinki after driving 50 mph in a 25 mph zone. Speeding tickets in Finland are linked to a driver's income, jacking up the rich heir's fine to $217,000. Other rich Finns have been fleeced in the past: in 2002, Anssa Vanjoki got a $103,000 fine for riding his motorcycle at 46 mph in a 31 mph zone; and in the 1990s, Internet millionaire Jaakko Rytsola paid a $74,600 speeding fine. (*Washington Post*, 2/15/04; *Birmingham News*, 5/26/02)

AMOUNT DOUG STEAD SPENT TO FIGHT A $100 SPEEDING TICKET: $150,000

Stead, the founder of a high-tech company in Canada, was issued the speeding ticket on Oct. 22, 1996. Claiming that the use of photo radar was unconstitutional, Stead spent 5 years and $150,000 fighting the ticket, but was ultimately required to pay. (*BC Business*, 10/03)

MOST EXPENSIVE PARKING SPACES EVER SOLD: $187,500

In February 2004, one-car parking spaces in the Knightsbridge section of London were hot properties at $187,500. One woman bought one for her 3-year-old son for when he was old enough to drive. (*Evening Standard*, 8/3/04)

WORLD'S LARGEST PARKING LOT: 20,000 SPACES (WEST EDMONTON MALL, ALBERTA, CANADA)

(Edmonton Sun, 4/22/01)

First car to have an automatic parallel parking system: 2004 Toyota Prius

The Intelligent Parking Assist System is a $2,100 option on Priuses, and is currently available only in Japan. All the driver needs to do is pull up next to the car in front of the space, push some directional arrows on a computer screen, and start to back up, after which a computer directs the car backward by itself, turning the wheels one way and then the other until the car is perfectly parked. (*Baltimore Sun*, 10/11/03)

PLAYBOY

1. FIRST ISSUE: DEC. 1, 1953
2. FIRST PLAYMATE: MARILYN MONROE
3. NUMBER OF COPIES SOLD: 53,000
4. HIGHEST CIRCULATION: 7,200,000

Sources: **1.** Founder Hugh Hefner initially intended to call the magazine Stag Party. Four weeks before publication, he received a registered letter from *Stag* magazine warning against infringing its trademark. Frantic, Hefner sought a new name, considering Top Hat, Bachelor Gent, Gentlemen, Satyr, and Pan, before a friend whose mother had once worked for the Playboy Motor Car Corporation of Buffalo, N.Y., suggested the name that stuck. (Gannett News, 1/27/94) **2.** *Playboy* paid $500 for the pictures. Hefner owns the burial plot next to Monroe's at Hollywood's Westwood cemetery. (*Washington Times,* 5/9/01) **3.** Hefner expressed the magazine's credo in the first issue: "Most of today's 'magazines for men' spend all their time out-of-doors. . . . We'll be out there too, occasionally, but we don't mind telling you in advance—we plan on spending most of our time inside. We like our apartment. We enjoy mixing up cocktails and an hors d'oeuvre or two, putting a little mood music on the phonograph, and inviting in a female acquaintance for a quiet discussion on Picasso, Nietzsche, jazz, sex." (Halberstam, *The Fifties*) **4.** That was in 1972. Current circulation is approximately 3 million readers. (*Washington Times,* 7/16/99)

1. WHAT THE PLAYMATE OF THE MONTH WAS ORIGINALLY CALLED: "SWEETHEART OF THE MONTH"
2. FIRST CENTERFOLD: MARCH 1956

Sources: **1.** *Financial Times* (London), 12/13/03. **2.** The first Playmate to have a centerfold was Marian Stafford. (Agence France-Presse, 11/30/03)

1. MOST COMMON TURN-ONS REPORTED BY PLAYMATES: MUSIC, ANIMALS, EATING
2. MOST COMMON TURN-OFFS: ARROGANT PEOPLE, LIARS, JEALOUSY, GETTING UP EARLY

(Playboy.com)

1. AVERAGE MEASUREMENTS OF A *PLAYBOY* PLAYMATE: 35-23-35
2. AVERAGE HEIGHT AND WEIGHT: 5'6", 115 POUNDS

Sources: **1.** According to a study conducted by psychologist Douglas Kenrick, men who are shown pictures of *Playboy* models later describe themselves as less in love with their wives than do men shown other images. Women shown pictures from *Playgirl* experience no such change in affection. (Playboy.com; *Time*, 8/15/94) **2.** The average American woman, in comparison, weighs 143 pounds and wears a size 14. (*Palm Beach Post*, 8/7/99)

Books most often cited as Playmate favorites:
The Prophet, Gone With the Wind

As of 1996, according to *The Playmate Book*. Each got 13 mentions by Playmates, closely followed by 12 mentions for books by Ayn Rand. (*Washington Post*, 12/22/96)

AMOUNT BY WHICH AVERAGE PLAYMATE WEIGHT HAS INCREASED SINCE THE 1960s: 1 POUND

The average height has increased about 2 inches. The average bust size has dropped about an inch, waist size has increased an inch, and hip size has remained about the same. (Playboy.com)

MOST COMMON PLAYMATE NAMES: SUSAN AND VICTORIA

(Playboy.com)

WOMEN WHO HAVE POSED IN *PLAYBOY*:

JAYNE MANSFIELD (FEBRUARY 1956) ZSA ZSA GABOR (MARCH 1957)

SOPHIA LOREN (NOVEMBER 1957) BRIGITTE BARDOT (MARCH 1958)

LIZ TAYLOR (JANUARY 1963) ANN-MARGRET (OCTOBER 1966)

JOAN COLLINS (MARCH 1969) RAQUEL WELCH (FEBRUARY 1977)

FARRAH FAWCETT (DECEMBER 1978) BO DEREK (MARCH 1980)

KIM BASINGER (FEBRUARY 1983) MADONNA (SEPTEMBER 1985)

SHARON STONE (JULY 1990) DREW BARRYMORE (JANUARY 1995)

(*Palm Beach Post*, 4/9/01)

State with the highest percentage of *Playboy* readers: Iowa

Mississippi has the lowest. (*New York Times*, 11/21/04)

PORN

1. ORIGIN OF THE WORD "PORNOGRAPHY":
FROM *PORNOGRAHOI*, GREEK FOR "PAINTERS OF PROSTITUTES"

2. ODDS THAT AN ADULT AMERICAN SURVEYED IN 2002 SAW A PORN FILM IN THE PAST YEAR: 1 IN 4

3. PERCENTAGE OF PORN USERS WHO SAY THEY FEEL GUILTY WHILE VIEWING PORN: 30%

4. PERCENTAGE OF PORN USERS WHO SAY THEY FEEL GUILTY AFTER VIEWING PORN: 16%

Sources: **1.** The term "pornography" was coined by a German art historian, and made its first appearance in English in 1850. Its first dictionary appearance was in 1857, in the *Oxford English Dictionary*. (Kendrick, *Secret Museum*) **2.** *Time*, 1/19/04. **3, 4.** Kinsey Institute survey for PBS's *Frontline*.

FIRST PORNOGRAPHIC BOOK: *SONNETTI LUSSURIOSI* ("LEWD SONNETS") (1524)

Written by Pietro Aretino, the book was popularly known as "Aretino's Postures," and consisted of sonnets about various sexual positions accompanied by illustrations. The book was banned by the pope, the illustrator was arrested, and Aretino narrowly escaped death by fleeing to Venice. His next book was a tell-all about Roman prostitutes and their clients. (*Times* [London], 10/21/02)

1. NUMBER OF ADULT FILMS PRODUCED ANNUALLY: 10,000
2. NUMBER OF PORN FILMS RENTED ANNUALLY IN AMERICA IN 1985: 79 MILLION
3. NUMBER RENTED TODAY: 800 MILLION
4. RATIO OF PORN VIDEOS TO REGULAR VIDEOS RENTED IN AMERICA TODAY: 1 IN 5

Sources: **1.** Only 4,000 are new productions—the remaining 6,000 are drawn from a massive production backlog of completed but unreleased titles. (*Video Business*, 4/19/04) **2.** *Atlanta Journal-Constitution*, 8/17/03. **3.** *Chicago Tribune*, 5/14/04. **4.** *Time*, 1/19/04.

1. Number of pages of porn online in 1998: 14 million
2. Number in 2004: 260 million
3. Readers of *Today's Christian Woman* magazine who admit to intentionally visiting porn sites online: 34%

Sources: **1, 2.** N2H2 Web Filtering. **3.** *Today's Christian Woman*, 10/03.

1. **RECORD IN 1995 FOR MOST MALE PARTNERS IN A DAY BY A PORN ACTRESS: 251 MEN**
2. **NEW RECORD SET IN 1998 FOR MOST MALE PARTNERS IN A DAY: 620 MEN**
3. **CURRENT RECORD FOR MOST PARTNERS IN ONE DAY: 646 MEN**

Sources: **1.** On January 19, 1995, Annabel Chong, a 22-year-old USC master's degree candidate and porn star, bedded 251 men over a 10-hour period. "Did it hurt?" Chong asked rhetorically. "Well, yeah. It's like running a marathon, you know, the pain is part of the high—part of the adrenaline rush." When asked why she did it, Chong said, "Why not? Having sex with 251 men for 10 hours is no different from having sex with one man for 10 hours." (CNN .com, 2/10/99) **2.** In late 1998, porn star Houston had sex with 620 men over a 10-hour period. Though she said "it was a great day," Houston abstained from sex for the next month because her neck was sore. (Penthouse.com) **3.** On Feb.10, 2002, Polish porn star Klaudia Figura set a new world sexual record by having sex with 646 men during a 1-day session. According to regulations, each sexual act had to take more than 30 seconds. (AVN, 4/02)

RECORD FOR MOST FEMALE PARTNERS IN ONE DAY: 55

In *The World's Luckiest Man,* porn actor Jon Dough had sex with 101 women, 55 in one day and then the other 46 two weeks later. (*Playboy,* 7/1/01)

FIRST PORN ACTRESS TO SUCCESSFULLY ENTER POLITICS: **ILONA STALLER**

Ms. Staller, popularly known by her stage name Cicciolina ("Honey Bunny" in English), appeared in numerous porn films before successfully running for a seat in the Italian Parliament in 1987 with a strategy that included repeatedly taking off her clothes at campaign stops. Staller served in Parliament until 1991; in 1990, she offered to have sex with Saddam Hussein if he freed foreign hostages being held in Iraq. (*People,* 7/6/87; *Los Angeles Times,* 8/24/90)

ACTUAL PORN FILM NAMES:

BEVERLY HILLS COPULATOR
BRASSIERE TO ETERNITY
MAY THE FORESKIN BE WITH YOU
WILLY WANKER
SPERMS OF ENDEARMENT
SHAVING RYAN'S PRIVATES
FORREST HUMP

(Google research)

PRESIDENTS

1. NUMBER OF TIMES THE CANDIDATE WITH THE THICKEST HEAD OF HAIR HAS LOST THE ELECTION SINCE 1960: 2

2. NUMBER OF TIMES THE TALLER CANDIDATE HAS LOST THE ELECTION SINCE 1888: 6

3. SHORTEST PRESIDENT: JAMES MADISON (5'4")

Sources: **1.** Except for John Kerry (2004) and Lyndon Johnson (1964), the candidate with the thickest head of hair has won 10 of the 12 presidential elections since 1960. (*Atlanta Journal-Constitution*, 11/7/00) **2.** That's out of 30 elections. The exceptions: 1888—5'11" Grover Cleveland beat 5'6" Benjamin Harrison in the popular vote in 1888—but lost the electoral college; 1940—6'2" Franklin Roosevelt defeated 6'2½" Wendell Wilkie; 1972—5'11½" Richard Nixon beat 6'1" George McGovern; 1976—5'9" Jimmy Carter beats 6' Gerald Ford; and 2004—6' George Bush beat 6'4" John Kerry. (*Rocky Mountain News*, 5/12/01) **3.** Abraham Lincoln was the tallest president, at 6'4", followed by Lyndon B. Johnson, at 6'3". (*New York Times*, 9/27/02)

Odds that a president was a lawyer: 6 in 10

Twenty-five of the 43 men who have held the office were lawyers. Twelve presidents have been generals, from Washington to Dwight Eisenhower. Seven did not have college educations, two were schoolteachers, and one—Andrew Johnson—was a tailor. (*Dallas Morning News*, 6/25/00)

1. LONGEST PRESIDENTIAL INAUGURAL ADDRESS IN HISTORY: 1 HOUR, 45 MINUTES

2. SHORTEST INAUGURAL ADDRESS: 2 MINUTES

Sources: **1.** Delivered by Pres. William Henry Harrison on March 4, 1841—during a snowstorm. Harrison refused to wear an overcoat, wanting Americans to see how tough he was. He died one month later of pneumonia. (*St. Louis Post-Dispatch*, 1/19/01; *U.S. News and World Report*, 1/11/93) **2.** A total of 135 words. Delivered on March 4, 1793, by George Washington at his second inauguration. (*St. Louis Post-Dispatch*, 1/19/01)

First president to travel abroad while in office: Teddy Roosevelt

In 1906, Roosevelt visited the Panama Canal. (*Bergen Record*, 12/21/99)

SECRET SERVICE CODE NAMES FOR PRESIDENTS:

RICHARD NIXON: SEARCHLIGHT

JIMMY CARTER: DEACON

RONALD REAGAN: RAWHIDE

BILL CLINTON: EAGLE

GEORGE W. BUSH: TRAILBLAZER

(*USA Today*, 5/14/98; *New York Post*, 4/22/01)

WORST PRESIDENT OF ALL TIME, ACCORDING TO A POLL OF 58 PRESIDENTIAL HISTORIANS: JAMES BUCHANAN

A consummate waffler, Buchanan disapproved of slavery as morally wrong, yet felt it had to be protected under the Constitution, and that, while no state had the right to secede, the president had no power to stop seceding states. Abraham Lincoln topped the list as the best president, followed by Franklin D. Roosevelt, George Washington, Theodore Roosevelt, and Harry Truman. (*USA Today*, 2/21/00)

NAME OF THE FIRST PRESIDENTIAL AIRCRAFT: SACRED COW

The press gave the nickname to the first plane designed specifically for a president's use—a Douglas C-54 Skymaster outfitted for FDR in 1944. The plane contained an elevator that allowed Roosevelt and his wheelchair to get onboard. Prior to the Kennedy administration, the Secret Service used the code name "Air Force One" for any military plane the president was flying in. Though the military preferred that the moniker be kept secret, Kennedy administration officials publicly starting using the name Air Force One to refer to the plane, and it has been known by that name ever since. (*U.S. News and World Report*, 5/19/03)

1. FIRST PRESIDENT TO THROW OUT A FIRST BALL AT A BASEBALL GAME: WILLIAM HOWARD TAFT
2. ONLY PRESIDENT SINCE TAFT NOT TO THROW OUT A FIRST BALL ON OPENING DAY: JIMMY CARTER

On April 15, 1910, Taft came as a spectator to watch the Washington Nationals take on the Philadelphia Athletics, but umpire Billy Evans thought it would be appropriate to have Taft throw out the first ball. He did, beginning an age-old Washington tradition. (*Washington Times*, 4/2/01)

PRESIDENTS WHO WERE ARRESTED WHILE IN OFFICE: FRANKLIN PIERCE (1853)

Franklin Pierce, driving back to the White House from a friend's home in his carriage, hit a woman identified as Mrs. Nathan Lewis. The woman was uninjured, but Constable Stanley Edelin arrested the president. The charges were later dropped. (*Washington Post*, 2/18/96)

1. Amount an ex-president receives annually in pension: $151,800
2. Amount received by a sitting vice president: $208,000

Sources: **1.** The president's pension is linked to the salary of a senior cabinet officer. (*Arkansas Democrat-Gazette*, 12/30/00) **2.** AP, 9/14/04.

1. MOST EMOTIONALLY STABLE PRESIDENT, ACCORDING TO A UNIVERSITY OF MINNESOTA STUDY: RONALD REAGAN
2. MOST EXTROVERTED: TEDDY ROOSEVELT
3. MOST OPEN TO NEW EXPERIENCES: THOMAS JEFFERSON

To come up with the results, the study asked 115 presidential biographers 592 questions regarding the character of the presidents. (*Minneapolis Star Tribune*, 8/6/00)

First public opinion poll: 1824

In 1824, a newspaper called the *Harrisburg Pennsylvanian* conducted the first public opinion poll, asking residents of Wilmington, Del., which presidential candidate they intended to vote for. The *Pennsylvanian* published the results, predicting that Andrew Jackson would win. Jackson won the popular vote, but failed to win a majority of electoral votes, and Congress picked John Quincy Adams to be president. (*Washington Times*, 8/6/92)

FIRST PRESIDENTIAL TV AD CAMPAIGN:
"EISENHOWER ANSWERS AMERICA"
(1952)

The spots featured a sympathetic Ike responding to ordinary citizens' concerns. In one ad, for example, an indignant New Yorker complains about how little $25 buys at the grocery store. Eisenhower responds by saying, "Yes, my Mamie [Ike's wife] gets after me about the high cost of living." (*Washington Post*, 8/3/04)

MUDSLINGING THROUGH THE AGES:

"A hero of many a well-fought bottle."
Slogan created by opponents of Franklin Pierce in the 1852 election, referring to Pierce's reputation as a heavy drinker

"Ma, Ma, Where's My Pa? Gone to the White House. Ha ha ha."
Republican rhyme used in the 1884 election against New York governor Grover Cleveland, who had fathered a child out of wedlock

"A Vote for Al Smith Is a Vote for the Pope."
Charge made by supporters of Herbert Hoover in 1928, who said that if Smith (a Catholic) were elected, the pope would move to Washington, and Protestant marriages would be outlawed

RADIO

1. NUMBER OF RADIO STATIONS IN AMERICA: 13,898

2. PERCENTAGE OF AMERICANS WHO LISTEN TO THE RADIO AT LEAST ONCE A WEEK: 94%

3. HOURS A WEEK THE AVERAGE AMERICAN LISTENS TO THE RADIO: 19 HOURS, 30 MINUTES

4. FIRST NAME FOR THE RADIO: "WIRELESS TELEGRAPHY"

Sources: **1.** Arbitron Radio 2004. **2, 3.** Americans listened to an average of 25 hours a week of radio in 1985. (*New York Times*, 7/19/04; *Washington Post*, 4/27/84) **4.** Known exclusively by that name until about 1906, when the terms "radiotelephony" and "radiotelegraphy" came into use, later shortened to "radio," which became the predominant term sometime around 1920. (Douglas, *Inventing American Broadcasting*)

FIRST WORDS SPOKEN ON RADIO:
"ONE, TWO, THREE, FOUR—IS IT SNOWING WHERE YOU ARE, MR. THIESSEN?"

Though skeptics like Thomas Edison had said that there was as much chance of transmitting wireless speech as "jumping over the moon," Canadian Reginald Fessenden transmitted these first-ever wireless words on Dec. 23, 1900, from a weather station on the Potomac River near Washington. His assistant, Thiessen, heard the words a kilometer away, and wired back. (Weightman, *Signor Marconi's Magic Box*)

DATE OF THE FIRST SCHEDULE COMMERCIAL RADIO BROADCAST: NOV. 2, 1920

On this date, Leo Rosenberg broadcast the returns of the Harding–Cox presidential race from the "studios" of radio station KDKA in Pittsburgh, Penn. (i.e., a wooden shack on the roof of a Pittsburgh factory). Because there were so few radios in existence, Rosenberg requested over the air that "anyone hearing this broadcast communicate with us." KDKA also broadcast the first baseball game (Pirates, Aug. 5, 1921) and football game (University of Pittsburgh, Oct. 8, 1921), both announced by Harold Arlin, the first full-time broadcaster. Like many early radio announcers, Arlin treated the new medium with such reverence that he would often wear a tuxedo while on the air, though no one could see him. (*Christian Science Monitor*, 11/1/95)

Longest-running radio program in history: The Grand Ole Opry, 79 years

On Nov. 28, 1925, WSM in Nashville debuted an unassuming old-time music hour titled the *WSM Barn Dance*, with a fiddler named Uncle Jimmy Thompson as the first act. The name "Grand Ole Opry" was created in 1927 when a radio announcer made fun of the "grand opera" broadcast on the previous show by calling the *Barn Dance* the "Grand Ole Oprey." The name stuck, and the show has been broadcasting from Nashville every Saturday night for 79 years. (*Tennesseean*, 10/8/00)

CITY WITH THE MOST RADIO STATIONS PER CAPITA IN THE U.S.: SALT LAKE CITY

Sixty-eight stations broadcast out of the Salt Flats of Utah—as many stations as in New York and Los Angeles. (*Deseret Morning News*, 1/31/03)

1. First disc jockey: Al Jarvis (1934)
2. First use of the term "disc jockey": Aug. 6, 1941

Sources: **1.** Up to the early 1930s, radio stations broadcast music either by employing musicians who played live in the studio or by broadcasting bands from other locations. Jarvis, an announcer for KFWB in Los Angeles, was set to emcee the broadcast of a dance band concert from a local ballroom when the band suddenly canceled. With hours of potential dead airtime on his hands, Jarvis rushed back to the studio and played a record of the band, telling the radio audience that the show was coming from "the make-believe ballroom." *The Make-Believe Ballroom* became the name of his show, the first radio show to rely almost exclusively on recorded music. (*Popular Music and Society*, 9/22/99; *New York Times*, 2/12/84) **2.** According to Allan Metcalf's *America in So Many Words*, the term "disc jockey" first appeared in the Aug. 6, 1941, issue of *Variety*. Other sources, however, indicate that the term was originally coined by Walter Winchell. (*New York Times*, 8/16/92)

1. FIRST CALL LETTER OF RADIO STATIONS EAST OF THE MISSISSIPPI: W
2. FIRST CALL LETTER WEST OF THE MISSISSIPPI: K

An international agreement in 1927 assigned call letters to every nation, each one code for its own location (C for Canada, X for Mexico). The U.S. received K and W for domestic stations. The Mississippi K–W divide wasn't formalized until the Federal Radio Act of 1934, which left some confusion in its wake (KDKA remains in Pittsburgh, and WOW is in Omaha). (*Austin American-Statesman*, 2/22/04)

TV SHOWS THAT BEGAN ON RADIO: CANDID CAMERA BOZO THE CLOWN GUNSMOKE FATHER KNOWS BEST FACE THE NATION PERRY MASON

Candid Camera was known on radio as *Candid Microphone*. (*Boston Globe*, 3/16/90; Nachman, *Raised on Radio*)

READING

1. Number of books Americans say they read each year: 16

2. Books and periodicals read annually by blind Americans: 20

3. Percentage of Americans in 1954 who said that comic books were at least in part to blame for the rise in juvenile delinquency: 70%

Sources: **1.** Eighty-three percent of Americans claim to have read all or part of at least one book in the 12 months preceding the poll. Ten percent claim to have read more than 50 books, and 5% more than 100. (Gallup poll, 12/02) **2.** National Library Service for the Blind. **3.** One in four adults said that comic books bore a "great deal" of blame for juvenile delinquency, while 31% said they bore some blame. (Gallup, 11/54)

YEAR READING TO ONESELF FIRST CAME INTO VOGUE: A.D. 383

That was the year St. Augustine observed that Ambrose, the bishop of Milan, read silently to himself. Until then, reading aloud had been the norm for mutual enjoyment and self-edification. (Manguel, *A History of Reading*)

1. ODDS THAT AN ADULT IN 1950 WAS ILLITERATE: 1 IN 2
2. ODDS TODAY: 1 IN 5

(*Economist*, 10/23/99 [quoting UNESCO figures])

MOST LITERATE COUNTRY ON EARTH: ICELAND

The literacy rate in Iceland is 99.9%, and Icelanders read more books per capita than anyone else. (*Columbia Encyclopedia*; U.S. State Department)

World's most prolific reader: Alexander Danilou, Russia

According to a 1988 article by the Russian Tass news agency, Danilou had read 24,752 books in the course of researching a reference book called *The People of the Blue Planet*. America's most prolific reader is probably Sydney Goldfield of Pikesville, Md., who, as of December 2004, had read over 9,700 books, hoping to reach the magic mark of 10,000. (*Baltimore Sun*, 11/8/99; *Los Angeles Times*, 10/7/88)

U.S. CITY THAT SPENDS THE MOST ON READING MATERIALS: SAN FRANCISCO

San Franciscans spend an average of $266 per year, compared to $144 nationally.
(Bureau of Labor Statistics survey, in the *San Francisco Chronicle*, 5/16/03)

1. MOST POPULAR MAGAZINE IN AMERICA: *AARP* MAGAZINE

2. WORLD'S MOST WIDELY READ MAGAZINE: *READER'S DIGEST*

3. MOST WIDELY READ SINGLE ISSUE OF ANY U.S. MAGAZINE: *SPORTS ILLUSTRATED* SWIMSUIT ISSUE

Sources: **1.** The magazine is sent to all members of the American Association for Retired Persons, and has a circulation of 22 million. *Reader's Digest* is ranked second, with an American circulation of 11 million, followed by *TV Guide* at 9 million and *Better Homes and Gardens* at 7.6 million. (*Los Angeles Times*, 4/4/04) **2.** William Roy DeWitt Wallace borrowed $600 from his family to launch his magazine, soliciting his first 1,500 subscriptions at $3 each and publishing his first issue in February 1922. Today, *Reader's Digest* claims to reach 100 million readers worldwide each month. (*New York Times*, 5/12/03) **3.** According to the magazine, some 55 million Americans take a peek at the swimsuit edition each year. (*Baltimore Sun*, 2/19/99)

1. READING SPEED OF THE AVERAGE PERSON: 250 WORDS PER MINUTE

2. READING SPEED OF THE WORLD'S FASTEST READER: 2,284 WORDS PER MINUTE

Sources: **1.** *Baltimore Sun*, 11/8/99. **2.** Anne Jones of Leicestershire, England, started speed-reading only 7 years before setting the record at the 2003 Mind Sports Olympiad. After taking into account comprehension, her rate was adjusted to 1,285 words per minute, which was still over twice that of her nearest competitor. (*Express*, 9/5/03; *Leicester Mercury*, 8/22/03).

PERCENTAGE OF AMERICANS WHO SAY THEY READ THE FINE PRINT:
When buying or selling a home—85% In credit card agreements—77% In housing rental agreements—70%
On sports/recreation liability waivers—67% In rental car agreements—63% On drug prescriptions—10%

(Ipsos-Public Affairs, cited in *Marketing News*, 9/29/03; *Formulary*, 11/1/03)

RESTAURANTS

1. MOST RESTAURANTS PER CAPITA: SAN FRANCISCO

2. MOST FREQUENTLY ORDERED RESTAURANT MENU ITEM: FRENCH FRIES

3. SECOND MOST FREQUENTLY ORDERED ITEM: HAMBURGER

4. MOST POPULAR MONTH TO EAT OUT: AUGUST

Sources: **1.** *Los Angeles Times*, 8/19/03. **2, 3.** NPD Group, reported in *Minneapolis Star Tribune*, 10/14/03. **4.** Saturday is the most popular day to eat out. (National Restaurant Association)

1. Opening of world's first restaurant: 1725
2. Opening of America's first Chinese restaurant: 1849

Sources: **1.** Several publications list Madrid's *Casa Botin* as the oldest restaurant in the world, and it is certainly the oldest continuously operating restaurant. The word "restaurant" was first used to describe an eating establishment in 1765 by Paris tavern keeper M. Boulanger, who served both soups and meat (a combination previously prohibited in France) with a promise to "restore" aching stomachs—*restaurabo* in Latin. The name stuck, and the word restaurant was born. (*People*, 12/14/87; *Boston Globe*, 6/28/91) **2.** San Francisco's Macao and Woosung offered a $1 all-you-can-eat buffet. Incidentally, medical literature discusses a disease called "Chinese restaurant syndrome," a reaction attributed to the consumption of food with monosodium glutamate (MSG). Symptoms include tingling and burning skin sensations, headache, and chest pain. (*Santa Fe New Mexican*, 11/26/04; *Mosby Medical Encyclopedia*)

SIZE OF A RESTAURANT MEAL IN COMPARISON TO A MEAL PREPARED AT HOME: 170% LARGER

(NPD Group, reported in *Minneapolis Star Tribune*, 10/14/03)

MOST EXPENSIVE RESTAURANT MEAL EVER: $62,679
(OR $10,446.50 PER PERSON)

To celebrate a business deal in the summer of 2001, six bankers racked up the bill at a London restaurant, including a $16,500 bottle of 1945 Chateau Petrus Bordeaux and several other vintage wines. The shocked restaurant staff wrote off the actual food bill, which totaled about $569. Because of publicity arising from the meal, five of the six diners lost their jobs. (AP Worldstream, 2/26/02)

WORLD'S MOST RIDICULOUSLY PRICED MENU ITEMS:
HAMBURGER: $59   CHICKEN ENTRÉE: $267 ABALONE FISH: $1,282

Sources: **1.** The cost of the burger and truffle sandwich at Manhattan's Bistro Moderne, easily eclipsing the $41 price of a burger at New York's Old Homestead Steak House (which the *New York Times* called "genuinely lousy"). (*New York Times*, 1/15/03) **2.** The *Poularde Alexandre Dumaine*, served at La Cote d'Or in France, is filled with julienned leeks and carrots, with truffles inserted under the skin. (*New Yorker*, 5/12/03) **3.** At the Forum Restaurant in Hong Kong, a serving of abalone cost the equivalent of $1,282 in 2003, and depending on the quality, can go much higher. (AP, 4/30/03)

WORLD'S DEADLIEST MENU ITEM: FUGU

Fugu, also known as puffer, globe, or swell fish, is a Japanese delicacy that can be deadly if prepared imperfectly. Improper fugu preparation kills several diners each year, and in 1958, 176 people reportedly died from consuming the fish. (*Times* [London], 12/23/01)

MEALS INTERRUPTED BY MOB HITS: 5

In 1972, "Crazy" Joe Gallo was gunned down at Umberto's Clam House in New York's Little Italy while enjoying shrimp and scungilli salad. Several months later, his avengers entered the Neopolitan Noodle and, in a case of mistaken identity, opened fire on four kosher-meat dealers. . . . In 1985, Gambino crime boss Paul Castellano was shot in front of New York's Sparks Steak House. . . . In 1989, Nicodemo S. Scarfo was shot eight times while chowing down on clams and linguine at a Philadelphia restaurant—and survived. . . . And in December 2003, low-level mobster Louie "Lump Lump" Barone shot Albert Circelli over an argument about a female singer who was entertaining diners at Rao's in East Harlem. (*Time*, 1/20/92; *Independent*, 1/11/03; *Mother Jones*, 1/1/02; *New York Times*, 1/5/04)

NUMBER OF FRENCH CHEFS WHO HAVE COMMITTED SUICIDE AFTER THEIR RESTAURANT WAS DOWNGRADED BY CRITICS: 2

Chef Bernard Loiseau committed suicide after the *GaultMillau* (a popular French restaurant guide) downgraded his restaurant's rating from 19 to 17 out of 20 points. In 1966, Parisian chef Alain Zick killed himself after losing a two-star rating in the *Michelin Guide*, France's best-selling book after the Bible. "Bravo, GaultMillau, you've won," declared legendary chef Paul Bocuse. "Your verdict has cost a man's life." (*New Yorker*, 5/12/03; *Wine Spectator*, 8/31/00)

REWARDS

1. AMOUNT AWARDED TO JUDAS FOR THE BETRAYAL OF JESUS: 30 PIECES OF SILVER

2. AMOUNT AWARDED TO PERSON WHO TIPPED OFF U.S. FORCES TO WHEREABOUTS OF SADDAM HUSSEIN'S SONS: $30 MILLION

3. AMOUNT AWARDED TO PERSON WHO TIPPED OFF THE FBI ABOUT THE POSSIBLE IDENTITY OF THE D.C. SNIPER: $350,000

Sources: **1.** *Atlanta Journal-Constitution*, 3/15/01. **2.** Hussein's sons were found in a home in the northern Iraqi city of Mosul in July 2003 after an informant who has never been identified, but is believed to be the owner of the house, contacted authorities to tell them of the brothers' whereabouts. (Agence France-Presse, 7/31/03) **3.** Robert Holmes, a 47-year-old car repairman from Tacoma, Wash., told the FBI during the 2002 killing spree that his friend John Allen Muhammad might be the shooter. In contrast, Whitney Donahue, a 38-year-old refrigerator repairman from Greencastle, Penn., who called police after he spotted the car at a Maryland rest area on Oct. 24, 2002, received only $150,000. (*Cincinnati Post*, 3/23/04)

AMOUNT AWARDED BY THE IRS IN 2003 TO PEOPLE WHO TURNED IN TAX CHEATS: $4.1 MILLION

People providing information to the IRS receive up to 15% of the additional taxes collected, depending on the value of their information. The record year for IRS reward money was 2000, when it handed out some $10.8 million to informants. (*Wall Street Journal* Abstracts, 2/12/04; *Philadelphia Daily News*, 7/18/01)

AMOUNT OFFERED BY THE D.E.A. FOR THE RETURN OF AN OBJECT THEY COULDN'T DESCRIBE: $25,000

The object was stolen from an unmarked Drug Enforcement Agency vehicle in Wilmington, N.C. " For security reasons, I can't say what it looked like," said Wilmington's DEA agent-in-charge. "It does work in the manner in which you would think, by looking at it, it would work. Obviously, I can't say how it works, but it works. It's also very expensive, and we want it back." (*Wilmington Star News*, 12/3/94)

LARGEST REWARD EVER OFFERED FOR THE RETURN OF A LOST DOG: $25,000

In the fall of 2002, Warren Patabendi of New York offered a $25,000 reward for the return of Bugsy, his parents' German shepherd. Patabendi raised the reward to $25,000 after signs offering a $10,000 reward drew no interest. (UPI, 11/8/02)

AMOUNT OFFERED FOR THE CAPTURE OF OSAMA BIN LADEN: $25 MILLION

This is the largest reward ever offered for a fugitive. In announcing the reward, President Bush said, "There's an old poster out West, as I recall, that said, 'Wanted: Dead or Alive.' All I want, and America wants, is [to see] him brought to justice." (*Insight on the News*, 4/1/03)

REWARD OFFERED BY O. J. SIMPSON FOR INFORMATION LEADING TO THE "REAL KILLER OR KILLERS" OF NICOLE SIMPSON: $500,000

(*USA Today*, 7/22/94)

CRIMINALS ARRESTED AFTER ASKING ABOUT REWARDS FOR THEIR CAPTURE: 2

March 1995:

Gerald Lydell Voyles, suspected in a 1981 murder, walked into the Polk County Prison in Bartow, Fla., and asked about the $3,000 reward for his capture. He was arrested after giving his real name. "We believe he was serious about the reward," said the local sheriff. "He will not be eligible."

(*Tampa Tribune*, 3/6/95)

March 1993:

Humallah Mendenhall, 18, fingered a friend as the murderer of a convenience store clerk to collect the reward. He neglected to mention that he drove the getaway car, for which he was promptly arrested and convicted of murder.

(*Houston Chronicle*, 10/11/95)

AMOUNT MICROSOFT OFFERED FOR INFORMATION LEADING TO THE CREATORS OF THE "MYDOOM," "MSBLAST," AND "SOBIG" VIRUSES: $250,000

In November 2003, Microsoft launched an Anti-Virus Rewards program with $5 million. Despite the reward, none of the virus creators has been captured as of the date of this writing. (*Newsweek*, 2/3/04)

RUNNING

1. NUMBER OF AMERICANS WHO SAID THEY JOGGED IN 1960: 6.9 MILLION

2. NUMBER WHO SAID THEY JOGGED IN 1980: ALMOST 25 MILLION

3. NUMBER WHO JOG TODAY: 36.2 MILLION

4. AMERICANS WHO COMPLETED A RACE IN 2002: 7,746,000

Sources: **1.** In a 1960 Gallup poll, 6% of adults said they occasionally ran. (Gallup, 1/30/83) **2.** Twelve percent of Americans said they jogged in 1980. (AP, 4/19/81) **3.** Running is the ninth most popular sports activity in America, just ahead of basketball and behind (among other sports) bowling, billiards, and fishing. In 2002, almost 25 million runners ran more than six times and 10.4 million ran at least 100 days (Sporting Goods Manufacturers Association, 5/7/04) **4.** Of these, some 39% ran in a 5-kilometer race, 13% in a 10-kilometer race, 6.7% in a half marathon, and 5.8% in a full marathon. (USATF.org)

Country where jogging for exercise was invented: New Zealand

In the late 1940s, Arthur Lydiard, a New Zealand factory worker trying to get rid of an expanding gut, started embarking on long slow runs in the New Zealand countryside. The sight was novel at the time; the few people who ran usually did so at top speed until they collapsed with exhaustion. Eventually, Lydiard not only lost weight with his jogging regimen, but became an accomplished coach espousing its benefits. After three of Lydiard's protégés won running medals at the 1960 Olympics in Rome, jogging became hugely popular in New Zealand, from where it spread around the world. (Galloway's *Book on Running*)

1. FIRST PERSON TO RUN A MARATHON: PHILIPPIDES

2. DISTANCE OF THE FIRST MARATHON: 24.85 MILES

3. CURRENT MARATHON DISTANCE: 26.22 MILES

4. WHY THE DISTANCE WAS CHANGED: SO THE ROYAL CHILDREN COULD SEE THE RACE

Sources: **1.** Legend has it that in 490 B.C., Philippides ran from Marathon in Greece to the city elders in Athens, to tell them the news that the Greek army had beat the Persians in the Battle of Marathon. After the words "Be joyful, we won!" left his mouth, Philippides collapsed and died from exhaustion and heat. (*South China Morning Post*, 5/2/04) **2.** Or 40 kilometers. (*Fort Worth Star-Telegram*, 8/22/04) **3, 4.** The Olympic Marathon was 24.85 miles in 1896 and 1900, and was slated to be that distance again until Princess Mary requested that the race start at Windsor Castle so that her children could watch from the windows. The distance from Windsor to the Olympic Stadium in downtown London was 26 miles, 385 yards, and was eventually adopted as the standard distance for all marathons. (*New York Times*, 11/6/94)

1. NUMBER OF AMERICANS WHO COMPLETED A MARATHON IN 1976: 25,000

2. NUMBER WHO COMPLETED A MARATHON IN 2002: 450,000

Sources: **1.** *Hartford Courant*, 8/9/02. **2.** USATF.org

MARATHON CHEATERS:

1896: After finishing in third place in the first Olympic Marathon in 1896, Spiridon Belokas was disqualified after admitting that he had hopped into a horse-drawn carriage for part of the race.

(*Dallas Morning News*, 8/3/96)

1904: American Fred Lorz appeared to be the winner of the 1904 Olympic Marathon, but was then disqualified after officials learned he had received a car ride for 11 miles. The actual winner, a Cambridge, Mass., metalsmith named Thomas Hicks, was given a bath by friends along the course during the race.

(*Dallas Morning News*, 8/3/96)

1980: A previously unknown runner named Rosie Ruiz came out of the blue to win the 1980 Boston Marathon, but was disqualified after no runners could remember seeing her on the course and she was unable to give her split times, or even explain the term "split time" to race officials. "I don't know how to explain what I did," Ruiz said, defending herself to the end. "I just got up this morning with a lot of energy."

(*Village Voice*, 5/25/99)

NUMBER OF MARATHONS COMPLETED BY RANULPH FIENNES IN 7 DAYS: 7

In an extraordinary feat of endurance, the 59-year-old Englishman ran *seven* marathons in *seven* days on *six* different continents, just *five* months after undergoing double bypass surgery. On October 27, 2003, Fiennes and a partner began the quest by running a marathon in Patagonia, Chile. They then flew to the Falkland Islands of Argentina where they ran another marathon on Tuesday; hopped a plane to Sydney, Australia, for a 26-mile run on Wednesday; off to Singapore for another 26-mile run on Thursday; followed by similar marathons in London and Cairo on Friday and Saturday; before completing the New York Marathon in 5 hours, 25 minutes on Sunday, Nov. 2, 2003. Over the course of the week, Fiennes ran 183.4 miles and covered some 45,000 miles in the air and on the ground. (*New York Times*, 11/3/03)

Year a barefoot runner won the Olympic Marathon: 1960

In 1960, Abebe Bikila of Ethiopia raced through the cobblestone streets of Rome without shoes, winning the marathon in a time of 2:15:16. Four years later in Tokyo, Bikila accomplished the same feat only 40 days after an appendectomy, although this time he wore shoes. (*Runners World*, 1/1/04)

1. INVENTOR OF THE MODERN TREADMILL: WAYNE QUINTON
2. LONGEST DISTANCE RUN ON A TREADMILL IN 24 HOURS: 153.6 MILES (EDIT BERCES, MAR. 8, 2004)

Sources: **1.** While man-powered treadmills had been used to torture prisoners in British jails in the 1800s, Quinton's 1953 version of the treadmill was the first to be used for health purposes, originally for testing cardiac patients at hospitals. (*Seattle Times*, 6/7/98) **2.** *Muscle and Fitness*, 6/1/04.

SANTA

1. HOUSES SANTA HAS TO VISIT ON CHRISTMAS EVE: 202,061,000
2. DISTANCE TRAVELED BY HIS SLEIGH: 761,594 MILES
3. NUMBER OF REINDEER NEEDED: 152,312

Sources: **1.** Our calculations are inspired by Roger Highfield's book *The Physics of Christmas*. We start with the total number of the world's children. Subtract Jews, Muslims, and other non-Christians. Exclude Orthodox Christian kids because they celebrate Christmas on January 6. Divide by the average number of children per household. Assume at least 10% of the remaining children are naughty. (See the 1934 song "Santa Claus Is Coming to Town") **2.** For the sake of simplicity, assume that each house is 20 feet apart (think your typical New York neighborhood), with no Jews, Muslims, or pagans living in between (forget your typical New York neighborhood). **3.** While Santa uses eight reindeer, reindeer can travel a maximum of only 40 miles a day. Thus, Santa needs to change his team every 40 miles, or about 19,039 times over the course of his journey.

AMOUNT THE AVERAGE AMERICAN SPENT ON CHRISTMAS PRESENTS IN 2004: $730

(Gallup, cited in *St. Louis Post Dispatch*, 12/6/04)

1. YEAR THE CELEBRATION OF CHRISTMAS BECAME ILLEGAL IN MASSACHUSETTS: 1659
2. YEAR IT AGAIN BECAME LEGAL: 1681

The Puritans believed that the day Christ was born should be celebrated not with gifts and feasts, but with prayer and hard work. In 1659, a law was passed in the Massachusetts Bay Colony decreeing that "anybody who is found observing, by abstinence from labor, feasting or any other way, any such days as Christmas day, shall pay for every such offense five shillings." (*Los Angeles Times*, 12/22/91)

FIRST STORE SANTAS:

Unknown (1841): In 1841, a Philadelphia store owner named J. W. Parkinson attracted thousands of children to his store by having a Santa Claus in the act of descending the store's chimney from his roof. However, it is unclear whether this Santa was actually real.

(Nissenbaum, *The Battle for Christmas*)

James Edgar (1890): In 1890, Edgar, the owner of a dry-goods store in Brockton, Mass., had a costume made up in Boston and, with his natural white hair and beard, walked through his aisles dressed as Santa. It was the first time children ever came face-to-face with the Christmas icon.

(*Boston Herald*, 12/15/96)

Number of Americans who've had their name legally changed to Santa Claus: 4

The most recent was a 44-year-old bus driver from Utah named David Porter, who won the right to do so from the Utah Supreme Court after a lower court judge said that it would create confusion. One court refused to allow an Ohio man to change his name, saying that the death of Santa would be devastating for children. "An obituary for Santa Claus would be the inevitable result of a name change to Santa Claus," the court wrote in refusing the request of Robert Handley. "The sorrow caused from the sight of such an obituary should be avoided." (*Salt Lake Tribune*, 8/11/01; AP, 3/17/00)

1. AVERAGE WEIGHT OF A MALL SANTA: 218 POUNDS
2. ODDS THAT A STORE SANTA HAS A MISDEMEANOR OR FELONY CONVICTION: 7%

Sources: **1.** Down from 225 pounds in 1997. (General Growth Properties Santa survey) **2.** The charges have included indecent exposure, harassment, assault on a female, soliciting prostitution, battery, and contributing to the delinquency of a minor. Forty-six percent of the malls surveyed hadn't run background checks on Santa or his helpers. (*State* [S.C.], 12/3/03)

First Christmas card: 1843

Up through the mid 19th century, it was customary to send letters to friends and relatives at Christmas. In the fall of 1843, however, Sir Henry Cole was too busy to write individual letters, and commissioned J. C. Horsely to design a Christmas card for him which bore the now familiar phrase "A Merry Christmas and a Happy New Year." Those not sent by Cole were offered for sale. The first Christmas card in America was sent out in 1850 by a store in Albany called Pease's Great Variety. (*Sunday Times* [London], 12/19/93)

FIRST MENTION OF DECEMBER 25 AS THE DATE CHRIST WAS BORN: A.D. 354

Since no one really knew when Jesus was born, early church leaders picked dates all over the spectrum: Bishop Clement of Alexandria said he was born on November 18, while another theologian placed his birth on March 28. Scholars suggest that December 25 was ultimately chosen because early Christians wanted to compete with and ultimately replace a major pagan festival on the Roman calendar occurring on the same day. (*U.S. News and World Report*, 12/23/96)

1. MOST FREQUENTLY RECORDED SONG OF ALL TIME: "WHITE CHRISTMAS"
2. OTHER NOTEWORTHY ASPECT OF THE SONG: IT MARKED THE END OF THE VIETNAM WAR

Sources: **1.** Among the hundreds of artists who have recorded the song since it was first performed by Bing Crosby on Dec. 25, 1941, are Alvin and the Chipmunks, Bob Dylan, Bob Marley, Charlie Parker, Elvis Presley, the Flaming Lips, the Backstreet Boys, the Three Tenors, Perry Como, Doris Day, and Kiss. The song has also been recorded in Japanese, Swahili, and Yiddish. (Rosen, *White Christmas*). **2.** On Apr. 29, 1975, as North Vietnamese troops advanced on Saigon, Americans in the city were secretly told that their evacuation would begin when "White Christmas" was played on the radio. (Rosen, *White Christmas*)

SCHOOL

1. Length of an average school day: **6 hours**
2. Attention span of an average student: **20 minutes**
3. Average annual teacher salary in 1900: **$328**
4. Average teacher salary today: **$45,771**

Sources: **1.** Hoover Institution. **2.** Of college students, that is; the attention span of your average grade-schooler is significantly less. (*High School Journal*, 2/1/00) **3.** *U.S. News and World Report*, 8/6/01. **4.** Indian teachers earn about $300 per month, Russian teachers $200, and Cuban teachers a paltry $20 per month. (*Gannett*, 7/23/04; *Washington Post*, 8/22/04; *Montreal Gazette*, 2/1/03)

1. ODDS THAT AN AMERICAN HAS A HIGH SCHOOL DIPLOMA: 17 IN 20

2. STATE WITH THE LOWEST PERCENTAGE O⁻ HIGH SCHOOL GRADUATES: TEXAS (77%)

3. STATE WITH THE HIGHEST PERCENTAGE OF GRADUATES: NEW HAMPSHIRE (92%)

(*Houston Chronicle*, 6/30/04)

PERSON FOR WHOM THE "DUNCE CAP" WAS NAMED: JOHN DUNS SCOTUS

(1266–1308)

Scotus was a respected theologian in his time, and inspired many followers, called "Duns men." Following his death, however, his views were widely discredited, and his followers were thought of as thickheaded for not seeing the truth. Because of this, the word "dunce" (first spelled that way in 1530) was created for someone too stupid to learn. (*Barnhart Dictionary of Etymology*)

PERCENTAGE OF D'S AND F'S GIVEN BY TEACHERS WHICH GO TO BOYS: 70%

(U.S. News and World Report, 7/30/01)

LENGTH OF THE SCHOOL YEAR IN VARIOUS NATIONS:

CHINA: 251 DAYS OF SCHOOL	ITALY: 216 DAYS
JAPAN: 243 DAYS	ENGLAND: 196 DAYS
GERMANY: 226 DAYS	UNITED STATES: 180 DAYS

The extended summer recess prevalent in America is a remnant of the time when children were needed to work on the family farm. Most other developed nations abandoned this outdated model years ago. (*Harvard Business Review*, 10/03; Cox News Service, 8/6/04)

First multiple-choice exam:

A. 1917 **B. 1931** **C. 1914**

Created by Frederick Kelly in 1914, the first multiple-choice exam was called the Kansas Silent Reading Test. (Aiken, *Tests and Examinations*)

1. NUMBER OF PENCILS MANUFACTURED ANNUALLY: 14 BILLION

2. YEARS AFTER THE PENCIL WAS INVENTED THAT THE ERASER CAME ALONG: 220

3. YEARS AFTER THE ERASER WAS INVENTED THAT IT WAS FIRST PLACED ON A PENCIL: 88

4. ODDS THAT A PENCIL IS YELLOW: 3 IN 4

5. WHAT THE NUMBERS ON THE PENCILS REFER TO: THE HARDNESS OF THE LEAD

Sources: **1.** Petroski, *The Pencil*. **2.** The lead (actually graphite) that now graces the inside of pencils worldwide was initially discovered in the 1550s near Keswick, England. It wasn't until 1770, however, that English chemist Joseph Priestly discovered that latex removes pencil marks. (*Christian Science Monitor*, 4/15/97) **3.** A Philadelphian named Hyman Lipman patented the idea of putting an eraser on a pencil in 1858. There was initial opposition to the marriage, however, with many educators believing that making errors easier to correct would ultimately result in more errors. (Petroski, *The Pencil*) **4.** There are two explanations for yellow being the predominant pencil color. The first is that an early manufacturer of the pencil located in Austria sought to honor his homeland by making his instrument in the yellow and black colors of the Austro-Hungarian flag (since the lead was black, the body had to be yellow). The second is that pencil makers sought to inform customers that their lead came from China (considered to be of the highest quality), and used the color Westerners associated with Asians. (Petroski, *The Pencil*) **5.** Most pencils are numbered from 1 to 4, with 4 being the hardest. (*Winston-Salem Journal*, 2/11/02)

SECRETS

1. NUMBER OF U.S. GOVERNMENT EMPLOYEES WHO CAN STAMP A DOCUMENT AS "TOP SECRET": 3,978

2. NUMBER OF DOCUMENTS CLASSIFIED AS SECRET IN 2003: 14 MILLION

3. NUMBER CLASSIFIED AS SECRET IN THE YEAR BEFORE SEPT. 11, 2001: 8 MILLION

4. AMERICANS WHO HOLD SOME TYPE OF SECURITY CLEARANCE: 2 MILLION

Sources: **1.** Gannett News, 6/21/04. **2.** Among the government's recently declassified documents is one detailing a concocted story about an Al-Qaeda plan to kidnap Santa Claus. (*Washington Post*, 9/3/04) **3.** *Boston Globe*, 5/4/04. **4.** GAO Reports, 8/1/04.

Levels of government secrecy:

CONFIDENTIAL:
Information whose loss would cause damage to national security, like the strength of American military forces and design and performance data of weapons.

SECRET:
Information whose loss would cause serious damage to national security, such as disclosing individual military plans or intelligence-gathering activities.

TOP SECRET:
Information whose loss would cause grave damage to national security, such as the disclosure of military codes or secret communications systems.

SIGMA 16:
Documents "containing nuclear weapons design specifications that would permit the reproduction and function of the weapon."

(Krutz, *Mastering the Five Domains of ISM*; Washington Post, 8/31/01)

SUBJECT OF A 1918 DOCUMENT THAT THE GOVERNMENT STILL REFUSES TO DISCLOSE ON NATIONAL SECURITY GROUNDS:

INVISIBLE INK

Several groups have been waging a decade-long battle to obtain the Mar. 16, 1918, document describing formulas for invisible ink, the oldest classified document in America. Though 1960s cereal boxes regularly published instructions on how to make invisible ink, the CIA refuses to declassify the document. "These formulas are so rudimentary that it's like taking Indian smoke signals and making them secret," commented the plaintiffs' attorney. (*Philadelphia Inquirer*, 2/27/02)

First president to be protected by the Secret Service: Grover Cleveland

Although the Secret Service was established in July 1865, its initial job was not protecting presidents, but battling counterfeiters (a role it retains today). It was not until the spring of 1894 that the agency clandestinely sent two agents to the White House to guard Pres. Grover Cleveland. That summer, three other agents were assigned to guard Cleveland's family at their summer home in Buzzard's Bay, Mass., after plots to kidnap the first family were uncovered. (Melanson, *Secret Service*)

SECRET RECIPES:

Coke:

Called "Merchandise 7x" by Coca-Cola employees, the formula for Coke is kept in a bank vault in Atlanta, Ga., but is seldom if ever seen. The company's bylaws specify that the formula is to be known to only two high-ranking Coke executives at any one time (who, reportedly, may not fly on the same plane), and is passed down by word of mouth. In 1977, the Indian government demanded to know Coke's ingredients, and Coca-Cola left that country rather than submit, not returning until 1993.

(U.S. News and World Report, 9/23/85; Griesing, I'd Like to Buy the World a Coke)

KFC Chicken:

The recipe for the Colonel's chicken is locked in a vault at Kentucky Fried Chicken headquarters in Louisville, Ky., accessible to only two people. To ensure secrecy, KFC has two companies prepare the chicken's coating, each preparing half the recipe, which (according to KFC) "is then blended in a way that it cannot be reverse engineered." In 2000, KFC sued the Kentucky couple who purchased the Colonel's house after they claimed that they had discovered the secret recipe in a book in the attic, but dropped the suit after determining that the ingredients listed were not the KFC recipe.

(CBS News, 1/30/01)

Krispy Kreme Doughnuts:

The company's signature glazed doughnut recipe was created in 1933 by a New Orleans cook, Joe LeBeau, and is kept in a manila envelope in a combination vault at the company's headquarters in Winston-Salem, N.C. To ensure the recipe's confidentiality, three separate groups of workers prepare separate portions of Krispy Kreme's glazed doughnut mix at its plant.

(Philadelphia magazine, 5/03)

1. NUMBER OF CIA AGENTS WHO HAVE BEEN KILLED IN THE LINE OF DUTY AS OF 2004: 83
2. NUMBER WHOSE NAMES REMAIN SECRET: 35

(AP, 5/21/04)

1. NUMBER OF PEOPLE WHO OFFICIALLY KNOW THE IDENTITY OF DEEP THROAT, THE *WASHINGTON POST*'S WATERGATE INFORMANT: 3

2. IDENTITY OF DEEP THROAT, ACCORDING TO WHAT CARL BERNSTEIN'S 9-YEAR-OLD SON TOLD A CAMPMATE: W. MARK FELT

Sources: **1.** Reporters Bob Woodward and Carl Bernstein and editor Ben Bradlee are the only people who officially know the identity of the informant who helped bring down the Nixon administration, and they have vowed to disclose it only after his death. (*Dallas Morning News*, 6/27/02) **2.** The name of the former associate director of the FBI slipped from young Jacob's lips while at summer camp in 1998. Though Bernstein denied that he would ever reveal Deep Throat's identity to a 9-year-old, Felt has remained a popular suspect with theorists after Jacob's faux pas. (*Dallas Morning News*, 8/1/99)

SECRET CIA PLOTS TO KILL OR HUMILIATE FIDEL CASTRO:

Exploding seashell (1963): According to a CIA report released in 1993, "the idea was to take an unusually spectacular seashell that would be certain to catch Castro's eye, load it with an explosive, and put it in an area where Castro went skin diving." The idea was shelved after the CIA could not find a "spectacular enough shell" that could hold enough explosives.

Poisoned cigars: CIA operatives in Cuba had cigars made with a chemical additive that was intended to produce "temporary personality orientation," with the plan to induce "Castro to smoke one before making a speech and then make a public spectacle of himself." The CIA abandoned the plan because no one could figure out how to get them to Castro.

Depilatories in Castro's shoes: CIA operatives hatched a plan to place a depilatory in Castro's shoes while he was on a foreign trip so that his beard, eyebrows, and pubic hair would fall out. After testing the chemical on animals, the scheme fell through after Castro did not make the trip.

(CIA Report on Plots to Assassinate Fidel Castro; *Seattle Times*, 11/30/99)

What a mafia member says at his initiation ceremony: "May I burn in hell if I betray my friends in the family"

In 1990, George Freslone, an FBI informant and mafia turncoat, secretly recorded his own initiation into the mafia, one of only two recordings of the ceremony that are known to exist. Before administering the oath, inductees have their trigger finger pricked by their "sponsor" until blood is drawn. (*Philadelphia Inquirer*, 11/8/94)

SHOPPING

1. **PERCENTAGE OF TOTAL PURCHASES IN AMERICA MADE BY WOMEN: 85%**

2. **ODDS THAT A WOMEN SAYS SHE ENJOYS SHOPPING: 4 IN 10**

3. **ODDS THAT A MAN ENJOYS SHOPPING: 2 IN 10**

4. **NUMBER OF AMERICANS AFFLICTED WITH ONIOMANIA (COMPULSIVE SHOPPING DISORDER): 15 MILLION**

5. **STRANGEST PURCHASE BY A COMPULSIVE SHOPPER: 2,000 WRENCHES**

Sources: **1.** *Newsday*, 9/26/04. **2, 3.** *Retail Forward*, 11/03. **4.** The condition was first identified nearly a century ago by a German psychiatrist. Oniomaniacs have an insatiable urge to shop, feel a tremendous rush when buying something, and then feel guilty for losing control. To counteract that feeling, they either hide their purchases or go shopping again. (*Orlando Sentinel*, 1/23/03) **5.** *Forbes*, 8/11/03.

1. **FIRST SUBURBAN SHOPPING CENTER IN AMERICA: COUNTRY CLUB PLAZA, KANSAS CITY, MO., 1922**

2. **FIRST INDOOR SHOPPING MALL: SOUTHDALE CENTER, EDINA, MINN., 1956**

Sources: **1.** When it opened in 1922, Country Club Plaza was revolutionary: a place that shoppers drove to, left their cars in a large parking lot, and shopped in a group of stores anchored by large tenants. In 1925, Country Club broke new ground again by becoming the first to have outdoor Christmas lights. (*New York Sun*, 1/6/03) **2.** The Southdale Center was the first fully enclosed, climate-controlled shopping mall, inventing the now familiar layout of a center pedestrian walkway surrounded by two levels of shopping floors. Its centerpiece was a multistory atrium (which the developers called "the Garden of Perpetual Spring"), which lured shoppers with orchids, azaleas, and palms that bloomed even in the midst of the harsh Minnesota winter. (Wrigley, *Reading Retail*)

Percentage of American shoppers who go to their right when entering a store: 85%

People tend to veer in stores the way they drive; thus, as studies have confirmed, shoppers in Britain and Australia walk to their left upon entering a store. (Underhill, *Why We Buy*)

1. AVERAGE TIME A WOMEN SPENDS IN A STORE IF SHE'S WITH ANOTHER WOMAN: 8 MINUTES, 15 SECONDS
2. IF SHE'S WITH HER CHILDREN: 7 MINUTES, 19 SECONDS
3. IF SHE'S WITH A MAN: 4 MINUTES, 41 SECONDS

The average amount of time a person who buys an item spends in a store is 11 minutes, 27 seconds. The average amount of time a person who doesn't buy anything spends in a store is 2 minutes, 36 seconds. (Underhill, *Why We Buy*; *St. Louis Post-Dispatch*, 12/3/97)

1. OLDEST STORE IN AMERICA:
LONDON HARNESS, BOSTON, MASS. (OPENED IN 1776)

2. OLDEST STORE IN AMERICA STILL OPERATED BY THE SAME FAMILY:
HILDRETH'S DEPARTMENT STORE, SOUTHHAMPTON, N.Y. (OPENED IN 1842)

Sources: **1.** Runners-up: Shreve, Crump & Lowe is the oldest jewelry store in America, selling baubles from its store in downtown Boston since 1796. In Chepachet, R.I., the Brown & Hopkins General Store has been in operation since 1809, making it the oldest continuously operated general store in the U.S. (*Washington Post*, 3/15/91; *Boston Globe*, 11/16/03) **2.** *New York Times*, 12/8/02.

1. NUMBER OF TIMES THE AVERAGE LIPSTICK HAS BEEN TOUCHED BEFORE IT IS BOUGHT: 8
2. NUMBER OF PEOPLE WHO'VE TOUCHED A TOWEL: 6.6
3. A GREETING CARD: 25

(Underhill, *Why We Buy*; *Bergen County Record*, 2/1/98; *Minneapolis Star Tribune*, 7/9/97)

1. NUMBER OF SHOPPING CENTERS IN THE U.S.: 47,835
2. NUMBER OF MALLS: 1,130
3. TOTAL SQUARE FOOTAGE OF RETAIL SPACE IN THE U.S.: 5.8 BILLION SQUARE FEET

Sources: **1.** In 1964, there were 7,600 shopping centers. (*Orlando Sentinel*, 2/12/04) **2.** National Real Estate Investor, 12/1/03. **3.** ICSC, 2/12/04.

Odds that a man will buy something he tries on:

6 in 10

Odds that a woman will do so:

1 in 4

(*The Palm Beach Post*, 7/29/99)

Percentage of women who decide which clothes to buy by themselves:

67%

Percentage of men who do so:

47%

(*Washington Post*, 8/22/99)

Percentage of men's clothing purchases made by women in 1985:

60%

Percentage of men's clothing purchases that are made by women today:

30%

(The NPD Group)

STATES WITH THE HIGHEST RATIOS OF SHOPPING CENTERS PER CAPITA:

1. CONNECTICUT—28.88 SQUARE FEET
2. DELAWARE—28.84 SQUARE FEET
3. FLORIDA—27.73 SQUARE FEET

(NRB Shopping Centers Census)

Instances where kids were accidentally locked overnight in toy stores: 1

On Jan. 21, 1996, every child's fantasy—and every parent's nightmare—came true for Antony and Jerome Cerezo of Quebec, Canada. The two children wandered off from their backyard and went to a nearby Toys R Us, where they fell asleep in a playhouse. When they woke up, the lights were out, and the store was closed. While about 150 people searched for them in the neighborhood, the boys were playing inside. They were discovered by the store manager the following morning. Asked why the alarm system didn't go off, a Toys R Us spokesman said: "They never tried the doors. . . . I'm told the trail of toys and chip bags confirms this." (*Montreal Gazette,* 1/23/96)

1. Percentage of shopping purchases made with cash in 1995: 60%
2. Percentage of shopping purchases made with cash in 2003: 32%

During the same period, purchases with credit or debit cards went from 10% of all shopping purchases in 1995 to 52% in 2003. (*Fortune,* 2/23/04)

ITEMS RECENTLY OFFERED FOR SALE ON EBAY:

A FULLY FUNCTIONAL KIDNEY on Sept. 2, 1999, after 6 days of bidding, the price of the kidney had ballooned to over $5 million. EBay put a stop to the sale because it is a federal offense to traffic in human organs.

(*Virginian-Pilot,* 9/12/99)

CHUNKS OF DEBRIS FROM THE WORLD TRADE CENTER went up on the auction block within minutes of the attack, though eBay was quick to remove the listings.

(*Newsweek,* 6/17/02)

USED LADIES' UNDERGARMENTS (particularly panties) could fetch up to $30 and remained a thriving niche market on the site before recently being banned.

(*Newsweek,* 6/17/02)

NAVEL LINT sold direct from a woman's belly button for $1.

(*People,* 8/4/03)

ARNOLD SCHWARZENEGGER'S USED COUGH DROP was offered in 2004 under the header "Schwarzenegger's DNA" with a starting bid of $500. EBay yanked the item after claiming it violated the site's prohibition against selling body parts.

(*Los Angeles Times,* 5/22/04)

SHOWS

1. HIGHEST BROADWAY TICKET PRICE IN 1893: $1.50

2. HIGHEST TICKET PRICE IN 2004: $480

3. LONGEST-RUNNING PLAY IN HISTORY: THE MOUSETRAP (53 YEARS)

4. LONGEST-RUNNING SHOW IN AMERICAN THEATER HISTORY: THE FANTASTICKS (42 YEARS)

Sources: **1.** On May 22, 1893, the American Theatre opened on 42nd Street with the U.S. premiere of *The Prodigal Daughter*, with ticket prices ranging from 25¢ to $1.50. (*USA Today*, 11/1/93) **2.** For the 150 VIP tickets that were offered per performance when Nathan Lane and Matthew Broderick starred as Max Bialystock and Leo Bloom in *The Producers* in 2002 and again in 2004. (*Variety*, 8/11/03) **3.** When it first opened in London on Nov. 25, 1952, one lead actor said, "We didn't think it was very good." The play, still running today, has been seen by over 10 million people in 44 countries. (*Mirror*, 8/25/01) **4.** The show, which opened May 3, 1960, at Manhattan's Sullivan Street Playhouse, closed in January 2002 after 17,162 performances. (*Newsday*, 9/5/01)

1. NUMBER OF TIMES HECTOR MONTALVO SAW CATS: 678

2. NUMBER OF TIMES LINDA RUSSAK SAW LES MISERABLES: 441

3. NUMBER OF TIMES LINDA RUSSAK SAW JEKYLL AND HYDE: 487

Sources: **1.** Montalvo first saw *Cats* on Oct. 11, 1982, which was 4 days after it opened on Broadway, and continued to see the show weekly until it closed in June 2000. "There is something in everybody's life that they do that becomes a part of them. For some, it may be a television show, a book or a movie. For me, it's *Cats*." (*Rocky Mountain News*, 9/15/98; *New York Times*, 4/21/00) **2.** And that's just as of September 1998. Russak started going to *Les Miz* as a way of connecting with her late husband, who had been a big fan of the musical. (*Rocky Mountain News*, 9/15/98) **3.** *Georgia Magazine*, 3/01.

First Broadway musical: Black Crook (1866)

Although this first show to feature a chorus line had a rather wooden plot, it featured young women costumed in "outrageously provocative" flesh-colored tights, which garnered censure—and increased ticket sales. Newspapers described the tights-wearing performers as "demons" with "scarcely a rag left upon them to take off" and the *New York Times* said the women wore "no clothes to speak of." (*NWSA Journal*, 6/22/02)

For their return to *The Producers* in 2004, Lane and Broderick each earned $100,000 a week. Other lavishly paid Broadway performers include Jerry Lewis, who earned $40,000 per week, plus a percentage of the box office, for his role as the Devil in *Damn Yankees*, and Glenn Close, who was paid $30,000 per week for her role in *Sunset Boulevard*. (*Variety*, 8/25/03; *Newsweek*, 3/6/95)

NUMBER OF TIMES YUL BRYNNER PERFORMED IN *THE KING AND I*: 4,625

Other iron horses of the stage include Bryan Hull, who played the Old Actor in the musical *The Fantasticks* 8,262 times from 1981 to 1998, and Catherine Russell, who played the lead in *The Perfect Crime* 6,892 times as of the end of 2003. (*Newsday*, 12/14/03)

MOST EXPENSIVE FLOP IN BROADWAY HISTORY:
Dance of the Vampires (2003)

The musical closed after 56 performances and a loss estimated at more than $12 million. Its less-than-kind reviews didn't help—the *Washington Post* called it "Count Drekula," while the *New York Times* said, "There are moments that climb into the stratosphere of legendary badness."

(*Washington Post*, 12/10/02; *The Stage*, 1/23/03)

SHOWS CLOSED ON OBSCENITY GROUNDS: 2
MAE WEST'S *SEX* (1926) AND *THE PLEASURE-MAN* (1928)

Sex, the story of a Montreal prostitute who goes straight, ran for almost a year before New York City's deputy police commissioner raided the theater. At her trial, the prosecution relied principally on the testimony of a police sergeant who testified that, during the play, "Miss West moved her navel up and down and from left to right." On cross-examination, however, he admitted that he could not swear he saw her navel. Nevertheless, West and her costars were convicted of lewdness and corrupting youth and spent 8 days in jail. (Watts, *Mae West: An Icon in Black and White*)

SIBLINGS

1. ODDS THAT AN AMERICAN HAS AT LEAST ONE SIBLING: 17 IN 20

2. ODDS THAT A PERSON HAS FIVE OR MORE SIBLINGS: 3 IN 10

3. PERCENTAGE OF SIBLINGS WHO HAVE GOOD RELATIONSHIPS WITH THEIR BROTHERS AND SISTERS: 78%

4. PERCENTAGE OF SIBLINGS WHO CHARACTERIZE THEIR RELATIONSHIP WITH BROTHERS OR SISTERS AS APATHETIC OR HOSTILE: 22%

Sources: **1.** When stepsiblings are taken into account, the number of multisibling families has been reported to be as high as 19 in 20. (*Time*, 12/18/00) **2.** *American Demographics*, 8/1/96. **3, 4.** *New York Times*, 8/18/92.

PERCENTAGE OF ADULT SIBLINGS THAT TALK TO EACH OTHER EVERY FEW DAYS: 20% AT LEAST ONCE A MONTH: 44% A FEW TIMES A YEAR: 29% NEVER: 7%

It's one thing to cut off contact with a sibling when living apart, but another when siblings share the same house, as is the case in a feud that's lasted 20 years between the Crocket brothers of Scotland. The brothers share the house left to them after their mother's death, but have barricaded the connecting doors to assure no unnecessary contact. The feud began over contested electricity bills and cleaning duties, and has escalated to a complete shutout—the two ignore each other if they ever meet. (*American Demographics*, 8/96; *Sunday Mail*, 2/23/03)

Number of the first 23 NASA astronauts that were firstborn: 21

The other two were only children, who share many of the same characteristics of firstborns. Popular theory has it that firstborns are reliable and well-organized, and strive for perfection. (*Washington Times*, 12/07/99)

RANK OF SIBLING RELATIONSHIPS IN ORDER OF CLOSENESS:

1. RELATIONSHIPS BETWEEN SISTERS
2. BETWEEN A SISTER AND A BROTHER
3. BETWEEN BROTHERS

(*Psychology Today*, 4/1/88)

1. PERCENTAGE OF SIBLINGS WHO SAY THEIR PARENTS PLAYED FAVORITES WHEN THEY WERE YOUNGER: 84%

2. PERCENTAGE OF MEN WHO SAY THEY WERE FAVORED BY THEIR MOTHER: 66%

3. PERCENTAGE OF WOMEN WHO SAY THEIR MOTHER FAVORED THEM: 27%

According to one study, fathers also tend to favor the opposite sex. When siblings said their father had a favorite, 62% of women and 49% of men said they were the one favored. (Klagsburn, *Mixed Feelings*)

BEST BIRTH-ORDER MIX FOR A HAPPY MARRIAGE: ELDEST-BORN FEMALE AND LAST-BORN MALE

According to psychologist Kevin Leman's birth order theory (based on a study of 3,000 families) many marriage problems stem from where in line spouses were born. The eldest-youngest combination works well because opposites attract and balance each other's characteristics, whereas two firstborn spouses are the worst match, as they constantly try to boss each other around. (*Washington Times*, 12/7/99)

SIBLINGS WHO WERE REUNITED AFTER . . . :

51 years: In 1950, Yap Sung was expelled from Malaysia to China by the British government, separating him from his parents and two sisters. Fifty-one years later, Sung came to Malaysia to look for his sisters. After a Malaysian newspaper printed their picture with an article about their long-lost brother, the siblings reunited in April 2001.

(*New Straits Times* [Maylasia], 4/17/01)

66 years: For 66 years, Binyamin Shilon thought his sister Rozia had been killed in the Holocaust. While he escaped to Russia and fought in the Russian army, Rozia was sent to Auschwitz, but miraculously survived. Both eventually made their way to Israel, but assumed the other had perished. Then, at the urging of a family friend, Rozia visited an Israeli museum devoted to the Holocaust in 2003, and learned that her brother was not only alive, but living not far from her. A few days later, Binyamin received a call. The caller asked whether he had a sister named Rozia. "Yes," he answered, expecting to hear what he had always feared about his sister's fate. The caller (Binyamin's nephew) then asked, "Would you like to talk to her?"

(*New York Times*, 12/23/03)

SLEEP

1. AMOUNT OF SLEEP REQUIRED BY A NEWBORN: 16.5 HOURS

2. AMOUNT OF SLEEP REQUIRED BY AN ADULT: 8 TO 9 HOURS

3. AMOUNT OF SLEEP THE AVERAGE ADULT ACTUALLY GETS PER NIGHT: 6 HOURS, 54 MINUTES

4. AMOUNT OF SLEEP THE AVERAGE ADULT GOT IN 1900: 8 1/2 HOURS

Sources: **1, 2.** Hauri, *No More Sleepless Nights*. **3.** National Sleep Foundation, cited in *Washington Times*, 4/1/01. **4.** Before electricity allowed people to turn night into day. (*Washington Times*, 4/1/01.)

AMOUNT OF TIME IT TAKES THE AVERAGE PERSON TO FALL ASLEEP: 15 MINUTES

(*The Washington Post*, 6/3/01)

PERCENTAGE OF ADULTS WHO SAY THEY WAKE EVERY NIGHT TO GO TO THE BATHROOM: 53%

(*Chicago Sun-Times*, 9/2/03)

1. Duration of the average yawn: 6 seconds

2. Percentage of people who yawn within 5 minutes of seeing someone else yawn: 55%

3. Test subjects who had the urge yawn after merely reading about yawning: 65%

Sources: **1.** *Chicago Sun-Times*, 8/1/03. **2.** *Columbian*, 4/4/03. **3.** *St. Petersburg Times*, 6/28/89.

1. LONGEST SCIENTIFICALLY DOCUMENTED CASE OF SLEEP DEPRIVATION: RANDY GARDNER (11 DAYS, 12 MINUTES)

2. TIME GARDNER RESTED AFTERWARD: 15 HOURS

Sources: **1.** By day 4, 17-year-old Randy Gardner was experiencing vivid hallucinations, including one in which he thought himself to be a famous football player. Despite his fatigue, in the final days of the test, he was able to defeat sleep researcher William Dement 100 times at pinball on day 11. According to Australian newspapers, a woman named Maureen Weston once reportedly went 18 days without sleep during a rocking chair marathon. (*Guardian*, 1/6/04; *New Scientist*, 4/26/97; *Courier-Mail*, 5/5/00) **2.** Gardner claimed he felt completely fine after waking up. (*New Scientist*, 4/26/97)

Percentage of car accidents caused by sleep deprivation: 54%

(*Times Newspapers*, 8/28/02)

PERCENTAGE OF PEOPLE WHO DREAM IN COLOR: 61%

Source: A 2003 study found 18% of people claiming that they never or rarely dreamed in color, versus 71% in 1942. (*New York Times*, 1/27/04)

1. DATE PRES. RONALD REAGAN FELL ASLEEP DURING AN AUDIENCE WITH THE POPE: JUNE 7, 1982

2. HOURS CHARLES LINDBERGH STAYED AWAKE DURING HIS 1927 SOLO FLIGHT OVER THE ATLANTIC: 33

Sources: **1.** Administration officials attributed the doze to jet lag. Reagan, a legendary sleeper, also reportedly overslept before his second inauguration, almost missing the event. (*Washington Post*, 1/11/92) **2.** Lindbergh fought the incessant urge to fall asleep by punching himself in the face and attempting to sleep with one eye open. Around the 20th hour, he suddenly awoke to find his plane plummeting toward the sea. (Martin, *Counting Sheep*, reported in the *Daily Telegraph*, 8/8/02)

SNEAKERS

1. AMOUNT AMERICANS SPEND ANNUALLY ON SNEAKERS: $16 BILLION

2. PERCENTAGE OF SNEAKERS SOLD IN AMERICA MADE FOR RUNNING: 28%

3. PERCENTAGE MADE FOR BASKETBALL: 23%

4. BEST-SELLING SNEAKER OF ALL TIME: CONVERSE ALL STARS

Sources: **1.** *New York Times*, 4/4/04. **2, 3.** Based on 2003 figures, running and basketball shoe styles rank 1 and 2 in the U.S. (*Footwear News*, 6/14/04) **4.** Introduced in 1917, the All Star was the first sneaker designed for basketball. An estimated 575 million pairs of the sneaker have been sold to date. (*Oregonian*, 7/10/03)

FIRST USE OF THE WORD "SNEAKER": 1873

The word comes from the shoe's rubber sole, which allows wearers to "sneak" around noiselessly. In 1862, a book titled *Female Life in Prison* said that prisoners referred to the rubber-soled shoes worn by a correction officer as "sneaks." Several years later, the use of "sneaks" to refer to rubber-soled shoes gained wide acceptance, and in 1873, store ads started referring to rubber-soled shoes by the name "sneaker." (*Chicago Tribune*, 4/18/93; *Rochester Democrat and Chronicle*, 5/13/01)

1. Nike's original name: Blue Ribbon Sports

2. Nike's sales revenue in 1964: $8,000

3. Nike's sales revenue in 2003: $12.3 billion

Sources: **1.** The company was started in 1964 by Phil Knight, a former University of Oregon runner and CPA, and Bill Bowerman, the track coach at Oregon, who made running shoes in his garage on the side. The company changed its name to Nike in 1972, although several founders fought hard to call the shoes "Dimension 6." (Strasser, *Swoosh*) **2.** Knight sold sneakers out of the back of his Plymouth Valiant at track meets around Oregon, and sold 1,300 pairs its first year. (*Footwear News*, 11/25/02) **3.** *Women's Wear Daily*, 8/12/04.

AMOUNT NIKE PAID FOR THE DESIGN OF ITS LOGO: $35

In 1971, Carolyn Davidson, a graphic design student at Portland State University, was approached by Nike founder Phil Knight and asked to design a logo for the then unknown athletic shoe company. When Davidson presented the swoosh design to Knight, his response was "Well, I don't love it but it'll grow on me." Davidson received $35 for her services. Eleven years later, Davidson was issued some Nike stock as a measure of the company's appreciation. (*Sports Illustrated*, 2/24/97)

RIOTS RELATING TO THE SALE OF AIR JORDANS:

Charlotte, N.C.: On Feb. 14, 2004, Charlotte police were called in to a shopping mall after 200 people waiting to purchase the new Jordan Retro 12 sneakers started pushing and fighting, resulting in one injury and one arrest.

(Charlotte Observer, 2/15/04)

Alexandria, La.: On Mar. 3, 2001, after 400 customers waiting to purchase the new Air Jordan Retro 11s broke the security gate of a sneaker store, police were called in, and used pepper spray to disperse the crowd. "It was like an animal attacking a bloody piece of meat," one customer said.

(Daily Town Talk, 3/4/01)

Sacramento, Calif.: Also on Mar. 3, 2001, 60 Sacramento police officers in riot gear were called in to quell disturbances caused by 200 customers fighting for 80 pairs of Jordan Retro 11s in a local mall.

(Scripps Howard News Service, 3/6/01)

LARGEST SNEAKERS IN NBA HISTORY:
1. SHAQUILLE O'NEAL: SIZE 23
2. WILL PERDUE: SIZE 22-4A
3. BOB LANIER: SIZE 22

(Fort Worth Star-Telegram, 9/17/99; Dallas Morning News, 2/17/99)

MOST SNEAKER ENDORSEMENT SWITCHES IN A SINGLE SEASON: 4 (DARRYL DAWKINS, 1982)

At the beginning of the 1982 NBA season, Dawkins had a promotional deal with Nike. Several weeks into the season, he told Nike he was going to Pro-Keds. A few months after that, he told Pro-Keds he wanted to go back to Nike, and got Nike to pay him a $20,000 advance. Several weeks later, Dawkins signed with Pony, and appeared in the playoffs in Pony shoes. Nike, which had just printed up 20,000 posters of Dawkins wearing its sneakers, got fed up and sued. (*Sports Illustrated*, 1/23/84)

SOCCER

1. NUMBER OF AMERICANS WHO PLAY SOCCER: 15 MILLION

2. NUMBER OF PEOPLE WORLDWIDE WHO PLAY SOCCER: 240 MILLION

3. AVERAGE ATTENDANCE FOR THE U.S. MAJOR SOCCER LEAGUE: 15,000

4. AVERAGE ATTENDANCE FOR BRITAIN'S TOP PROFESSIONAL LEAGUE: 35,000

5. SOCCER TEAM WITH THE WORLD'S HIGHEST AVERAGE ATTENDANCE: BORUSSIA DORTMAND, GERMANY (78,000)

Sources: **1.** *New York Times*, 5/26/02. **2.** *Washington Post*, 4/22/01. **3.** *Sports Illustrated*, 7/5/04. **4.** *New Straits Times* (Malaysia), 6/27/04. **5.** Agence France-Presse, 1/8/04.

1. First reference to the word "football": **1424**

2. First use of the word "soccer": **1889**

3. Countries that call soccer "football": **188**

4. Countries that call soccer "soccer": **4**

Sources: **1.** According to the *Oxford English Dictionary*, the first use of the word "football" was in an edict put out by King James I that banned the playing of the sport: "The king forbids that any man play at the fut ball under the pain of jail." (*Independent*, 6/6/96) **2.** The word "soccer" (or "socca" or "socker" as the word was originally spelled) came into being as a means of distinguishing the two types of football played in England—rugby football and "association" football. In print, the latter was often abbreviated "assoc. football," which was itself subsequently shortened in the U.S. to "socca" and then to "soccer." (*Knoxville News-Sentinel*, 5/16/03) **3, 4.** Every country except for the U.S., Canada, Australia, and New Zealand calls the sport "football."

YEAR FIRST WAR FOUGHT OVER SOCCER: 1969

On June 8, 1969, Honduras beat El Salvador in the first half of a World Cup qualifying match held in the Honduran capital. The previous night, Honduran fans had surrounded the hotel where the Salvadoran team was staying, creating a deliberate racket so the Salvadoran team could not sleep. Angry at these tactics, the Salvadorans responded in kind when the series moved back to El Salvador. On game day, the Honduran team had to be brought to the stadium in armored cars. A dirty dishtowel was hung from the flagpole in place of the Honduran flag, and hundreds of visiting Honduran fans were beaten. The "Soccer War" began the following night, killing 3,000 before a cease-fire was declared. (Kapuscinski, *The Soccer War*)

INSTANCES WHEN SOCCER BRIEFLY LED TO PEACE: DEC. 25, 1914

During a spontaneous Christmas Day cease-fire in World War I, British and German soldiers who had been killing each other hours before put down their guns and met in no-man's-land to bury their dead and play a game of soccer. According to a diary report, the Germans won 3–2. (*Washington Times*, 7/15/03)

MOST LOPSIDED SCORE IN SOCCER HISTORY:
AUSTRALIA 32, AMERICAN SAMOA 0

The slaughter occurred in a World Cup qualifier on Apr. 11, 2001. There were so many goals that the official scorekeeper apparently lost count and it took several days to determine whether the score was actually 31–0 or 32–0. (*Toronto Star*, 4/11/01)

BIGGEST UPSETS IN SOCCER HISTORY:

North Korea 1, Italy 0 (1966 World Cup)

North Korea, an unknown entity in the soccer world, beat the mighty Italians on their way to the World Cup finals. Korea's lone goal scorer was rewarded with a Mercedes and a luxury apartment on his return to North Korea, while Italians greeted their team with rotten fruit.

(*New York Times*, 6/7/99)

U.S. 1, England 0 (1950 World Cup)

On June 29, 1950, a hodgepodge of Americans (led by a player who stayed out partying the night before) beat the vaunted English. When editors at the *New York Times* received the score, they thought there had been an error, and refused to print it without confirmation.

(*New York Post*, 6/29/00)

Uruguay 2, Brazil 1 (1950 World Cup)

On July 16, 1950, tiny Uruguay beat host Brazil before a crowd of 199,584 Brazilians, the largest crowd ever to see a sporting event in a stadium.

(*Agence France-Presse*, 7/14/00)

275

SPELLING

1. MOST FREQUENTLY MISSPELLED WORD IN THE ENGLISH LANGUAGE, ACCORDING TO THE *OXFORD ENGLISH DICTIONARY*: RESTAURATEUR

2. SECOND MOST FREQUENTLY MISSPELLED WORD: MILLENNIUM

3. MOST MISSPELLED AMERICAN CITY: PITTSBURGH

Sources: **1.** Most people spell it "restauranteur." Given its weird spelling, it is surprising the word is misspelled only 20% of the time it's used. (*Washington Post*, 5/27/99) **2.** "Millenium" is spelled incorrectly 10% of the time. In May 1999, the *Houston Chronicle* misspelled "millennium" 16 times over a 1-year period. (*Washington Post*, 5/27/99) **3.** In 1890, the U.S. Board of Geographic Names ruled that the final "h" should be dropped from the names of all cities ending in "burgh." The citizens of Pittsburgh resisted, however, and in 1911 the board restored the "h" to "Pittsburgh." Apparently, people remain confused. Other cities that made the list include Tucson; Cincinnati; Albuquerque; Culpeper, Va.; Asheville, N.C.; Worcester, Mass.; Manhattan; Phoenix; Niagara Falls; Fredericksburg, Va.; Philadelphia; Detroit; Chattanooga, Tenn.; and Gloucester, Mass. (UPI, 8/3/01)

Number of National Hockey League champions whose names are misspelled on the Stanley Cup: 4

The worst spelling error for a team: The home of the 1971 champion Boston Bruins is spelled "BQSTON." The biggest spelling goof of a player's name: Jacques Plante played with the Montreal Canadiens, champs between 1955 and 1960, and they spelled his name five different ways. "It adds to the tradition," says Phil Pritchard, a director of the Hockey Hall of Fame. (*Dallas Morning News*, 6/10/99)

1. NUMBER OF TIMES THE *NEW YORK TIMES* HAS MISSPELLED "MISSPELLED" SINCE 2000: 14

2. NUMBER OF TIMES "MISSPELLED" IS MISSPELLED ON THE WEB: 16,900

Sources: **1.** Spelling it with one "s" rather than two. In comparison, the *Boston Globe* misspelled "misspelled" only 5 times since 2000, the *Los Angeles Times* only once, and the *Washington Post* has yet to misspell the word. (LexisNexis) **2.** Spellweb.com.

WHAT THE *WASHINGTON POST* MISSPELLED ON MAY 30, 2003: THE NAME OF THE NATIONAL SPELLING BEE WINNER

Said the paper in its correction: "The last name of National Spelling Bee winner Sai R. Gunturi was misspelled in a May 30 KidsPost article and on the front-page promo and caption." (*Washington Post*, 5/30/03)

WINNING WORDS FROM THE MOST RECENT NATIONAL SPELLING BEE:
2004: AUTOCHTHONOUS
2003: POCOCURANTE
2002: PROSPICIENCE

"Autochthonous" means indigenous, "pococurante" means indifferent, and "prospicience" means the act of looking forward; foresight. There are 3,750 words eligible to be used in round one of the spelling bee and more than 460,000 for the later rounds. Other winning words from past years include "elucubrate" (to produce something through intensive effort; 1980); "croissant" (a flaky bread roll; 1970); "troche" (medicinal lozenge; 1960); "haruspex" (an ancient Roman soothsayer; 1950); "therapy" (treatment of a physical or mental disorder; 1940); "fracas" (a noisy fight or loud quarrel; 1930); and "gladiolus" (plants from the iris family; 1925). In 1936, MacNolia Cox became the first African American to advance to the final round. She lost on the word "nemesis," which was not on the official list of words, and which most people believe was given to her at the behest of southern judges who didn't want a black spelling champion. (*Washington Post*, 6/01/00, 6/13/04)

PERCENTAGE OF PEOPLE WHO SAY THEIR NAME IS OFTEN MISSPELLED: 71%

(Douglas, *The Mother of All Baby Books*, cited in the *Chicago Sun-Times*, 6/12/03)

ONLY WORD IN THE ENGLISH LANGUAGE THAT HAS THREE CONSECUTIVE SETS OF DOUBLE LETTERS: BOOKKEEPER

If you allowed for hyphenated words, "sweet-toothed" and "hoof-footed" would also qualify.
There is one word that has four sets of double letters in a row—balloonneer. (AskOxford.com)

Words that have five consecutive vowels: 2
Queueing, Rousseauian

(AskOxford.com)

SPORTS CONTRACTS

1. AVERAGE NBA SALARY IN 2004: $4.9 MILLION
2. AVERAGE MAJOR LEAGUE BASEBALL SALARY: $2.49 MILLION
3. AVERAGE NFL SALARY: $1.26 MILLION
4. AVERAGE NHL SALARY: $1.79 MILLION
5. AVERAGE WNBA SALARY: $48,000

Sources: **1.** Up from $171,000 in 1980, and $900,000 in 1990. (*Daily News* [New York], 2/22/05; *Chicago Tribune*, 11/8/91)
2. Up from $52,300 in 1976, $146,500 in 1980, and $589,000 in 1990. (*Sports Illustrated*, 4/19/04; *USA Today*, 11/11/98)
3. Up from $17,000 in 1960, $23,000 in 1970, $78,000 in 1980, and $363,000 in 1990. (*Los Angeles Times*, 12/26/04; *USA Today*, 1/24/01)
4. Up from $108,000 in 1980, and $276,000 in 1990. (*Toronto Sun*, 6/1/04; *Toronto Star*, 11/13/01) **5.** WNBA

HIGHEST PAID AMERICAN PROFESSIONAL ATHLETES EXCLUSIVE OF ENDORSEMENTS:
SHAQUILLE O'NEAL: $27.69 MILLION
ALEX RODRIGUEZ: $25.2 MILLION
PEYTON MANNING: $14 MILLION

Chris Webber and Alan Houston have the second highest NBA salaries at $17.5 million annually, while Manny Ramirez earns $22 million from the Boston Red Sox. (*Sports Illustrated*, 5/17/04; *Los Angeles Times*, 12/1/04; *Atlanta Journal-Constitution*, 2/17/04)

1. PAYROLL OF THE FIRST ALL-PROFESSIONAL SPORTS TEAM: $9,300 (CINCINNATI RED STOCKINGS, 1869)
2. SALARY OF HIGHEST PAID PLAYER: $1,400

Sources: **1.** Nemec, *Great Baseball Feats, Facts and Firsts*. **2.** Paid to George Wright, brother of the manager, who batted .519 in 1869, scored 339 runs, and hit 59 homers. (*U.S. News and World Report*, 8/29/94)

HIGHEST ANNUAL SALARY EARNED BY:

1. BABE RUTH: $80,000

2. LOU GEHRIG: $39,000

3. JOE DIMAGGIO: $100,000

4. JACKIE ROBINSON: $42,500

5. TED WILLIAMS: $135,000

6. MICKEY MANTLE: $100,000

7. SANDY KOUFAX: $130,000

8. WILLIE MAYS: $180,000

9. HANK AARON: $200,000

Sources: **1.** When told that he was making more than Pres. Herbert Hoover, Ruth replied, "I had a better year than he did." (*Arizona Republic*, 12/12/00). **2.** *Minneapolis Star Tribune*, 7/5/95. **3.** After driving in 167 runs in 1937, DiMaggio demanded a $45,000 contract in 1938. He had to settle for $25,000, but by the time his holdout ended he had been vilified by the press. (*USA Today*, 3/9/99) **4.** U.S. *News and World Report*, 3/24/97. **5.** In 1959, after Williams batted below .300 for the first time (.254), he asked for a huge slash in salary—from $125,000 to $95,000—possibly the first and last time that's happened in professional sports. (Salon.com) And in the year he hit .406, Williams said: "If I was being paid thirty thousand dollars a year, the very least I could do was hit .400." (Baseballalmanac.com) **6.** When Mantle signed for $100,000 in 1963, he became only the fourth person in baseball history to be paid this much. **7.** Koufax and fellow Dodger Don Drysdale held out together during spring training in 1966, asking for a $1 million, 3-year contract between them. They eventually signed separate 1-year contracts 2 weeks before the season started, $130,000 for Koufax and $115,000 for Drysdale. (*Fort Worth Star-Telegram*, 8/4/99) **8.** *USA Today*, 8/29/94. **9.** Says Aaron about today's salaries, "If the owners will pay them that money, fine. I made as much money as I could while I was playing. Is it healthy for the game? Only they can tell." (*Atlanta Business Chronicle*, 8/23/96)

1. NFL MINIMUM SALARY IN 2004: $230,000
2. TOP SALARY EARNED BY OTTO GRAHAM: $25,000
3. TOP SALARY EARNED BY JIM BROWN: $85,000
4. TOP SALARY EARNED BY JOHNNY UNITAS: $275,000

Sources: **1.** *Dallas Morning News*, 9/24/03. **2.** Graham never missed a game as a pro while passing for 23,584 yards and 174 touchdowns, finishing his career with a 105–17–4 regular-season record. (*Sarasota Herald-Tribune*, 12/28/03) **3.** With 12,312 career rushing yards before retiring in 1966, Brown is widely regarded as the greatest running back in NFL history. (*Colorado Springs Gazette*, 9/26/01) **4.** Unitas threw at least one touchdown in 47 consecutive games from 1956 to 1960. Unitas earned more in his last 2 years with the San Diego Chargers than in his previous 17 years with the Baltimore Colts. "I never had an agent, I did all my own negotiations," said Unitas. (*Toronto Star*, 2/15/91)

1. Meal money given daily to NBA players: $96
2. To NHL players: $85
3. To NFL players: $85
4. To Major League baseball players: $80.50

(Dallas Morning News, 5/25/04; NFL; MLB)

STOCKS

1. BEST MONTH FOR STOCKS HISTORICALLY: APRIL
2. WORST MONTH FOR STOCKS: SEPTEMBER
3. PERCENTAGE BY WHICH THE STOCK MARKET'S PERFORMANCE ON SUNNY DAYS EXCEEDS ITS PERFORMANCE ON CLOUDY DAYS: 25%

Sources: **1.** According to the *Stock Traders Almanac*, April is the best month for performance of the Dow, offering an average uptick of 1.9%, and April 1999 was the first (and only) time the Dow rose 1,000 points in a single month. December is the top performer for the S&P 500, and the second best Dow performer. January is by far the best performer on the NASDAQ, up an average 3.9% each year. (*2005 Stock Traders Almanac*) **2.** Though the greatest one-day stock market disasters have all occurred in October (the crash of 1929, the carnage of 1978 and 1979, Black Monday 1987), September has actually been the worst performing month for both the Dow and the S&P 500 over the past 50 years. (*2005 Stock Market Almanac*) **3.** As a possible reason for the weather differential, Ohio State University professor David Hirshleifer suggests that sunny weather makes people feel happier and more optimistic. (*Psychology Today*, 11/1/01)

FIRST PUBLICATION OF STOCK TABLES: JULY 3, 1884

First published in something called the *Customer's Afternoon Letter*, a two-page daily that subsequently became the *Wall Street Journal* in 1889. The first stock index featured 11 stocks. Nine of them were railroads, because industrial stocks were felt to be too risky at the time. (*Baltimore Sun*, 4/9/00)

Only day of the week that has not been called "black" by Wall Street: Wednesday

Save for Wednesday, each day of the week evokes specific memories of past economic disasters. Here's the rundown:

Black Monday: Oct. 19, 1987—the historic 1987 one-day stock crash, in which U.S. stocks dropped 23%.

Black Tuesday: Oct. 29, 1929—the Great Stock Market Crash, which began the Depression. More money lost in one day than in all of World War I.

Black Thursday: Sept. 18, 1873—Jay Cooke & Co, a leading railway bank, collapsed, forcing Wall Street to shut down for 10 days.

Black Friday: Sept. 24, 1869—in an unsuccessful attempt to corner the gold market, railway speculator Jay Gould tried to trick President Grant into selling all the government's bullion after amassing huge stores for himself. Gould inadvertently collapsed the market in the process. Loan rates soared as investors lost millions all across the board.

(*Esquire*, 5/1/01; *Scotland on Sunday*, 9/15/02)

280

1. YEAR *CFO* MAGAZINE GAVE ITS EXCELLENCE AWARD TO SCOTT SULLIVAN, CHIEF FINANCIAL OFFICER OF WORLDCOM: 1998

2. YEAR SULLIVAN WAS ARRESTED: 2002

3. YEAR *CFO* MAGAZINE GAVE ITS EXCELLENCE AWARD TO ENRON'S ANDREW FASTOW: 1999

4. YEAR FASTOW WAS ARRESTED: 2002

Sources: **1, 2.** Noted for excellence in "mergers and acquisitions," Sullivan was arrested for hiding billion of dollars in WorldCom's expenses and for overstating earnings by billions more. **3, 4.** Noted for his excellence in "capital-structure management," Fastow pled guilty to cooking Enron's books. (*American Prospect*, 11/18/02)

1. PRICE OF ONE SHARE OF BERKSHIRE HATHAWAY STOCK IN 1965: $18

2. PRICE OF ONE SHARE OF BERKSHIRE HATHAWAY ON DEC. 20, 2004: $86,300

In other words, if you invested $250 in Warren Buffett's company in May 1965, your shares would be worth well over $1 million. And Berkshire Hathaway's not even close to being the market's best performer. Want to kick yourself some more? While $1 invested in Berkshire Hathaway in 1976 grew to $1,044 at the end of 2000, a single dollar invested in a company called Mylan Laboratories in 1976 would have been worth $1,545 by the end of 2000; a buck invested in Applied Materials Inc. would have been worth $1,419; and a dollar invested in Wal-Mart would have reached $1,108. (*Pensions and Investments*, 7/8/02; *Newsweek*, 4/8/96)

1. DATE ON WHICH ESTEEMED ECONOMIST IRVING FISHER SAID THAT "IN A FEW MONTHS I EXPECT TO SEE THE STOCK MARKET MUCH HIGHER THAN TODAY": OCT. 14, 1929

2. DATE ON WHICH THE STOCK MARKET CRASHED: OCT. 29, 1929

Sources: **1.** Major newspapers joined in the volley of good cheer that preceded the crash. "Good Times Are Predicted in 1929" read the *Washington Post*. The *Chicago Tribune* confirmed: "New Year Begins with U.S. at Peak of Prosperity" and "Joyous Bulls Confident in 1929 Market." The *New York Times* voiced the one sour note: "The . . . rash abuse of credit . . . the fantastic illusions that are entertained of the economic future and the public's appetite, in the face of unsettled credit, for the most reckless stock speculation are distinctly disquieting." (*Columbia Journalism Review*, 3/1/99) **2.** Experts were as adept at predicting the future after the crash as they were before. Days after the crash, *BusinessWeek* reported: "[The crash] doesn't mean that there will be any general or serious business depression." And presidential economic advisor Bernard Baruch wrote a telegram to Winston Churchill on Nov. 15, 1929, in which he said four words—"Financial storm definitely passed." (Cerf, *The Experts Speak*)

SUCCESS

1. NUMBER OF TIMES HENRY FORD LOST EVERYTHING BEFORE DESIGNING THE MODEL T: 2

2. TIMES BABE RUTH STRUCK OUT: 1,330

3. FUEL REMAINING WHEN MAN FIRST LANDED ON THE MOON: 15 SECONDS' WORTH

Sources: **1.** *BusinessWeek*, 8/4/86. **2.** *Fortune*, 5/1/95. **3.** *Washington Times*, 7/18/99.

KURT WARNER'S POSITION BEFORE BECOMING A PRO BOWL QUARTERBACK: SUPERMARKET CLERK, CEDAR FALLS, IOWA

Less than 5 years before winning the Super Bowl MVP Award, Warner was working the 9:30 P.M. to 5:30 A.M. shift at the Hy-Vee Grocery stocking shelves for $5.50 an hour. Late at night, Warner would toss bags of candy to other workers cutting down the frozen food aisle, promising them that one day he was going to play in the NFL. "They were probably thinking this guy is working in a supermarket, how's he going to play in the NFL?" Warner said. "They listened to me, probably humored me with their smiles. But I'm sure nobody expected this. You can't blame them." (*Calgary Sun*, 1/26/00)

ODDS THAT UPSET WOULD BEAT MAN O' WAR IN THE 1919 SANFORD STAKES: 100 TO 1

Considered the greatest upset in horse racing history, Upset beat Man o' War by half a length on Aug. 13, 1919. Man o' War—perhaps the greatest horse ever—had never before lost, and would never lose again. Though the term had occasionally been used before, Upset's win popularized the use of the word "upset" to describe an unexpected victory over a seemingly superior foe. (ESPN.com)

JACK FLECK'S JOB WHEN HE WON THE 1955 U.S. OPEN:
GOLF COURSE MANAGER, DAVENPORT, IOWA

Fleck left the Duck Creek Golf Club in care of his wife and a couple of assistants so he could try to qualify for the Open. In the final round, Fleck was two behind Ben Hogan on the 15th hole, with Hogan done for the day. Everyone was so certain Hogan won that TV coverage ended. But Fleck birdied two of the last three holes to force a playoff the following day. "Unknown Golfer Birdies Last Hole to Deadlock Ben," read the headline in the *San Francisco Chronicle*. The following day, Fleck won by three strokes. (*Independent*, 6/16/98)

ODDS AGAINST JAMES "BUSTER" DOUGLAS WHEN HE DEFEATED MIKE TYSON TO WIN THE HEAVYWEIGHT CROWN:
42 TO 1

On Feb. 11, 1990, Douglas knocked Tyson out in the 10th round, perhaps the greatest upset in the history of boxing. Douglas, a 29-year-old journeyman fighter, was given no chance to win, and faced several additional challenges in the months before the fight: first, his wife left him, then his mother died of a stroke. "Something great must be about to happen to me," Douglas said several weeks before the fight, "because something out there is definitely trying to deter me." (*Sports Illustrated*, 2/19/90)

Length of Dan "Rudy" Ruettiger's football career at Notre Dame: 27 seconds

Ruettinger—"a 5-foot-nothing" guy without a speck of athletic ability—had one consuming goal in life: to play a down of football for Notre Dame. "Our attitude at first was, 'Go away,' " said former teammate Willie Fry. "But he wouldn't go away. Basically you had to like Rudy because you couldn't get rid of him." After serving as the team's tackling dummy in practice for a year, Rudy finally got his chance. On Nov. 8, 1975, Rudy suited up and was brought into the final home game against Georgia Tech with 27 seconds left. He sacked the quarterback and was carried off the field a hero. The movie *Rudy* was later made about his life. (*People*, 11/1/93)

1. Attempts by Thomas Edison to invent the lightbulb: 10,000
2. Attempts by Michael Jordan to make his high school team: 2

Sources: **1.** Edison responded to the difficulties he was encountering by saying, "I haven't failed. I've just found 10,000 ways that won't work." (*Edmonton Sun*, 1/11/00) **2.** Jordan was cut the first time he tried out in his sophomore year. "I wasn't afraid to fail," Jordan says. "It's part of life. I used to love constructive criticism. I used to look in the mirror and say, 'He's right.'" (*Arlington Morning News*, 7/29/00)

SUICIDE

1. ODDS THAT A PERSON COMMITTING SUICIDE IS MALE: 4 IN 5

2. ODDS THAT A PERSON ATTEMPTING SUICIDE IS FEMALE: 3 IN 4

3. ODDS THAT A SUICIDE ATTEMPT IS SUCCESSFUL: 1 IN 25

Sources: **1.** There were 31,655 suicides in 2002, the most recent date for which figures are available, with males responsible for about 80% of that total. (American Association of Suicidology) **2.** In total, an estimated 765,000 Americans attempt suicide each year. (American Academy of Suicidology) **3.** American Academy of Suicidology.

Only country in which more women than men kill themselves: China

About 21% of the world's females live in China, yet 55.8% of the women who commit suicide worldwide are Chinese. (*Time* [Spanish edition], 7/28/03)

WORLD'S HIGHEST SUICIDE RATE: LITHUANIA

Lithuania has 44.7 suicides per 100,000 inhabitants; Russia is ranked second with 88.7 suicides per 100,000. In the U.S., New Mexico has the highest suicide rate, and Massachusetts the lowest. (UPI, 9/9/04)

1. ONLY STATE IN U.S. WHERE IT IS ILLEGAL TO COMMIT SUICIDE: NORTH CAROLINA

2. LAST PROSECUTION OF PERSON WHO ATTEMPTED SUICIDE: 1961

Sources: **1.** Both suicide and attempted suicide remain illegal under the common law of North Carolina. Suicide was also a crime in England—the victim's family would forfeit his possessions and the victim would be buried beside a roadway with a stake through his body. In 1824, the law was changed to allow suicide victims to be buried in churchyards, but without religious ceremony and between 9 P.M. and 12 A.M. (*State v. Willis*, 121 S.E.2d 854 [1961]) **2.** In 1961, North Carolina charged one Edger Willis with the crime of attempted suicide for (in the words of the indictment) "unlawfully and feloniously slashing and cutting his throat and hanging himself by the neck from a barn rafter, which acts failed to cause death." (*State v. Willis*, 121 S.E.2d 854 [1961])

Most common method of suicide: Guns

Fifty-five percent of all suicides are by firearms, followed by suffocation/hanging (20%) and poisoning (17%). (American Academy of Suicidology)

WORLD'S MOST POPULAR SUICIDE LOCATION:
GOLDEN GATE BRIDGE

In 1937, just 3 months after the bridge's opening, Harold Wobber, a 47-year-old First World War veteran, was the first to jump to his death. Twenty-six people have survived the plunge from the bridge. . . . The Jacques Cartier Bridge in Canada reportedly has the world's second highest number of suicides, and as of December 2004, 34 people had jumped from the top of the Empire State Building to their deaths. (*New Yorker*, 10/13/03; *Montreal Gazette*, 10/16/03; *Daily News*, 12/19/04)

NUMBER OF SUICIDES SINCE BRIDGE'S OPENING IN 1937: ABOUT 1,300

In 1995, as the number of suicides approached 1,000, a San Francisco radio station offered a case of Snapple to the family of the 1,000th victim. . . . In 1973, 14 people tried to be the bridge's 500th suicide victim, including one man who wore a T-shirt emblazoned with "500" in oversized numbers. (*New Yorker*, 10/13/03)

saddest note from a bridge jumper:

```
I'm going to walk to the bridge. If one
   person smiles at me on the way, I will
not jump.
```

(*New Yorker*, 10/13/03)

NUMBER OF PEOPLE OFFICER KEVIN BRIGGS HAS TALKED OUT OF JUMPING: 250

Briggs told the *New Yorker* that he begins talking to a potential jumper by asking, "How are you feeling today?" Then, "What's your plan for tomorrow?" If the person doesn't have a plan, Briggs says, "Well, let's make one. If it doesn't work out, you can always come back here later." (*New Yorker*, 10/13/03)

SUPERMARKETS

1. NUMBER OF ANNUAL HOUSEHOLD TRIPS TO THE SUPERMARKET: 73

2. ODDS THAT A PERSON ACTIVELY DISLIKES GROCERY SHOPPING: 2 IN 3

3. TIME IT TAKES THE AVERAGE SHOPPER TO BUY GROCERIES: 47 MINUTES

4. SECONDS A SHOPPER'S EYE LINGERS ON EACH PRODUCT: 2.5

Sources: **1.** Down from 90 visits annually in the 1990s. (*Detroit News*, 6/15/03) **2.** *American Demographics*, 7/97. **3.** *South Florida Sun-Sentinel*, 4/17/04. **4.** *American Demographics*, 8/1/98.

First self-service grocery: 1916 (Piggly Wiggly, Memphis, Tenn.)

In 1916, Clarence Saunder's Memphis Piggly Wiggly had one long shopping aisle, and was the first to allow customers to pick their own goods. In 1940, 10% of the nation's groceries were sold in self-service supermarkets. By 1950, that had grown to 30%, and then doubled to 60% in less than 5 years. (*Chicago Tribune*, 10/23/85; 2/3/91)

FIRST GROCERY COUPON: 1895

1¢ OFF ON GRAPE NUTS CEREAL

(Atlanta Journal-Constitution, 1/17/94)

1. INVENTION OF THE SHOPPING CART: JUNE 1937
2. DISTANCE THE AVERAGE GROCERY CART TRAVELS IN ITS LIFE: 30,000 MILES

Sources: **1.** In 1936, Sylvan Goldman, the owner of a chain of Humpty Dumpty markets in Oklahoma City, realized that if grocery shoppers could carry more, they would buy more. The question was how to improve on the small handheld baskets then in use. One night, Goldman's eyes fixed on a folding chair in his tiny office. As Goldman later told the *Smithsonian*, "I had the thought . . . that if I would put wheels on the bottom of those folding chairs, raise the seats some so I could have room to put a rack at the bottom of the chair . . . and let the back upright of the chair be the handle of the basket carrier, this could be shopping in ease." The first shopping cart debuted at one of Goldman's Humpty Dumpty markets in June 1937, consisting of two baskets at different levels. Goldman added the baby seat to his shopping carts in 1947. (*Chicago Tribune*, 2/3/91; Unarco.com) **2.** *Minneapolis Star Tribune*, 04/16/95.

WHAT FROZEN FOOD WAS CALLED BEFORE IT BECAME FROZEN FOOD: "FROSTED FOOD"

Clarence Birdseye was a fur trader who switched careers after a trip to Newfoundland, where he discovered that food that was quickly frozen retained its freshness until cooking. In 1930, Birdseye established Birds Eye Frosted Foods, with frozen peas, cherries, chicken, and fish among his first products. The word "frosted" was chosen because at that time "frozen" typically denoted food that was ruined by cold weather. (*Los Angeles Times*, 1/24/01; Straser, *History of American Housework*)

RATIO OF SHOPPERS WHO PUT AN UNWANTED FOOD ITEM BACK WHERE THEY FOUND IT: 1 IN 3

Almost half of shoppers—45%—leave an unwanted grocery item where they are, 8% ask a stock boy to put it back, 6% leave it at the checkout line, and 5.2% hide it. (Kanner, *Are You Normal?*)

1. Year the bar code was invented: 1952
2. First item scanned: Wrigley chewing gum, 1974

Sources: **1.** In 1952, Norman Woodland and Bernard Silver patented the first system in which a light scanner read coded information on a product label, but their system was viewed as impractical. With no customers on the horizon, they sold the patent to IBM in the late 1950s. (*Baltimore Sun*, 6/29/04) **2.** On June 26, 1974, at Marsh Supermarkets in Troy, Ohio, a 10¢ pack of Wrigley's was scanned by cashier Sharon Buchanan, the first item ever scanned. The pack of Wrigley's and the scanner are now on display at the Smithsonian National Museum of American History. (*Baltimore Sun*, 6/29/04)

TATTOOS

1. NUMBER OF AMERICANS WITH TATTOOS: 30 MILLION

2. PERCENTAGE OF AMERICANS ABOVE 60 WHO HAVE TATTOOS: 3%

3. PERCENTAGE BETWEEN 40 AND 60 WITH TATTOOS: 9%

4. PERCENTAGE OF THOSE UNDER 40: 30%

Sources: **1.** *Atlanta Journal-Constitution*, 10/18/02. **2–4.** Survey conducted by Scripps Research Center, reported in *San Mateo County Times*, 1/23/03.

Origin of the word "tattoo": From the Tahitian word *tatau*

Tatau, which means "to mark something," may have first been picked up by sailors—the first to popularize tattooing in the West—who likely learned techniques from their travels at sea. The actual origins of tattooing are unknown, since evidence traces it to nearly all ancient cultures, from Maori tribesmen to the Thracian women of fifth-century Greece. (*Los Angeles Times*, 8/27/04; *Jerusalem Post*, 3/21/03)

1. NUMBER OF STATES WHERE TATTOOING IS ILLEGAL: 2 (SOUTH CAROLINA AND OKLAHOMA)

2. NUMBER OF PEOPLE ARRESTED FOR TATTOOING IN SOUTH CAROLINA SINCE 1966: 1

Sources: **1.** *Dermatology Times*, 11/1/02. **2.** In 1999, 10 days after Ronald White appeared on a Myrtle Beach, S.C., television station tattooing a customer, 10 police officers dressed in combat gear and bulletproof vests arrested him at his home. White was sentenced to a year in prison and a $2,500 fine for illegal tattooing, later reduced to 5 years probation. He appealed all the way to the U.S. Supreme Court, claiming that tattooing was a form of art entitled to First Amendment protection. Though he was represented by former special prosecutor Kenneth Starr, the Supreme Court refused to hear the case, and the ban remains in place. (*Washington Times*, 10/30/02)

WORLD LEADERS WITH TATTOOS: 3

WINSTON CHURCHILL: ANCHOR

JOSEPH STALIN: DEATH'S HEAD

FDR: FAMILY CREST

(*USA Today*, 3/24/97)

Lawsuits arising from misspelled tattoos:

Dan O'Connor:
Sued after "Fighting Irish" tattoo was spelled "Fighing Irish"

Jeremy Van Camp:
Sued after he found out that Chinese letter tattoo that was supposed to say "Jeremy" said "Kung Po Karate"

Lee Beck:
Sued after finding out that Chinese tattoo that was supposed to say "Love, honor and obey" actually said "This boy is ugly"

Joseph Beahm:
Sued after the phrase "Why not, everyone else does" was misspelled "Why not, everyone elese does"

(*Record*, 10/26/95; *Independent*, 6/16/02; *Christian Science Monitor*, 8/26/99)

AMOUNT JIM NELSON WAS PAID TO HAVE A CORPORATE LOGO TATTOOED ONTO HIS HEAD: $7,000

Nelson put his head on *eBay* for auction, which was won by CI-Host, a web-hosting company based in Dallas, entitling it to tattoo its bright orange and blue logo onto Nelson's head. (*Telephony*, 5/19/03)

PERCENTAGE OF PEOPLE WHO REGRET GETTING A TATTOO: 17%

According to a 2003 Harris poll, Republicans were more likely to regret getting a tattoo than Democrats. The chief reason for regret? "Because of the person's name in the tattoo." (*Adweek*, 11/3/03)

TAXES

1. TOTAL NUMBER OF PAGES IN THE ORIGINAL U.S. TAX CODE IN 1913: 14

2. NUMBER OF PAGES IN THE U.S. TAX CODE IN 2004: 4,766

3. NUMBER OF PAGES INTERPRETING THE TAX CODE IN 1913: 400

4. NUMBER OF PAGES INTERPRETING THE TAX CODE IN 2004: 60,044

Source: **1.** The income tax system began in 1913. (*Washington Times*, 12/4/02) **2.** The code is almost 2.8 million words. In comparison, the novel *War and Peace* contains 660,000 words. (House Republican Conference, 4/11/03) **3, 4.** A total of the pages in the tax code, regulations and IRS rulings. (*Newsday*, 4/5/04)

1. Person who said that "in this world nothing is certain but death and taxes": Benjamin Franklin

2. Person who said "we don't pay taxes—only the little people pay taxes": Leona Helmsley

Sources: **1.** Franklin made the comment in a Nov. 13, 1789, letter written to a friend, Jean Baptiste-Leroy, in which he expressed concern about the stability of the new American republic: "Our constitution is in actual operation. Everything appears to promise that it will last; but in this world nothing is certain but death and taxes." (*Los Angeles Times*, 10/8/96) **2.** Helmsley's former housekeeper testified about the hotel mogul's comment at her 1992 trial for tax evasion, for which she served 18 months in prison. (*New York Times*, 8/1/04)

LONGEST TITLE FOR ANY U.S. TAX FORM:

"SEPARATE LIMITATION LOSS ALLOCATIONS AND OTHER ADJUSTMENTS NECESSARY TO DETERMINE NUMERATORS OF LIMITATION FRACTIONS, YEAR-END RECHARACTERIZATION BALANCES, AND OVERALL FOREIGN LOSS ACCOUNT BALANCES"

(Form 1118)

FIRST PERSON TO RECEIVE A TAX DEDUCTION FOR BREAST ENLARGEMENTS: CYNTHIA HESS
(A.K.A. CHESTY LOVE)

In 1988, the Wisconsin stripper claimed a $2,088 deduction for depreciation on implants that increased her breast size to a 56FF. The IRS rejected the deduction, contending that the implants constituted personal expenses because they were designed to improve her appearance. A court accepted the deduction, however, concluding that the implants substantially increased Hess's business income, and that given their size (each of her new breasts weighed 10 pounds), she could not possibly have derived any personal benefit from the implants. (*Los Angeles Times*, 4/13/94)

Odds of being audited by the IRS: 1 in 129

(AP, 11/18/04)

1. HIGHEST U.S. TAX RATE FOR INDIVIDUALS TODAY: 37.6%
2. HIGHEST U.S. TAX RATE IN 1913: 7%
3. HIGHEST INDIVIDUAL AMERICAN TAX RATE OF ALL TIME: 94%

Sources: **1.** *U.S. News and World Report*, 2/3/02 **2.** Davis, *Future Wealth*. **3.** In 1944 and 1945, America's highest income earners paid 94¢ out of every dollar earned to taxes. Indeed, the tax rate on the highest-income Americans remained at about 90% throughout the 1950s, decreased to 70% in the 1960s and '70s, and to 50% in the early '80s before reaching a post–World War II low of 28% in 1998. (IRS)

NUMBER OF STATES THAT REQUIRE DRUG DEALERS TO PAY TAXES ON THE SALE OF POT, CRACK, AND HEROIN: 24

Under these little-known laws, drug dealers must typically pay a tax of about $3.50 per gram of marijuana, $200 per gram of heroin and crack, and $2,000 per 50 doses of LSD and ecstasy. The tax is paid through tax stamps, which the dealers are required to buy from the state's department of revenue. Drug dealers do not have to provide their names, and the revenue department is prohibited from giving the names of tax-stamp purchasers to the police. "They will come in and tell us they need to purchase enough stamps for, say, a pound of marijuana," says a Tennessee tax official. "We will calculate that and issue them the stamps." (*Memphis Business Journal*, 8/20/04; *Boston Globe*, 2/7/94)

HIGHEST INCOME TAX RATE IN THE WORLD: DENMARK

Which taxes its wealthiest taxpayers at a rate of 62% (Danish Consulate)

TEAM NAMES

1. MOST COMMON HIGH SCHOOL AND COLLEGE TEAM NICKNAME: EAGLES

2. ONLY PROFESSIONAL SPORTS TEAM TO BE NAMED AFTER A PERSON: CLEVELAND BROWNS

3. YEAR PEKIN (ILL.) HIGH SCHOOL CHANGED ITS NICKNAME FROM THE "CHINKS" TO THE "DRAGONS": 1981

4. TEAM NAME OF COACHELLA VALLEY (CALIF.) HIGH SCHOOL: THE ARABS

Sources: **1.** As of 2004, 1,029 high schools were named the Eagles, and 125 colleges. For college teams, Eagles were followed by Cougars (111 schools), Bulldogs (98 schools), Tigers (97 schools), and Panthers (70 schools). For high school: Tigers (852 schools), Bulldogs (784 schools), Panthers (747 schools), and Wildcats (655 schools). (*Clell Wade Coaching Directories*) **2.** Named after Paul Brown, the team's original coach. Before they moved from Fort Wayne, Ind., to Detroit, the Pistons were known as the Fort Wayne Zollner Pistons, after their owner Fred Zollner. (*USA Today*, 6/4/04) **3.** According to school officials, the name "Chinks" was adopted because the town was believed to be on the opposite end of the globe from Peking, China. (*Palm Beach Post*, 2/4/02) **4.** *Palm Beach Post*, 2/4/02.

PERIOD THE CINCINNATI REDS CHANGED THEIR NAME TO RED LEGS TO AVOID CHARGES OF COMMUNIST SYMPATHY: 1953–58

(*San Francisco Chronicle*, 9/15/94)

BASEBALL TEAM NAMED AFTER WARM BREAD: MONTGOMERY BISCUITS (CLASS AA SOUTHERN LEAGUE)

Thought to be the only current edible vegetarian team nickname, though the Atlanta Braves were known as the Boston Beaneaters in the early 1900s. (*Atlanta Journal-Constitution*, 4/18/04)

1. First college to change its nickname in deference to Native Americans: Stanford

2. Percentage of Native Americans in recent poll who said that pro teams should not stop using Indian nicknames: 83%

3. First college to cancel a game because of its opponent's team name: University of Iowa

Sources: **1.** Stanford changed its name from Indians to Cardinals in 1972. (*Christian Science Monitor*, 4/14/00) **2.** *Sports Illustrated*, 3/4/02. **3.** On May 4, 2004, Iowa canceled a baseball game against the Bradley University Braves, enforcing a decade-old and seemingly forgotten university rule forbidding the university from competing against opponents with Native American nicknames. (*Charleston Gazette*, 5/13/04)

UNUSUAL COLLEGE TEAM NICKNAMES:

UC SANTA CRUZ—*BANANA SLUGS*

WHITTIER COLLEGE—*POETS*

OHIO WESLEYAN—*FIGHTING BISHOPS*

SCOTTSDALE COMMUNITY COLLEGE—*ARTICHOKES*

CENTRE COLLEGE—*PRAYING COLONELS*

HAVERFORD COLLEGE—*BLACK SQUIRRELS*

UNIVERSITY OF VIRGINIA—*WAHOOS*

RHODE ISLAND SCHOOL OF DESIGN—*NADS*

CAL STATE LONG BEACH—*DIRT BAGS*

COLLEGE OF THE ATLANTIC—*BLACK FLIES*

HAMPSHIRE COLLEGE—*FROGS*

Teams that have been named in contests:

Philadelphia 76ers Cleveland Cavaliers **Buffalo Bills**
Cleveland **Browns Milwaukee Bucks** San Jose Sharks
Chicago Cubs Seattle Mariners

Although the Cubs was informally referred to as the White Stockings and the Colts in its early years, a Chicago paper held a contest and the name Cubs was chosen in 1900. . . . Early entries for the contest to name the Sharks included the Microchips and the Screaming Squids. The most common suggestion was the Blades, but it was nixed because of gang connotations. . . . R. D. Trebilcox won the 1968 contest to name Milwaukee's NBA team, explaining that bucks are "good jumpers, fast and agile." . . . A railroad worker, Jimmy Dyson, came up with the name Buffalo Bills, explaining that, like Buffalo Bill Cody, Buffalo was opening up a new frontier in sports. (*Toronto Star*, 1/7/92; *New York Times*, 5/2/93; *USA Today*, 9/15/89; *Chicago Tribune*, 11/5/96)

TEETH AND SMILES

1. NUMBER OF ACTIVE DENTISTS IN AMERICA: 166,383

2. STATE WITH LEAST NUMBER OF DENTISTS PER CAPITA: MISSISSIPPI

3. PERCENTAGE OF AMERICANS WHO AVOID THE DENTIST BECAUSE OF FEAR: 15%

Sources: **1.** The U.S. has one dentist for every 1,691 people. (*Journal of Dental Hygiene*, 9/22/03) **2.** Mississippi has one dentist for 2,694 people. (*Journal of Dental Hygiene*, 9/22/03) **3.** In England, some 36% avoid regular visits to the dentist for the same reason. (*Washingtonian*, 2/03; *Sunday Mercury*, 9/26/99)

1. MOST TEETH LOST BY A SINGLE HOCKEY PLAYER: 12

2. NUMBER OF TEETH HOCKEY HALL OF FAMER GORDIE HOWE LOST IN HIS FIRST NHL GAME: 4

3. ODDS THAT AN NHL PLAYER WEARS A MOUTH GUARD: 6 IN 10

Sources: **1.** Ken Daneyko, who retired in 2003 after 20 seasons with the New Jersey Devils, lost 12 teeth throughout his career. Among other things, Daneyko is now an advertising spokesperson for cosmetic dentistry. (*Times* [London], 1/17/04) **2, 3.** *New York Times*, 1/14/04.

INVENTOR OF THE SMILEY FACE: HARVEY BALL (1963)

Harvey Ball, a freelance graphic artist from Worcester, Mass., was paid $45 in 1963 to design an emblem that would ease tensions between workers at two insurance companies that merged. Unfortunately for Ball, he never trademarked or copyrighted the face, but a Belgian entrepreneur named Franklin Loufrani did, and has been reaping millions from the face since 1971. (*Boston Globe*, 10/4/99)

FIRST USE OF THE E-MAIL SMILEY FACE: SEPT. 19, 1982

The text-based "emoticon" smile was first used by Scott Fahlman, a research professor, on a bulletin board discussion at Carnegie Mellon University. The idea arose after an online joke was misconstrued, prompting the idea of a sign explicitly indicating that a post was supposed to be funny. Among the rejected signs before Fahlman proposed the ":-)": *, %, *%, &, and [#] (which was supposed to represent teeth between lips). (*Software Development*, 1/1/03)

Inventor of dental anesthesia: Horace Wells

On Dec. 11, 1844, the American dentist experimented on himself, inhaling nitrous oxide and then allowing an assistant to pull his teeth. He later killed himself after not receiving formal credit for his discovery. There is a statue of Wells in his hometown of Hartford, Conn. (*Washington Post*, 9/8/99)

FIRST USE OF THE WORD "CHEESE" TO ENCOURAGE A SMILE: 1920

Used on students of the Oundle School in England. (Trumble, *A Brief History of the Smile*)

WHAT PHOTOGRAPHERS SAY IN OTHER COUNTRIES TO COAX A SMILE:

KOREA: "KIMCHI"
(PICKLED CABBAGE)

JAPAN: "WHISKEY"

SPAIN: "PATATA"
(POTATO)

CZECH REPUBLIC: "FAX"

CHINA: "QIEZI"
(EGGPLANT)

SWEDEN: "OMELET"

(Trumble, *A Brief History of the Smile*)

AGE AT WHICH A BABY BEGINS TO DELIBERATELY SMILE: 8 WEEKS

(NPR's *Talk of the Nation*, 1/20/04)

TELEPHONES

1. DERIVATION OF THE WORD "TELEPHONE": GREEK FOR "FAR-OFF SOUND"

2. FIRST WORDS SPOKEN ON A PHONE: "MR. WATSON, COME HERE. I WANT TO SEE YOU."

3. FIRST AREA CODE: 201

4. WHAT AMERICA DID TO HONOR ALEXANDER GRAHAM BELL DURING HIS FUNERAL: SUSPENDED TELEPHONE SERVICE NATIONWIDE FOR 1 MINUTE

Sources: **1.** *American Heritage Dictionary.* **2.** On Feb. 14, 1876, as Bell placed that very first call to his assistant, he accidentally spilled a beaker of acid on his leg and barked over the line, "Mr. Watson, come here!" (*Toronto Star*, 12/16/99) **3.** New Jersey received the nation's first area code because the state was home to AT&T. Area codes were initially designed with rotary phones in mind. Large cities were assigned numbers near the beginning of the dial, so New York got 212 and Los Angeles 213. (*Bergen County Record*, 4/18/01) **4.** Bell's funeral took place on Aug. 4, 1922. (*Washington Post*, 2/6/87)

1. INVENTOR OF THE WORD "HELLO": THOMAS EDISON

2. WHAT ALEXANDER GRAHAM BELL PROPOSED AS THE INITIAL TELEPHONE GREETING: "AHOY"

Phone inventor Alexander Graham Bell insisted that the proper phone greeting should be "ahoy!" Thomas Edison preferred "hello"—a word he created in 1877. Though some early phone users promoted the greeting "What is wanted?", "hello" soon won out, and appeared in the *Oxford English Dictionary* in 1883. (*New York Times*, 3/5/92)

NUMBER OF HOURS AFTER ALEXANDER GRAHAM BELL FILED HIS TELEPHONE PATENT THAT ELISHA GRAY FILED HIS: 2

Gray had invented a telephonelike device several months before Bell, but didn't bother to immediately patent it, focusing instead on improvements to the telegraph. When Gray did finally get to the Patent Office to file his invention at 4 P.M. on Feb. 14, 1876, Bell had beaten him to the office by exactly 2 hours. (Huurdeman, *The Worldwide History of Telecommunications*)

1. FIRST TELEPHONE BOOK: NEW HAVEN, CONN. (1878)
2. FIRST YELLOW PAGES: CHEYENNE, WYO. (1883)

Sources: **1.** Printed by the New Haven Telephone Company in 1878, the *List of Subscribers* was a single-page directory that listed 50 locals by name. Subscribers dialed in to the operator, and asked for parties by name. (*Wisconsin State Journal*, 2/22/03)
2. Printed in Cheyenne, Wyo., the pages ended up yellow because it was the only color available. (*Hartford Courant*, 10/22/99)

Inventor of the telephone number: Dr. Moses Parker

While dealing with a measles epidemic in his native Lowell, Mass., in 1879, Parker became concerned that the exchange operators would become sick, and that their replacements wouldn't know which people were associated with the several hundred jacks on the telephone switchboards. He therefore suggested that each person be given a "number" consisting of two letters and five digits. (Grigonis, *Voice Over DSL*)

FIRST OVERSEAS CALL: 1900

The first overseas call was made on Christmas Day, 1900, from Key West to Havana. The garbled signal came over the line, and Havana reportedly responded to the historic moment with: "I don't understand you!" (*Palm Beach Post*, 1/1/01)

FIRST CELL PHONE CALL: APRIL 3, 1973

Clutching a 2-pound contraption to his ear, Martin Cooper, a Motorola VP, dialed his competitors at Bell Laboratories from a New York sidewalk and informed them that he was calling from the first-ever handheld mobile phone, thereby prompting the cell phone's first awkward silence. The first cell phone was priced at over $3,000. (*Wireless Week*, 10/15/03; NPR's *Morning Edition*, 4/3/03)

PERCENTAGE OF PEOPLE WHO USE CELL PHONES IN THE BATHROOM: 62%

(Business Wire, 10/28/03)

Inventor of voice mail: Gordon Matthews

The eureka moment came in the 1970s when Matthews noticed a large pile of pink memo slips
in a trash can and thought there had to be a better way. (*Toronto Star*, 2/26/02)

ODDS THAT A CALL TO INFORMATION RESULTS IN A WRONG NUMBER: 1 IN 3

A poll conducted by the *Chicago Sun-Times* in 2000 revealed that at least a third of the numbers given by directory assistance
are wrong. A recent survey in England found that the operator gave incorrect numbers 40% of the time. (NPR, 7/29/00; UPI, 11/20/03)

WOMAN WHO RECORDED "THE NUMBER YOU HAVE DIALED IS NOT IN SERVICE": JANE BARBE

Barbe, who died in 2003, is heard by an estimated 40 million people a day, chanting lines like
"*The number you have dialed is not in service*" and "*Please press one for more options*." (*New York Times*, 7/30/03)

Busiest day for long-distance calls in telephone history: Sept. 11, 2001

AT&T received 101 million more call requests on September 11, 2001 (431 million total) than on its previous busiest day. (AP, 5/20/04)

RECENT INSTANCES OF CELL PHONE RAGE: 2

Pachuca, Mexico: After a man's cell phone fell into a lion cage at a Mexican zoo, the man snuck into the cage in an effort to retrieve the phone. The phone began ringing, however, waking the lion, who then attacked the man.

(Coventry Evening Telegraph, 3/22/00)

Stratford, Conn.: A 77-year-old man drove a 19-year-old woman driving with a cell phone in her hand off a highway. When questioned by police, the septuagenarian stated he "was prejudiced against people who talk on cell phones while driving."

(Connecticut Post, 10/1/02)

COUNTRY THAT BANNED THE PLAYING OF "ON HOLD" MUSIC: SAUDI ARABIA

In recent years, Islamic courts in Saudi Arabia have banned the music that gets played when you're on hold. In a related note, testimony in Martha Stewart's trial revealed that she found Merrill Lynch's hold music so objectionable that she threatened to take her business elsewhere unless it was changed. *(Daily News, 2/6/04; New Yorker, 1/5/04)*

ONLY TWO LETTERS THAT ARE NOT ON A PUSH-BUTTON PHONE: Q AND Z

Because telephone manufacturers were prohibited from placing any letters on 1 and 0 when they first began alphabetizing the dial pad, placing three letters on each of the eight remaining numbers left them two letters short of completing the alphabet. *(Rocky Mountain News, 8/17/02)*

1. BUSIEST CALLING HOLIDAY OF THE YEAR: MOTHER'S DAY
2. BUSIEST COLLECT-CALLING DAY OF THE YEAR: FATHER'S DAY

(Indianapolis Star, 5/7/04)

Number of years after David Towles died that a phone bill was sent to his cemetery: 5

David Towles died in 1997, at the age of 60. Five years later, Sprint found him at Hillside Cemetery with a telephone bill for 12¢, 10¢ of which were for a call made years after Mr. Trowles had passed away. *(AP Worldstream, 3/13/03)*

TELEVISION

1. AMOUNT OF TV THE AVERAGE HUMAN BEING WATCHES EACH DAY: 3 HOURS, 39 MINUTES

2. TV WATCHED DAILY BY THE AVERAGE AMERICAN HOUSEHOLD: 4 HOURS, 25 MINUTES

3. COUNTRY THAT WATCHES THE MOST TV: JAPAN (4 HOURS, 29 MINUTES)

4. FIRST COMMERCIAL TV STATION IN THE U.S.: WNBT

Sources: **1.** Study by Eurodata TV, cited in the *International Herald Tribune*, 4/5/04. **2.** *Daily Variety*, 3/31/04. **3.** The average Greek citizen watches the most TV in Europe—3 hours, 54 minutes. (*International Herald Tribune*, 4/5/04; Agence France-Presse, 4/1/04) **4.** WNBT began broadcasting from New York on July 1, 1941.

SOME EARLY NAMES FOR TELEVISION:

RADIOVISION PHOTOTELEGRAPHY TELEPHONOSCOPE RADIO MOVIES TELECTROSCOPY FARSCOPE RADIO KINEMA

(Dyson, *History of Great Inventions*)

First image shown on television: Statue of Felix the Cat

In 1927, RCA broadcast the first TV images over experimental station W2XBS. Since the lighting was extremely hot, technicians used a small Felix the Cat figurine instead of a human being. (NBC, *Brought to You in Living Color*)

FIRST PERSON SHOWN ON TV: TOM SARNOFF (1932)

Sarnoff was the son of RCA founder David Sarnoff. When he was 5 years old, his father hosted a group of dignitaries at his New York apartment, where a rudimentary television was hooked up to a camera at an RCA office building nearby. Unbeknownst to his father, Tom had snuck off to the office, and when David Sarnoff triumphantly announced to his guests: "Now, ladies and gentlemen, I give you your first look at television," they were met with Tom's image on the set, waving and saying, "Hello, Daddy." (*Broadcasting and Cable*, 11/6/95)

FIRST OFFICIAL TELEVISION BROADCAST: MAY 1, 1939
(OPENING OF NEW YORK WORLD'S FAIR)

On May 1, 1939, RCA televised the opening ceremonies of the New York World's Fair, at which Pres. Franklin Roosevelt and Albert Einstein both spoke. Since there were only about 200 working televisions in all of New York, people jammed in front of store windows to see the new technology. One newspaper reported that, while television watching was reported to be tiring, "not a single one" of the people the reporter was watching with "reported any fatigue." (*Christian Science Monitor*, 5/2/39)

COST OF FIRST COMMERCIAL EVER BROADCAST: $9

On July 1, 1941, the Bulova Watch Company paid $9 to WNBT-TV in New York to have a Bulova clock ticking on the air for 20 seconds as an announcer read the time. (*Entertainment Weekly*, 3/28/97)

1. Number of televisions in American homes in 1946: 7,000
2. Number in 1950: 4.4 million

The emergence of television abruptly changed leisure activities in the U.S. In 1951, cities with television reported a 20–40% drop in movie attendance, libraries saw a precipitous drop in the number of books taken out, and radio listeners departed in droves (Bob Hope's radio ratings dropped from 23.8 in 1949 to 12.7 in 1951). (Neuhaus, *Manly Meals and Mom's Home Cooking*; Barnouw, *Tube of Plenty*)

FIRST RERUN: DICK TRACY

In February 1951, the first rerun was broadcast when ABC began replaying prime-time episodes of *Dick Tracy* on Saturday mornings. (*Encyclopedia of Daytime Television*)

FIRST ON-AIR FIRING: JULIUS LAROSA

LaRosa, a regular on *The Arthur Godfrey Show*, had just finished singing his weekly number on Oct. 19, 1953, when Godfrey walked up to him, placed his hand on the crooner's back, and told the TV audience, "Thank you, Julie. That, folks, was Julie's swan song." Though letters flooded the ABC mailroom, Godfrey held his ground, citing an "improper lack of humility" by the singer. (*Washington Post*, 11/7/83)

COVER SHOT OF THE FIRST *TV GUIDE*: DESI ARNAZ, JR.

The first *TV Guide* came out on Apr. 3, 1953. At the peak of its popularity, *TV Guide* sold 20 million copies an issue, and still sells 9 million copies. (*Deseret Morning News*, 4/13/03)

MOST WATCHED TV EPISODES OF ALL TIME:

1. *M*A*S*H* (FINAL EPISODE)
2. *DALLAS* ("WHO SHOT J.R.?")
3. *ROOTS* (FINAL EPISODE)

Sources: **1.** The final episode was watched by 60.2% of American homes with TV sets, or 106 million viewers, nearly half the U.S. population at the time. (*Entertainment Weekly*, 5/1/98) **2.** The "Who Shot J.R.?" episode of Dallas in 1980 was watched by 53% of households with TVs, or 83.6 million people. (*USA Today*, 5/18/98) **3.** ABC's *Roots*, part 8, which aired on Jan. 30, 1977, was watched by 51.1% of people with TVs. (*Christian Science Monitor*, 5/8/98)

First TV cartoon series: *Crusader Rabbit* (1949)

TV's first cartoon lasted 2 years, featuring Crusader along with his sidekick, Ragland T. Tiger. The show's creators later went on to produce *The Rocky and Bullwinkle Show*. The first single cartoon broadcast was "Donald's Cousin Gus," which aired on NBC's experimental station W2XBS on May 19, 1939. (*Edmonton Journal*, 8/26/03; TVAcres.com)

FINAL LINES OF TV SERIES:

1. "SORRY, WE'RE CLOSED": *CHEERS*
2. "I'LL SEE YOU ALL IN THE CAFETERIA": *SEINFELD*
3. ". . . THE DAY THE RUNNING STOPPED": *THE FUGITIVE*
4. "GOOD-BYE": *M*A*S*H*

Sources: **1.** Spoken by bartender Sam Malone to a customer at the door of the bar in the concluding episode. (TVAcres.com) **2.** Seinfeld, in jail for failing to come to the aid of a fat carjacking victim, is performing before a less than enthusiastic prison audience. "You've been a great audience," he says sarcastically as he's carried away by prison guards. "See you all in the cafeteria." (CNN) **3.** TVAcres.com. **4.** The word was not actually said, but spelled out in stones by B. J. Hunicutt as Hawkeye leaves the deserted Mobile Army Surgical Hospital for the last time by helicopter. (*Entertainment Weekly*, 5/29/98)

First use of the term "couch potato": July 15, 1976

Coined by a man named Tom Iacino, the term owes its origin to an earlier phrase used to refer to the TV-obsessed—
"boob tuber." Iacino and his friends were TV fanatics, and sought a fresh word to describe themselves. Since a potato was a type of
vegetable tuber, and since TV was watched from a couch, the phrase was born. (*San Diego Union-Tribune*, 7/16/03)

TV THEME SONGS TO HIT #1:

"BALLAD OF DAVEY CROCKETT" (1955)
"THEME FROM *S.W.A.T.*" (1975)
"WELCOME BACK, KOTTER" (1976)
"THEME FROM *MIAMI VICE*" (1985)
"HOW DO YOU TALK TO AN ANGEL" (1992)
(FROM FOX'S THE HEIGHTS)

(*Billboard Book of Top 40 Hits*)

MINUTES OF DEAD AIR AFTER DAN RATHER WALKED OFF THE CBS *EVENING NEWS*: 6

On Sept. 11, 1987, when CBS chose to continue coverage of a tennis match rather than cut to the *Evening News*
at 6:30, Dan Rather walked off the set in protest. When the tennis match ended at 6:33 P.M., the network switched to the CBS studio
and the anchorman's empty chair. Six long minutes of dead air time ensued until Rather finally returned to the studio at 6:39. "I would
have fired him," Walter Cronkite was quoted as saying. "There's no excuse for it." (*Los Angeles Times*, 9/14/87)

1. First infomercial: Chop-o-Matic
2. Frequency of infomercial airings: 225,000 times per month
3. Ronco best-sellers: Inside-the-Shell Egg Scrambler; Spray-On Toupee

Sources: **1.** Much of the magic of infomercials is due to the smooth sales tactics of one Ron Popeil, who in 1951
kicked off the infomercial revolution by introducing the Chop-o-Matic to the consumer masses. Selling for $3.98, it sliced,
it diced, it vanished from shelves faster than viewers could dial 8-0-0. (ABC News, 5/6/98) **2.** *Fortune*, 11/11/02. **3.** The last
of which came in nine colors, and was used every day by Popeil. (FSB, 11/1/02; ABC's *Primetime Live*, 5/6/98)

THERAPY

1. **ORIGIN OF THE WORD "SHRINK":** FROM THE WORD "HEADSHRINKER"

2. **NUMBER OF PSYCHIATRISTS FOR EVERY MILLION PEOPLE IN THE U.S.:** 142

3. **NUMBER OF PSYCHIATRISTS FOR EVERY MILLION PEOPLE IN CHINA:** 15

Sources: **1.** "Shrink" came from the word "headshrinker," and probably originated as a disparaging comparison between psychotherapy and the tribal practice of boiling the heads of enemies. The first recorded use of the term was in 1966. (*Rocky Mountain News*, 5/27/97; *Barnhart Dictionary of Etymology*) **2.** National Mental Health Information Center **3.** *Time*, 11/24/03.

1. State with the highest percentage of psychiatrists: Massachusetts (32.5 per 100,000)

2. State with the lowest: Mississippi (6 per 100,000)

Sources: **1, 2.** New York is second with 30.3 per 100,000. California has only 15.8. (National Mental Health Information Center)

COUNTRY WITH THE HIGHEST PERCENTAGE OF THERAPISTS IN THE WORLD: ARGENTINA

Buenos Aires is said to have the highest number of analysts per capita of any city in the world, with many working in a neighborhood that has become known as Villa Freud. Interestingly, Woody Allen is perhaps the most popular filmmaker in Argentina; his angst-ridden films rank among the highest-grossing films in the country's history. . . . France has more psychiatrists than any other European country. (*Newsday*, 1/5/02; *Dallas Morning News*, 9/14/98)

1. **Number of prescriptions for antidepressants written in the U.S. in 1995:** 43 million

2. **Number of prescriptions for antidepressants written in 2003:** 145 million

Sources: **1.** *Chicago Tribune*, 4/21/96. **2.** *Mental Health Weekly Digest*, 8/11/04.

YEAR THAT THE NOBEL PRIZE WAS AWARDED TO THE CREATOR OF THE PREFRONTAL LOBOTOMY: 1949

The prefrontal lobotomy is a surgical procedure in which cells in the frontal lobes of the brain are destroyed by the insertion and rotation of a knife. One surgeon described the operation like this: "There's nothing to it. I take a sort of medical ice-pick, bop it through the bones just above the eyeball, swiggle it around, cut the brain fibers, and that's it. The patient doesn't feel a thing." Approximately 100,000 lobotomies were performed before the practice was discontinued in the 1960s. Shortly after winning the Nobel Prize, Egas Moniz was shot by one of his former patients. (*Independent*, 11/8/99)

ONLY PRESIDENT KNOWN TO HAVE BEEN TREATED BY A PSYCHIATRIST: RICHARD NIXON

In 1951, Nixon, then a senator from California, went to see a New York psychotherapist named Dr. Arnold A. Hutschnecker complaining of pain in his neck and back. Nixon continued to see the therapist intermittently throughout his political career, and Hutschnecker visited him at least twice in the White House. While Hutschnecker never discussed his treatment of Nixon while the ex-president was still alive, after Nixon's death, he said that while Nixon "didn't have a serious psychiatric diagnosis," he had "a good portion of neurotic symptoms." (*New York Times*, 1/3/01)

Device invented in the early 1900s to cure women suffering from "hysteria": Vibrators

In the 1880s, women were thought to experience "hysteria," characterized by tightening of the chest, choking, convulsive fits, and loss of memory. The vibrator was invented and operated by doctors during office visits to induce "hysterical paroxysms" (orgasms) in "afflicted" women. (*Psychology Today*, 12/1/99)

ODDS THAT AN ADULT IN AMERICA WILL SUFFER A BOUT OF DEPRESSION DURING THEIR LIFETIME: 1 IN 6

Women are about 56% more likely than men to experience depression. (*San Francisco Chronicle*, 6/18/03)

THINGS TO FEAR

1. **ANNUAL RISK OF BEING MURDERED: 1 IN 15,440**
2. **RISK OF BEING KILLED IN A CAR ACCIDENT: 1 IN 3,014**
3. **RISK OF BEING KILLED BY A SHARK: 1 IN 264 MILLION**

Sources: **1, 2.** Harvard Center for Risk Analysis. **3.** Four people were killed by sharks in 2003, down from 11 fatal shark attacks in 2000. Florida has the highest concentration of unprovoked shark attacks in the world (31 in 2003), though the only shark fatality in America in 2003 occurred in California. (*Houston Chronicle*, 6/6/04)

ODDS OF THE EARTH BEING STRUCK BY A HUGE METEOR DURING YOUR LIFETIME: 1 IN 9,000

As one scientist stated in recent congressional testimony: "There are at least 2,000 asteroids of the class that could strike the Earth which are more than 2/3 of a mile across. Of the 2,000, we have discovered and charted the paths of only about 245, or 12%. None of them, we have learned, are targeted towards Earth within the foreseeable future. But any one of the other 88% could strike at any time, even this afternoon, without warning. We simply haven't been looking hard enough." (*Arizona Republic*, 10/27/98; Testimony of Clark Chapman, 5/21/98)

Amount by which the likelihood of getting into a car accident at 35 mph exceeds car accidents at 65 mph: 500%

(*Consumers' Research*, 10/1/97)

ODDS OF GETTING STUCK IN AN ELEVATOR: 1 IN EVERY 100,000 ELEVATOR TRIPS

The only time an elevator has been known to go into freefall happened at the Empire State Building in 1945, after a B-25 bomber struck the building in a heavy fog and cut the elevator cables. A woman fell more than 70 floors and survived.... If an elevator is falling, it will do no good to try and jump at the exact moment of impact.... In 1999, magazine editor Nicholas White was stuck in an elevator in Rockefeller Center for 40 hours until someone finally noticed him on a video monitor. (AP Online, 10/20/99; UPI, 4/1/03)

AMERICANS KILLED BY FLYING COWS: 3

In February 1999 a motorist in Vacaville, Calif., was killed when a cow hit by another car was propelled through the windshield of his pickup. The same thing happened to another driver in 1998, and a Wisconsin farmer in 1993. (*San Francisco Chronicle*, 2/26/99; *Madison Capital Times*, 12/28/93)

ODDS OF BEING STUNG TO DEATH BY BEES: 1 IN 85,882

In Weymouth, England, in 1988, about 20,000 bees covered Jane Clark's house, trapping her and her family inside for 2 days until the bees finally flew off. Clark claims that she called twice for a rescue team, but Weymouth council said it could not intervene as bees are a protected species. Mrs. Clark said, "There were thousands swarming over the house. It was like something out of a horror movie. There was a horrendous noise." (National Safety Council; *Daily Mail*, 5/26/98)

ODDS OF BEING INJURED BY AN AMUSEMENT PARK RIDE: 1 IN 124,000 RIDES

Amusement park deaths in the U.S. average about 3 to 4 per year, or about 1 in 150 million rides. (*Dallas Morning News*, 2/19/02)

ODDS OF DROWNING IN THE BATHTUB: 1 IN 11,469

Canadian prime minister R. B. Bennett died in a bathtub in England in 1947. Jim Morrison, lead singer of the Doors, died in a Paris bathtub at age 27 in 1971. . . . In what became known as the "Brides in the Bath" trial, George Joseph Smith was charged with murder after his fourth wife was found dead in the bathtub on their honeymoon. Three other wives had also died in the bathtub while honeymooning with him. (*Rocky Mountain News*, 1/7/00; *Toronto Star*, 4/17/99)

ODDS THAT A MAN WILL SUFFER A HEART ATTACK DURING INTERCOURSE: 1 IN 1 MILLION

Although the incidence of such fatalities is rare, studies have shown that up to 80% of men who die during intercourse are in bed with someone other than their wives. A case in point: former vice president Nelson Rockefeller, who died while in flagrante delicto with his 25-year-old personal assistant. And French president Francois Faure died in a bordello in 1899 during an act of copulation. (*Daily Mail*, 12/5/02; *Current Psychiatry Reports*, 6/01)

TIPPING

1. ORIGIN OF THE WORD "TIPS": ACRONYM FOR "TO INSURE PROMPT SERVICE"
2. AVERAGE AMERICAN RESTAURANT TIP IN 2004: 18.6%
3. STANDARD TIP IN 1955: 5%

Sources: **1.** The practice of tipping allegedly began in English teahouses, where the tea often arrived lukewarm. If you wanted hot tea, you left a few coins in a box on the table marked "T.I.P.S." ("To Insure Prompt Service"). (*Washington Post*, 5/4/01) **2.** *Zagat Survey.* **3.** *Money*, 12/1/00.

NUMBER OF STATES IN WHICH TIPPING WAS PROHIBITED IN THE EARLY 1900S: 7

An organization called the Anti-Tipping Society of America, made up of 100,000 traveling salesmen, successfully lobbied to have tipping prohibited in seven states from about 1905 to 1919. (*Christian Science Monitor*, 10/23/00)

COUNTRIES IN WHICH TIPPING IS NOT EXPECTED OR IS ACTIVELY DISCOURAGED:
JAPAN, NEW ZEALAND, SINGAPORE, THAILAND

(*Independent*, 6/28/03; *New York Times*, 2/15/04)

1. City that gives the most generous tips: Philadelphia
2. City that gives the smallest tips: Seattle

According to the latest *Zagat Survey*, Philadelphians are the most generous diners in America, leaving an average tip of 19.2%, followed closely by Atlantans at 19.1%. Western diners give less—San Franciscans and Angelinos give 18.2% and people from Seattle give 18%, still not a measly sum. (*Zagat Survey*, 2005)

1. GENDER THAT TIPS MORE WHEN THE SERVER IS FEMALE: MEN

2. GENDER THAT TIPS MORE WHEN THE SERVER IS MALE: WOMEN

(AP Online, 7/4/02)

1. LARGEST RESTAURANT TIP EVER GIVEN: $2.4 MILLION

2. SECOND LARGEST RESTAURANT TIP: $11,232

Sources: **1.** On Feb. 29, 2000, Erich Sager walked into the Federalist, a swank Boston restaurant, and ordered lunch. Though lunch was no longer being served, Gwen Butler, the bartender, persuaded the kitchen to make him a plate of lobster salad. After the bartender told Sager she wanted to open a restaurant, Sager agreed to finance it, and gave her $2.4 million. Alas, the money wasn't sufficient to open the eatery, and Butler is now back to tending bar. (*Boston Globe*, 6/16/00) **2.** In April 2001, two Wall Street bankers spent some $6,207 at Nello's, a New York restaurant, then added a tip of $11,232. The motivation for leaving such a substantial tip was never revealed. (*Independent*, 4/11/01)

1. PERCENTAGE BY WHICH TIPS HAVE BEEN FOUND TO *INCREASE* WHEN A *WAITRESS* DRAWS A HAPPY FACE ON THE CHECK: 18%

2. PERCENTAGE BY WHICH TIPS *DECREASE* WHEN A *WAITER* DRAWS A HAPPY FACE ON THE CHECK: 3%

Other findings from the annals of tipping research: Waitresses who squatted next to tables when talking with diners increased their tip by 3% of the total check; waitresses who wrote "thank you" on the back of the check increased their tip by 2%; candy offered with the check increases the tip percentage by 6%; waitresses who touch customers increase their tip by 2–5%; and providing the check on a tray with a credit card logo increases the tip by 4.5% compared to when the check is presented on a tray with no logo, even if the customer is paying with cash. (*Hotel and Motel Management*, 9/2/96; *Restaurant Hospitality*, 9/1/96; *Wilson Quarterly*, 1/1/03; *Minneapolis Star Tribune*, 1/1/97)

Amount waitress Phyllis Penza won from a lottery ticket given to her instead of a tip: $3 million

In April 1984, Penza, a waitress at Sal's Pizzeria in Dobbs Ferry, N.Y., was serving one of her longtime customers, police sergeant Robert Cunningham, who jokingly offered her half of the winnings from a lottery ticket he had in place of a tip. Penza accepted, thinking nothing of it, until the impossible happened, and the $1 ticket ended up being worth $6 million. True to his word, Cunningham split the winnings two ways. (UPI, 4/3/84)

TOYS

1. NUMBER OF TOYS SOLD EACH YEAR IN THE U.S.: 3 BILLION

2. AMOUNT SPENT ANNUALLY ON TOYS FOR THE AVERAGE CHILD WORLDWIDE: $32

3. AMOUNT SPENT ANNUALLY ON TOYS FOR THE AVERAGE AMERICAN CHILD: $328

4. AMOUNT SPENT FOR THE AVERAGE AFRICAN CHILD: $2

Sources: **1.** Toy Industry Association. **2–4.** Several studies have shown that children become overwhelmed when they have too many toys, and play less than children with fewer. (World Toy Facts and Figures; *Daily Mail*, 2/26/01)

First toy to be mass-produced: Marbles (1884)

The first factory for American marbles was S. C. Dyke & Co. in Akron, Ohio, which was turning out 30,000 clay marbles a day in 1884. (*Cleveland Plain Dealer*, 8/21/94; Cohill, *A Spin on the Past*)

FIRST TOY ADVERTISED ON TELEVISION: MR. POTATO HEAD (1952)

Mr. Potato Head was originally arms, legs, eyebrows, and hair that kids pushed into a real potato borrowed from the kitchen. The plastic body came in 1964. Mr. Potato Head's children are named Spud and Yam. (*Houston Chronicle*, 11/24/95)

FIRST TOY FAD: TEDDY BEARS

On Nov. 14, 1902, Pres. Theodore Roosevelt—though a passionate hunter—refused to kill a young bear tied to a tree for his pleasure. Newspapers told the story, which inspired Morris Michtom to create a stuffed bear and place it in the window of his Brooklyn, N.Y., store alongside a sign that said "Teddy's Bear." When Michtom wrote to the president asking if he could market the bears under his name, the president wrote back, "I don't think my name is likely to be worth much in the toy bear business, but you are welcome to use it." (*Chicago Sun-Times*, 1/25/02)

OTHER TOY FADS OF NOTE:

Slinkys (1945): Created by Richard James after he saw a spring fall off a table and "walk." His wife was so uncertain of the idea that she asked a friend to buy one when they were first offered at Gimbels. Over 250 million have been sold to date.

Silly Putty (1949): Invented by accident as scientists were looking for a rubber substitute during World War II, the "nutty putty" was strictly for the amusement of a few scientists until Peter Hodgson bought 21 pounds of the stuff and resold it as Silly Putty. Apollo 8 astronauts used it to keep tools from floating around.

Yo-Yos (1962): Meaning "come back" in Tagalog, a Filipino language, the yo-yo was brought to this country by Pedro Flores in the 1920s but did not really break out until the Duncan Yo-Yo company bought TV advertising in the early '60s. An amazing 45 million yo-yos were sold by Duncan in 1962.

(*Washington Post*, 1/13/04, 1/13/02; *FSB*, 12/03; *Los Angeles Times*, 6/30/02; *San Diego Union-Tribune*, 4/29/01; *New York Sun*, 6/18/03)

CRACKER JACKS PRIZES DISPENSED SINCE 1912: 23 BILLION

(*Chicago Tribune*, 5/24/04)

1. YEAR THE FIRST TALKING DOLL WAS CREATED: 1889
2. FIRST SUCCESSFUL TALKING DOLL: CHATTY CATHY (1963)
3. FIRST PEEING DOLL: BETSY WETSY (1937)
4. FIRST POOPING DOLL: BABY ALIVE (1973)
5. FIRST PEEING AND POOPING DOLL: BABY UH-OH (1990)

Sources: **1.** Thomas Edison created a rather homely doll with a small phonograph inside on which he recorded snippets of nursery rhymes and other phrases. Edison made about 8,000 of the dolls, but sold just 294, and moved on to other ventures. (Wood, *Edison's Eve*; *Atlanta Journal-Constitution*, 1/31/93) **2.** Cathy spoke 11 phrases, such as "Please brush my hair" when a child pulled a string. Cathy's original voice was provided by June Foray, who also did the voice of Rocky the Flying Squirrel in the Bullwinkle cartoon series (in a later incarnation, Maureen McCormick [Marcia on *The Brady Bunch*] provided Cathy's voice). (*National Post*, 11/8/03) **3.** *Deseret Morning News*, 12/17/99. **4.** Depending on the "food" served to the doll, Baby Alive excreted a red-, yellow-, or green-tinted substance into a tiny diaper. (*Washington Post*, 2/19/96) **5.** When fed a bottle, Baby Uh-Oh wet her diaper, revealing yellow stains on one side and brown stains on the other. She even got diaper rash on her tush. (*Newsday*, 2/14/90)

TREES

1. WORLD'S RAREST TREE: WOLLEMI PINE, DISCOVERED IN 1994

2. WORLD'S FATTEST TREE: 190 FEET AROUND

3. TREES THAT OWN THEMSELVES: 1

Sources: **1.** There are only 43 Wollemi pines in the world, located on 1.2 acres in a national park 125 miles from Sydney, Australia. They were discovered by David Noble, out on a hike when he veered from the trail and came upon the grove of trees, which were thought to have disappeared some 150 million years ago. "The discovery is the equivalent of finding a small dinosaur still alive on Earth," said Carrick Chambers, director of the Royal Botanic Gardens. The Wollemi pines' exact location is kept secret to protect them from hordes of tourists and rare tree thieves, who already stole a transplanted Wollemi pine from the Brisbane Botanic Gardens. (AAP General News, 8/16/02) **2.** The staggering Montwezuma cypress in the small Mexican town of Tule measures more around (190 feet) than up (140 feet), and it takes more than 50 people to encircle its base. In the early 20th century, someone carved into its trunk, "Tree, you are a god." A later visitor, equally inspired, saw it differently: "God," he carved, "you are a tree." (*Christian Science Monitor*, 7/16/98) **3.** The tree that owns itself is a large white oak at the corner of Dearing and Finely Streets in Athens, Ga. In the 1890s, Col. W. H. Jackson deeded the tree and the land around it to itself to protect it from development. (*Newsday*, 7/15/96)

Recent funerals for trees: 2

In March 1994, the City of New York held a 45-minute funeral service for a 63-year-old cedar tree that died in a Queens park. Sixty park workers attended the service, at which flags were lowered to half staff, taps was played, and a eulogy was given by the New York City Parks Commissioner Henry Stern. "We wanted to commemorate the happy 63 years of the tree," Stern said. . . . Five years later, residents of Annapolis, Md., held a funeral service for a 400-year-old tulip poplar, the last of the so-called Liberty Trees where American patriots plotted against the British, which was mortally wounded by Hurricane Floyd. On Oct. 25, 1999, after a speech by the governor and the tolling of bells, the tree was cut down. (*Washington Post*, 10/26/99; *Newsday*, 3/26/94)

LONGEST TIME SPENT LIVING IN A TREE IN THE U.S.: 737 DAYS (JULIA HILL, STAFFORD, CALIF.)

On Dec. 10, 1997, Hill climbed up into an ancient redwood outside of Stafford after getting word that a logging company threatened to cut the tree down. Food and other supplies were delivered to Hill's 6-by-8-foot platform 160 feet off the ground by bucket; other buckets served as toilet and sink. Through 2 years, she washed herself in rainwater, fought efforts to have her arrested, and survived numerous fierce winter storms. Finally, on Dec. 18, 1999, Hill climbed down after the logging company agreed to spare the tree. (*Toronto Star*, 12/24/99; *San Francisco Chronicle*, 12/3/00)

NUMBER OF SHOES IN THE WORLD'S LARGEST SHOE TREE: 1,000

Perched on a lonely stretch of U.S. Highway 50 near Middle Gate, Nev., 3 miles from the nearest building, the massive cottonwood Shoe Tree is festooned with hundreds of boots, sneakers, high-heeled shoes, sandals, and even a pair of roller skates. According to locals, the first pair of shoes was thrown by a newly married husband passing through town who threw his bride's shoes into the tree after she threatened to leave. They eventually made up, and several years later, threw their baby's first pair of shoes into the tree. . . . Other shoe trees bloom in Eureka Springs, Ark.; Marengo, Ind.; Alpena Springs, Mich.; Priest Lake, Idaho; Leetsville, Mich., and a Florida nudist colony. Shoe trees have also spawned other clothing crops, such as the bra trees located at the Crested Butte ski area in Colorado, Vail's China Bowl, and Bob's Biker Bar near Marlow, Okla. (*Las Vegas Journal*, 8/8/99; *Outside*, 5/01)

WHAT RONALD REAGAN SAID TREES CAUSE MORE OF THAN CARS: POLLUTION

Reagan said that "trees cause more pollution than automobiles." Even his own staff teased him about the comment. Once when Air Force One was flying over a wooded area, Press Secretary James Brady pointed out of the window and said: "Look, Mr. President: killer trees!" . . . Actually, recent studies indicate that some tree species, such as the oak, the poplar, and the white willow, do emit significant amounts of pollution. (*Time*, 2/12/90; *Independent on Sunday*, 11/24/02)

Place where people live in trees: Irian Jaya, Indonesia

Known as the Tree People of Irian Jaya, the Korowai tribe lives in a cluster of tree houses that can be as high as 150 feet off the ground. (*Insight Guides: Indonesia*)

HIGHEST AMOUNT EVER PAID FOR A PIECE OF FRUIT FROM A TREE: $67,000

The price was paid for a rare lychee produced by a 400-year-old tree whose fruit had been eaten exclusively by emperors during the Qing Dynasty (1644–1911). (*Houston Chronicle*, 7/2/02)

TV SEX

1. YEAR AN ACTOR'S PREGNANCY WAS FIRST INCORPORATED INTO A TELEVISION PLOT: 1952 (*I LOVE LUCY*)

2. ELVIS'S FIRST PELVIC THRUST ON NATIONAL TV: 1956 (*THE ED SULLIVAN SHOW*)

3. YEAR A MARRIED TV COUPLE WAS FIRST ALLOWED TO SHARE A BED: 1947 (*MARY KAY AND JOHNNY*)

Sources: **1.** This despite the fact that Lucy and Ricky Ricardo slept in twin beds (mandated by network censors), which were separated by a nightstand. Nor was the term "pregnant" allowed to be used to describe Lucy's condition. On the air, Lucy was merely "expecting," or "with child." Lucy and Desi arranged for the delivery episode—titled "Lucy Goes to the Hospital"—to air on the day Ball actually gave birth to their real-life child, elevating the event to a level of national importance that overshadowed even the coverage of the Eisenhower inauguration. (*Washington Times*, 1/13/01; *Washington Post*, 6/18/89) **2.** The Sullivan show avoided televising Elvis below the waist. (NPR, 8/16/97) **3.** *Mary Kay and Johnny* starred real-life wife and husband Mary Kay and Johnny Stearns, and aired on the DuMont network from 1947 to 1950. In 1951, however, the networks adopted a TV content code, which required even married couples like Rob and Laura Petrie on *The Dick Van Dyke Show* to reside in separate twin beds. When couples did meet for the occasional kiss across the divide, at least one foot always had to be on the floor. (*New York Times*, 7/2/04; *Daily News*, 11/14/02)

YEAR A BELLY BUTTON WAS FIRST SHOWN ON A NETWORK SERIES: 1964 (*DR. KILDARE*)

In an episode called "Tyger, Tyger," guest star Yvette Mimieux wears a bikini, which exposes her navel for all to see. A year later, NBC insisted Barbara Eden conceal her belly button on *I Dream of Jeannie*. Jeannie's bottle could also never be seen in the bedroom. (*USA Today*, 9/24/99)

YEAR OF FIRST INTERRACIAL KISS: 1968 (*STAR TREK*)

It was *Star Trek*'s third season, and Kirk and Uhuru weren't acting out of their own desire, but were being controlled by the rulers of the planet Platonius, who created a play in which the two were forced to kiss. The first interracial couple on TV were Tom and Helen Willis, George Jefferson's neighbors on *The Jeffersons*. (*Record*, 4/27/97; *Columbus Dispatch*, 6/4/03)

YEAR FIRST (AND ONLY) LEAD TV CHARACTER HAD AN ABORTION: 1972 (*MAUDE*)

(*USA Today*, 9/24/99)

YEAR A TELEVISION EPISODE FIRST SHOWED A CONDOM: 1987 (*VALERIE*)

In an episode titled "Bad Timing," Valerie Harper's 17-year-old son David buys some condoms for a planned tryst with houseguest Lori. Although NBC censors were uneasy, the show—and the word "condom"—was aired uncut. (*People*, 5/11/87)

YEAR A DERRIERE WAS FIRST GLIMPSED: 1983 (*BAY CITY BLUES*)

(*USA Today*, 9/24/99)

Year a kiss between women was first shown on TV: 1991 (*L.A. Law*)

Partner C. J. Lamb plants a longer-than-casual kiss on the lips of her shocked associate Abby Perkins. (*Evening Standard*, 10/2/03)

YEAR A TV EPISODE FIRST DEALT WITH MASTURBATION: 1992 (*SEINFELD*)

The episode was called "The Contest," in which Jerry, Kramer, George, and Elaine attempt to abstain from playing with themselves, though the word "masturbation" is never uttered. (*USA Today*, 9/24/99)

UFOs

1. PERCENTAGE OF AMERICANS WHO BELIEVE ALIENS HAVE VISITED THE EARTH: 30%

2. PERCENTAGE WHO SAY THEY OR SOMEONE THEY KNOW HAS SEEN ONE: 7%

3. STATE WITH MOST UFO SIGHTINGS: NEW MEXICO

Sources: **1.** *Life*, 3/00. **2.** Twenty-one percent of Americans say they would board an alien spacecraft if invited. (*Life*, 3/00) **3.** Followed by Wisconsin, where on a lonely stretch of highway outside of a small town called Dundee, sightings are so common that there is a tavern named Benson's Hideaway and UFO Bar. (*Milwaukee Journal-Sentinel*, 12/28/03)

Date of alleged meeting between Pres. Dwight Eisenhower and aliens: Feb. 20, 1954

Ike was on a Palm Springs golf vacation when, on the night of February 20, he made an unscheduled departure from where he was staying. Several hours later, the Associated Press reported that "Pres. Eisenhower died tonight of a heart attack in Palm Springs," but then retracted the story minutes later. On the following day, officials claimed he was only at the dentist fixing a chipped tooth. American University professor Michael Salla and other researchers believe that Eisenhower secretly met with aliens that evening at Edwards Air Force Base. The claim has been repeatedly made in UFO books and the media, and emphatically denied by those close to Eisenhower. (*Washington Post*, 2/19/04)

NUMBER OF PEOPLE WHO BELIEVED MARTIANS HAD INVADED THE EARTH ON OCT. 30, 1938: 1.2 MILLION

On Oct. 30, 1938, CBS Radio interrupted the music of Ramon Raquello and his orchestra to broadcast what sounded like live news footage of a Martian invasion of Grovers Mill, N.J. By the time an actor portraying a reporter announced, "I can see the thing's body. It's large as a bear and it glistens like wet leather" over the radio, one woman had already tried to poison herself, while another ran into a church shouting, "New York has been destroyed. It's the end of the world. Go home and prepare to die." Fifteen people were treated for shock in one Newark, N.J., hospital alone. In New Jersey, people wrapped their heads in wet towels to ward off toxic gases and jammed up the highways to New York and Philadelphia. (*Hartford Courant*, 11/18/98; *Los Angeles Times*, 10/31/03)

AMERICAN PRESIDENTS WHO'VE SEEN UFOS:
JIMMY CARTER RONALD REAGAN

During a routine flight while he was governor of California, Reagan reported seeing a bright white light zigzagging through the sky. After having his plane give chase for a few minutes, Reagan told the *Wall Street Journal* that "all of a sudden to our utter amazement it went straight up into the heavens." Jimmy Carter had a similar experience in 1969, 7 years before he was elected president. "It was the darndest thing I've ever seen," Carter said during the 1976 campaign. "It was big; it was very bright; it changed colors and it was about the size of the moon. We watched it for 10 minutes, but none of us could figure out what it was. One thing's for sure. I'll never make fun of people who say they've seen unidentified objects in the sky." (*Augusta Chronicle*, 1/28/01)

NUMBER OF HOURS A RUSSIAN AIRPORT WAS SHUT DOWN BECAUSE OF AN ALLEGED UFO HOVERING OVER THE RUNWAY: 1 1/2 HOURS

On Jan. 26, 2001, the crew of an Il-76 cargo aircraft refused to take off due to a glowing object hovering over Barnaul Airport's runway in Siberia. Crew of another craft refused to land for the same reason, taking their cargo to a nearby airport instead. The UFO vanished some 90 minutes after first appearing. (Agence France-Press, 1/27/01)

NUMBER OF NEAR MISSES REPORTED BETWEEN AIRPLANES AND UFOS: 56

According to Richard Haines, a former NASA executive and head of the National Aviation Reporting Center on Anomalous Phenomena, the incidents include the following:

In 1981, Capt. Phil Schultz was piloting a TWA flight over Lake Michigan when a large silver object descended directly toward his airplane, avoiding it only by making a high-speed turn at the last second.

In 1995, an Aerolineas Argentinas flight was approached by a luminous object as it tried to land at Bariloche Airport. Before the UFO disappeared, the lights at the airport mysteriously went out and instruments in the control tower started fluctuating wildly.

In 1997, a Swissair 747 over Long Island narrowly avoided a glowing white object approaching the plane.

(*Providence Journal*, 5/8/01; *Times* [London], 2/5/03; *Toronto Star*, 8/12/95)

317

UMPS AND REFS

1. SALARY OF A VETERAN MAJOR LEAGUE UMPIRE: $185,000
2. OF A VETERAN NBA REFEREE: $300,000
3. OF A VETERAN NFL REF: $8,000 PER GAME
4. OF A VETERAN NHL REF: $250,000

Sources: **1.** According to the *Cleveland Plain Dealer*, an ump with 10 years' experience makes about $185,000, first-year umps make about $85,000 per year, and an ump who has been in the majors for 26 years makes about $340,000. (*Cleveland Plain Dealer*, 5/30/04) **2.** *Washington Post*, 4/18/04. **3.** NFL refs chosen for the playoffs make $15,000 per game, while those chosen for the Super Bowl make $20,000 (NFL Officiating Department) **4.** *Edmonton Journal*, 2/22/04.

INSTANCES WHERE SOCCER REFS HAVE BEEN KIDNAPPED OR MURDERED:

Alvaro Ortega

Shot dead in Medellín, Colombia, in 1989 after he failed to call a penalty in a crucial game between Cali and Medellín.

(*Guardian*, 11/18/89)

Armando Perez

Kidnapped in Colombia in 1988 after a gang feared a rival drug gang had bribed soccer refs, and was released after 24 hours with a warning that corrupt officials would be killed.

(*Los Angeles Times*, 7/3/94)

FIRST NBA REF TO EJECT A BROADCASTER: STEVE JAVIE (MARCH 1, 1994)

On March 1, 1994, Portland Trailblazer radio analyst Mike Rice was ejected by Javie after throwing his hands in the air in exasperation after Javie called a technical foul on Portland. The two got into an argument in which Javie ended with "Shut up and do your piddly little job" but promptly threw Rice out instead. (*St. Louis Post-Dispatch*, 3/7/94)

ONLY ORGANIST TO BE EJECTED BY AN UMP: WILBUR SNAPP (JUNE 26, 1985)

On June 26, 1985, Snapp played "Three Blind Mice" in response to a questionable call against the Clearwater Phillies at the team's Jack Russell Stadium. Hearing this, umpire Kevin O'Connor walked up to the screen, gestured to Snapp, and threw him out of the game. (*New York Times*, 9/10/03)

First use of hand signals to call balls and strikes: 1906

Although there is some evidence that signaling balls and strikes may have occurred several decades earlier in the minors, National League umpires Bill Klem and Cy Rigler are generally credited with bringing the innovation to the majors in 1906. While most scholars attribute the invention of hand signals to a need to communicate balls and strikes to a deaf player named William "Dummy" Hoy, others say Hoy was out of the league by that time. (Ritter, *Story of Baseball*)

1. FIRST PROFESSIONAL FEMALE UMPIRE: BERNICE GERA (JUNE 24, 1972)

2. FIRST FEMALE NBA REF: VIOLET PALMER (OCT. 31, 1997)

Sources: **1.** It took 3 years of lawsuits before Gera won the right to become an umpire. On June 24, 1972, she made her debut in the first game of a Class A New York–Penn league doubleheader. After the game, she quit, saying she was treated poorly by the players and other umpires, and never umped again. Gera was followed by Pam Postema, who had a 13-year umpiring career in the minor leagues from 1977 to 1989, and worked major league spring training games in her last year. (*Greenville News*, 7/11/03; *Dallas Morning News*, 5/21/03) **2.** After debuting in a game between the Vancouver Grizzlies and the Dallas Mavericks, Palmer was praised for her composure and her calls. Some were still split on the issue of women referees, however, including Michael Jordan, who said: "certain things you do with other referees you can't really do to female referees. You can't pat them on the butt anymore." (ABC News, 11/2/97)

CRITICAL ERRORS INVOLVING NFL COIN TOSSES: 1

On Nov. 26, 1998, the Pittsburgh Steelers and Detroit Lions were tied at the end of regulation play. As referee Phil Luckett tossed a coin to determine who would receive the ball first in overtime, a national TV audience clearly heard Jerome Bettis call tails on behalf of the Steelers. Though the coin landed tails, Luckett gave the Lions the choice of receiving, after which they scored a touchdown to win the game. "How can you blow the coin toss?" Steeler linebacker Earl Holmes said after the game. (*New York Post*, 11/28/98)

UNDERWEAR

1. PAIRS OF UNDERWEAR BOUGHT BY THE AVERAGE ADULT AMERICAN EACH YEAR: 7

2. PAIRS OF SOCKS BOUGHT BY THE AVERAGE ADULT AMERICAN ANNUALLY: 9

3. PERCENTAGE OF AMERICAN BUYERS OF MALE UNDERWEAR WHO ARE WOMEN: 75%

4. NUMBER OF WEEKLY UNDERWEAR CHANGES BY ASTRONAUTS ON THE MIR SPACE STATION: 1

Sources: **1.** According to the NPD Group, American women bought 894 million pairs of underwear in 2003, while men bought 601 million. The average Frenchman buys only three pairs of underwear a year. (Agence France-Presse, 12/7/03) **2.** American men bought 1.2 billion pairs of socks in 2003, and American women, 891 million. (NPD Group) **3.** (*Chicago Tribune*, 1/15/99). **4.** Astronauts on the International Space Station change their underwear once every 3 or 4 days. (*Sunday Times* [London], 12/13/98)

Debut of thong underwear: 1981

Thong underwear was created by and first sold at Frederick's of Hollywood, though many historians say the thong was actually invented in 1939, when exotic dancers in New York created a thonglike G-string to avoid threats of arrest by Mayor Fiorello La Guardia during the World's Fair held in New York. Today, at least 19 million Americans own a pair of thong underwear. (*Palm Beach Post*, 6/23/03)

YEAR WOMEN BEGAN WEARING UNDERWEAR IN THE WESTERN WORLD: 1800

According to costume historian C. Willett Cunnington, prior to 1800, drawers were considered "a purely masculine or children's garment, and the adoption of them by women was at first regarded as savoring of depravity." In Paris, they were allowed only for use by actresses as late as 1783, and when they did become acceptable, female underwear literally came in pairs: one for each leg, plus garters, and no crotch. This remained the standard until the 1880s. (*Palm Beach Post*, 9/15/97; *Independent*, 1/21/95)

EVENT THAT PRECIPITATED THE ADOPTION OF UNDERWEAR BY JAPANESE WOMEN:
A TOKYO DEPARTMENT STORE FIRE (1932)

On Dec. 16, 1932, a fire broke out on the fourth floor of Tokyo's Shirokiya Department Store. Up to a dozen women in the store reportedly died because they hesitated to climb down rescue ropes, which would have exposed their bare bodies underneath their kimonos to the crowds below. (*Daily Yomiuri*, 12/16/98; *Financial Times* [London], 6/10/00)

AMERICAN MALE UNDERWEAR BREAKDOWN:
50% WEAR BRIEFS   40% WEAR BOXERS   10% WEAR BOXER BRIEFS

(*Rocky Mountain News*, 7/1/04)

1. INVENTOR OF MEN'S BRIEFS: ARTHUR KNEIBLER (1935)
2. STORE WHERE THE FIRST PAIR OF BRIEFS WERE SOLD: MARSHALL FIELD

Sources: **1.** Kneibler, an executive at a Kenosha, Wisc., underwear company, got the idea for men's briefs after seeing a photo of a man wearing a short swimming suit on the Riviera in 1934. Kneibler adapted the bathing suit, adding a new material called elastic to the waistband, and on May 29, 1935, Kneibler's invention received Patent No. 21,999. A 1935 magazine ad touted the underwear's "scientific suspension" and "restful buoyancy." (*Ottawa Citizen*, 12/30/93; *Chicago Tribune*, 1/22/85) **2.** Kneibler's briefs debuted during a January 1935 Chicago blizzard. The contrast between the weather outside and the skimpy briefs seemed so ridiculous to Kneibler that he sought to pull the display, but was convinced otherwise after he had sold 600 pairs by noon. (*Chicago Tribune*, 1/22/85)

UNDERWEAR SOLD AT AUCTION:

The queen of England's panties: sold for $420 at a London auction in 1979

(*Washington Post*, 3/3/79)

Marilyn Monroe's bra: sold for $1,400 at Sotheby's in 1981

(*Herald Sun*, 8/19/95)

Madonna's panties: garnered $15,000 from an anonymous bidder at a 1991 London auction

(*USA Today*, 8/23/91)

JFK's boxers: worn by the future president during World War II, bought for $5,000 by an Irish businessman in 2003

(*Houston Chronicle*, 7/30/03)

VEGETABLES

1. INVENTION OF THE WORD "VEGETARIAN": 1847

2. WHAT NON-MEAT-EATERS WERE KNOWN AS BEFORE 1847: PYTHAGOREANS

3. PERCENTAGE OF AMERICANS WHO ARE VEGETARIANS: 2.8%

4. PERCENTAGE OF AMERICANS WHO ABSTAIN FROM DAIRY PRODUCTS AND EGGS: 1.8%

Sources: **1.** The word "vegetarian" was coined in 1847 by the first members of the Vegetarian Society of Great Britain to describe people who did not eat meat, poultry, or fish. Some suggest that the word comes from the latin *vegetus*, meaning "full of life," though the prevailing view is that it comes from its obvious source—the word "vegetable". (Stepaniak, *Vegan Sourcebook*) **2.** Named after Pythagoras, inventor of the famous mathematical theorem, who became a vegetarian after studying with members of an Egyptian sect who abstained from eating meat. (*Independent* [London], 4/3/93) **3.** From a 2003 survey Harris cited in the *Chicago Tribune*, 10/5/03. **4.** Strict vegans abstain from eating all animal products, including honey (because bees are destroyed in the honey-making process) and white sugar (because some companies use bone matter to whiten the sugar). (*Chicago Tribune*, 10/31/01)

Number of vegetarians in India: 220 million

India has the largest vegetarian population in the world, made up mostly of Hindus (but also Buddhists and Jains) whose religion prohibits the killing of anything living or with the potential for life (Indian vegetarians eat milk products but not eggs). (*New York Times*, 3/24/04)

COLOR OF CARROTS BEFORE THEY BECAME ORANGE:

WHITE, PURPLE, BLACK, GREEN, RED

It was not until the 17th century that carrots turned orange, when growers from Denmark (the royal family of which was known as the House of Orange) crossbred yellow and red carrots to create what has become the vegetable's universal color. (*New York Times*, 11/30/03)

FRUITS THAT ARE WIDELY THOUGHT OF AS VEGETABLES:

TOMATOES CUCUMBERS EGGPLANTS PEPPERS STRING BEANS

The word "fruit" means the fleshy meat growing from the ripened ovary of a plant, and contains the seeds. (*Los Angeles Times*, 3/11/02)

YEAR THE SUPREME COURT DETERMINED THAT
THE TOMATO WAS IN FACT A VEGETABLE: 1893

In *Nix v. Hedden*, tomato importers sought to challenge a 10% tax imposed on tomatoes by claiming that tomatoes were a fruit (which was not subject to the tax) rather than a vegetable. Though the Supreme Court found that the tomato was technically a fruit, since Americans ate it with the main meal rather than dessert, it could be taxed as a vegetable. (*Providence Journal*, 3/10/03)

PERSECUTED VEGETARIANS:

K. D. LANG:

After the singer said that "meat stinks" on national television, her records were banned from more than three dozen radio stations in the U.S. and Canada. In her hometown of Consort, Alberta, a sign announcing it was "Home of k. d. lang" was defaced with the words "Eat beef, dyke." The backlash in the town was so intense that Lang's mother was temporarily forced to move.

(*American Scholar*, 9/22/00)

MANI:

Founder of a religious movement in the third century, called Manichaenism, which espoused meatlessness, he was tortured and executed by the leaders of Persia in A.D. 276. In the fourth century, Timothy, the Patriarch of Alexandria, tested Christian clergy in Alexandria by requiring them to eat meat; those who refused were interrogated.

(*Spencer, Vegetarianism*)

WAR

1. SHORTEST WAR IN HISTORY: 38 MINUTES
2. LONGEST-RUNNING CURRENT WAR: 29 YEARS
3. NUMBER OF SUITCASE-SIZED NUCLEAR BOMBS DEVELOPED BY THE SOVIET UNION: 132
4. NUMBER THAT ARE CURRENTLY MISSING: 84

Sources: **1.** On Aug. 25, 1896, the Sultan of Zanzibar died and his cousin was appointed his successor by the British, the colonial ruler at the time. When a competing claimant to the sultancy took control of the royal palace along with several thousand supporters, the British issued an ultimatum—either surrender by 9:00 A.M. or the British would open fire. When the ultimatum was ignored, British warships in the harbor opened fire on the palace at 9:02 A.M. At 9:40 A.M., the surviving rebels surrendered. (*Independent*, 1/4/97) **2.** Rebels in southern Sudan have been engaged in a 29-year struggle with the Sudanese government in the north for autonomy and independence. The war began in 1955, was stopped by a peace treaty that lasted from 1972 to 1983, and has been continuing ever since, resulting in 2 million deaths. Intensive peace talks began in December 2004. (AP, 12/27/03) **3, 4.** *New York Times*, 9/5/04.

1. NUMBER OF ACTIVE WARS IN THE WORLD IN 2003: 30
2. PERCENTAGE OF RECORDED HISTORY THAT THE WORLD HAS SPENT "ENTIRELY AT PEACE": 8%

(Hedges, *What Every Person Should Know about War*)

Years after World War II ended that the last Japanese soldier surrendered: 29

On Mar. 10, 1974, villagers on the Philippine island of Lubang discovered Hiroo Onoda, a Japanese soldier who had been hiding in the jungle since August 1945, completely unaware that World War II had ended. Onoda refused to believe Japan had been defeated, forcing Philippine authorities to locate Onoda's former commanding officer, who flew to the Philippines and ordered him to surrender. On Mar. 11, 1974, Onoda presented his sword in formal surrender to Pres. Ferdinand Marcos. (*Time International*, 6/3/96)

NUMBER OF WIDOWS OF CIVIL WAR VETERANS STILL SURVIVING AS OF DEC. 2004: 1

In December 1927, Alberta Martin, 21, became the third wife of Civil War veteran William Jasper Martin, who was 81. She was believed to be the last Confederate widow at her death on May 31, 2004, at the age of 97. Weeks later, however, Maudie Celia Hopkins, 89, of Arkansas, was discovered: in the 1930s she became the teenage bride of an octogenarian Confederate veteran, making her not only the new last surviving Confederate widow, but the only surviving Civil War widow today. (*New York Times*, 6/16/04

ONLY PLACE ON THE AMERICAN MAINLAND WHERE DEATH RESULTED FROM ENEMY ACTION DURING WORLD WAR II: BLY, ORE.

From late 1944 to April 1945, the Japanese released more than 9,000 balloons with attached bombs, hoping the winds would carry them across the ocean to the western United States. An estimated 1,000 actually reached North America, and on May 5, 1945, Elsie Mitchell and five children were killed outside Bly, Ore., by an explosion from one such device they found in the woods. (*New York Times*, 5/6/85)

1. ODDS THAT AN AMERICAN SOLDIER WAS ACCIDENTALLY KILLED BY AMERICAN FIRE IN WORLD WAR II: 1 IN 50

2. ODDS THAT AN AMERICAN SOLDIER WAS ACCIDENTALLY KILLED BY AMERICAN FIRE IN THE 1991 PERSIAN GULF WAR: 1 IN 4

Sources: **1.** Perhaps the worst instance of friendly fire during World War II occurred on July 25, 1944, when 111 Americans were accidentally killed by Allied air strikes during the invasion of Normandy. (Reuters, 12/5/01) **2.** Thirty-five of the 148 U.S. fatalities in the Persian Gulf War were accidentally killed by their fellow combatants. (Reuters, 12/5/01)

Bloodiest single day for one army in military history: July 1, 1916, Battle of the Somme (19,240 British soldiers dead, 38,000 wounded)

At 7:30 A.M. on July 1, 1916, 11 British divisions spread over the Somme region of France, attacked entrenched German troops following a continuous 5-day bombardment that had done little to break the German lines. Wave after wave of British soldiers were mowed down by German machine guns. This did not diminish the enthusiasm of the British commander, however, who reported back to London, "It all went like clockwork. Our troops are in wonderful spirits and full of confidence. The way to capture machine guns, is by grit and determination." By the time the battle ended in November, the Germans had been pushed back a grand total of 5 miles, at a cost of 420,000 British casualties, 194,000 French and 465,000 German. (*Independent*, 10/18/99, 7/1/01)

WATER

1. GALLONS OF WATER USED PER DAY ON THE WORLD'S GOLF COURSES: 2.5 BILLION
2. GALLONS OF WATER USED PER DAY BY THE AVERAGE AMERICAN 100 YEARS AGO: 5 TO 10
3. GALLONS OF WATER USED BY THE AVERAGE AMERICAN TODAY: 100

Sources: **1.** About the same amount it would take to keep 4.7 billion people alive at the U.N. daily minimum. (*World Watch*, 3/1/04) **2.** *Washington Post*, 7/31/03. 3. Americans consume more water on a per capita basis (1,870 cubic meters of water per year) than any other country in the world, with Canada (1,471 cubic meters) a close second. (*National Geographic*, 9/1/02; Canadian Press, 12/3/03)

Number of years a Kenyan man went without a bath before his neighbors forced him to wash: 10

According to the BBC, his odor became so overpowering that his neighbors abducted him, tied him up, and put him in a tub. (*New York Times*, 3/9/04)

1. AMOUNT OF BOTTLED WATER BOUGHT BY THE AVERAGE AMERICAN IN 2003: 22.6 GALLONS
2. CELEBRITIES WHO REPORTEDLY BATHE WITH BOTTLED WATER: MICHAEL JACKSON RAQUEL WELCH
3. PERCENTAGE OF BOTTLED WATER SOLD IN AMERICA THAT IS DRAWN FROM MUNICIPAL TAP SOURCES: 25%

Sources: **1.** Sales of bottled water in America now surpass beer, milk, and coffee, and are behind only soda in the beverage category. The world's leading bottled water consumers are France and Italy. (*Washington Post*, 4/29/04) **2.** According to the *Chicago Tribune*, Michael Jackson orders 32 cases of Evian at a time because he bathes in it, while Raquel Welch uses it to wash her hair. (*Chicago Tribune*, 5/16/01) **3.** The tap water is then filtered. (*Beverage Industry*, 4/1/03)

1. FIRST HEATED SWIMMING POOL: FIRST CENTURY B.C.
2. RESIDENTIAL SWIMMING POOLS IN THE U.S. TODAY: 8 MILLION
3. CELEBRITY POOLS: LIBERACE'S POOL: SHAPED LIKE A PIANO
SAMMY SOSA'S POOL: SHAPED LIKE A 21 (SOSA'S NUMBER)
EVANDER HOLYFIELD'S POOL: SHAPED LIKE A BOXING GLOVE
SALVADOR DALI'S POOL: SHAPED LIKE A PENIS

Sources: **1.** Built by Gaius Maecenas, a rich Roman landlord. (*Miami Herald*, 9/2/02) **2.** About 40% are aboveground. Arizona has the highest number of pools per capita of any state. There are also 5.6 million hot tubs. (*Washington Post*, 8/3/03) **3.** *Sports Illustrated*, 1/17/00; *El Paso Times*, 5/30/02.

1. NUMBER OF YEARS NEW YORK CITY HAS BEEN CONSTRUCTING A NEW 60-MILE WATER TUNNEL: 36
2. NUMBER OF YEARS OF CONSTRUCTION REMAINING: 14

Workers (called sandhogs) 600 feet underground advance about 50 feet per day on what has been billed as "the greatest nondefense construction project in the history of Western civilization." The new water tunnel is expected to allow New York to retire its two existing water tunnels (88 and 67 years old), which are thought to be leaking extensively and potentially on the brink of collapse. To date, 24 sandhogs have been killed digging the tunnel, about one per mile. (*New Yorker*, 9/1/03)

1. LARGEST WIND-GENERATED WAVE OF ALL TIME:
113 FEET (FEB. 6, 1933)

2. LARGEST WAVE TO HIT A CRUISE SHIP:
95 FEET (QE2, SEPT. 11, 1995)

3. LARGEST WAVE EVER SURFED: 66 FEET

Sources: **1.** Measured on Feb. 6, 1933, from the bridge of the oil tanker USS *Ramapo*, which was plowing through a typhoon in the North Pacific. (*St. Louis Post-Dispatch*, 5/11/95) **2.** On Sept. 11, 1995, a 95-foot wave washed over the *Queen Elizabeth 2* off of Newfoundland, reaching the height of the bridge. "It looked as if we were going straight into the white cliffs of Dover," said Capt. Ronald Warwick. Other than bent rails, little damage was caused to the ship. (*Washington Post*, 9/16/95) **3.** On Jan. 19, 2001, surfer Mike Parsons rode a 66-foot wave for approximately 20 seconds at Cortes Bank, an offshore reef approximately 120 miles off the coast of California. (*Orange County Register*, 3/30/01)

WEATHER

1. **Average global temperature in 2004:** 57° Fahrenheit
2. **Hottest year on record:** 1998 (58.15° average)
3. **Coldest year on record:** 1907 (56.41° average)
4. **Number of the ten warmest years on record that have occurred since 1990:** 10

Sources: **1-3.** National Climatic Data Center. **4.** *Los Angeles Times*, 6/28/04.

1. **INVENTOR OF THE "WEATHER FORECAST":** ADMIRAL ROBERT FITZROY (1861)
2. **WHAT WEATHER FORECASTS WERE CALLED BEFORE FITZROY CAME ALONG:** WEATHER INDICATIONS AND WEATHER PROBABILITIES

Sources: **1.** Though the word "forecast" with regard to weather was first used in 1533, it was Robert FitzRoy who coined the term "weather forecast" in 1861. FitzRoy gathered telegraph reports from various correspondents around England, at first providing them to coffeehouses frequented by ship captains, and subsequently newspapers. FitzRoy called his reports "forecasts," and emphasized that they were based on science rather than "prognostications" or "prophecies." By 1889, "weather forecast" had become the official term for chronicling the weather. Ironically, FitzRoy committed suicide in 1865, which many attributed to despondency over an inaccurate forecast. (*Daily Telegraph*, 12/24/01; Lockhart, *Weather Companion*) **2.** Cox, *Storm Watchers*.

1. **First TV weatherman:** Wooly Lamb   2. **First network TV weather forecast:** May 1949

Sources: **1.** On Oct. 14, 1941, a puppet named Wooly Lamb made the first weather forecast on New York's WNBT-TV (later WNBC), and continued for 7 years thereafter. Each day, Wooly opened the forecast by singing, "It's hot. It's cold. It's rain. It's fair. It's all mixed up together. But I, Wooly Lamb, predict tomorrow's weather." (*Weatherwise*, 10/93). **2.** In May 1949, John Youle, a local Chicago weatherman, made the first national weather broadcast on NBC's *Camel News Caravan* with John Cameron Swayze. Youle's only visual aid was a store-bought Rand McNally map on which he would diagram the weather with a black magic marker (he added a red marker when color TV became popular). (*New York Times*, 7/31/99)

PERCENTAGE OF WEATHER CHANNEL VIEWERS WHO WATCH FOR AT LEAST 3 STRAIGHT HOURS: 1 IN 5

The company refers to these people as "weather-involved," while others at the station refer to them as "weather weenies." Criticism over obsessive Weather Channel–watching allegedly contributed to a recent Washington, D.C., divorce. "To tell you the truth, I found it very hard to understand how my husband could sit there and watch old episodes of *Ironside* again and again," said Bobby Meyer. "The weather is always new." (*Times Union*, 10/7/98; *Washington Post*, 5/27/98)

Formula for finding out the outdoor temperature from crickets:

Number of times a cricket chirps in 13 seconds + 40 = temperature (°F)

(Boston Globe, 7/31/03)

LENGTH OF PRISON TERM FACED BY A BRAZILIAN WEATHERMAN AFTER A WEATHER FORECAST THAT TURNED OUT TO BE INCORRECT: 6 MONTHS

On Dec. 30, 2001, Luiz Carlos Austin, a weatherman on a Rio, Brazil, television station, forecast heavy rains for New Year's Eve and advised people to stay indoors. Torrential rains in early December had led to mudslides that killed 71 people in the Rio area, and Austin's warnings were taken seriously. The rains never came, however, and Austin was charged with "sounding a false alarm." Said prosecutor Alberto Guimaraes, Jr.: "Making those kinds of declarations on the most-watched television station in the country could have caused a massive panic." (*Knoxville News-Sentinel*, 10/3/02)

NUMBER OF WEATHERMEN WHO WERE ALLEGEDLY KILLED FOR INCORRECT FORECASTS: 1

According to the *San Jose Mercury News*, in April 1996 a Peruvian television weatherman named Francisco Arias Olivera predicted 2 inches of rain would fall on the town of Sicuani, Peru, rather than the 19 inches that actually fell and which resulted in a flood that killed 17 people. Grief-stricken townspeople lynched Olivera and hung him from a tree outside the television station. (*San Jose Mercury News*, 2/24/04)

1. Accuracy of the *Old Farmer's Almanac*'s weather predictions: About 60%
2. Year the almanac predicted snow in July: 1816

Sources: **1.** Though far from authoritative, even this level of accuracy is remarkable when one considers that the almanac makes predictions 18 months in advance for 16 separate regions of the U.S. (*Washington Post*, 11/30/03) **2.** In 1816, a typesetter for the *Farmer's Almanac* accidentally replaced a weather forecast for July with a wintry forecast intended for the month of February. The gods were with the almanac, however, because a volcanic eruption in Indonesia that year caused one of the coldest summers on record, including snow in New England on the very day it was predicted. (*Washington Post*, 11/30/03)

1. NUMBER OF WORDS FOR SNOW REGULARLY ATTRIBUTED TO THE ESKIMO LANGUAGE: 100 TO 400
2. ACTUAL NUMBER: 12 TO (AT MOST) 24

For over a century, newspapers and books have repeatedly made the claim that the Eskimo language has anywhere from 100 to 400 words for snow. Recent studies estimate the actual number of Eskimo words for snow from two to (at most) a couple of dozen, not much more than English (which has snow, sleet, blizzard, squall, slush, dusting, etc.). (Pullum, *The Great Eskimo Vocabulary Hoax*; Pinker, *The Language Instinct*)

ODDS THAT A TORNADO OCCURS IN THE U.S.: 3 IN 4

About 1,125 of the world's 1,500 annual twisters occur in the U.S. The deadliest tornado in history occurred on Mar. 18, 1925, when a twister in Missouri, Illinois, and Indiana killed an estimated 710 people. (Grazuli, *Nature's Ultimate Windstorm*)

PERCENTAGE OF WEATHER FORECASTERS WHO WERE WOMEN IN 1961: 75%

In 1952, 26-year-old Carol Reed became America's first female weather forecaster on New York's WCBS-TV, spawning a slew of what were known as "weathergirls" whose qualifications had more to do with their figures than meteorological experience. One New York weathergirl even gave midnight forecasts in a slip as she tucked herself into bed. (*Weatherwise*, 10/93; *New York Times*, 2/18/96)

1. HIGHEST TEMPERATURE EVER RECORDED IN ALASKA: 100°F
2. HIGHEST TEMPERATURE EVER RECORDED IN HAWAII: 100°F

Sources: **1.** Recorded at Fort Yukon on June 27, 1915, it's the only such temperature Alaska has experienced. (*Milwaukee Journal-Sentinel*, 8/21/00) **2.** Set at Pahala on Apr. 27, 1931. (*San Antonio Express-News*, 8/22/03)

1. HIGHEST TEMPERATURE EVER RECORDED IN THE U.S.: 134°F
2. HIGHEST TEMPERATURE EVER RECORDED IN BRITAIN: 100°F
3. HIGHEST TEMPERATURE EVER RECORDED AT THE SOUTH POLE: 7.5°F

Sources: **1.** Recorded in Death Valley, Calif., on July 10, 1913. (Lingenfelter, *Death Valley*) **2.** Temperatures in England had never exceeded 100° F prior to the heat wave of summer 2003, with the previous high 98.7° F in 1990. When Heathrow Airport reported reaching 100° on Aug. 10, 2003, bookies lost millions of pounds in payouts from people betting on the temperature. Though beer and sunscreen sales rocketed, so did the death toll—to a grim 900. (*Weatherwise*, 11/1/03) **3.** *Rocky Mountain News*, 5/12/01.

STRANGE WEATHER EVENTS:

RAINING FISH:

On Aug. 6, 2000, residents of Yarmouth, England, experienced a seafood shower of small bite-sized sprats that were sucked up by a waterspout over the sea and then rained down on the town. "I thought at first I might have had something wrong with my eyes," said one resident, whose house was covered in fish.

(*Guardian*, 8/7/00)

RAINING FROGS:

On May 19, 1860, a tornado over Lake Wilcox in Ontario, Canada, emptied half of the lake and rained frogs, fish, and turtles over nearby areas.

(*Toronto Star*, 5/10/02)

WEDDINGS

1. **COST OF THE AVERAGE AMERICAN WEDDING (2003):** $22,360
2. **LENGTH OF THE AVERAGE AMERICAN ENGAGEMENT:** 16 MONTHS
3. **NUMBER OF GUESTS AT THE AVERAGE WEDDING:** 125
4. **LARGEST NUMBER OF WEDDING GUESTS IN HISTORY:** 200,000

Sources: **1.** *Washington Post*, 1/22/04. **2.** During this time, engaged couples in America register for or purchase some $4 billion worth of furniture, $3 billion worth of housewares, and $400 million worth of plates and utensils. (*New Yorker*, 5/21/03) **3.** According to theknot.com, cited in the *Wilmington Morning Star*, 5/17/03. **4.** Invited to the 1995 wedding of the son of a wealthy Indian government minister to the granddaughter of an Indian movie star. Five thousand goats and 25,000 chickens were reportedly slaughtered and prepared by some 3,000 cooks. (*Miami Herald*, 9/10/95)

1. Percentage of women who say they cried at their wedding: **45%**

2. Percentage of men who cried: **25%**

(Sinrod, *Just Married*)

MOST POPULAR FIRST DANCE SONG IN 2003:

"AT LAST," ETTA JAMES (U.S.)

"WONDERFUL TONIGHT," ERIC CLAPTON (U.K.)

In Britain, the Clapton track edged out Robbie Williams's "Angels" and Carly Simon's "Nobody Does It Better."
(Poll by *Bride's Magazine*, reported in *Adweek*, 6/23/03; *Manchester Evening News*, 8/21/03)

1. **AMOUNT THE AVERAGE AMERICAN BRIDE SPENDS ON HER WEDDING DRESS:** $799

2. MOST EXPENSIVE WEDDING GOWN EVER WORN IN THE U.S.: $300,000

Sources: **1.** Condé Nast Bridal Survey, as reported in *Newsday*, 9/21/03. **2.** The gown, made from 1,100 diamonds totaling 300 carats, 3,000 Swarovski crystals, and 50 yards of silk, was worn by a 23-year-old bride in Brooklyn, N.Y., in 2003. (*New York Post*, 7/17/03)

1. Odds that a newly married couple does not make love on their wedding night: 3 in 10

2. Average times per day a couple makes love on their honeymoon: 2.28

In a 1918 book called *Married Love*, British author Marie Stopes warned brides about the dangers surrounding the wedding night, in which she would engage in "physical relations with her husband fundamentally different from those with her brother. . . . There have been not a few brides whom the horror of the first night of marriage . . . has driven to suicide or insanity." (Kanner, *Are You Normal About Sex, Love, and Relationships?*)

UNUSUAL WEDDING LOCATIONS:

2 1/2 MILES UNDERWATER:

In July 2001, David Leibowitz and Kimberly Miller descended 2 1/2 miles in a miniature submarine and exchanged vows above the wreck of the *Titanic*.

(*Independent*, 7/30/01)

240 MILES ABOVE THE EARTH:

In August 2003, Russian cosmonaut Yury Malenchenko married Yekaterina Dmitriyeva, in what was the first wedding in space. Malenchenko, aboard the International Space Station, exchanged vows with his bride (on the ground in Houston) via a televised hookup. An American astronaut aboard the space station served as best man. The couple went ahead with the ceremony, despite official Russian opposition. "Marriage is a cosmonaut's own business," Malenchenko told the Tass news agency.

(Agence France-Presse, 8/10/03)

OTHER STRANGE WEDDING INCIDENTS:

Tampa, Fla. (1992)—bride throws macaroni salad at groom at wedding reception; groom responds by shooting bride

(*Washington Post*, 5/3/92)

Bridgeport, Conn. (1993)—wedding couple arrested when, while feeding each other wedding cake, the groom shoves wedding cake in his bride's face, after which she hits him over the head with a chair

(*Herald Sun*, 8/5/93)

Cleveland, Ohio (2000)—10 police officers respond to fight at wedding which breaks out when groom's father gets angry after bride's father introduces groom by the wrong first name

(*Newsday*, 6/28/00)

Long Beach, Calif. (1993)—angered by the location of his seat, wedding guest fires handgun at the dance floor, killing another guest

(*Los Angeles Times*, 2/15/93)

WORK

1. FIRST MINIMUM WAGE: 25¢ PER HOUR

2. ESTIMATED NUMBER OF WORKDAYS EACH YEAR IT TAKES FOR YOU TO PAY YOUR TAXES: 101

3. ODDS THAT SOMEONE WOULD CONTINUE IN THEIR CURRENT JOB IF THEY WON $10 MILLION IN THE LOTTERY: 1 IN 3

Sources: **1.** The minimum wage was first introduced in 1938. It hit $1 in 1956, $2 in 1974, $3 in 1980, $4 in 1991, and $5 in 1997. (*Minneapolis Star Tribune*, 1/10/96) **2.** Typically in late April or early May, "Tax Freedom Day" is the day on which the average American, if they worked every workday since January 2, had earned enough to pay the year's taxes and could begin to think about feeding their family. (*Daily Telegraph*, 5/29/04; *San Francisco Chronicle*, 4/11/04) **3.** Forty percent say they would stop working, while 23% say they would find some other profession. (Gallup poll, 8/29/97)

Odds that a worker says that they are "always" or "often" under stress at work: 3 in 10

(National Opinion Reseach Center, reported in the *International Herald Tribune*, 9/6/04)

1. PERCENTAGE OF WORKWEEK THE TYPICAL WORKER SPENDS IN MEETINGS: 25%

2. ODDS THAT A PERSON AT A MEETING DOESN'T KNOW WHY THEY'RE THERE: 1 IN 3

Senior executives spend the equivalent of 4 workdays a week in meetings, according to professor Roger Mosuick. According to other surveys, 80% of participants daydream in meetings and 25% occasionally fall asleep in them. (*Christian Science Monitor*, 3/8/99; *Financial Management*, 12/00)

1. RANK OF "OFFICE TOO HOT" AS PRINCIPAL WORKPLACE COMPLAINT AMONG EMPLOYEES: SECOND
2. RANK OF "OFFICE TOO COLD": FIRST

Among other more unusual workplace complaints found in a study conducted by the International Facility Management Association: "the ice is not cold enough," "I'm allergic to the color green," and "coworker eats too loud." (*St. Louis Post-Dispatch*, 9/1/97)

1. NUMBER OF JOBS HELD BY THE AVERAGE AMERICAN BY THE TIME THEY'RE 32: 9
2. NUMBER OF JOBS HELD SIMULTANEOUSLY BY SEAMUS MCSPORRAN, RESIDENT OF THE SCOTTISH ISLAND OF GIGHA: 16

Sources: **1.** U.S Department of Labor. **2.** Including postman, fire chief, ambulance driver, undertaker, constable, insurance agent, and gas station attendant. "I was often the only person willing or able," McSporran says, "and the list seemed to grow longer and longer." (*People*, 5/8/00)

Year the office cubicle was invented: 1968

Until the 1970s, the basic workspace was a big room housing row upon row of identical desks. In 1968, Bob Probst had an idea to break up these open areas to give each worker a space of their own. He did this by designing a lightweight portable wall that surrounded each worker on three sides. His invention—which he called the Action Office—is what we now call the cubicle. (*Fortune*, 10/2/00)

NUMBER OF JAPANESE WORKERS IN 2002 WHO DIED OF KAROSHI, OR OVERWORK: 162

The word "karoshi" made its first appearance in the *Oxford English Dictionary* in 2002, meaning "death brought on by overwork or job-related exhaustion." In 2001, a Japanese company was forced to pay $1,100,000 to the family of a deceased employee who worked for 17 months without a single day off. Ichiro Oshima averaged 30 minutes to 2 hours of sleep a night. (*Daily Yomiuri*, 6/11/03; AP, 5/24/02)

WORLD TRADE CENTER

1. Time it took to build the World Trade Center: 6 years, 8 months

2. Time it took to destroy the towers, from the first crash to the second collapse: 104 minutes

Sources: **1.** Critics thought the towers were cold and soulless. "There is a fascination with the towers' ugliness," a *Washington Post* architecture critic wrote in 1973. Yet, according to *Newsweek*, more postcards of the World Trade Center were mailed each year than of any other building in the world. (*Fortune*, 10/1/01; *Newsweek*, 9/24/01) **2.** American Airlines Flight 11, bound for Los Angeles, took off from Boston at 7:59 A.M. and hit the World Trade Center's North Tower at 8:45. United Flight 175, bound for Los Angeles, left Boston at 7:58 A.M. and hit the South Tower at 9:06. The South Tower collapsed at 10:00. The North Tower came down at 10:29. Ironically, 7 days before the attack, the Trade Center's structural engineer told a terrorism conference in Germany that he had designed the building to withstand the impact of a Boeing 707. (UPI, 9/11/01)

1. Odds that an American knew someone hurt or killed in the attack: 1 in 5

2. Total number of World Trade Center victims: 2,752

3. Number of firefighters: 343

4. Number of police officers: 60

5. Number of rescue dogs: 1

Sources: **1.** *New York* magazine, 9/02. **2.** On Oct. 29, 2003, the New York City Medical Examiner's Office reduced the death toll, which had stood at 2,792 since December 2002, by 40 people who they could not prove had died or in some cases whether they ever existed. Among the removed names were the only children said to have died on the ground in the attack. (AP, 10/30/03) **3.** The number represents almost half the deaths in the FDNY's hundred-year history. (*USA Today*, 9/10/02) **4.** Comprising 23 NYPD officers and 37 Port Authority police officers. **5.** Sirius, a bomb-sniffing dog stationed at the Twin Towers, was in a basement kennel when the towers collapsed. The 5-year-old lab was the first Port Authority police dog killed in the line of duty. (AP, 4/25/02)

1. Estimated units of blood donated to the New York Blood Center in the aftermath of 9/11: 36,000

2. Total units of donated blood actually used for victims: 258

(*New York* magazine, 9/02)

Last person pulled alive from the Trade Center rubble:
Genelle Guzman McMillan (12:30 P.M., Sept. 12, 2001)

Walking down from her 64th floor office, McMillan had reached the 14th floor of the North Tower when it collapsed. Somehow her falling body found an air pocket. She landed atop a dead firefighter, and was finally rescued 27 hours after the towers fell. (*Bergen Record*, 9/10/03)

Date last remains were found near the site: Sept. 8, 2003

On Sept. 8, 2003, almost 2 years to the day after the attack, workers found bone fragments on a scaffolding put up before the attacks at 90 West Street, one block south from where the Trade Center stood. These are believed to be the last remains recovered from the Trade Center. (*New York Times*, 9/9/03)

Date the fire at Ground Zero was finally put out: Dec. 19, 2001

For 99 days, the fire continued to be fueled by documents and office furniture. Flare-ups would occur as recovery crews exposed pockets of fire to the air. (AP, 12/20/01)

Amount of money the 9/11 attacks took to execute:
$400,000 to $500,000

(*New York Times*, 7/23/04)

Final cost of cleaning up Ground Zero: $582 million

(*New York Times*, 9/11/03)

New York Lottery's winning number on Sept. 11, 2002: 9-1-1

The odds of those particular numbers coming up on Sept. 11 were 1,000 to 1. (Agence France-Presse, 9/13/02)

AUTHOR BIOS IN THIS BOOK: 1

Paul Grobman is an attorney who lives with his wife, three kids, a dog, and two parakeets on the Upper West Side of Manhattan. This is his first book. Please visit www.vitalstatistics.info for more information.